An Economic History of Twentieth-Century Europe

Economic Regimes from Laissez-Faire to Globalization

IVAN T. BEREND
University of California, Los Angeles

CAMBRIDGE UNIVERSITY PRESS

Cambridge, New York, Melbourne, Madrid, Cape Town, Singapore, São Paulo

Cambridge University Press
The Edinburgh Building, Cambridge CB2 2RU, UK

Published in the United States of America by Cambridge University Press, New York

www.cambridge.org
Information on this title: www.cambridge.org/9780521672689

First published 2006

Printed in the United Kingdom at the University Press, Cambridge

A catalogue record for this publication is available from the British Library

ISBN-13 978-0-521-85666-9 hardback
ISBN-10 0-521-85666-3 hardback
ISBN-13 978-0-521-67268-9 paperback
ISBN-10 0-521-67268-6 paperback

An Economic History of Twentieth-Century Europe

ınd economic performance
looks at the historic devel-
ny, examining both its fail-
enges of this crisis-ridden
surveys the rise and fall of
and introduced in Europe
ıows the roots and charac-
faire, the regulated market
ıon-market regime, the rise
ıd of century globalization.
: European regions that had
isappear during the course
ries reached a similar level
ill be required reading for
cs, and modern European

f History at the University
ions include (with György
Ránki) *The European Periphery and Industrialization 1780–1914* (1982),
Decades of Crisis: Central and Eastern Europe Before World War II (1998),
History Derailed: Central and Eastern Europe in the 'Long' 19th Century (2003),
and *Central and Eastern Europe, 1944–1993: Detour from the Periphery to the
Periphery* (1996).

To my beloved grandchildren, Benjamin, Daniel, and Esther

Contents

List of boxes   *page* ix
List of figures   x
List of tables   xii
Acknowledgments   xiv

Introduction   1

1 Europe's laissez-faire system and its impact before World War I   10
The rise of Britain and the laissez-faire system   10
Rising modern sectors   15
Europe's position in the world   20
Rising disparity within Europe   23
The beginning of Scandinavia's catching-up   28
The Southern and Eastern peripheries remaining behind   30
The challenge of globalized laissez-faire   39

**2 Decline of laissez-faire and the rise of the regulated
market system**   42
The turning point: war economy 1914–18, postwar chaos, and
the agony of laissez-faire   47
Failed attempts to return to "normalcy"   55
The death of laissez-faire, and extreme state regulations during
the Great Depression   61
The theory of the regulated market   72
War economy, 1939–45   74
The impact of the regulated market economy: European
economic performance   79
Europe's deteriorating role in the world   89

3 Economic dirigisme in authoritarian–fascist regimes   92
The origins and characteristics of economic dirigisme   95

Functions and programs of the state 102
Self-sufficiency, planning, and the populist welfare system 109
Dictated regional economic integration 124
Economic results 129

4 The centrally planned economic system 133
Marxist theoretical legacy, Lenin and the Bolshevik program 133
Forced industrialization and central planning: "socialism in
one country" 142
From an isolated Soviet system to the Soviet bloc 150
The characteristics of the centrally planned economic system 157
Safeguarding and attempts to legitimize the regime 164
Regional integration system of planned economies 166
The goal and balance sheet of the centrally planned economy 169
Rapid growth and industrialization – reproduced backwardness 172
Reform attempts that failed 178
Crisis and collapse 182

**5 Mixed economy and welfare state in an integrated
post-World War II Western Europe** 190
Postwar international regulations 192
Economic integration and the rise of the European Union 197
The emergence of *Sozialpartnerschaft* and the mixed economy 212
Planning in mixed economies 223
The rise of the welfare state 226
Educational revolution 236
Economic growth and structural changes 238

6 Globalization: return to laissez-faire? 263
Globalization and its characteristics 263
Globalization of the laissez-faire ideology and system 275
The impact of globalization on Europe 278
The challenge of mixed economy and welfare state 300
Globalization and inequality 305
Rising global environmental considerations and regulations 312
Europe: a rising economic superpower 320

Bibliography 327
Index 350

Boxes

1.1	The Brown Boveri Company	*page* 16
1.2	The Paris Metro	18
1.3	Aspirin	27
1.4	Tungsram	32
1.5	The Agnellis	35
2.1	John Maynard Keynes	43
2.2	KLM	85
3.1	The autobahn	104
3.2	Hjalmar Schacht	113
3.3	Volkswagen	119
3.4	Radar and the ballistic rocket	121
4.1	Dnieprostroi	147
4.2	The Danube–Black Sea Canal	155
5.1	Jean Monnet	202
5.2	The Channel Tunnel	207
5.3	Sir William Beveridge	231
5.4	Marks and Spencer	249
6.1	The World Wide Web	265
6.2	Nokia	272
6.3	Benetton	274

Figures

I.1	Urbanization, 1913–90	*page* 2
I.2	Birth rates, death rates, and population growth in Europe	3
I.3	Life expectancy at birth, 1900–2000	4
I.4	Population growth of Europe and the world	5
1.1	Disparity in economic growth, 1897–1913	38
2.1	Industrial recovery, 1928–37/8	71
2.2	Soviet industrialization and war preparations in the 1930s	76
2.3	Economic growth, 1900–50	80
2.4	Restructuring of British industry, 1912–38	82
2.5	Restructuring of French industry, 1929–38	83
2.6	Labor productivity USA – Europe, 1913–50	87
2.7	Regional disparities, 1900–50	89
3.1	Changes in sectoral employment, Italy and Spain, 1950–73	131
3.2	Rise of tourism: Spain	132
4.1	Industrial output in the peripheries	151
4.2	Decline of agricultural population: Central and Eastern Europe	170
4.3	Labor productivity in the peripheries, 1950–73	176
4.4	Indebtedness of Central and Eastern Europe, 1970–90	184
4.5	Per capita income in the Soviet Union	187
4.6	Per capita GDP in Central and Eastern Europe and the former Soviet Union, 1989–98	187
5.1	Nuclear energy as % of energy used in 1998	240
5.2	Labor productivity in Southern and Eastern Europe, 1950–90s	246
5.3	Spending on food and clothing: Switzerland, 1912–2000	247
5.4	Spending on basics (food, clothing, etc.); 15 best-developed EU countries	248
5.5	Spread of telephone lines, TV and radio licenses in Europe	252

5.6 Telephone lines per 100 inhabitants, 1979   252
5.7 Number of cars in 10 best-developed EU countries   254
5.8 Europe's catching-up (GDP per capita), 1950–73   257
6.1 Foreign direct investment, 1973–2000   267
6.2 Daily foreign exchange transactions globally, 1973–95   268
6.3 German investments abroad, 1961 and 1990   270
6.4 Unemployment rate, 1950–90s   281
6.5 De-industrialization of Western Europe, 1960s–90s   288
6.6 Europe's exports, 1950–2000   290
6.7 Service revolution: services in the European Union
     (15 countries) in % of total value added   292
6.8 Employment structure by sectors of economy, 1900–2000   293
6.9 Labor productivity in Western Europe, 1913–90s   294
6.10 Ireland's per capita income level, 1973–2000   298
6.11 Aging of population, Western Europe, 1900–2000   302
6.12 Regional disparities (GDP per capita), 1973–2000   308
6.13 Poverty in Central and Eastern Europe (7 countries),
     1980s–1990s   309
6.14 Personal computers per 1,000 inhabitants, 1995   310
6.15 Gross domestic product: continents, regions, 1973–2000   322
6.16 Population and GDP, EU–USA, 2000   323
6.17 Labor productivity, EU–USA, 1950–90   324
6.18 Foreign direct investment by countries of origin, 1973–2000   325

Tables

1.1	The world's GDP growth by continents	*page* 21
1.2	The world's per capita GDP growth by continents	21
1.3	The share of the continents in world's total GDP	21
1.4	The slowing down of old leaders, and the rise of new Western economic powers	30
1.5	Railroads in peripheral Europe in 1913	31
1.6	GDP per capita	39
1.7	GDP per capita disparities between European core and peripheries	39
2.1	Decline of GDP (in percent) in belligerent countries, 1913–19	52
2.2	Tariffs in % of value of imported goods, 1927–31 compared	66
2.3	GDP and GDP per capita in Europe and the world, 1900–50	80
2.4	Output of electric energy of 23 European countries	81
2.5	The spread of telephone and radio in 21 European countries	83
2.6	Number of motor vehicles in Europe	84
2.7	Labor productivity in Western Europe and Scandinavia	86
2.8	GDP per capita in three European regions, 1913 and 1950	88
2.9	Regional income disparities within Europe, 1900–50	88
2.10	Number of cars and telephone lines per 1,000 inhabitants	90
3.1	German share in foreign trade in %	127
3.2	GDP per capita in Southern Europe in 1990 ppp dollars and %	130
4.1	Catching-up process of the Soviet Union, 1900–50	150
4.2	Labor productivity	177
4.3	Per capita GDP 1989–98 in million 1990 international dollars	188
4.4	GDP growth rate per capita	188
4.5	Per capita GDP in % of the European Union	188
5.1	Public expenditures in % of gross social product	227
5.2	Radio and TV licenses in Western Europe	251

5.3   Volume of exports, 1913 = 100%   256
6.1   Rate of growth in constant prices and unemployment   283
6.2   From peak to trough: fluctuation in foreign trade between
      1973 and 1983 – maximum percentage peak to trough fall or
      smallest rise per annum   283
6.3   Annual R&D spending in the European Union, early 1990s   285
6.4   Average annual percentage change in private consumption   289
6.5   Merchandise exports as % of GDP in 1990 prices   290
6.6   Service revolution: value added in services as % of total
      value added   291
6.7   Labor productivity, GDP per hour at international 1990 $ 294
6.8   Leaders in catching up (GDP per capita 1973–98)   300
6.9   Mediterranean and Northern countries: GDP per capita   300
6.10 The growth of GDP per capita   321
6.11 Per capita real GDP growth   321
6.12 Regional disparity, GDP per capita, regions in % of the West,
      1950–98   322
6.13 The level of GDP per capita in 1990 ppp dollars, 1950–92   324
6.14 Stock of foreign direct investment in 1998   326

Acknowledgments

Writing an economic history of an entire continent over the course of an entire century is probably an over-ambitious enterprise. Several inspirations, however, have prompted me to write one.

I lived through and survived more than two-thirds of that century, and closely watched the latter half of it. I had personal experiences with a war economy and various economic regimes. I actively participated in economic regime change in Hungary. I feel fortunate for this unique, motivating experience.

Roughly twenty years ago, with my late friend and co-author György Ránki, I published an economic history of nineteenth-century Europe – *Európa gazdasága a 19. században 1780–1914* (*Europe's Economy in the 19th Century 1780–1914*, Budapest: Gondolat Kiadó). Some of my good friends and colleagues published even broader economic histories: David Landes's classic *The Unbound Prometheus*, and Sidney Pollard's *Peaceful Conquest* on the industrialization of Europe covered roughly two centuries between 1760 and 1970. Derek Aldcroft pioneered his *The European Economy, 1914–1970*, and then expanded it to the end of the century in 2001. Several excellent works covered the interwar period – among others, the thin but essential *The European Economy Between the Wars* by Charles Feinstein, Peter Temin, and Gianni Toniolo. Even more works were published on the unique prosperity after World War II and its sudden end in the 1970s; Barry Eichengreen's important studies, the edited volumes of Nicholas Crafts and Gianni Toniolo, and Andrea Boltho deserve special attention among them. Herman Van der Wee published a world economic history on the post-World War II prosperous third of a century. My most inspiring friend, Eric Hobsbawm, produced a gigantic opus on the complex world history of the entire twentieth century.

I cannot cease this fragmentary list without mentioning Angus Maddison's excellent historical statistics, which offer a unique source for comparative figures. These works and experiences encouraged me to make my own contribution. They also enabled me to bypass several aspects of the twentieth-century economic history of Europe. In this volume, I will not discuss the various factors of economic growth and the major cyclical pulsation of the economy they vividly discussed and analyzed. I will concentrate on a much less discussed aspect of the century's political economy: the rise and fall of various economic regimes, their interrelations, and impacts. It may also help in understanding the political economy of the process of economic homogenization, which gained momentum in the second half of the century. The European peripheries in the South and East of the continent remained much less industrialized and developed than the advanced core countries in the West until the mid-twentieth century. Tremendous attempts were made and new economic models and policies introduced to catch up with the West. These efforts failed for a long time but, at least in certain peripheral areas, gained momentum during the second half of the century. The failure and the progress of convergence and catching-up with the more advanced regions is an important aspect of the analysis.

I am very grateful to all of my friends and colleagues who provided encouragement and made it possible for me to find a new focus to investigate the century. I include in this list the anonymous reviewers of Cambridge University Press who gave valuable advice to finalize the manuscript.

As always in my life, research and writing are closely connected with teaching. The courses I have taught over the past fifteen years at the University of California Los Angeles on the economic history of nineteenth- and twentieth-century Europe, and on the European Union, helped me in working on and thinking about this project for years. I am very grateful to my great colleagues in the History department, and to thousands of my students over those years, who created an inspiring intellectual environment for my work. UCLA's Young Research Library, with its unique collections and superb services, offered the best possible resources. The grants from UCLA's Academic Senate helped me manage the immense statistical work. I am especially grateful to David Summers for his excellent work in copyediting my manuscript, and for the most professional staff of Cambridge University Press who took special care preparing the publication.

Last but not least, I want to mention my wife, Kati, for her invaluable contributions, from library research and chart compositions to critical reading and commenting on several versions of the manuscript. I accomplished this book with her collaboration, which, I must confess, sometimes threatened to endanger the heavenly harmony of our marriage, but which, despite a few emotional minutes, in the long run strengthened it tremendously – and the manuscript as well.

Ivan T. Berend

Introduction

Looking back over the twentieth century, one may imagine Charles Dickens's feelings when he reflected on the bloody ending of the eighteenth century. He opened his 1859 *A Tale of Two Cities* with the words: "It was the best of times, it was the worst of times, it was the age of wisdom, it was the age of foolishness, it was the epoch of belief, it was the epoch of incredulity, it was the season of Light, it was the season of Darkness, it was the spring of hope, it was the winter of despair . . ."

Indeed, as Sir Isaiah Berlin expressed it, the twentieth century was the most horrible century of Western history. Eric Hobsbawm characterizes it as the Age of Extremes, "a sort of triptych or historical sandwich: a quarter of a century of a 'Golden Age' between two, equally long periods of catastrophes, decomposition and crisis" (Hobsbawm, 1994: 1, 6). Mark Mazover gave the provocative title *Dark Continent* to his book on Europe's twentieth century, which "brought new levels of violence into European life, militarizing society . . . killing millions of people with the help of modern bureaucracies and technologies" (Mazover, 1998: 404).

The twentieth century, nevertheless, radically changed Europe and the life of its peoples in a positive way. A person could produce ten times more value in an hour by the year 2000 than a century before. The amount of goods and services, food, clothing, housing, summer vacation and travel, health and educational services available to an average European family in 2000 was five times greater than that available to a similar family in 1900. The monthly consumption spending of an Italian working-class family of four was $180 in the 1890s, but one hundred years later – in comparable dollars – $1,600. Moreover, in the latter period health care and education were free to them. People moved from remote villages to rising cities and changed their lives dramatically (see Figure I.1). "The transformation of the daily life of ordinary European people . . . is the most revolutionary event, to date, in the history of the continent" (Feinstein, Temin, Toniolo, 1997: 5).

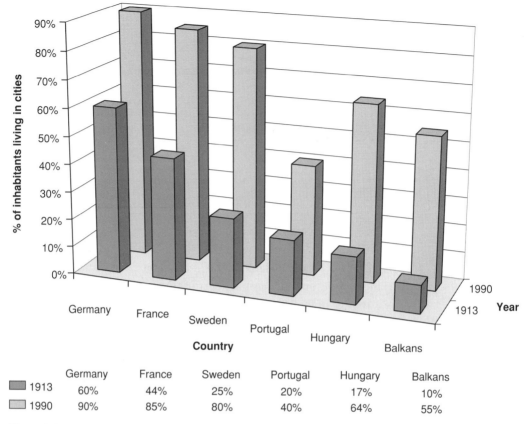

	Germany	France	Sweden	Portugal	Hungary	Balkans
1913	60%	44%	25%	20%	17%	10%
1990	90%	85%	80%	40%	64%	55%

Figure I.1
Urbanization,
1913–90

The death rate decreased drastically (see Figure I.2) and life expectancy at birth, as an average, nearly doubled in twentieth-century Europe (see Figure I.3) – in the advanced part of the continent it was forty-six years in 1900 and seventy-eight years by 2000, while in the poorer parts it increased from thirty-two to sixty-seven years. The population of the continent increased throughout the century (see Figure I.4). An average person spent three times the number of years in school and became incomparably better educated at the end of the century than at the beginning. Progress of this kind – concurrent with new economic policies – was an everyday experience for twentieth-century Europeans. Best of times, worst of times.

European people of the twentieth century long believed in their role in promoting human development and social progress. This idea had reigned since the Enlightenment as a kind of secular religion. People longed, as the German philosopher Georg W. F. Hegel opined, for the absolute knowledge of Truth, the earthly realization of the "absolute spirit," as Jews longed for the coming of the Messiah. People of the age accepted that history had a goal and was advancing toward higher stages, and they wanted to make this goal identical with their own goals and ideals.

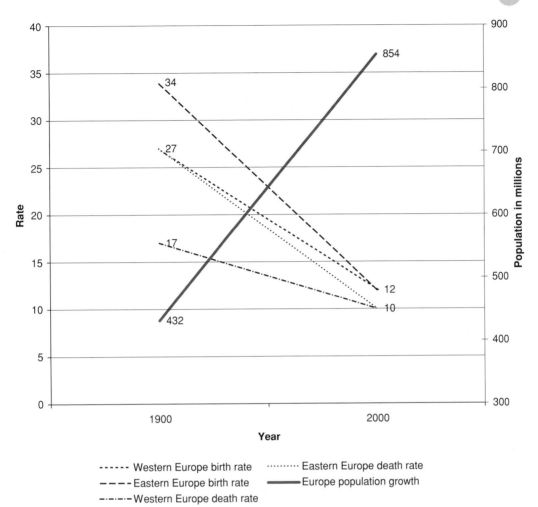

Figure I.2 Birth rates, death rates, and population growth in Europe

They were convinced that understanding history and the requirements of the age, the knowledge of Truth, created an unshakable base for human actions. People believed they could mould history and influence progress through rationally based actions and interventions. Twentieth-century economic thinking and practice were, in a way, the crowning of this idea of Enlightenment. An unbroken chain of economic experiments based on different kinds of interventions attempted to influence human development.

History and experience teach us, according to G. W. F. Hegel, that people and governments have never learned anything from history. Twentieth-century Europe, despite early and repeated signs to the contrary, eventually proved this bitter conclusion at least partially wrong. European countries sought lessons from the past and developed policies, rightly or wrongly, accordingly. Cicero's description of history as *testis temporum, magister vitae* – "witness of times, teacher of life" – characterizes the experience of

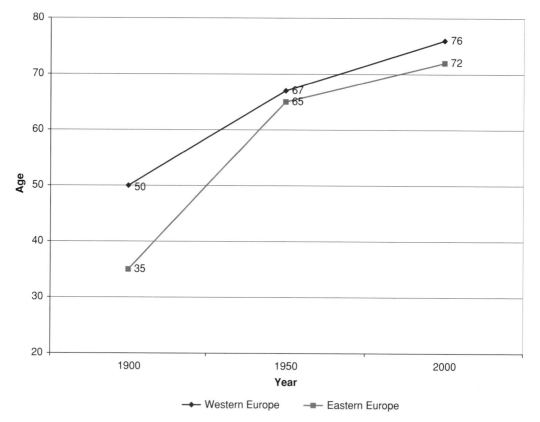

Figure I.3 Life expectancy at birth, 1900–2000

the past century. The unprecedented catastrophes and cataclysms of the "age of extremes" scarred three generations: two bloody wars that killed 50–60 million Europeans and eliminated entire minorities, revolutions and civil wars that turned sons against fathers and brothers against each other. The social fabric was strained by decades of economic chaos, including depression, and hyper-inflation that abolished the value of money and pushed countries back hundreds of years to the barter system. Economic warfare among nations in peacetime, and poverty and suffering in epidemic proportions, cried out for resolution.

These experiences mobilized the masses, educated economic and political thinkers, and influenced governments. People learned from their suffering and thought that they understood the requirements of the age: they knew the Truth and were able to act accordingly. Economists worked out counter-cyclical policy measures to avoid bottomless economic decline. From their war experience, they learned new methods to stabilize international financial markets, create jobs, and achieve specific economic goals which in "normal times" had been out of reach. They changed their attitudes toward colonialism, once considered an essential policy. They

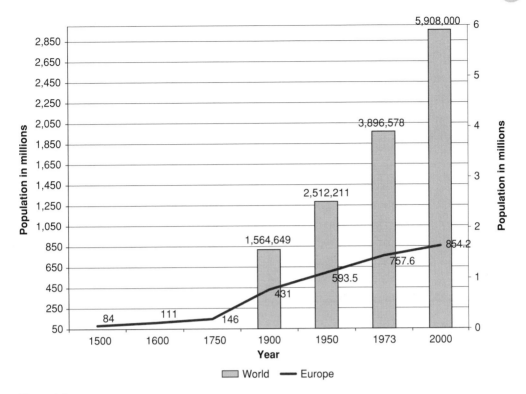

Figure I.4
Population growth of Europe and the world

gave up their colonies, sometimes reluctantly but mostly peacefully, under the pressure of the post-World War II de-colonization drive. The people of twentieth-century Europe became more entrepreneurial, took more risks, and introduced several new economic systems.

Economic growth became the new "golden calf" or the *Zeitgeist* of the age. State planners introduced new regulations and interventions aimed at higher economic growth. Though the ideal of growth through market automatism predominated at the beginning of the century, most of the new experiments were based on market corrections with an explicit social goal. Redistributive systems were created to decrease sharp income differences among different layers of society and among various regions.

Less developed countries tried economic measures to generate higher capital accumulation and investment, and to force rapid economic development. The strict regulations and planning of the war economy taught valuable lessons. Regulated markets became the norm in the interwar decades. Authoritarian regimes, mostly Mediterranean dictatorships, went further with economic dirigisme, establishing state sectors and economic targets to be achieved by state planning and assistance. The less developed European periphery, Russia and Central and Eastern Europe, went even further. Regimes in this region eliminated private property and market prices, and introduced a centrally planned, non-market system, because they believed that backwardness could be eliminated by central state policy. Modernization dictatorships subordinated unions, oppressed all kinds of resistance, and, behind the shield of dictatorial regimes, implemented rapid, forced industrialization to catch up with the advanced West.

All of these regimes were isolationist. They equated independence with self-sufficiency. When prohibitive, protectionist policies failed in a national framework, they were supplemented by dictated economic cooperation. The German Nazi leadership created a *Grossraumwirtschaft*. The Soviet Bloc's centrally planned economies established the Council for Mutual Economic Aid (CMEA, or Comecon) under Soviet leadership. For a while, these regimes accelerated economic growth, but eventually these planned economies proved too rigid for the requirements of the new technological revolution and gradually globalizing world economy. Moreover, because they imposed isolation and terror, anachronistic to the age, none of them survived the century.

Several promising elements of these regimes, however, were taken over by the post-World War II West European governments. New international monetary and trade agreements created a different economic environment, and post-World War II economic development avoided dramatic cyclical fluctuations. These regimes used strict regulations and counter-cyclical policy in a mixed welfare-state economy, and preserved or established state-owned sectors in transportation, communication, and industry, often using planning to achieve specific goals.

But most of all they introduced a system of redistribution based on high taxation and built up a strong social safety net made up of free education, health benefits, insurance, maternity leave, guaranteed pensions, and long paid vacations. However, universal welfare services guaranteed as citizen rights did not achieve utopian egalitarian goals; private ownership and income differences were preserved. Social solidarity nonetheless became a leading principle, with a reinterpretation of citizen rights to include the right to employment and social security. These measures, aside from contributing to general welfare, also strengthened domestic markets and increased consumption, which became the engine of prosperity. These regimes also introduced a corporative type of collaboration between employees and employers, which reinstated the unions destroyed by the dictatorial regimes. Instead, the system worked in a democratic and voluntary way, as a *Sozialpartnerschaft* or social partnership as it was called in Austria, and led to wage and profit moderation.

Furthermore, all of these state interventions were implemented with the market environment basically intact. State-owned companies acted as private ones in a free market. Planning was not based on compulsory state command but used market incentives for the realization of goals. Regulatory state intervention was not combined with protectionism but free trade. Instead of economic confrontation, called economic nationalism between the two wars, European governments introduced a European free market zone, a system of cooperation, on an equal and democratic basis. They created a customs and then an economic union, introducing a common currency, the Euro, and a common central bank. Collaboration began with six countries. The Union gradually expanded to nine, then twelve, then fifteen, and in 2004, to twenty-five countries.

The introduced economic systems influenced economic growth, structural changes, and regional restructuring. The European economy was transfigured from an industrial–agrarian structure to a communication service-led economy. The continent made progress in narrowing the traditional gap between the advanced Western core and the less developed peripheries with less than half the core's income level. Some of the peripheries caught up with the West. Scandinavia remained outside the main industrialization drive of the West until the late nineteenth century, but gradually industrialized and caught up with the Western income level between the 1870s and 1930s. Mediterranean Europe, Ireland, and Finland achieved a much higher-than-average growth rate and a catching-up process only in the second half of the twentieth century, especially following European Community membership and assistance during the last third of the century. The Central and Eastern European periphery was unable to follow this trend. State socialism led to rapid industrialization but was accompanied by isolation, and the rigid non-market economy reproduced technological backwardness. The gap between East and West grew larger than it had ever been in modern history. This last remaining periphery on the continent, nevertheless, has begun to shrink with the acceptance of eight of the region's countries into the European Union. Their EU membership heralds the beginning of their catching-up process in the early twenty-first century. Although a European continent without peripheries remains a long way off, so far that it may yet prove to be a utopian dream, the way to full integration is now paved for at least a few countries of the region.

Most of these changes and innovations were introduced during the real "body" of the "short" twentieth century, concentrated into roughly six decades between 1914 and 1973. The last decades of the century and the transition to the twenty-first century saw dramatic political and regime change as well as breathtaking globalization of the world system in which regulations often proved counterproductive, and social welfare expenditures became a burden in an arena of unlimited international competition. At the end of the twentieth century, people lost the comfortable, long-held belief in their ability to change historical processes. Skepticism has arisen from attempts to change history that have been compromised, violent actions in the name of peace, and the degradation of human ideals. A conservative reaction to that century's ideals totally rejected even the possibility of understanding history and discovering Truth. The laissez-faire ideology re-emerged triumphant.

Human intervention to generate progress and change countries' destinies spanned the entire century. The results were mixed and setbacks in the transformation of Europe were unavoidable. In the interwar decades the future looked bleak. Post-World War II Europe grew euphoric during history's most striking economic development. After the oil crisis and a dramatic structural crisis in the 1970s and 1980s, adjustment to the requirements of the new technological-communication revolution shocked the people of the continent again. Globalization, especially during the final two decades of the century, created an unprecedented international economic environment. New economic phenomena appeared and remained incomprehensible. A new search for Truth began.

The engine of economic development, which previously moved national economies with the assistance of nation states, shifted. Multinational companies led technological development and established a different kind of division of labor among their subsidiaries all over the world. The unprecedented increase in direct foreign investment, bank loans, and financial transactions of a globalized cutthroat free market facilitated technological explosion and dramatic restructuring of the economy. With the changes came reinterpretation of the nature of competition, of "social burdens," and of expensive welfare benefits.

Can Europe adjust to these new requirements? Although only the future will tell, Europe has already made impressive progress. The integration process has expanded the size and power of the European Union. Both the modernized division of labor within the Union and the rise of European multinational companies as equal competitors in the world market have repositioned Europe to meet the demands of the twenty-first century. Europe is an economic superpower with potential equal to that of the United States. Reform of the welfare state is on the way. Will these reforms succeed without abolishing the welfare state? Several signs point in this direction, but the answer is not yet clear.

This book looks at the story of Europe as the laboratory of economic regimes, presenting its "development trend," which is to say, both the failures and the successes in responding to the challenges of a crisis- and tragedy-ridden but highly successful age. This book has a central hypothesis: the leading trend of the twentieth century was the gradual synthesis of diametrically opposing and sharply confronting economic systems. The invented and newly introduced regimes were like day and night – free market system versus centrally planned regime, democratic market economy versus dictatorial economic dirigisme. These opposing regimes that fought each other at the end of the day also learned from one another. Thus, they experienced a kind of synthesis, combining elements of laissez-faire and of regulation, of private and public ownership, and of planned and interventionist systems. Furthermore, though invisible at first glance, the analysis reveals that the vast disparity among European regions, inherited from the entire period of early modern and modern history, gradually began to disappear and although disparity increased in some cases, more and more of the continent's countries reached a similar economic level.

The process itself was highly controversial. Like counterpoints in music that combine individual melodies, economic transformation was characterized both by broadening and narrowing diversity, diverging and merging economic regimes. Some regimes were "antidotes" or "counterpoints" to others. Some regions exhibited the opposite development trend from others. Several elements of certain economic regimes terminally failed and disappeared. By the end of the century, however, a kind of Hegelian dialectical synthesis was emerging.

Nevertheless, an economic synthesis is far from complete. Will it ever be completed in a more or less homogeneous federal Europe? Will new economic regimes emerge? Will Europe experience another revolt against globalization? Only the twenty-first century will provide the answers to these questions.

CHAPTER 1

Europe's laissez-faire system and its impact before World War I

The rise of Britain and the laissez-faire system

The "long" nineteenth century, from the 1770s–80s to 1914, was the most spectacular period of economic change in Europe. The British Industrial Revolution opened a new chapter of economic history. By the middle of the eighteenth century Britain had achieved the prerequisites for sustained economic growth. More than 1,000 miles of navigable canals and waterways, 300 Newcomen steam engines, a revolutionized agriculture, and dynamic proto-industrial development made Britain the center of world trade. Domestic markets played a dominant role during this period (Flinn, 1966: 62); only 5–9% of British output was exported during the eighteenth century. However, higher profits in foreign markets increased the role of exports to 10–12% (Bairoch, 1976: 196). Export activity, nevertheless, became the driving force of industry: during the first half of the eighteenth century the output of export industries increased by 76%, while output in other industries grew only 7%. The value of British exports doubled between 1700 and 1750, and then more than tripled by 1800. The leading textile industry by then exported half its output. Eric Hobsbawm concludes that the origins of British industrialization were rooted in foreign trade, especially with less developed areas such as India and other colonies (Hobsbawm, 1968: 49).

In the early eighteenth century, Britain defended its domestic market in a traditional mercantilist way. For example, the so-called Calico Law banned the imports of Indian cotton goods. Exports flourished, especially in the leading textile sector. The value of British exports increased thirty-fold during the long nineteenth century to 40% of the national income (Schlote, 1952: 53). The rate of export growth also increased, from 2% to 4%, and then to 6% during the 1860s to 1870s. Already by 1820 the value of British merchandise exports surpassed the value of merchandise exports of France, Switzerland, Austria, the Low Countries, and Italy combined. By 1870, British exports reached 40% of total Western European exports, and by World War I still accounted for more than one-third (Maddison, 2001: 361). British industrial development also intensified. During the first four decades of the nineteenth century industrial output grew at rates of 23%, 39%, 47%, and 37%. Britain gradually gave up agricultural self-sufficiency.

Free trade became a prerequisite for the country's further economic expansion. No other country had such a vested interest in eliminating trade obstacles. Following early attempts in the eighteenth century such as the Methuen Agreement with Portugal (1703) and the Eden Treaty with France (1786), Britain from the 1840s steadily advanced toward free trade. Sir Robert Peel produced a balanced budget without huge tariff incomes in 1842. Freed from reliance on tariffs to finance the state budget, he was able to reduce import duties for 750 articles and export duties on British manufactured products. Peel made further radical tariff reductions in 1845. The severe Irish famines in these years led to the elimination of the Corn Laws (1846 and 1849), which defended domestic agricultural markets and had reflected agricultural interests. The repeal of the Navigation Law (1849) ended restrictions on mooring foreign ships in British ports. However, it took another quarter of a century and a series of balanced budgets by Gladstone in the 1860s before tariffs were lifted and free trade policy was institutionalized in Britain.

The Cobden–Chevalier Treaty between Britain and France (1860) was the first milestone in establishing a laissez-faire system throughout Europe. The most-favored-nation clause of this treaty became the vehicle for the internationalization of free trade through the mechanism of automatically invoking tariff reductions subsequently negotiated with any third party. Indeed, through a series of agreements with Germany, Italy, Belgium, Sweden, Norway, Spain, Holland, Austria, and Portugal, Europe effectively became a free trade zone during the last decades of the nineteenth century.

This was facilitated by the development of a multilateral payment network. Although the bulk of trade transactions remained bilateral until World War I, at least 20–25% became multilateral. This encouraged international trade because countries could offset a trade deficit with one partner by a trade surplus with another so that less gold and hard currency was needed for balanced trade. This reduced a major obstacle to international trade – the lack of sufficient gold and hard currency reserves. The crowning move toward a laissez-faire system was made with the introduction of the gold standard. Until the 1870s, most European countries had a bimetallic (silver and gold) system (France), a silver standard (Holland, Scandinavia, the German states), or inconvertible paper money (Russia, Greece, Italy).

Most currencies thus were not convertible, a major obstacle for the expansion of foreign trade. The pioneer of the gold standard was again Britain, which made important progress in this direction at the end of the eighteenth century, and fully introduced the gold standard in 1821. Other European countries followed much later. In 1867 the European Monetary Congress in Paris advocated the introduction of the gold standard. In that year, Holland went on the gold standard, followed by the Scandinavian countries. United Germany introduced its new currency, the mark, based on gold. By 1878, the Latin Monetary Union also adopted the gold standard, so that Western Europe was in conformity. By the 1890s, when Austria-Hungary and Russia joined, the gold standard became common throughout Europe. Each currency unit had a fixed gold content, and thus currencies became easily exchangeable. Exchange rates became stable, dominated in gold, with only arbitrage determined by supply conditions affecting its fixity and causing some fluctuations. The British pound sterling, unchanged in value between 1821 and 1914, was practically equal to gold and became the international currency (Kenwood and Lougheed, 1971).

Together with the gradual transformation from protectionism cum bimetallism toward free trade cum gold standard, the theory and ideology of laissez-faire was born. It was a slow process, partly because of a dominant kameralist-mercantilist concept of the eighteenth century, and partly because economics was not yet an independent discipline but part of political theory. In the early centuries of commercial capitalism mercantilist economic policy sought to increase exports to gain gold and silver. The state played a central role in promoting domestic production, regulating trade, and increasing state revenues. It was a dynamic concept recognizing the need for domestic industrial development to increase the export capacity of the country. Because the accumulation of precious metal within a country could be guaranteed only through export surplus, strict control of foreign trade and protective tariffs to limit imports were inherent to mercantilism. With industrial development, nevertheless, an increasing number of political thinkers realized the need for "emancipation of capitalism from state tutelage":

It has been said that mercantilism is the theory and ideological justification of commercial capitalism, whereas the value problem, which is the chief concern of the classical school of economists, emerged only when the transition to industrial capitalism [progressed]. (Heimann, 1964: 35, 39)

First the physiocrats, and especially François Quesnay, changed the way of thinking by attacking the mercantilist belief in trade and money as the only source of wealth. Instead, they emphasized the role of land and the production of goods by the extractive branches for creating wealth. They turned toward free trade and economic freedom. Even stronger arguments followed.

This concept was rooted in the individualist ideal of John Locke and David Hume. Eighteenth-century British philosophers were convinced of a "divine harmony between private advantage and the public good." The term laissez-faire was, however, introduced by a Frenchman, the Marquis d'Argenson, in the mid-eighteenth century. To govern better, he stated, one must govern less. Jeremy Bentham in his *A Manual of Political Economy* (1793) formulated a law: "The general rule is that nothing ought to be done or attempted by government." The nineteenth century was characterized by the gradual rise and then the unchallenged domination of the laissez-faire economic system.

Almost everything which the State did in the eighteenth century in excess of its minimum functions was, or seemed, injurious or unsuccessful. The Economists were teaching that wealth, commerce, and machinery were the children of free competition . . . But the Darwinians could go one better than that – free competition built the Man . . . The principle of the Survival of the Fittest could be regarded as a vast generalization of Ricardian economics. (Keynes, 1927: 13–14)

The pioneers of a comprehensive economic theory and ideology of the industrial age, however, were the first great generations of British economists: Adam Smith, David Ricardo, and John Stuart Mill. Their ideas were based on two foundations: the *Zeitgeist* of Newtonian physics and the Enlightenment on the one hand, and British practice and self-interest on the other. In the perspective of physics, the universe is governed by internal natural laws in a self-perpetuating harmony, which includes humankind. In a departure from previous concepts, the new perspective suggested that free man could employ knowledge of natural laws to create harmony in society and the economy. Outside intervention is harmful. British practice suggested the same: a free economy and trade without state intervention are advantageous. The new theories consequently were formulated as natural laws, expressing the general interest of the world. The British economists firmly believed that free trade was the only system in which each country could be a beneficiary.

Adam Smith, professor of Logic and Rhetoric and later Moral Philosophy at Glasgow University, in his milestone *Wealth of Nations*, the foundation of modern economics, propounded an economic concept of preordained harmony, governed by the "invisible hand" of the market. In Smith's laissez-faire system, self-interest serves the public interest because of free competition. Division of labor results in productivity increases both in the factory and on an international level. Smith proved that "the greatest improvement in the productive powers of labour, and the greater part of the skill . . . seem to have been the effects of the division of labour" (Smith, 1970: 8). Like individual factories, countries also must specialize in the production of goods they can produce in the most efficient way. Intervention and protection create artificial obstacles to the most productive employment.

David Ricardo was born four years before the *Wealth of Nations* appeared, entered the family business, and became a broker in the City of London. The self-made millionaire became a self-made economist and, without university education, one of the finest ever. His theory of comparative advantage maintained that free trade is advantageous for both partners, since each of them is selling what they can produce in the most efficient way and buying what they cannot. Trade between industrial and agrarian countries is thus not a zero-sum game, in which one of the parties wins while the other loses.

John Stuart Mill received the best possible education and became one of the finest intellectuals of the mid-nineteenth century. He made fundamental contributions to economics and political philosophy with the concepts of unrestricted private property and a free market as the sole basis of human rights and freedom. In his essay "On Liberty" (1859), Mill stated:

It was once held to be the duty of governments . . . to fix prices, and regulate the process of manufacture. But it is now recognized . . . [that it is much better to leave] the producers and sellers perfectly free, under the sole check of equal freedom to the buyers . . . Restrictions . . . are indeed restraints; and all restraints, *quâ* restraint, are evils . . . they do not really produce the results which it is desired to produce by them. (Mill, 1946: 695–8)

In the social-political arena, Mill envisioned the same divine harmony, described in his "Considerations on Representative Government" (1861), when

manual labourers and their affinities on the one side, employers of labour and their affinities on the other, should be . . . equally balanced . . . in Parliament . . . A balance preserved among personal interests, as may render any one of them dependent for its success, on carrying with it at least a large proportion of those who act on higher motives, and more . . . distant views. [Representative government is the] ideal type of a perfect government. (Mill, 1946: 823–4)

In British classical economic and political theory the connection between laissez-faire economy and personal liberty and democracy was seen as natural, and also as the expression of universal interests and guarantor of universal liberty and harmony. The unique success of Britain, the model country of industrialization during the nineteenth century, gradually became a validation of British devotion to free trade and economic thinking. Laissez-faire ideology became broadly accepted, and by the dawn of the twentieth century it became the *Zeitgeist* in the advanced countries, although it remained shallow in practice and was shelved if the national economy was endangered.

Under the banner of laissez-faire ideology, internationalization, or the first globalizing trend of the European economy, made great progress and became institutionalized. The rapid spread of free trade and the gold standard created a no- or low-tariff zone in Europe and a convertible currency with extremely stable exchange rates during the entire period. The British pound sterling, as good as gold, became the international currency. Free trade was accompanied by the building of an international communication network, in particular transoceanic trade and communication, and the European railroad system. After the first railroad line was opened in Britain in 1825, nearly 363,000 kilometers of rail lines were built on the European continent by 1910. Each country became connected with others. The time and cost of transportation decreased significantly.

Other international institutions were established, such as the International Telegraph Union (1865) and the International Postal Association (1875), together with the internationalization of the major European waterways (first the Rhine in 1868), and the metric system (1875). During the 1880s, most of the countries joined the new international patent and copyright agreements. All these paved the way for an international laissez-faire regime in Europe. However, although the continent remained committed to this international laissez-faire system, in domestic policy many countries soon turned to protectionism and state interventionism, especially after 1873 when American competition hit the European market, strongly endangering agriculture. This was particularly so in the peripheries, which were unable to compete with the core countries.

Rising modern sectors

Nineteenth-century economic development reached its peak during the first decade of the twentieth century thanks to the scientific achievements at the turn of the century. These included advances in modern chemistry, which led to the rise of new industries. Electricity, its generation, and a series of secondary and tertiary innovations of its applications created a new source of energy and led to the renewal of transportation as well as existing industries such as metallurgy and engineering. Countries

Box 1.1 The Brown Boveri Company

Founded in 1890 in a remote township of 4,000 inhabitants in Baden, Switzerland, the Brown Boveri Company was born as an international company. One of its founders, Charles Brown, was the son of an English engineer who moved to Switzerland. He studied engineering in Winterthur and worked for the Oerlikon Engineering Company from the age of twenty-two. The other founder, Walter Boveri, from a French family which emigrated from Savoy to Bavaria in the early seventeenth century, studied engineering and moved to Oerlikon. Brown and Boveri worked together and, in 1890, signed a contract of partnership, founding their own company in Baden, where one of the first electric power stations was also established at that time.

Though a small company with 200 workers, Brown Boveri began producing for exports from the beginning. The key to success lay with the founders themselves, especially Brown's engineering talent. He succeeded in transforming low-voltage electricity into high-voltage power and transporting it as early as the late 1880s. This was the last word in turn-of-the-century technology. Switzerland, lacking coal resources, began exploiting its rich water resources and initiated the widespread construction of hydroelectric power stations. The company had plenty of orders. The Swiss market, however, was too narrow and the company became multinational: the Frankfurt and Mannheim power stations also ordered generators and both required Brown Boveri to establish repair shops on the spot. Subsidiaries in Germany (1893), France (1894), Norway (1902), Italy (1903), and Austria (1910) were thus established.

By 1900, the firm had become a joint-stock company. During the first years of the century, Brown Boveri delivered generators for power stations and built transmission lines throughout Europe. The electrification of the newly built Simplon tunnel opened a new market. The company developed marine turbines for the new Dreadnought battleships, the largest of the time. Around the turn of the century, Brown Boveri's foreign sales already accounted for 80% of output of its highly reputed precision engineering products. This required the formation of an international sales organization, gradually established in more than 100 countries. Various kinds of cooperative agreements, joint investments, and subsidiaries enlarged the Brown Boveri Group: the British Charles Parsons, and Vickers, the German AEG, the Brown Boveri in Mannheim, the Compagnie Electro-Mécanique in Paris, Tecnomasio Italiano Brown Boveri in Milan, and similar companies in Prague, Budapest, Warsaw, Rotterdam, Brussels, Madrid, and even in Canada, Brazil, Argentina, and New York. Post-World War II prosperity led to skyrocketing turnover from 200 million to 3 billion Swiss francs in twenty years, while employment climbed to 80,000.

In small countries of Europe, several companies in cutting-edge industries emerged from the beginning as multinationals (Brown Boveri, 1966).

without coal, which had been at a severe disadvantage during the nineteenth century, suddenly became energy-rich through the construction of hydroelectric power stations. Switzerland, Norway, and Italy profited greatly from these developments.

Electricity conquered Europe relatively quickly. Paris declared itself to be the *capitale électrique* and 900,000 people surged to see the International Exhibition of electricity in November 1891. By 1906, nearly 3,000 communities were connected to the network (Beltran and Carré, 1991: 64, 103, 106, 124). London did not remain behind: in 1890, roughly 38 gigawatt-hours of electric energy were sold; in ten years this quantity increased by five times. "Before the First World War … [electricity] had concentrated … [in] the commercial city center areas and in wealthy suburbs" (Hannah, 1979: 189). By 1903, with the exception of two, all towns in Britain with more than 100,000 inhabitants had electricity supply, although no more than 6–7% of the urban population used electric lighting. By 1919, half a million houses were connected to electricity in Britain (Byatt, 1979: 25).

At the same time, the spider web of electric tramlines began forming the new European city transportation networks. The first electric trams appeared in Berlin and Prague in 1884 and in the 1890s, respectively. The London network expanded to 921 kilometers by 1900 and to 3,533 kilometers by 1906. In 1912, the Paris tram network was 2,004 kilometers long. At the same time, Budapest had a 172 kilometer-long electric tram network, used by 214,000 people in a year.

The world's first subway system began operating between Paddington and Farringdon Street in London in 1863. For decades, the London "tube" operated by steam, but electrification began at the end of the century, and by 1905 the Inner Circle was electrified (Byatt, 1979: 46–50). In 1896 the 2 kilometer-long Budapest subway system began operating; in 1900, the Paris Metro was opened and carried half a million passengers daily before the war.

Electricity also made possible the telephone. Before World War I, nearly 3.5 million telephone lines existed in Europe and 5.3 billion calls signaled the spread of new technology. The other major revolutionizing

Box 1.2 The Paris Metro

The Paris Metro system grew into a gigantic monument of twentieth-century urban transportation. After decades of debate over a railroad system for the city, the decision was made in 1898 to construct six lines of the subway system, the *Métropolitain*. Fulgence Bienvenüe, an official of the French national railroad, was appointed Director General of construction, responsible for building the tunnels and bridges, while the electrification, access to the stations, and operation of the system was run by a Belgian engineer, Baron Empain. Construction of the first six lines began in February 1899.

It was not the first modern metro, since London already had a large system, and a single 2 kilometer-long metro line was opened in Budapest in 1896. The Paris system, however, was ambitious. Bienvenüe decided to use the open trench method (unlike London, but like Budapest). The lines were not deep and the trenches were dug by hand, then the tracks were laid and walls and ceilings were built to complete the tunnels. After a strikingly short sixteen months, the first line with eighteen stations was opened in July 1900 between Port Maillot (later from the Grande Arche de La Défense) to Château de Vincennes, linking the west and east sides of the city. By the end of the year, 16 million Parisians traveled by Metro, an immense success in the year of the Paris World Expo.

Bienvenüe continued working on the planned six lines. From the construction of the fourth line, instead of bridges, tunnels were built under the river Seine. Another five lines followed. Meanwhile, a private company began building two north–south metro lines in 1909, which, in 1929, became part of the Paris Metro system as lines 12 (between Porte de La Chapelle and Mairie d'Issy) and 13 (between Châtillon-Montrouge and Saint Denis-Université). By the time Bienvenüe retired in 1934, the bulk of the thirteen lines was ready. A fourteenth line between Bibliothèque François Mitterrand and Madeleine was added in 1998.

In 1899, the design of stations and entrances also began with the participation of twenty companies, but the Compagnie Métropolitain de Paris was dissatisfied with the plans and commissioned the famous Art Nouveau architect Hector Guimard to design all of the stations and entrances by 1913. They became art historical monuments of the city.

The Metro is a symbol of Paris, and certainly the best, most dense network, and most accessible subway system in Europe. In the last decade of the twentieth century 1.2–1.3 billion trips were taken annually on the Paris Metro (Plotkin, 2000).

technological change was the appearance of the motor car as the most important private transportation vehicle. From the very beginning, cars were popular, though in the early days they were luxury toys. They improved fast, and by 1913 the person-to-car ratio was 437:1 in France, 890:1 in Switzerland, and 1,567:1 in Germany (Merki, 2002: 40–1, 78, 91, 95–7). Public transportation also adopted cars and buses early on. In Berlin, the first taxicab appeared in 1900, increasing to nearly 2,000 by 1912. Taxis were first used in the streets of London in 1904. The famous horse-drawn Paris omnibus made its last run in April 1913, by which time 927 buses already carried 206 million passengers.

The other main application of the combustion engine, the airplane, was closely connected to war efforts. In October 1911, for the first time in history, Italy used airplanes against the Turks near Tripoli, and a few days later, at the beginning of November, history's first air bombing occurred. World War I spurred this trend. The German Junkers–Fokker Works geared up for serial production of all-metal airplanes in 1917 (Morrow, 1993: 154). The German Air Force attacked London with its Me-109 fighters during the war. Civil aviation and air transportation, nevertheless, developed simultaneously. The world's first airline company, the German DELAG, was founded in 1909.

Although new technology opened up previously non-existent spheres of endeavor, it had a tremendous impact on old technology sectors as well. The symbol of nineteenth-century modernity, the railway, began to be modernized; the first lines were electrified around the turn of the century. Electricity, cars, and airplanes, however, were in their infancy; they did not yet affect the everyday life of the population, but heralded the future. The new sectors, nevertheless, gave tremendous impetus to economic development and Europe's industrial output more than doubled between 1890 and 1913 (Bairoch, 1976).

The service sector became the most dynamic area of growth for the economies of advanced countries. Before the war, more than one-third (and in some cases such as Norway and Britain around 50%) of the active population worked in services, mostly in trade, transportation, banking, and personal service branches, which produced 30–45% of the gross domestic product (GDP) in Western Europe. Indeed, the continent's economy reached a zenith: between 1900 and 1913 European GDP increased by an impressive 27%.

By the early twentieth century, the Western European countries essentially ruled the world and forged ahead along their chosen path toward economic progress. The established leaders maintained their positions at the top of the ladder. Both in 1900 and in 1913, Britain, Belgium,

Holland, Switzerland, and France were the richest countries on the continent, although by 1913 Germany and Denmark had joined this elite group.

Europe's position in the world

Western Europe nearly tripled its income level during the nineteenth century. While Southern and Eastern Europe had a somewhat slower growth, these regions profited from Western prosperity and also more than doubled their per capita income. At the beginning of the twentieth century, Europe was dominant in the world economy, representing nearly half (46%) of the world's total gross domestic product, and 41% of the world's per capita GDP.

From the 1870s, however, new competitors emerged. Taken together, the United States, Canada, Australia, and New Zealand increased their GDP by 43 times during the century, although they reached only 79% of the total West European GDP level by 1913. If measured on a per capita basis, the picture was somewhat different. In 1820 and 1870, these overseas countries were far behind Britain, reaching only 69% and 75% of its per capita income level respectively, but from the 1870s they broke through and by 1913 they already surpassed Britain by 4% and Western Europe in general by more than 40%.

Latin America, part of the international system but in a peripheral position, more than doubled its per capita income level during the nineteenth century. Asia, Oceania, and Africa, on the other hand, mostly outside the world system, increased their per capita income during the nineteenth century by only 28–35%. See Tables 1.1, 1.2, and 1.3.

Economic growth and development level were closely connected with industrialization. At the beginning of the nineteenth century, the majority of the world's population worked in agriculture, the only exception being Britain, where the agricultural population was historically small. As a consequence of the Industrial Revolution, however, only 38% of Britain's population remained in agriculture, with 33% in industry and 29% in services. (At that time 70% of the United States' population worked in agriculture, and 15% each in industry and services.) By 1860–70, in Britain the industrial/agricultural employment ratio was 42:23, while agriculture continued to account for 50% of the workforce in the United States, Germany, and France, roughly 70% in Scandinavia, 60% in Japan and nearly 90% in Russia.

By 1913 Britain had 12% and Western Europe roughly 28% agricultural employment (the same as in the United States), but the world remained still mostly agricultural: the Scandinavian countries had more

Table 1.1 The world's GDP growth by continents (GK dollars† 1990, billion)
(Maddison, 1995a: 227)

Year	WE*	%	E**	%	O***	%	LA****	%	A&O*****	%	A*	%	W**	%	Europe % of world
1820	133	100	230	100	14	100	14	100	405	100	33	100	695	100	33
1870	305	229	502	218	112	800	29	207	446	110	40	121	1,128	162	45
1913	735	552	1,242	540	583	41643	115	821	723	179	63	191	2,726	392	46

*Western Europe, 23 countries; ** total Europe (39); *** overseas (4); **** Latin America
(44); ***** Asia & Oceania (56); * Africa (56); ** world total, 199 countries
†Geary–Khamis dollars

Table 1.2 The world's per capita GDP growth by continents (in 1990 GK dollars)
(Maddison, 1995a: 228)

Year	WE	%	E	%	O	%	LA	%	A&O	%	A	%	W	%	WE % of W
1820	1,292	100	956	100	1,205	100	679	100	550	100	450	100	651	100	199
1870	2,110	163	1,434	150	2,440	202	760	112	580	106	480	107	859	132	236
1913	3,704	287	2,381	249	5,237	435	1,439	212	742	135	575	128	1,539	236	241

Table 1.3 The share of the continents in world's total GDP in %
(Maddison, 1995a: 227)

Year	E	O	LA	A&O	A
1820	33	2	2	58	5
1870	45	10	2	40	3
1913	46	21	4	27	2

than 40%, Japan 60%, Russia 70%, China and the Balkan countries more than 80% agricultural population (Maddison, 1995a: 39; Berend and Ránki, 1982: 159).

The European core was the most important supplier of processed industrial products in the world: Europe produced 52% of the world's industrial output in 1913. Three countries – Great Britain, Germany, and France – produced 72% of all European manufactured products and delivered roughly the same share of the continent's manufactured exports. Britain alone delivered more than half of the world's textile exports. Meanwhile, the same three Western European countries bought 63% of the world's food and raw material exports. Europe became the center of the world economy with 62% of world trade in 1913, while the combined share of Asia, Latin America, Africa, and East India was only 25%.

Europe also became the world's banker by exporting more than $40 billion, roughly 90% of total international capital exports, during the nineteenth century. The world economy became a European world economy.

Although the European economic system was strongly internationalized, and characterized by cooperation, the most powerful players of industrialized Europe were competitive, potentially hostile rivals for world leadership. An exalted expansionism and deadly race in colonial empire building began. This proved extremely successful. During the last third of the century, the Western core countries conquered the unoccupied territories of the world. Britain built an empire of 345 million people. France controlled 56 million in Africa, Asia, and the Pacific region. Some of the small Western countries such as Belgium conquered African territories eight times larger than Belgium itself, and Holland ruled 35 million people in Asia. Even their significance has been exaggerated, maintained Patrick O'Brien: "Supplies from the European colonies and settlements overseas played a complementary role that increased in scale and scope . . . [P]olitical conquest and colonization overseas was vital for success" (O'Brien, 2004: 19, 35).

To conquer and rule other continents was hypocritically dubbed *mission civilisatrice* (the civilizing mission) by the representatives of the "superior" French culture among "barbarous-primitive peoples" (Conklin, 1977). Rudyard Kipling in his poem "The White Man's Burden" described patronizing, self-sacrificing British who served the interests of their "half devil and half child" captives.

What fueled this feverish expansionism? Colonialism gained a new incentive from industrial capitalism. J. A. Hobson, in 1902, called this new phenomenon "imperialism" in the title of his book. The main initiative of expansion was, in his interpretation, colonial profit, which was necessitated by the gradual decline in investment opportunities in Britain, where rates of return were falling as technological senescence was taking root (Hobson, 1902). Karl Kautsky, the leading theorist of the German Social Democratic Party, in 1907 developed the concept of a new phase of capitalist development from the 1880s, characterized by monopolization of markets, "empire building," colonization of "agricultural areas," competition among the great powers with an increasing militarization, arms production, and the danger of war. Rosa Luxemburg, another leading Marxist theoretician, maintained in 1913 that capitalism could not reproduce itself without additional markets, raw material and labor resources. Consequently, it needed a "third person," outside the capitalist sector, the agrarian peripheries, which later were called the "third world" (Luxemburg, 1975). This view was shared by Vladimir I. Lenin, who in his 1917 study discussed the imperialist phase as a natural developmental stage of capitalism (Lenin, 1988).

Empire building, no doubt, was closely connected with the breathtaking advance of capitalist economy and had strong economic motivations. However, it also became a major status symbol of the great powers. As Heinrich von Treitschke phrased it in 1887, expressing the German ideology but also a characteristic latecomer's attitude:

All the great nations . . . want to leave their mark on the barbarian lands . . . [T]hose who do not participate in this race will play a miserable role in the future. Colonization became a vital question of the great nations. (Treitschke, 1887)

At the end of the nineteenth century the German geographer Friedrich Ratzel, a social-geographical Darwinist, coined the phrase *Lebensraum* (living space), a theory of the "struggle for space" (Ratzel, 1897), which became an ideological base for German expansionism. Russia, which occupied huge Asian, Central Asian, and European territories during the eighteenth and nineteenth centuries, continued using a policy that Lenin called "domestic colonization." Russia did not turn toward faraway continents but expanded the empire in every possible direction, absorbing and "Russifying" neighboring territories.

Rising disparity within Europe

The high level of prosperity in Europe in the early twentieth century was the product of a century of sustained growth, most commonly associated with the industrial revolution. The generally rapid growth, nevertheless, was uneven. Some advanced countries could adjust better to and profit more than others from the technological and structural transformation. Most of the old leaders, too comfortable in their leading positions, were relatively slow in their response to turn-of-the-century structural challenges, especially compared with the United States, but also with faster-growing France, Germany, and Scandinavia.

Britain had reached its peak as the world's industrial leader and began a slow decline relative to other Western countries. During the half century before World War I, the rate of increase of British exports dropped from 5–6% to 3% per year. The growth in industrial output, 30–35% per decade before 1870, declined to 17% after 1870. The British chemical industry, for example, produced only one-half and one-third of that produced by the Germans and the Americans respectively before the war. Industrial productivity increased rapidly but still represented only half of American, Swedish, and German productivity growth.

Holland made economic progress in supplying its domestic market with industrial consumer goods. Important new industrial branches emerged as well. The traditional sectors, however, continued to dominate the economy: food processing and textiles employed more than 40% of industrial employees. The most important sector of the Dutch economy remained its highly specialized agriculture, which employed about a quarter of the labor force through World War I. Before the war, Holland's per capita industrial output was by far the lowest (ranking twelfth) in Western Europe (Jansen and Smidt, 1974: 36).

Among the old leaders, France was an exception, although here too remained some indications of the old leader's *maladie*: the old export branches were preserved – textiles, toys, and luxury goods still represented 54% of French exports in 1913. As a consequence, the country lost ground to European competitors. Smallholder peasants represented 41% of the active population in 1913, a much higher percentage than in most other Western countries. At its high point, France's share of European trade reached nearly 20%, but by 1913 it had dropped to 12.6% (Broder, 1976: 305). Investment activity was relatively slow. This was due to the rapidly increasing export of capital, which consumed 20–25% of its capital formation (Girault, 1979: 226; Lévy-Leboyer, 1977: 74).

Despite such signs of certain weakness, the French economy exhibited impressive strength and an ability to renew itself. New technologies and leading sectors emerged. Electric power generation jumped from 340 million kW to 1,800 million kW, and before the war electric engines represented nearly 25% of steam-engine capacity. The electricity industry continued to increase its output by 14% per year. Around Grenoble, the most modern electro-metallurgical industry developed on the basis of Alpine hydro-electric power generation. France also fostered one of the world's most modern steel industries, which showed robust growth at a rate of 4.6% per year (three times faster than textiles) between 1892 and 1913. The country also took a leading role in aluminum-metallurgy, producing 16% of the world's output (Lévy-Leboyer, 1968). One of the greatest new successes was the rise of the automotive industry. The Peugeot and Renault companies (and in connection with them the Michelin tire maker) gained worldwide importance. By 1913 France produced 45,000 cars, second in the world behind the United States and first in Europe in this new industry.

The French economy responded quickly to the new requirements of the twentieth century. Per capita GDP increased by 32% between 1897 and 1913 (Maddison, 1995a). Considering the volume of output, France remained the third largest industrial power in Europe, behind Britain and Germany. On the basis of per capita industrial output it held fifth place behind Britain, Germany, Switzerland, and Belgium.

France's success, nevertheless, was only partial, compared with the sky-rocketing successes of its new and more vigorous neighbor and rival. Germany became the technological leader and home to some of the most modern industrial sectors of the age. What was the secret behind united Germany's unique success? From the *Gründerzeit* of the early 1870s, when the capital of joint-stock companies doubled in four years, Germany became the home country of the new industrial revolution, along with the United States. The country emerged as a great power with its strong economic performance and highly developed transportation and banking network. Without the "burden" of obsolete older technology, Germany was able to concentrate on the emerging science- and new technology-intensive industries, developing an industrial structure much more modern than that of its old rivals.

Already at the turn of the century Germany was the first to build an industrial core that would become typical of twentieth-century Europe. The textile industry which had driven the first industrial revolution played a secondary role in German industrialization and nearly lost its importance altogether before the war, employing roughly 10% of the industrial labor force. Coal, iron, and steel formed the real engine from the late nineteenth century. The Ruhr region became the heart of German industry: in 1913, nineteen companies produced more than one million tonnes of coal. Iron and steel emerged as the most technologically modern, leading industry from the turn of the century. Between 1890 and 1913, iron and steel output reached an unparalleled three- and four-fold growth. By 1913, these branches produced one-sixth of Germany's entire industrial output, and the country produced three times more steel than France and twice as much as Britain.

On the solid foundation of these basic industries, Germany successfully challenged Britain's leading position and created one of the world's strongest engineering industries, which employed more than 15% of the industrial workforce before the war. Superb science and technology education helped to build a labor force that formed the bedrock of shipbuilding and other engineering branches, which doubled employment and tripled output between 1890 and 1913 (Fischer, 1978: 535–41). In the older industrial countries of Europe, textiles and other consumer goods industries continued to dominate production at an average ratio of 3:1 and even 4:1, compared with the so-called heavy industries. In Germany alone after the turn of the century, the heavy industries enjoyed a 2:1 advantage over consumer goods industries (Hoffmann, 1931).

The overwhelming strength of German industry, however, lay in those branches that emerged as part of the new industrial revolution. The spectacular development of the production of electric power deserves special attention. Germany produced more electric energy than Britain, France, Italy, and Sweden combined by 1913. The Siemens-Schuckert Company (from 1903, when the two firms merged) employed 57,000 workers at home and 24,000 abroad, and dominated electrical power station building in Europe. Electro-metallurgy and the electro-chemical industry followed. The giant AEG Werke introduced a series of electrical household appliances.

Germany's greatest industrial achievements, however, were its breakthroughs in the modern chemical industry. As early as the 1870s, German companies, among them Badische Anilin, Agfa, and Bayer, dominated half the world's chemical market. During the half century before World War I, the German chemical industry posted a 6.2% annual growth and increased output tenfold (Fischer, 1978). Before the war, Germany sold nearly one-third of the world's total exports of chemical products and 90% of its synthetic dyes. The country's chemical output was 60% higher than that of the United States and five times higher than that of the Swiss, who were second on the continent. The country's exceptional strength in the sciences and its uniquely advanced system of technical education provided a strong foundation for new science-based industries. Overall, Germany's economic growth was one of the fastest in early twentieth-century Europe: per capita GDP increased by 32% between 1897 and 1913 (Hoffmann, 1971: 31–5; Köllmann, 1978: 17).

Box 1.3 Aspirin

Aspirin, a simple drug, became the most successful miracle medicine of the twentieth century. Hippocrates had already mentioned that grained willow tree bark was a good pain and fever reliever. During the nineteenth century several German, Italian, and French scholars isolated the active ingredient from willow bark, called salicin, and improved it into salicylic acid. Though invented and reinvented, it was forgotten and had to wait until the end of the century to become a recognized medicine.

The story of the aspirin was connected with Friedrich Bayer and Company, a small German dye factory established in 1863 and one of the pioneers in synthetic dye production. In 1884, the almost bankrupt company employed a young chemist, Carl Duisberg, who invented synthetic dyes and soon became the head of the research and patent department. He also transformed the company by introducing various pharmaceutical products. By 1890, in a newly built three-story research laboratory, ninety chemists worked in the Eberfeld factory. Duisberg, a business genius, took over the company and built a second research laboratory, Eberfeld, which specialized in pharmaceutical research, and added a huge factory in Leverkusen. The new laboratory began research to produce a refined version of salicylic acid by eliminating its dangerous side effect of destroying prostaglandins, produced by the stomach lining to defend the stomach from its own acid. Felix Hoffman, a young chemist, succeeded in 1899 when he produced the corrected version, acetylsalicylic acid, named Aspirin.

Duisberg was the first industrialist to introduce brand names for drugs rather than their difficult chemical names. He also initiated a new way of marketing by sending free samples to hospitals and doctors. In three years, more than 160 reviews and studies on aspirin were published. The drug was first sold in powder form and became a popular pain and headache killer and anti-inflammation medicine. In 1904, the trademark Bayer Cross was introduced, and by 1915 production of tablets began.

Extraordinarily, research into the unique qualities of aspirin never stopped. In 1950, in a little-known American medical journal, a study announced that aspirin, by reducing thrombi formation in blood, prevents heart attacks. Nobel Laureate John Vane's study proved this convincingly in 1988, and became one of the most cited works in pharmaceutical research. Aspirin turned out to be an excellent drug against arthritis as well. The body's immune system turns against the body's tissues in certain circumstances. The disease of the autoimmune system, rheumatoid arthritis, may destroy joints. Aspirin may prevent the attack against tissues. Thus it was successfully used against two of the most widespread diseases, heart attack and arthritis. Meanwhile, aspirin remained one of the most effective pain, headache, and fever killers. As a testament to the drug's remarkable qualities, more and more people take 1–2 pills daily. Although several aspirin brands were in competition with each other, and successful substitutes conquered huge markets, the Bayer Cross Aspirin remained one of the leading brands (Mann and Plummer, 1991).

Prior to World War I, Britain, France, and Germany represented less than a third of Europe's population, produced 72% of the continent's industrial output, 93% of its coal, 78% of its steel, 80% of its engineering, and 74% of its chemical products, and consumed 73% of its cotton imports.

The beginning of Scandinavia's catching-up

The Scandinavian countries, which were among the non-industrialized, food and raw material deliverers until the late nineteenth century, profited tremendously from the globalization process, produced for export, and received important foreign investment, especially to infrastructure. In addition, Scandinavia enjoyed sufficient internal socio-economic potential to adjust and begin a catching-up process to join the European core. In the early twentieth century the region became an economic champion. Denmark, Sweden, and Norway were able to adjust to the new technological-structural requirements of the turn of the century, and progressed rapidly along the road toward modern industrialization. The export of unprocessed goods, most of all wood, timber, and iron ore, was replaced by industrial exports produced by a rapidly developing processing industry, most of all pulp and paper. Between 1891 and 1900, 38% of Swedish exports consisted of unprocessed wood and 8% of pulp and paper; by 1911–1913, the share of wood exports dropped to 26%, while pulp and paper increased to 18% (Fridlizius, 1963). Between 1896 and 1912, the Swedish pulp and paper industry, an export sector par excellence with 75–80% of its production exported, increased its output by 11% annually and became the most dynamic branch of industry.

From the 1890s, the Swedish iron and steel industry had recovered sufficiently from the shock of the British industrial revolution to be able to renew itself according to the newer technology of the Siemens-Martin process. Iron and steel exports represented 10% of Sweden's total exports (Nilsson, 1972). Engineering, especially electrical engineering, also emerged as an important new sector and increased output sixfold. In 1913 this sector employed 19% of the industrial workforce, produced 14% of its total output, and supplied 10% of total exports.

In several respects, Norway followed a similar path. Until 1866, its economy consisted mostly of fishing and fish exports (47% of total), along with wood and timber output and exports (42% of total). Industrialization in Norway practically began with the processing of what had until that time been unprocessed wood exports. By 1910, 43% and 23% of wood was exported as pulp and paper, respectively (Hodne, 1975: 33). Hydroelectric power generation marked a real turning point for energy-poor Norway: by 1914 there were 123 power stations with a 920,000 horsepower capacity. These abundant and cheap energy sources initiated the development of the artificial fertilizer, aluminum, and electro-steel industries as well as a number of other modern sectors. On the eve of World War I, exports from Norway's chemical industry surpassed those of its wood industry.

Norway's service sector deserves special attention, for its important role was a peculiar feature of the Norwegian economy. Norway emerged as a great shipping power at the end of the nineteenth century. The capacity of its merchant fleet, more than 1.5 million tonnes by 1910, represented the world's third largest merchant fleet, and shipping produced one-third of the country's export income (Johnsen, 1939). In 1910, services produced 50% of the GDP.

While Swedish and Norwegian industrialization was strongly export driven, Denmark's export economy remained agriculturally based, with a strong food-processing industry. An export-oriented, modern agricultural sector was, in fact, the bedrock of the Danish economy. Between 1893 and 1914 pig stocks increased more than threefold. Food processing emerged as a leading sector and made up one-third of Denmark's industrial output (Milward and Saul, 1977: 504). The country profited from turn-of-century globalization. Britain became the single most important market for Danish exports: between 1885 and 1910, Danish exports to Britain increased by nearly three times. Based on substantial export incomes, industrialization in Denmark gained ground from the late nineteenth century. Denmark's industrialization had an import-substituting character. By World War I, the country covered 70% of its domestic consumption of industrial products. Danish economic development represented the most successful example of a complementary, export-oriented economy.

The GDP of Scandinavian countries increased rapidly in the early twentieth century (see Table 1.4). Sweden achieved a rate of economic growth that was three times faster than that of Europe as a whole, while the region

Table 1.4 The slowing down of old leaders, and the rise of new Western economic powers (GDP per capita in $ 1990 ppp[†]) (Maddison, 1995a: 194–6)

Year	Old leaders*	1870 = 100	France and Germany	1870 = 100	Scandinavia**	1870 = 100	USA	1870 = 100
1870	2,679	100	1,886	100	1,631	100	2,457	100
1900	3,827	143	2,992	159	2,408	148	4,096	167
1913	4,330	162	3,644	193	3,046	187	5,307	216

[†]Purchasing power parity; * Holland, Britain, Belgium, Switzerland; ** Sweden, Denmark, Norway

came closer to matching West European income levels before World War I, with Denmark reaching 98% and Sweden 84%.

The Southern and Eastern peripheries remaining behind

While Scandinavia began catching up with the Western core, European economic development exhibited major disparities. The Mediterranean and Central and Eastern European countries could not follow in the footsteps of the West and were unable to repeat the Scandinavian miracle. They, however, were an integral part of the global European economy, and some of them profited from its internationalization. Sidney Pollard speaks about a unified and interrelated process of European industrialization; closed economic models for independent national economies no longer applied (Pollard, 1973).

One of the most important elements of this globalization was the dramatic growth of foreign trade. The export possibilities to the growing Western markets were among the key elements behind peripheral transformation. The West European countries imported two-thirds of world imports, nearly two-thirds of which were made up of food and raw materials, and nearly two-thirds of these products came from other European countries (Kuznets, 1967).

The rich West European countries began investing in and funding their less developed partners. By 1913 the stock of exported capital reached $46 billion, and 26% of it went to peripheral European countries (Kuznets, 1967; Woodruff, 1966). Western markets and capital exports led to agricultural modernization and generated a belated agricultural revolution in

Table 1.5 Railroads in peripheral Europe in 1913 (Berend and Ránki, 1982: 98, 100)

Region	Length of railroads (in 1,000 km)	Land area/1 km railroad (in sq km)	Length of railroads (in km)/100,000 inhabitants
Western core	167.7	10.14	90.2
Mediterranean Europe	38.4	25.14	61.0
Central & Eastern Europe	98.8*	20.49**	50.4***

* With Russia. The figure without Russia is 28.6 km; ** Without Russia. The Russian figure is 324.17 sq km; *** Without Russia. The Russian figure is 42.3 km

the European peripheries. This process began mostly during the last third of the nineteenth century and reached its zenith before World War I. As a result, Central and Eastern European agricultural output generally doubled during the half century before the war. The Mediterranean countries were less successful. In the best cases they developed a self-sufficient agricultural economy.

The industrialized Western countries rushed to invest in raw material extraction in the European peripheries. Russia and Romania became Europe's most important crude oil producing and exporting countries. Around the turn of the century the leading British, Dutch, and American companies opened the Romanian oilfields and almost the entire production was exported. Half of the Spanish mining companies were in foreign hands and they extracted rich iron resources at Vizcaya Bay, copper at Rio Tinto, and lead from Cartagena Mountain. Of this output, 90% was exported (Plaza-Prieto, 1955; Voltes, 1974: 179).

Modern railroads were built as part of a united European system, mostly with Western investment. By 1913, the length of Russian railroads reached 70,200 kilometers of track (Khromov, 1950: 462; Bovikin, 1973: 35) (see Table 1.5). In the four countries of Mediterranean Europe the length of railroads increased by 45% between 1890 and 1913. Before World War I, a modern transportation network, though less developed than in the West, connected the peripheries with the West.

Exports of agricultural products and raw materials increased tremendously in response to growing demand in the West. Russia delivered nearly a quarter of the world's wheat exports, exporting 8 million tonnes of grain annually by 1910–13 (Khromov, 1963: 59, 207). Romania delivered another

8% of the world's wheat exports. Serbian pig, cattle, dried plum, and copper exports, Greek raisins, tobacco, and olive deliveries, Italian, Portuguese, and Spanish wine, citrus fruits, Spanish ores, Italian raw silk, Russian grain, timber, and oil played important roles in Western markets. These exports increased by leaps and bounds.

Some of the more successful peripheral countries also began processing a part of their agricultural products. Hungary developed the world's second largest flour mill center in Budapest (next to Minneapolis) so that two-thirds of wheat production could be exported in processed form, which represented a quarter of world wheat flour exports. Food processing became the leading branch of the emerging industries, producing 32% of the industrial output of the Dual Monarchy (26% of the Austrian-Czech, and 39% of Hungarian industrial output). Some important steps were taken in the most modern sectors as well: for example, the United Incandescent Lamp Co. emerged as a European leader (Berend and Ránki, 1955).

Box 1.4 Tungsram

Egyesült Izzólámpagyár (United Incandescent Lamp Co.) was established in 1896 in Budapest. It was a promising signal of modernization, a pioneer of electro-technical industry in Hungary, where 68% of the population was still engaged in agricultural activities, and nearly 40% was illiterate. In this environment the new, strongly export-oriented company introduced the most modern technology of the age: it produced light sources for newly electrified cities. By 1901, the company had also established telephone exchanges. The International Cartel Agreement of the top European companies in 1903 gave United Incandescent an equal market share with the Dutch Phillips Co. (11.3%) in the incandescent bulb market, behind the leading German AEG and Siemens companies (22.6%).

The company, which was established with 700 workers, employed more than 3,000 before World War I, when production reached 30,000 bulbs daily. The company was among the first to change to the more effective Wolfram filaments (1906), and replaced the vacuum by filling the bulb with gas (1913). By 1913, five-sixths of the company's production was exported. United Incandescent, which later became Tungsram, closely followed the most advanced managerial and technological achievements of the advanced countries. Lipót Aschner, an American-type manager, launched an unending campaign of vertical expansion and technological progress. In 1921, he established one of the first world-class research laboratories. When the leading research engineer, Imre Bródy, invented the krypton gas filling process, the company established a krypton gas factory and bought a glass factory. Production required a huge amount of coal, so Aschner bought coal mines in 1936. By 1938, the firm produced more than 23 million bulbs and employed 5,000 workers. It had companies in Vienna and Warsaw. Before the war, 85% of output was exported to 53 countries.

During the state socialist postwar decades, the company was nationalized and lost its foreign connections. It continued to grow, and the central role Tungsram played in the country's industrial exports to the West did not change. At the end of the 1980s, the company employed 20,000 people. It was the crown jewel of Hungarian industry with a 5–6% share of the West European markets, and a 2–3% share of the roughly $12 billion in world trade.

Nevertheless, the company could not keep up with the rapid technological developments. Small wonder that the American General Electric (GE) bought 50% of the company's shares at the end of the 1980s, before the communist regime collapsed. By 1994, GE owned the entire company and invested roughly $600 million in modernizing Tungsram – certain production lines and branch subsidiaries were closed down, while production was concentrated on high-margin products. The number of employees was reduced from 20,000 to 9,000. Productivity increased by double-digit numbers annually during the 1990s. GE decided to concentrate a great part of its worldwide R&D capacities in Hungary – a unique step from a multinational company which invests in transforming or developing countries. Out of GE's eight major worldwide research programs, four are running in the Cleveland headquarters, and another four, with half of the company's professional R&D employees, are in Budapest. Tungsram became the world's largest light-source producer, selling, via GE's commercial network, 40% of its output in Western Europe, 30% in the Middle East and Asia, nearly 20% in the United States, and roughly 10% in Hungary and Eastern Europe (Berend and Ránki, 1955, 1966; Marer and Mabert, 1996).

Food processing also became the leading export sector of Ireland, the Western periphery of Britain. Ireland remained basically agricultural: only one-third of the net output of agriculture and industry combined was produced by industry. Beer and whiskey, produced mostly by the Dundalk, Dublin, and Belfast distilleries and the Dublin brewers, Guinness first among them, represented more than 40% of Irish exports in 1907 (Cullen, 1987: 134–5; 157–61).

During the half century prior to World War I, European exports grew by 2.8% per year on average. Russian exports grew by 3.8% and Bulgarian exports by 5.3% per year (Bairoch, 1973). Capital accumulation from export incomes also increased. Initial steps toward industrialization were taken in some of these countries, though only a few of them were able to become agricultural-industrial – most remained entirely agricultural.

Russia, a great European power and military giant, preserved its traditional agriculture (Liashchenko, 1952). It more or less stagnated in the 1890s, and output even decreased on a per capita basis. Overtaxed and exploited by the state, it provided a rather weak and fragile domestic market. Important steps toward industrialization were taken, however, and as a result per capita GDP increased by 61% between 1890 and 1913 (even by 22% between 1900 and 1913). GDP levels were still rather low in 1913, at only 71%, 60%, and 40% of the Hungarian, Italian, and average West European levels, respectively. Russian modernization was thus a partial failure, but at least industrialization had begun.

Poland, Finland, and the Baltic countries, the Western rim of the Russian empire, began to industrialize in response to export opportunities presented by Russian markets. Measured by per capita output, these countries also achieved growth rates twice as high as their Russian counterparts and were able to build agrarian-industrial economies.

Several peripheral countries in the Mediterranean and Balkan regions were not able to adjust to the technological-structural requirements of the early twentieth century and lagged even more behind than before. Italy was the only exception, and represented one of the greatest successes of the peripheries. During the period of major regional changes, though still far behind the West, Italy achieved spectacular annual 6.7% growth before World War I (Gerschenkron, 1962). Although the largest regions of the country remained backward and pre-industrial, and more than 58% of the active population was still working in agriculture in 1911, an "industrial triangle" emerged between Turin, Milan, and Genoa. By 1911, Italy had built an industrial base that employed nearly 24% of the labor force. Moreover, this industrialization process achieved its best results in the newest sectors of the economy. In 1898, the first hydroelectric power station was built, and Italy's hydroelectric power capacity, from a small base, increased 32-fold between 1895 and 1914, making it a leader in this area (Mori, 1977: 195, 360). This energy provided the basis for the rise of modern metallurgy, which increased its output by 12% annually from the turn of the century. The engineering, electrical, automotive, and chemical industries became the most dynamic sectors of the economy.

Box 1.5 The Agnellis

The two Giovanni Agnellis, grandfather and grandson, changed the economic history of Italy when they built up one of the world's largest business empires of the twentieth century. The family comprised rather undistinguished, wealthy landowners in the mid-nineteenth century when they moved to Villar Perosa, near Torino, in 1853. That was the birthplace (in 1866) of Giovanni Agnelli, who became a cavalry officer, soon resigned, married, and settled in Torino. He had some interest in technology. Having heard about the automobile – four years before Henry Ford – he established with a partner the Fabbrica Italiana di Automobili Torino – better known as Fiat – with 50 employees in 1899. In the early years the factory produced around 100 cars annually, but by 1914, with 4,000 employees, it was producing 4,000 cars a year. Agnelli fostered special connections with the powerful prime minister, Giovanni Giolitti, whose expansionist adventures greatly helped Fiat. The company began producing trucks, machine guns, and airplane engines as well. The war years proved to be a bonanza: the factory was flooded with military orders, the labor force soon increased to 10,000, and Fiat, the thirtieth biggest industrial firm in Italy, grew to become the third largest by the end of the war.

Giovanni Agnelli turned out to be an excellent manager, with great instinct for employing the best people. He was also a master builder of political connections and cultivated a good relationship with Mussolini, who appointed him senator for life in 1923. Agnelli even joined the Fascist Party in 1932 and profited from the connections lavishly. He was ready to sell his soul to the devil, including Nazi Germany, if it furthered Fiat's development with huge military orders. The founder, Giovanni, dishonored by collaboration, died in 1945 at the age of seventy-nine.

Giovanni's only son, Edoardo, also a cavalry officer, married an aristocrat, and named his first son, born in 1921, after his grandfather, but called him Gianni.

Gianni Agnelli, following family tradition, joined the cavalry, but also earned a law degree. The young officer of the fascist army was sent to the Russian and then North African fronts, but he changed sides in time. After the war and the death of his grandfather (his father had died in an air accident in 1935) he became vice-president of Fiat, and from time to time performed various services for the company. However, he did not take a real job or responsibility; that role was assumed by an efficient, ironhanded manager, Vittorio Valetta, who ran the family empire for nearly twenty years. Gianni, meanwhile, indulged in a flamboyant playboy lifestyle, a real

Dolce Vita, enjoying the company of a great number of celebrity women, flitting between his twenty-eight-room Côte d'Azur villa, using his yacht and airplane, his Fifth Avenue home in New York, or his forty-five-room family home near Torino. In 1953 he married, and in 1966, at the age of forty-five, finally took over the chairmanship of the company. He proved to be an instinctive business talent, besides a charming diplomat who spoke several languages and was familiar with those in the highest political circles. The Agnelli empire was enormous by that time: Fiat employed 130,000 people, produced as many cars in a day in 1966 as it had in an entire year when his grandfather died in 1945, and became the number two carmaker in Europe. The Fiat 124 became the best-selling model in the country. The family controlled civil engineering, cement, newspaper, merchant ships, and food industry interests. Engineering subsidiaries worked in Monte Carlo, Pakistan, and Turkey, and car factories were opened in the Soviet Union, Poland, Spain, and Argentina. The prosperous multinational company was one of the few in the world still under family ownership and management.

However, the troubled second half of the 1970s, with skyrocketing prices, declining markets, and deep political turmoil in Italy, rocked the company. The Red Brigades terror group killed or wounded twenty-seven Fiat managers. The Agnellis traveled in bulletproof cars, escorted by bodyguards. Nevertheless, from 1979 Fiat emerged from its difficulties, and in 1980 an outstanding new top manager, Cesare Romiti, took over the operation, forming an excellent tandem with Gianni Agnelli. Fresh modernization plans and investments paved the way toward new prosperity. The new Fiat Uno became an immense success. Diversification of production led to greater heights: a robot assembly system was created and itself became an export item. Fiat bought Alfa Romeo and monopolized nearly two-thirds of the domestic car market.

During the 1980s, the Agnellis' interests included telecommunications, aerospace, bioengineering, department stores, insurance companies, and newspapers. The firm ran 569 subsidiaries and 190 associated companies in 50 countries, generating income of $33 billion. Gianni Agnelli became the uncrowned king of Italy (Friedman, 1989).

Italy achieved the highest rates of growth in early twentieth-century Europe with a 66% increase in per capita GDP. By 1918, still far behind Western Europe, Italy belonged to the world's eight most important producers of steel, cement, electrical energy, cars, superphosphates, and artificial silk.

The least successful countries of early twentieth-century Europe were those of the Iberian Peninsula and the Balkans. What were the main causes of their failure to progress? Their social capability, inherited cultural traditions, and, in some cases, educational backwardness – mostly in the Balkans – together with their limited resource base, weakened their development opportunities. They could not adjust to modern technological sectoral requirements, and as a consequence lost further ground. Portugal, for example, missed out on the prosperity enjoyed elsewhere in early twentieth-century Europe, with most of its industries remaining local and small scale. Total per capita GDP was essentially stagnant in the late nineteenth century, but then decreased by 4% between 1900 and 1913, so that income levels were below those of Russia and only 37% of the West European average.

A similar failure to modernize characterized the Balkans, which remained almost entirely agricultural, with 75–80% agricultural employment, and only about 10% of the workforce employed in industry. Foreign capital, which played such a crucial role in peripheral modernization, was used mostly to build up the new state apparatus, the army, and more glamorous capital cities with representative public buildings. In other words, they were used, at least in part, for "symbolic modernization." Twenty percent of foreign capital went toward modernizing the army in Romania. In Serbia, 40% was used to pay for the army and to cover budgetary deficits. Small wonder, then, that both Bulgaria and Serbia became insolvent around the turn of the century.

The Romanian oil industry became important, but remained a foreign enclave, and its output was exported while Romania continued to import processed oil products. The Bulgarian and Serbian industries employed between 14,000 and 15,000 workers each before the war. Only about one-third of the low level of domestic consumption of industrial goods was satisfied by domestic production in prewar Bulgaria. The industrial revolution still had not arrived in the Balkans. On the eve of World War I Serbia's per capita GDP had reached only slightly more than one-quarter of West European levels. Figure 1.1 illustrates the disparity in economic growth between 1897 and 1913.

The failure of industrialization in the Iberian Peninsula was little affected by the fact that Spain did make some progress toward industrialization in the early twentieth century (Sánchez-Albornoz, 1968; Nadal, 1971: 275). The leading iron and steel industries, and those branches of engineering which produced for the railroads, also began to establish themselves in the Basque industrial zone. On the other side of the peninsula, in Catalonia, textiles became the leading sector (Voltes, 1974: 241). Though 71% of the labor force still worked in agriculture, as in 1860, those who did work

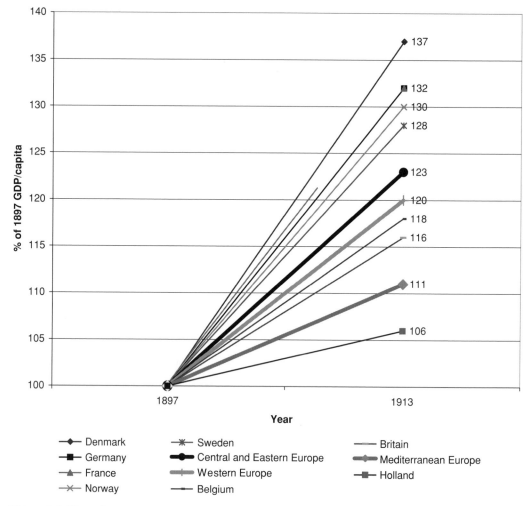

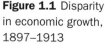

Figure 1.1 Disparity in economic growth, 1897–1913

in industry (17%) produced more than one-fifth of the GDP. Spain's per capita GDP reached 64% of Western levels. However, the eastern and southern peripheries of Europe, especially the Balkans, preserved their obsolete economic character and remained far behind the West (see Table 1.6).

Although Central and Eastern European growth rates were similar to the Western trend, they were not fast enough to generate a catching-up process with the core countries. The gap between the West on the one hand and Southern and Eastern Europe on the other remained wide and, regarding Southern Europe, even broadened. Industrialization had more or less failed in this region. Agricultural employment continued to dominate, at 75–80% of the active population in Russia and the Balkans, and 55–70% in Italy, Portugal, Hungary, Poland, and Spain. Industrial employment remained below one-fifth of total employment, and industrial output accounted for

Table 1.6 GDP per capita ($ 1990 ppp) (Maddison, 1995a: 228)

Year	Central & Eastern Europe*	%		Southern Europe**	%		Western Europe***	%	
1870	1,085	100	79	1,108	100	70	2,110	100	68
1900	1,373	127	100	1,572	142	100	3,092	147	100
1913	1,690	156	123	1,750	158	111	3,704	176	120

* 9 countries; ** 7 countries; *** 23 countries

Table 1.7 GDP per capita disparities between European core and peripheries (Maddison, 1995a: 228)

Year	Western Europe	Southern Europe	Eastern Europe
1820	100	62	60
1870	100	53	51
1913	100	47	46

less than one-quarter of GDP by 1910 (Berend and Ránki, 1982: 159). Economic growth remained slow; between the turn of the century and 1914 there was only 10% growth in Ireland and Spain, and a 4% decline in Portugal. Most of the Balkan countries experienced negative growth. Russia, Poland, and Hungary, though having taken important steps toward industrialization, could not surpass significantly the rates of Western growth. Regional, core–periphery disparities did not disappear (see Table 1.7). In some cases, they even broadened. The entire pre-World War I experiment of export-led industrialization could not lead to a breakthrough and, at least, the beginning of catching up with the West.

The challenge of globalized laissez-faire

Most of the countries of Southern and Eastern Europe, though they tried to adopt the Western model of laissez-faire policies, were increasingly unable to generate successful industrialization. Both the exaggerated nineteenth-century optimism and enthusiasm to follow in the Western footsteps and copy the Western economic model, and the near-religious belief in progress along the path taken by the West, evaporated (Berend, 2003: 1–4). Globalized laissez-faire did not live up to its promise in some of the peripheral countries of Europe, and it faced increasing challenges. State interventionism gained ground.

Eventually, from the 1870s, during the European grain crisis, there was skepticism about free trade and the deliberate use of various kinds of weapons to generate economic modernization and growth. In Russia and most of Central and Eastern Europe various kinds of substitutions were offered to bridge the gaps in the resources for industrialization. State investments, subsidies for newly established firms, railroad tariff reductions on state-owned railroads, and free building plots for companies were used to promote industrialization. A shift from laissez-faire to proto-economic nationalism characterized particularly the late nineteenth century in the peripheries (David and Spilman, 2000). Some of the countries of the region, such as Russia and Spain, which were free to turn to high tariffs, did so.

Free markets, the first wave of globalization, capitalist individualism, "selfish materialism," as well as parliamentary democracy were questioned frequently and rejected angrily by rebellious political groupings and militants, though not yet by the governments of these countries. Right-wing populism and proto-fascist ideologies emerged in many countries: in Russia, Romania, Italy, and, for very different reasons, in a disappointed France and Germany (Mosse, 1966; Arendt, 1966). Left-wing radicalism was on the rise as well in Eastern and some parts of Southern Europe. Bolshevik ideology offered a revolutionary solution for Russia. These revolutionary political trends, in different ways and through different means, challenged the European world system with its economic, social, and political institutions and rejected the parliamentary political system combined with free market economy. The seeds of severe conflicts and revolts had been sown.

The first decades of the twentieth century, though still a period of passionate expansion of colonial rule, triggered the first premonitions of a changing balance of world power. Colonial rule was challenged. The European settlements, or "white colonies," moved toward independence. Canada, Australia, New Zealand, and South Africa became "dominions" with internal autonomy; "Home Rule" in Ireland signaled the same direction. India's National Congress adopted the idea of "self rule" in 1906 and the movement steered toward independence. The Ottoman Empire, after five centuries' rule in the Balkans, was virtually expelled from Europe. After World War I Russia lost its conquered and incorporated European possessions. Germany, already the strongest industrial power in Europe, mobilized to challenge the existing world order and began organizing an alliance system. Its Western rivals responded and Europe rapidly shifted toward a deadly war.

As a clear sign of the end of the European century, the United States emerged as the world's leading economic power. In 1900, Britain was still the richest country in the world, and the four rising overseas countries – the United States, Canada, New Zealand, and Australia – reached only 84% of its per capita income level; by 1913, the four countries' average equaled the British level. The combined average per capita level of the United States and Australia, which already surpassed the British level by 4% in 1891, was 24% higher by 1913. The per capita GDP of the four overseas countries, former white colonies, surpassed the West European average income by 45% in 1913.

In that year the stock of machinery, equipment, and business buildings per employed persons in the United States was more than three times higher than in Britain. American labor productivity became the highest. The British and Dutch levels remained 15–20% behind; the Belgian, German, and Swiss levels lagged by a third. The symbol of a new age, the automobile, became widespread in America, which had eleven times more cars than Britain, and more than three times the number in Western Europe as a whole. The population growth rate in the United States, partly because of massive immigration from Europe, was 2.3 times higher than in Europe before World War I. During the war, the United States became the world's leading industrial power. Before the war, Europe produced 43% of the world's output, but this dropped to 34% after the war and remained behind the American level. The United States produced nearly 36% of the world's manufacturing production in 1913, more than Britain, Germany, and France together. Britain and Germany produced only 40% of American manufacturing output. The American share surpassed 42% of world production after the war, and it was already one-third more than the three European leaders together. Europe lost one-third of its prewar foreign investments and the United States took over as the leading international creditor. Europe lost its predominant role as leader of the world economy. Europe was challenged.

CHAPTER 2

Decline of laissez-faire and the rise of the regulated market system

John Maynard Keynes, in his Sidney Ball Lecture at Oxford University in 1924, challenged the biases in favor of laissez-faire. As in the title of his essay, *The End of Laissez-faire*, Keynes prophesied a new age. War experiences certainly played an important role in forming his revolutionary views and negating the basic principle of Adam Smith:

War experience in the organization of socialized production, has left some near observers optimistically anxious to repeat it in peace conditions. War socialism unquestionably achieved a production of wealth on a scale far greater than we ever knew in Peace . . . The world is not so governed from above that private and social interest always coincide. Many of the greatest economic evils of our time are fruits of risk, uncertainty, and ignorance . . . For the same reason big business is often a lottery, that great inequalities of wealth come about; and these same factors are also the cause of the Unemployment of Labour . . . Yet the cure lies outside the operations of individuals . . . I believe that the cure for these things is partly to be sought in the deliberate control of the currency and of credit by a central institution . . . [savings and investments should be regulated] I do not think that these matters should be left entirely to the chances of private judgment and private profits . . . We do not dance even yet to a new tune. But a change is in the air. (Keynes, 1927: 5, 35, 39, 47–9, 52–3)

The twentieth century, especially after World War I, began with a major challenge to the laissez-faire regime with the emergence of alternative economic systems. The entire continent gave up free trade and laissez-faire market economy and turned toward protectionism, state interventionism, and a regulated market system.

World War I was a turning point. It "marked the true watershed between the nineteenth and twentieth centuries" (Feinstein et al., 1997: 18). One could add, it accelerated the collapse of laissez-faire. German experiments in state regulation of the war economy became a kind of model for all

Box 2.1 John Maynard Keynes

John Maynard Keynes, the most influential economist of the twentieth century, was both a product and maker of Cambridge. He was born in Cambridge in 1883. His father was an economist and logician, and for a long time the registrar, the chief administrative officer of Cambridge University. His mother became Mayor of Cambridge. Maynard, as friends called him, gained the best possible English education at Eton and then King's College, Cambridge, where he graduated in 1905. His interest was mathematics, but he turned to economics, and in 1902 was elected to the Cambridge Apostles, the highest-level intellectual group of the time, and began teaching monetary economics as a lecturer. By 1909 he became a life-long fellow of King's College.

Keynes was a larger-than-life figure. As bursar, the chief economic officer of King's College, he made excellent investments and significantly furthered the wealth of the college. As a private person, his first task every morning was to read the stock-market news and to make investments to be financially independent. Eventually, he became a millionaire. He married the beautiful prima ballerina of the Diaghilev Ballet, Lydia Lopkova, collected paintings and books, and was friends with the best minds of the age. He served on the boards of several insurance and investment companies, worked as unpaid advisor to the Chancellor of the Exchequer during World War II, and influenced the Beveridge Report, which was instrumental in introducing the welfare state. Meanwhile he served as chairman of what came to be the Arts Council of Great Britain. As his last gigantic practical achievement, he was the father of the Bretton Woods Agreement (1944), which created a new international monetary system and established the World Bank and the International Monetary Fund.

During all of this Keynes was an extremely productive scholar, the author of writings collected in twenty-seven volumes.

His professional life masterfully combined theory and practice. His first job was a two-year civil service posting to the India Office, during which he published a book on *Indian Currency and Finance* (1913). During World War I, he was a civil servant at the Treasury, and Chief Treasury Representative of Britain at the Paris Peace Conference in 1919, the year he published *The Economic Consequences of the Peace*. The latter was not only a first-class analysis of the counterproductive reparation clause of the Treaty, but became a prophecy, which brought Keynes international fame. The same was true of his 1925 pamphlet *The Economic Consequences of Mr. Churchill*, in which he sharply and rightly attacked the reintroduction of the gold standard with an overvalued pound, the work of Winston Churchill, then Chancellor of the Exchequer.

During the 1930s, Keynes became a member of the Prime Minister's Economic Council. Meanwhile he published influential theoretical works, among them the milestone *The General Theory of Employment, Interest, and Money* (1936), which transformed economics. The Keynesian Revolution, as the change was called, proved that classical economics was wrong in assuming that "each supply creates its demand," since not all of the incomes were spent. The essence of Keynesian theory was the creation of effective demand. A new school of Keynesian economics was established and influenced economic practice throughout the world for decades.

John Maynard Keynes, Lord of Tilton, died of a heart attack in April 1946 before his sixty-third birthday. His memorial service was held at Westminster Abbey.

combatant countries, including Britain. Instead of further building an international economic system, these countries adopted economic nationalism and sought self-sufficiency. State interventions, which had an important pre-history dating from the end of the nineteenth century, played a successively more important role during the Great Depression of the early 1930s, the war preparations in the second half of the same decade, and in World War II itself. The war economy clearly demonstrated a new possibility of coping with enormous economic tasks by multiplying the countries' efforts. It was for this reason that a regulated market economy came to dominate the peripheral countries of Europe, which had failed to industrialize under the rules of laissez-faire, and revolted against nineteenth-century globalization.

It is a fallacy to suppose that, because Great Britain and the United States have an interest in the removal of trade barriers, this is also an interest of Yugoslavia . . . International trade may be weaker . . . But Yugoslavia and Colombia will be better off than they would have been under the regime of European or world prosperity, which reduced them to the position of satellites . . . *Laissez-faire, in international relations* . . . is the paradise of the economically strong. State control is the weapon of self-defence invoked by the economically weak. (Carr, 1964: 59–60)

Karl Polanyi also stated that "the liberal creed assumed its evangelical fervor only in response to the needs of a fully deployed market economy" (Polanyi, 1964: 135). The one and a half decades prior to World War I, indeed, marked both the zenith and the early decline of this system. "Nineteenth century civilization," quoting the opening sentence of Polanyi's *The Great Transformation: the Political and Economic Origins of Our Time*, "collapsed" in the dawn of the twentieth century. The foundation of that civilization, according to Polanyi, was the self-regulated market, with the gold standard as one of its main symbols (Polanyi, 1964: 3). The collapse of the system, in his view, was in fact the paradoxical response to the success of the gold standard, which provoked the idea of a "realistic self-protection of society." Polanyi speaks about "social and national protectionism," i.e. "social legislation and customs tariffs." Against the backdrop of economic liberalism, a product of developed market economies,

the protection of man, nature, and productive organization amounted to an interference with markets . . . [which] *ipso facto*, impaired the self-regulation of the system. Since the purpose of the intervention was to rehabilitate the lives of men and their environment . . . giving stability to incomes, continuity of production . . . [free markets] were forced upon [backward countries and] a helpless people in absence of protective measures . . . [were] suffering . . . Nations and peoples . . . shielded themselves from unemployment and instability with the help of central banks and customs tariffs . . . These devices were designed to counteract the destructive effects of free trade . . . (Polanyi, 1964: 214, 216–17)

Parallel to the accomplishments of the laissez-faire system, its dissolution also began during the 1870s, when the first "Great Depression" and the deep European grain crisis hit several countries of the continent. At the same time, an ambitious Germany sought to catch up with its Western counterparts, while a desperate agrarian-peasant South, Central and Eastern Europe could only dream about modernization and industrialization according to the Western model. "By the end of the Depression," concluded Polanyi, "Germany had surrounded herself with protective tariffs . . . [and] set up an all-round social insurance system . . ." (Polanyi, 1964: 216).

The appearance of laissez-faire ideas, together with British economic hegemony and Napoleonic political domination, actually generated a very early opposition among economists and political thinkers of non-industrialized countries. Alexander Hamilton, in his *Report on Manufactures* to the American Congress in 1791, argued for protective tariffs, industrial subsidies, and self-sufficiency. He maintained that protection could free infant industries from the competition posed by the more advanced countries and thus ensure that they could catch up with these rivals:

Not only the wealth but the independence and security of a country appear to be materially connected with the prosperity of manufactures. Every nation . . . ought to endeavour to possess within itself all the essentials of national supply. (Hamilton, 1904: 69)

Johann Gottlieb Fichte, in his *Der geschlossene Handelsstaat* (1800), indicated that Germany was in a similar position. The Napoleonic challenge convinced him of the need for strong state interventions in Germany. An almighty state must regulate every aspect of social and economic life. The key words of his concept, instead of the Smithian market automatism and harmony, were *Gesetz und Zwang* (law and compulsion). He advocated strong state regulation and isolation, including fixing prices, banning imports and communications with foreigners, and issuing paper money with only local value in order to halt international economic connections. Trade would be a state monopoly and the state would establish self-sufficiency and an egalitarian distribution (Fichte, [1800] 1920).

Friedrich List repeated the argument in 1841. His *The National System of Political Economy* was an explicit debate with Adam Smith and the English school of economics. He sharply criticized Smithian "cosmopolitanism," "materialism," and "individualism," and stressed the importance of national economy. Import-substituting industrialization has a distinct national mission. List maintained that laissez-faire was advantageous only for advanced, industrialized countries. He advocated a strict policy of protection – so-called "educational tariffs" – during the transition from agrarian to industrial structures (List, [1841] 1922). His theory was popular in non-industrialized countries. Lajos Kossuth, the revolutionary leader of Hungary during the 1840s, used List's metaphors and argued that the industrialized and agrarian countries were connected in ways much like the innkeeper and the barrel: the first can tap the other freely.

The United States followed Hamilton's advice and introduced moderate protective tariffs as early as 1816, but protection was strongly increased through successive tariff acts after 1824, 1862, and 1864. Most important of all, however, were those introduced by the McKinley Act of 1890 and the Dingley Tariff of 1897. These measures increased tariffs to 57% of the value of imported goods. America entered the twentieth century with high protectionism.

The first successful attacks against the laissez-faire system, nevertheless, came during the so-called first Great Depression of 1873–96. In 1879, Germany introduced moderate tariffs on both agricultural and industrial products. Here, too, tariffs were increased in 1885 and 1888. By 1902, a new general tariff introduced very high levels of protection for finished manufacturing and agricultural products. Around the turn of the century, the dual interests of agriculture, strongly hit by overseas competition since the 1870s, and growing industry made protective tariffs popular all over Europe: Italy introduced effective protection in 1887, Switzerland in 1884 but most critically in 1906. France's Méline Tariff of 1892 granted protection for agriculture and industry, but the 1910 measures further increased tariffs for chemical, rubber, and electrical manufacturing. Russia emerged as the most protective country in all of Europe: the 1868 tariffs defended its infant industry from foreign competition, but tariffs were heavily increased in 1891, 1893, and 1900. By World War I, only Britain, Holland, and Denmark preserved a free trade system (Kenwood and Lougheed, 1971: 83–5).

In addition to tariffs, state interventionism became a popular strategy among non-industrialized countries of the continent. Various kinds of state subsidies supported industrialization in Russia, Hungary, Romania, and Bulgaria. Alexander Gerschenkron considered state interventionism to be a substitute for missing internal factors of industrialization in Eastern Europe (Gerschenkron, 1962).

The turning point: war economy, 1914–18, postwar chaos, and the agony of laissez-faire

World War I intensified protectionism. It was a natural consequence of both exalted nationalism, which equated self-defense and independence with economic self-sufficiency, and military necessity to counterbalance the effects of the naval blockade of the Atlantic. The war economy had to be as independent as possible from other countries in times when the reliable supply of imports was jeopardized. In addition to the impulse toward self-sufficiency and protectionism, the war economy embodied a strictly state-directed and regulated economic system. Wolfram Fischer noted:

The influence of the state reached a new quality during the First World War. All belligerent countries, but most of the neutral ones as well introduced raw material and food regulations, many besides the control of strategic products. In connection with this, war supplies and suppliers, often the transportation sector and sometimes agriculture were also controlled and regulated. (Fischer, 1978: 171)

Britain, the pioneer and model of laissez-faire, halted the operation of undisturbed market rules. By October 1914, the state, through the War Office, began market purchasing and established controls over trade and the production of certain products. At the beginning, the government tried to limit private enterprise and the rule of supply and demand. The need for physical control, nevertheless, soon became necessary. The Defence of the Realm Act (DORA) of March 1915 mandated the takeover of munitions-producing factories. At the same time, the Treasury Agreement sought to guarantee the labor market by entering into an agreement with the unions to restrict some of the freedoms of labor. The Munitions of War Bill of July 1915 introduced the government-directed production of weapons and then state ownership of munitions factories. The government also regulated the supply of raw materials. The Ministry of Munitions, established in June 1915 and led by Lloyd George, managed 250 state-owned factories with 2 million workers, supervised another 20,000, and controlled private establishments with another 1.4 million workers. In July of 1915, a special department was founded to promote industrial research, named the Department of Scientific Research in 1916. The Ministry of Munitions itself grew from 20 employees of the Army Contracts Department of August 1914 to 65,000 employees by the end of the war. Coal mining was also under government direction. Price control and export licensing were introduced in 1915. In the end, the mines became virtually nationalized and the state decided upon investments and supply. Railways were taken over and managed by the Railway Executive Committee, which also controlled fares. As of November 1915, the Port and Transit Executive Committee directed shipping, which included canal transportation. The McKenna Act of 1915 introduced protective tariffs even in Britain. The laissez-faire of the late nineteenth century was over.

State control spread to raw materials and the food supply. By April of 1918, all slaughtering and wholesaling companies had become government agents. Price control of food – first wheat, sugar and meat, then all the main categories of food – was introduced in the summer of 1917. Rationing followed soon after. The Cotton Control Board, established in June 1917, rationed cotton and restricted the output of cotton goods. The Food Production Department of the Board of Agriculture distributed fertilizer, tractors, and even the labor force, in the form of prisoners of war. By the end of the war, the government purchased roughly 90% of all imports and marketed more than 80% of food in the domestic market.

The war economy was also financed by the state. The government introduced new taxes and revenues, which more than doubled during the war in real terms. War expenditures still outpaced revenues, so that during the war years the total war budget deficit surpassed £7 billion. This had to be covered by government borrowing, which reached three times the prewar level of savings. By 1917–18 the deficit amounted to 40% of the national income. Inflationary financing became unavoidable. Currency notes were issued and their circulation increased nearly tenfold between 1914 and 1918. Britain eventually abandoned the gold standard, at least temporarily (Pollard, 1983: 20–5, 28–30, 32–4).

The German war economy was even more complex and centralized, to the point that it was practically a new economic model. Shortly after the outbreak of the war, in August 1914, the Prussian War Ministry established its Kriegsrohstoffabteilung (KRA) under the direction of Walther Rathenau, head of AEG and one of the country's leading industrial captains, to direct the production and supply of raw materials. Free market prices were abolished by October of 1914. The KRA fixed prices, allocated materials, and developed *Ersatz* (substitute) products. Among the innovations were synthetic nitrogen fixation, rayon, synthetic rubber, synthetic fat (from snails), and coffee (from acorns). At the end of the war, the KRA supervised two dozen corporations that produced and marketed raw materials. In May 1916, a special office, the Kriegsernährungsamt, was established to regulate and ration the food supply.

From August 1916 the Hindenburg Program introduced a new kind of planning to increase war production, mostly in strategic "heavy industries." The program also introduced the total mobilization of labor. In December 1916, a special law, the *Gesetz über den Vaterländischen Hilfsdienst*, mobilized the entire male population between the ages of seventeen and sixty for compulsory labor service. Meanwhile, *Betriebsräte,* or workers' committees, were established in companies with a minimum of fifty workers to assure mediation in factories. As a symbol of collaboration between the government and the unions, a representative of the unions became a member of the Kriegsamt. The state took the upper hand in price formation and, from January 1915, introduced food rationing. A huge bureaucracy directed rationing, which bought, stored, and sold food products.

In November 1916, the Oberstes Kriegsamt, or Supreme War Office, was founded within the Prussian War Ministry, but was as a matter of practice under the direction of the Supreme Army Command, which accomplished the total militarization of the German economy. It also gained an upper hand over industry. With a network of government offices, among them the powerful Kriegsersatz- und Arbeitsdepartement and the Waffen- und Munitionsbeschaffungsamt, the Supreme War Office had the authority to close down ineffective firms and reorganize industrial branches via compulsory cartelization. Industries for civil consumption were restricted; the number of shoe factories, for example, dropped from 1,500 to 400. The entire German economy was directed by an almighty state.

War financing was also a state responsibility and was assured by war loans, short-term state debts via treasury bills, and increased taxes – these covered war expenditure totaling 150 thousand million marks. The final source of war financing was, however, the printing of paper money. The money supply quintupled and prices increased: the war led to an accelerating rate of inflation (Zunkel, 1974; Feldman, 1966). The term *Planwirtschaft* (planned economy), so important during the twentieth century, was invented and introduced during World War I in Germany (Carr, 1964: 116).

State direction, control, and ownership became general practice in war economies. In France, war supply was mostly produced by state-owned factories, and an independent ministry was founded for war production in 1916. The Ministry of War established a special department for directing the economy. In Austria-Hungary, war production was under military control and a widespread organizational network was created according to the German pattern.

The consequences of war and the war-time economic system had a tremendous impact on the interwar economy. Europe was unable to return to "normalcy" in terms of the laissez-faire system of the nineteenth century. Military and civilian death tolls, combined with a fall in the birth rate, left Europe (without Russia) facing a 22–24 million population deficit. Another 7 million people were permanently disabled. Russia lost nearly 16 million people during the war, revolution, and civil war, and suffered a birth deficit of around 10 million. Between 1914 and 1921, thanks to the decline in the birth rate and the "Spanish" flu epidemic, Europe lost 50–60 million people (Aldcroft, 2001: 6–8).

Physical destruction was pronounced in Belgium, France, Poland, Serbia, and Russia, countries which had become battlefields. The Allied Reparation Commission assessed their war damages at £6.6 billion (Kenwood and Lougheed, 1971: 192). Belgium lost roughly 6% of its housing, half of the steel mills, and three-quarters of the rolling stock of the railroads.

France emerged [from the war] almost bankrupt, with large debts and some 10% of her territory devastated. Industrial and agricultural output was some 40% down in 1913 with exports a fraction of their prewar level. (Aldcroft, 2001: 36)

Pig iron and coal output declined by roughly 50% between 1913 and 1919, and did not recover until 1922 and 1924, respectively. France, a creditor country before the war, emerged from the war deeply in debt, and was forced to repay $3.7 billion to the United States and Britain.

Defeated and exhausted, Germany experienced a nutrition crisis. The Versailles Treaty cut off 15% of the country's arable land, 75% of its iron ore, and 26% of coal resources. Iron and steel production capacities dropped 44% and 38%, respectively. Germany lost roughly 90% of its merchant fleet, its entire navy, a great part of its railway rolling stock, and all of its foreign investment. By 1919, German industry produced little more than one-third of its 1913 output levels. By 1923, industrial production overall still had not reached half the prewar level (Berghahn, 1987: 276–7).

Within the new borders of Poland, 1.8 million buildings were destroyed. Half of the railway bridges and station buildings were ruined. Serbia, also a battlefield, lost half of its animal stocks. Bulgarian agricultural output dropped to 57% of the pre-Balkan wars levels, while industrial production was still 20% lower in 1921. Romanian crude oil output did not reach half the prewar level until 1921. War exhaustion hit Austria hard – by 1918, agricultural production had fallen by half, and milk consumption in Vienna dropped to 7% of prewar levels; cut off from former raw material resources, industrial output reached only one-third of prewar levels in 1919 (Berend and Ránki, 1974: 174–7).

To various degrees, the first postwar years were characterized by decline. One of the most frightening phenomena was runaway inflation, due to the financing of the war economy, the accumulation of huge debts, severe declines in agricultural and industrial production, the heavy burden of reconstruction, and, in some cases, reparation payments. Five countries – Germany, Austria, Hungary, Poland, and Italy – were hit hard by hyper-inflation. Romania and Bulgaria also suffered. Germany was particularly badly affected. In November 1923 $1 attained the astronomical rate of 4.2 billion marks. Thirty paper mills, 150 printing firms, and 2,000 printing presses worked 24 hours a day to supply the valueless paper money (Tipton and Aldrich, 1987: 176). The price of a kilogram of butter reached 5 billion marks and the Reichsbank printed 1,000 billion mark notes. Money, however, was not accepted and the country fell back on barter trade: the price of a haircut was four eggs, a first-class burial, forty eggs. In Hungary, by 1919 the value of one prewar gold crown became equal to ten paper crowns; by the spring of 1924, it was equal to 18,400 paper crowns. The crown, which had been on a par with the Swiss franc before the war, was valued at 1 franc:3,500 crowns by the summer of 1919. By the spring of 1924, 1 Swiss franc was equal to 1.8 million crowns (Berend and Szuhay, 1978). In the fall of 1918, one Polish mark was equal to $1. By the spring of 1924 $1 was equivalent to 9.3 million marks (Berend and Ránki, 1974: 181–3).

Countries that lost huge territories, as well as, paradoxically, those that gained territories required a long time to reconstitute and consolidate their new national economies. Austria, Hungary, Poland, Romania, and Yugoslavia took decades to cope with their new circumstances.

Several European countries were more fortunate. Britain's direct war losses, nevertheless, were still severe. Of nearly 6 million mobilized men,

Table 2.1 Decline of GDP (in percent) in belligerent countries, 1913–19
(Maddison, 1995a: 180, 182)

Austria	Belgium	France	Germany	Britain
−38	−20	−25	−28	+01

more than 600,000 died. The British commercial fleet was decimated. Exports dropped to 40% of prewar levels, and in 1918 re-exports of imported goods, mostly from the Empire, stood below one-fifth of 1913 levels. As B. W. E. Alford phrased it: "Trade was an early casualty of the war." As a result, industrial production declined. Output in 1920 stood at 1913 levels, but then fell by roughly 20% in 1921, and did not recover until 1924. GDP, which in 1919 had reached 1913 levels (see Table 2.1), subsequently declined between 1920 and 1922 by 16% and did not recover until 1927. Before World War I, Britain was the world's leading foreign investor and financial power. This position partly evaporated during the war: its overseas capital holdings declined by 25%, and the so-called invisible income from financial transactions decreased by 25–33%. "The advance of the nation's prosperity had depended in a major way on its ability to generate large and increasing surpluses on international financial transactions. This capacity was lost . . ." (Alford, 1996: 107–9, 120; Pollard, 1983: 52).

Unlike the countries at war, most of the neutral states emerged from the war and the immediate postwar years with a stronger economy and higher incomes: the Netherlands, Spain, Norway, and Switzerland increased their per capita GDP by 19, 15, 11, and 9%, respectively, between 1913–14 and 1922–24. At the end of the war, however, because of shortages of energy, raw materials, and markets, and because of revitalized international competition and sharply restricted export possibilities, the neutral countries suffered setbacks. None of the European countries escaped the negative consequences of the war.

Most of the European countries, at least as a consequence of temporary dislocation, lost the work and achievements of one or two generations. The income level of Austria and Belgium declined to that of the 1870s–80s, i.e. by two generations. The levels of Germany, France, the Netherlands, and Britain dropped to that of the 1890s and lost the work of one generation (Maddison, 1995a).

Besides war losses, an ugly wave of deadly great power rivalry continued, and fundamental nationalism and various forms of extremism flooded the continent. The victors sought to strengthen their dominant role. The disillusioned peripheral and defeated countries, and those who believed they had been cheated by the victors, revolted. Victors and the defeated, rich and poor countries alike, were looking for the new rules of the game. Those nations that had lagged behind the core *ante bellum* refused to continue as before.

An idealistic President Wilson spoke about "peace without victory," freedom and equal status for all nations without great power interference, collective security, guaranteed by a newly established League of Nations, and the right of self-determination for all nationalities. America, how-ever, soon withdrew from international politics and peacemaking. Instead of taking the lead and helping to build an international world order, the United States became preoccupied with domestic affairs. The Versailles Peace Treaty became the peace of the victors, and, paraphrasing Karl von Clausewitz, the peace was nothing more than the continuation of war by other means. France planned to destroy its archenemy, Germany, as much as possible: Article 233 of the Versailles Treaty declared that Germany would have to pay for the destruction and damage of the war, and the amount "shall be determined by an inter-Allied commission, to be called the Reparation Commission." The Commission, under strong French pressure, decided on a $33 billion reparation obligation for Germany in April 1921. This was far too excessive. "French claims were at the outset of a most extrav-agant character," Lloyd George, postwar prime minister of Britain, wrote later. France demanded, for example, 75 billion francs for devastation of buildings in north-east France, which represented 4% of the territory of the country, while official French statistics in 1917 had valued the housing properties of the entire country at only 59.5 billion francs (Lloyd George, 1932: 18–20).

J. M. Keynes denounced the Treaty as "Carthaginian" and "outrageous" and strongly opposed an excessive reparation burden in his *Economic Con-sequences of the Peace*. He considered it counterproductive and believed the victors would in effect punish themselves by exacting more from Germany than it was able to pay.

[T]he bankruptcy and decay of Europe, if we allow it to proceed, will affect everyone in the long-run. The only safeguard against revolution in Central Europe . . . [if] even the minds of men who are desperate, revolution offers no prospect of improvement whatever. (Keynes, 1920: 296, 283, 287)

Even the hard-nosed French soldier Marshal Foch realized that the "peace," in reality, was nothing else but an "armistice for twenty years." His *bon mot* turned out to be a prophetic forecast. Versailles, realizing Prime Minister

Georges Clemenceau's 1918 idea, decided to destroy Austria-Hungary, the "natural" ally of Germany, and by using and abusing the Wilsonian "right of self-determination," hammered out an alliance behind Germany. Clemenceau envisioned an alternative eastern barrier in a chain of newly established independent allied countries, a Little Entente, of Poland, Czechoslovakia, Yugoslavia, and Greater Romania. The Versailles Treaty system thus redrew the map of Central Europe. Robert Seton-Watson's influential journal, *The New Europe,* spoke about a *tabula rasa* in the region (Berend, 1998: 152–3). Austria-Hungary, with its 676,443 square kilometers of territory and 51.4 million inhabitants, was replaced by Austria (85.5 thousand square kilometers and 6.5 million inhabitants), Hungary (92.6 thousand square kilometers and 7.6 million inhabitants), and a newly created Czechoslovakia (140.4 thousand square kilometers with 13.6 million inhabitants). Transylvania and some additional territories were given to the newly created Great Romania, which was enlarged from 137.9 to 304.2 thousand square kilometers and from 7.5 to 17.6 million inhabitants. Croatia and Slovenia, together with Voivodina and Bosnia-Herzegovina, joined Serbia, Montenegro, and Macedonia and became part of the newly established Yugoslavia (249 thousand square kilometers with 12 million inhabitants). Partitioned Poland was reunited and then expanded to include 388.3 thousand square kilometers and 27.2 million people. Besides "Russian Poland," the three Baltic countries and Finland also separated from Russia and became independent. Germany lost 14% of its territory and 10% of its population. Both Alsace-Lorraine, which had been occupied by the Germans, and Western Poland, which had been incorporated into Prussia, were returned to France and Poland, respectively.

Once the borders were redrawn, thirty-eight independent economic units replaced the prewar twenty-six, and twenty-seven currencies were in use instead of the prewar fourteen. The frontiers, i.e. tariff borders, increased by 2,000 kilometers. These territorial changes generated tremendous nationalist upheaval. Austrians believed that their new country was not viable and both Left and Right advocated an *Anschluss* or merger with Germany. The Vorarlberg province wanted to join Switzerland. The dismemberment of Hungary (which lost two-thirds of its prewar territory) and Bulgaria (which lost 10% of its territory) and the creation of Great Romania, Czechoslovakia, and Yugoslavia, partly artificial constructions, generated a new wave of hostility among neighboring nations. Irredentism became the driving force of Hungarian and Bulgarian politics. Tensions within the new, smaller, multinational states rather quickly reproduced the struggle among nationalities. German nationalists sought revenge. The defeated Central European countries dreamt of the revision of the Versailles Treaty system.

Minorities, who felt oppressed and declared themselves nations without a state, often turned to aggressive, revisionist powers, which openly advocated the elimination of the Versailles system. The stage was set for revolts (Berend, 1998).

The Bolshevik Revolution in Russia, left-wing revolutions in Hungary, Bavaria, Bulgaria, and revolutionary attempts in Germany and Austria challenged the capitalist system. They were defeated everywhere except in Russia. At the same time, right-wing extremism was born. In January 1919, a right-populist German Workers Party was established, adding "national socialist" to its name in 1921, and adopting the pan-German ideology of expansionism and anti-Semitism under the leadership of Adolf Hitler. Hitler's Nazi Party "translated" the idea of Marxian class struggle as the solution of social and economic ills into a concept of racial struggle, an anti-Jewish revolution of the Aryan people. Hitler attempted a *putsch* in Munich in November 1923, which failed at the *Feldherrnhalle*. Nevertheless, the Nazi movement's march toward power had begun. A wave of counter-revolution followed and authoritarian nationalist regimes were established across the crisis-torn Baltic, Balkans, and Central European region.

If communism often mixed with nationalism, as it did in Hungary and Russia, right-wing extremism, during the same period and under similar revolutionary conditions, was born of a fundamentalist nationalism. Mussolini's fascism in Italy in 1922 offers the most telling example. The leader of the Nationalist Party, Enrico Corradini, "translated" the Marxian concept of class struggle into a nationalist concept of international class struggle between the "proletarian nations and the bourgeois nations." In contrast to proletarian socialism, he preached national socialism. In the context of revolutionary postwar Italy on the brink of civil war, after the "Red Biennium" of 1920–1, Benito Mussolini took over the nationalist program. The European peripheries sought new roads to development: Russia began its communist experiment, while most of Central and Eastern Europe and all of Mediterranean Europe were ruled by right-wing authoritarian dictatorships.

Failed attempts to return to "normalcy"

What were the economic consequences of the new political setting on interwar Europe? The radical transformation of the political environment of postwar Europe had immediate and long-lasting economic consequences. The victors were not confident of preserving their gains, the victims looked for revenge. In this environment, the bitter lessons of war, starvation, and economic exhaustion inspired programs of self-sufficiency in food as well as in basic strategic materials production. All of the peripheral countries refused to follow prewar export-led industrialization. They "de-linked" themselves from the West and turned toward import-substituting industrialization. Since earlier attempts to catch up had failed, these countries sought to avoid competition in a free market with their more industrially advanced rivals in the West. Self-sufficiency, based on the prohibition of imports and their replacement with domestic products, became the ideal. High tariffs, state interventionism, and even state ownership became widespread. The newly independent countries equated national and economic independence with self-sufficiency. The thirty-year period between 1914 and 1944, sometimes called the twentieth century's "Thirty Years War," was characterized mostly by deep economic and political turbulence.

Europe hardly recovered from the deep postwar chaos. Turning toward "normalcy" was signaled by stabilizing the currencies and the restoration of the gold standard by sixteen countries between 1923 and 1926, and by another four in 1927–9, but the international economic system was ruined; the lack of economic leadership weakened cooperation, conserved international economic chaos, and increased risk. In this situation, international agreements remained on paper and attempts to reconstruct prewar conditions failed. The League of Nations remained powerless. The former lending countries of Europe became debtors to the United States.

Britain's main ambition and activity focused on the reconstruction of the international monetary mechanism as a guarantee of international trade and prosperity. The Cunliffe Committee initiated the move toward a return to gold as early as 1918. This was indeed accomplished between 1924 and 1928. Britain, led by nineteenth-century knowledge and habits – or as B. W. E. Alford called it, this "innate sense of superiority," enhanced by imperial sentiments (Alford, 1996: 129) – sought to re-establish its prewar position and forced the return to the gold standard. As the Chancellor of the Exchequer, Winston Churchill, stated in his budget speech:

every Expert Conference since the War . . . every expert Committee in this country, has urged the principle of return to the gold standard . . . in international affairs at the earliest possible moment . . . [Britain] resume[s its] international position as a gold standard country [and] will facilitate the revival of international trade, [and Britain's] central position in the financial systems of the world. (Churchill, 1925)

The Gold Standard Act in May 1925, in an orthodox and counterproductive way, restored the prewar exchange rate and effectively overvalued the pound by 10–20%. "In short, the British economy was crucified on a cross of gold which bore the inscription $4.86 to the pound" (Alford, 1996: 129). By 1926, thirty-nine countries, including most of those in Europe, followed. Together with Britain, the Scandinavian countries (and Sweden even before that, in 1922) and Switzerland also returned to prewar parity, which in some cases caused a "parity crisis." The Netherlands valued its currency at higher than prewar parity. Overvalued currencies stifled exports by making them more expensive.

The potential benefits of the stabilization, were partly frustrated because the exchange rates did not always closely reflect the relative price level in the various countries. (Zacchia, 1976: 516)

The Bank of England and its governor, Montagu Norman, made another attempt to help re-establish British financial and economic leadership in the world when he tried to organize an "internationale" of central banks and launch cooperative actions to maintain stable financial order in Europe. The central banks, according to his vision, would become "a third independent branch of global power side by side with the market and governments." However, rivalries and nationalism in Europe eliminated his plan (Péteri, 2002: 34, 194).

The victorious great powers sought to restore prewar international conditions, as well as their own leading roles. Since free trade had been a prime mover of the prewar economy, they believed it was necessary for rapid reconstruction and mobilized the League of Nations to reach this goal. The first international conferences under the aegis of the League were held in Brussels in 1920 and Geneva in 1922. A series of so-called prohibition conferences was organized by the Economic Committee of the League between October 1927 and September 1929. A special conference of the League of Nations in 1927 advocated the return to a free (or low-tariff) trade system. At that time the situation seemed closer to "normal" and the great powers acted accordingly. The report of the 1927 Geneva conference sought to convince governments that protectionism was less a guarantee of national security than a source of conflicts among nations.

Economic peace will largely contribute to security among nations . . . During the great war, nations were driven temporarily to live to a quite abnormal extent on their own resources . . . The attempts after the war to seek prosperity through the policy of economic isolation have, after an experience of nearly nine years, proved a failure . . . A simple return to prewar conditions seemed in the circumstances the appropriate objective of economic policy which would be sufficient to cure the current difficulties. [Certain countries] maintain . . .

recently established industries in existence by means of tariffs . . . the desire of certain nations to attain a degree of economic independence . . . [and] to stimulate artificial industries . . . [instead of those] most naturally suited is not justified. (World Economic Conference, 1927: 10–29)

Several countries signed the resolution. In January 1931, however, the League returned to the issue to examine the results. It turned out that none of the signatory governments followed the initiative. The attempt had failed. Vojislav Marinković, Yugoslavia's minister of foreign affairs, offered reasons for the failure during the debate. Laissez-faire economists, he argued, had expected the restoration of economic equilibrium by free trade. Free trade, however, served only the advanced countries. How could the poor agricultural countries compete with their overseas competitors? The imposition of protective tariffs was irrational and threatened to undermine world trade. But what rational solutions were there for countries in an emergency?

Last year, when I was in the Yugoslav mountains I heard that the inhabitants of a small mountain village, having no maize or wheat . . . were simply cutting down a forest, which belonged to them . . . I said to them: "You see that your forest is becoming smaller and smaller. What will you do when you cut down the last tree?" They replied . . ."what would we do now if we stopped cutting down our trees?" I can assure you that the agricultural countries are in exactly the same situation. You threaten them with future disasters; but they are already in the throes of disaster. (Carr, 1964: 58)

In other words, an irrational situation resulted in an irrational economic policy. The great powers and their League of Nations, however, continued their attempts to restore the old order. The *Draft Annotated Agenda* for another world economic conference in 1933 condemned the "worldwide adoption of ideals of national self-sufficiency, which cut unmistakably athwart the lines of economic development." The Van Zeeland Report of 1938 repeated the old gospel that free trade is "fundamentally preferable . . . [to] autarchic tendencies . . . [It] shall offer to all participants advantages greater than those offered by the position in which they now find themselves" (Carr, 1964: 56). By that time, however, few people shared this view. Instead, most governments of the less developed countries of Europe agreed with remarks made by Hjalmar Schacht at the Economic Council of the German Academy in November 1938, even though they were clearly an expression of the Nazi political strategy to present Germany as the leader of the victims of the victorious great powers. The wealthy great powers, said Schacht, do not understand "that a poor nation has nevertheless the courage to live by its own laws instead of suffering under the prescriptions of the well-to-do" (Schacht, 1938). Tariff increases, tariff wars, and the quest for self-sufficiency, though counterproductive and dangerous for the international economy in the long run, offered the only immediate line of self-defense for various countries of the peripheries. A return to laissez-faire was out of the question.

The postwar situation naturally led to the continuation of the type of regulations that had presided during wartime. "In areas of severe war destruction both in East and Western Europe, the state played the role of organizer and financer of reconstruction" (Fischer, 1978: 175). Rebuilding transportation systems often went hand in hand with nationalization of railroads. Both France and Germany turned to state railroad systems. In countries of dominant big estates and mass landlessness, such as Poland, Czechoslovakia, Hungary, Yugoslavia, and Bulgaria, land reforms, trimming or abolishing big estates were carried out by the state (Berend, 1985: 152–161).

All of the countries, having learned from their bitter war experience, wanted to secure their own supply of food. Agricultural protectionism was a central demand of farmers, who represented a powerful political bloc protecting their interests, which became a strong government preference. Newly established independent countries created independent customs units to hammer out an independent national economy. All these developments encouraged trade restrictions and exchange controls. Tariffs, import quotas, licensing foreign trade, and other restrictive measures continued to be applied after the war.

Another major political factor, the increasing role and influence of social democracy, also contributed to the rise of a regulated market system. The idea of state regulation of the national economy emerged in the early twentieth century German social democratic movement. Eduard Bernstein, the leading theorist of the party, in his series of studies, *Probleme des Sozialismus* (1896), argued that capitalism developed in a different direction from the one prophesied by Marx. Poverty was not growing because of welfare reforms achieved by the organized mass movement through parliament. He replaced the concept of proletarian revolution with the idea of reforms realized by parliaments as a peaceful road toward socialism (Bernstein, 1899). Rudolf Hilferding, in 1923, at a keynote speech to the refounding congress of the Second Socialist International in Hamburg, went further by stating the possibility of "eliminating the faults of capitalism" within the system. Four years later, at the Kiel congress of the German Social Democratic Party, he presented a matured new concept of socialism:

We arrive at a capitalist organization of the economy, where the road leads from an economy determined by the free play of forces to an organized economy . . . In reality, organized capitalism means that the capitalist principle of laissez-faire is replaced by the socialist principle of planned production. This planned, deliberately managed form of economy is much more susceptible to the conscious influence of society, which means to the influence of the . . . compulsory organization of the whole society, the state. (Protokoll, 1923: 58; Protokoll, 1927: 166–8)

The social democratic parties, after World War I, became decisive political factors in West European politics. In 1919 they won 41% and 39% of votes in Austria and Germany respectively, and about one-third of the votes in Belgium, Denmark, Finland, Italy, Norway, Sweden, and Britain in postwar elections. During the early 1930s, they gained between 46% and 54% of votes in the Scandinavian countries. Several socialist parties such as the German, British, Austrian, French, and Swedish formed governments or participated in government coalitions in the interwar decades. They successfully promoted cooperation between unions and employers' organizations, and prepared a large-scale public works program.

The interwar years witnessed a blossoming of employer-union pacts from the Stinnes-Legian pact of 1918, which established the joint labour-management board for economic regulation (the *Zentralarbeitsgemeinschaft*) in Germany, to the largely ineffectual "Whitley Councils" in Britain, the Matignon Accords of 1936 following the victory of the Popular Front in France . . . the employer-employee pacts in the Nordic countries such as the Saltsjöbaden Agreements in Sweden (1938), and the so-called Main Agreement between the LO and the NAF in Norway (1935) . . . Ever since the 1914–18 war years, there had been a growing interest in planning in both "bourgeois" and social democratic circles. (Sassoon, 1996: 60–2)

E. H. Carr went further:

In Europe after 1919, the planned economy, which rests on the assumption that no natural harmony of interests exists and that interests must be artificially harmonized by state action, became the practice, if not the theory, of almost every state. (Carr, 1964: 51)

Protectionism was one of the main elements of state interventionism. Postwar governments used wartime restrictions to ban imports and exports. These restrictions remained in effect in Czechoslovakia and Yugoslavia until 1923, and until 1924 in Hungary and Romania. In Britain, the McKenna Tariff remained in force and was even extended. Both the Safeguarding the Industries Act and the Dyestuffs Importation Act of 1921 provided safeguards for a great number of key industries. The country, nevertheless, soon returned to decontrol of wartime regulations.

The European trend was also influenced by restrictive policies in the United States, a country that was on the rise as an economic powerhouse. The Fordney-McCumber Tariff of 1922 increased American protectionism to its highest level. France, Germany, Belgium, and Holland introduced or increased import tariffs. This new trend, tariffs as the *ultima ratio* of economic self-defense, emerged by the mid-1920s. New and higher tariffs were introduced in the new countries: in 1922 and 1924 in two steps in Bulgaria; in January 1925 in Austria, and in the same year in Yugoslavia and Hungary; in 1926 in Czechoslovakia; in 1924 and 1927 in two steps in Romania. New tariffs were more specialized and contained thousands of items to exclude new trade partners from the advantages of duty reductions granted in previous trade agreements for other partner countries. The levels of the new tariffs were also much higher than ever before. Romania increased tariffs from 30% to 40% of the value of imported goods; Hungary raised them from 20% to 30% and, in several cases, to 50%. Yugoslav tariffs for industrial consumer goods reached 70–170% of the value of imports. The new tariffs were considered to be *tarifs de combat,* bargaining weapons against trade partners all over Europe. The strategy was to force future partners to make compromises by mutual tariff reductions. The second half of the 1920s was characterized by bitter trade wars. Economic nationalism, the effort to establish self-sufficiency, undermined international trade. Czechoslovak exports to the Danubian countries dropped from 52% to 31%, while Yugoslav imports from the area of former Austria-Hungary declined from nearly 75% to 28% during the first postwar decade (Berend and Ránki, 1974: 202–8).

The death of laissez-faire, and extreme state regulations during the Great Depression

The last nail in the coffin of the laissez-faire system was struck with the Great Depression in the early 1930s. The first sign of a decline appeared in agriculture. Overwhelming overseas competition undermined Europe: wheat exports from the United States, Canada, Argentina, and Australia increased from less than 7 million tonnes before the war to roughly 19 million tonnes by 1929. With the recovery of European agriculture during the 1920s, a huge world surplus accumulated. Agricultural overproduction was a global phenomenon. As a consequence, the combined average price of basic agricultural commodities declined by roughly 30%. Farmers all over the world reacted by further increasing output to counterbalance the decline in price. Worldwide production of basic agricultural commodities increased 30–80% during the second half of the 1920s. A deep crisis became unavoidable. From the winter of 1930 to the spring of 1931 sixteen international conferences were held in an effort to find a solution, but all failed.

Another cause of the end of quasi-prosperity was the drying up of American investments and credits, which played an important role in assisting and developing Europe, from the middle of 1928. In one single year, capital inflow was reduced by half. Germany received only $482 million in 1929, compared with $967 million in the previous year. As a bitter consequence, debtor countries already had to pay back more in interest, dividends, and principal than they received in 1928. By 1930, the financial crisis had deepened as net capital exports dropped to $363 million, i.e. by 85% (Aldcroft, 1978: 263–4). Commodity prices began falling by the middle of 1928. Limited prosperity came to a halt in 1928 and 1929, by the end of which time the European economy had collapsed.

The "Black Thursday" of the American Stock Exchange in 1929, nevertheless, was a turning point. It caused a tremendous shock, which discouraged entrepreneurs from investing and consumers from buying, and made bankers especially cautious and thus borrowing more difficult. Since the United States was the chief lender country, and because a great number of the credits during the 1920s were short-term transactions, immediate repayment became impossible without new credits. International financing virtually stopped. Other factors also contributed: the slowdown of money growth in the United States, and the gold reserve decline of the Bank of France. The two leading lenders, the United States and Britain, which continued to disburse almost $1.5 billion of credit in 1930, decreased their lending to $30 million in 1931 and to $32 million in 1932. Because of massive repayment obligations, the leading capital exporting countries already had a $1.424 billion capital inflow from their debtors in 1931. Germany, which received $1.037 billion in 1927 but only $129 million by 1930, had a net capital repayment of $540 million by 1931, since repayment greatly surpassed borrowing. Poland, which received $124 million in 1928, received only $3 million in 1930, and by 1931 net repayment stood at $1 million (International, 1949: 11–12). Heavily indebted Germany, which owed half its debt in short-term credits, lost 2 billion marks in gold and foreign exchange in six weeks during the summer of 1931. The reserves of the National Bank dropped from $512 million in July 1929 to $58 million in June 1931. Depositors stormed the banks to withdraw their money. In July, the Darmstädter- und Nationalbank, one of the three largest, went bankrupt. The German banking system, the powerhouse of the German economy since the mid-nineteenth century, collapsed; within two days, all the banks were closed. Something similar happened in Austria. The Central European headquarters of the Rothschild empire, the Vienna Creditanstalt, center of vast Central and Eastern European operations, went bankrupt in May 1931. The Austrian National Bank rushed to help, but its payments also dried up; by the summer of 1932 its reserves had dropped by nearly 90%. The gold basis of the schilling declined from 87% to 25%. At that point, a further 1 billion schillings in debt was recalled and Austria reached the point of financial collapse. Financial crisis spread like wildfire. During the 1930s, when new credits were not available but the debtor countries had to repay at least part of their debts, capital outflow became characteristic on the continent. About $7 billion was pumped out from a crisis-ridden Europe (Feinstein et al., 1997: 168). The high degree of indebtedness made repayment in several countries practically impossible.

Due to the *Zeitgeist* of the age, each country turned inward to find domestic solutions. The consequence, paradoxically, was an utterly international crisis. The duration, intensity, and worldwide scope of the depression were unique indeed. World industrial output dropped by 30%, coal and iron production by 40–60%, grain prices declined by 60%, the volume of European trade fell from $58 billion to $21 billion between 1929 and 1935, and 20 million Europeans became unemployed.

The first reaction was a more exalted economic nationalism. This took the form of further exaggeration of precrisis protectionism. The United States rushed to introduce the Smoot-Hawley Tariff Act in June 1930, which was a "crushing blow to European industry" (Garraty, 1986: 15). Britain, an advocate of a return to the prewar international system, also made steps toward economic nationalism after 1925. Lack of confidence itself became devastating. In the panic situation of September 1931, Britain abandoned its "natural child," the gold standard, and in the same year introduced a temporary "Abnormal Importations Act," which generally imposed 50% tariffs on manufactured goods, but permitted duties up to 100% *ad valorem*. German and French tariffs were doubled between 1927 and 1931, and reached 40% *ad valorem*.

Import quota and licensing measures were also added and were even more restrictive than high tariffs, since they operated independently of price movements. They limited imports in an effort to defend domestic markets. France was the first to introduce this new weapon, but nineteen other European countries followed during the 1930s. International trade, ailing already in the 1920s, virtually collapsed. The value of European imports dropped from nearly $32 billion to $12 billion, and exports declined from

$26 billion to $9 billion between 1928 and 1935, or roughly one-third of precrisis levels. All efforts to return to "normalcy" faltered between 1929 and 1933, and by 1936 the gold standard collapsed all over Europe.

The German government closed the banks on July 13, 1931 and ceased the exchange of national currency for foreign currency. All payment in foreign currency had to be permitted by the Central Bank. Hungary followed Germany's lead: on July 17, 1931 the government closed the banks for three days and authorized the withdrawal of only 5% of deposits. As of December 22, a transfer moratorium stopped currency payments of foreign debts. Austria and other debtors followed. "In such an atmosphere, the regulation of foreign trade and financial transactions was a natural and inevitable development" (Kenwood and Lougheed, 1971: 210).

Most European governments introduced strict measures of exchange control, which transformed international trade. Debtor countries pioneered the transformation. Because of their difficulties in making payments, and the lack of hard currency and gold, these countries returned to barter trade, i.e. they paid each other in kind. Germany played the central role in introducing these arrangements. In 1932 and 1933, bilateral agreements with Brazil and Egypt established the pattern. In most cases barter compensation deals went beyond private agreements and were organized by governments. Partner countries signed bilateral clearing agreements and centralized all payments for imports and exports via their national banks. The President of the National Bank of Austria, Dr. Richard Reich, suggested this idea at the conference of national banks in Prague in 1931. The two partner countries created accounts for international payments, and importers paid with their own currency to the account of their own national banks. These payments served for payments to the exporters of the same country. As a consequence, the partner countries did not have to use hard currency. The imports of a country were thus determined by its exports. Since balanced bilateral trade was rarely realized, the governments paid the difference to each other at the end of each year. The first clearing agreement was signed by Austria and Yugoslavia in January 1932, followed by agreements with Hungary, Italy, and Bulgaria. Germany signed its first clearing agreement with Hungary in 1932, followed by a series of similar agreements with other Central and Eastern European countries.

All of the Central European countries devalued their currency in hidden and partial ways, since the bonus system devalued the currency in trade transactions but not in financial transactions such as interest and principal repayments. The system also allowed them to pay export subsidies by using higher exchange rates for exports. Between exchange control countries (of Central and Eastern Europe) and free exchange countries (of Western Europe), agreements about payments regulated economic communications. The first such agreement, which served as a model for similar agreements between creditor and debtor countries, was signed between Britain and Germany in November 1934. It limited German imports from Britain to 55% of German exports to Britain (based on deliveries during the previous month but one), while the remaining 45% served German debt repayments.

Tariffs remained among the most effective weapons of government economic policy. Between 1929 and the mid-1930s, tariffs, as a rule, were increased. Britain, the cradle of free trade, also turned to protection. On February 4, 1932, Neville Chamberlain, Chancellor of the Exchequer, referring to the "catastrophic" price decline and the "extraordinary growth of trade restrictions" in the world, announced this step:

We propose, by a system of moderate Protection, scientifically adjusted to the needs of industry and agriculture, to transfer to our own factories and our own fields work which is now done elsewhere, and thereby decrease unemployment . . . (Parliamentary Debates, 1932: col. 279–96)

Britain returned to postwar protectionism, which was gradually eased in the mid-1920s. Indeed, the Import Duties Act of March 1932 introduced a general *ad valorem* tariff of 10%. In April of that year, that level was doubled, while it reached 33.3% for luxury goods, steel, and chemicals. "The Import Duties Act inaugurated the protectionist era in Britain" (Pollard, 1983: 121). Import quotas were also introduced – in 1933, quotas for agricultural imports were put in place. Austria and Czechoslovakia meanwhile increased their wheat tariffs by two and three times, respectively, between 1930 and 1934.

The level of tariffs as a percentage of the value of imported goods jumped, and for fifteen European countries averaged 64% higher in 1931 than in 1927 (see Table 2.2 for examples).

Most of the countries did not consider the consequences of this market defense satisfactory: France was the first country to introduce import quotas and import licenses, which became the most widespread method of defending domestic markets. "Import quotas were even more damaging to international trade than tariffs, since a quota directly limits the level of permissible imports and thus operates independently of the price mechanism" (Kenwood and Lougheed, 1971: 216–17). While tariffs remained relatively low in Belgium, limited quotas were introduced for sugar, fertilizers, and coal by June 1931, and then expanded in 1932–3 to various agricultural products, and, in 1933–4, to textiles. By 1939, nineteen European countries

Table 2.2 Tariffs in % of value of imported goods, 1927–31 compared (Hogg, 1986: 11)

Country	General tariff 1927	General tariff 1931	Agricultural tariff 1927	Agricultural tariff 1931
Germany	20	41	27	83
France	23	38	19	53
Italy	28	48	25	66
Belgium	11	17	12	24
Switzerland	17	27	22	39
Sweden	20	27	22	39

were using this weapon. Additionally, many countries banned the imports of certain products.

Fixed quotas or the prohibition of imports were often combined with a state monopoly of trade. In Czechoslovakia, the Československá obilní společnost was founded in 1934 to monopolize cereal trade (Olšovský and Průha, 1969: 219). Tariff increases and bans on imports were rather efficient in countries with net agricultural imports. In the agrarian countries of the peripheries, however, which were net agricultural exporters, other measures of state intervention were needed. They would be summarized as state assistance in the reduction of the cost of production, subsidization of output and export, and debt alleviation to prevent the collapse of peasant farming.

Yugoslavia established Privilegovano Akcionarsko Društvo (Prizad), a grain trade monopoly, in 1930. The government also established the Privilegovana Agrarna Banka to assume bad debts from 654,000 peasant farms and rescue them from bankruptcy. In 1930, Bulgaria founded direktsiya khranoisnos, a Directorate of Grain Export, which controlled the domestic market and monopolized foreign trade of cereals and seeds. Exports of tobacco and rose oil were monopolized by the Bulgarian Agrarian Cooperative Bank. In Hungary, hangya szövetkezet and Futura Rt., 70% and 100% state-owned companies, respectively, monopolized 80–85% of agricultural exports (Szuhay, 1962).

Multilateralism nearly disappeared, with the exception of several international cartel agreements, which mostly regulated primary goods markets. The tin and sugar schemes of 1931, the tea and wheat agreements of 1933, rubber and copper agreements of 1934 and 1936, respectively, which controlled nearly 90% of exports, introduced price controls and quantitative limits on output. Before World War II, as many as 180 international cartel agreements regulated market cooperation. They were, however, largely replaced by state-organized regional economic agreements. The Rome Agreement of February 1934, for example, created an economic bloc, consisting of Italy, Austria, and Hungary, which regulated exports and opened markets to each other. At the same time, a German-led Central and Eastern European economic bloc was created, based on strictly bilateral agreements, between 1934 and 1939. During these same years, the "Oslo Group" of Denmark, Sweden, Norway, Finland, Holland, Belgium, and Luxembourg established some economic cooperation among member countries. Britain also initiated the Ottawa Agreement in 1932 by introducing import preferences and tariff reductions for British Commonwealth countries, while imposing tariffs against others.

In the early 1930s, most of the governments had to intervene to save collapsing banks and industrial companies, to assist and defend farmers, and create jobs. During the most severe crisis in modern world history, practically all governments took action. Although Britain did not move too far in the direction of state interventionism, the "cheap money" policy (in addition to money market forces) of a 2% bank rate helped to keep prices and interest rates stable. The policy also contributed to a construction boom in the 1930s, which was responsible for fully 30% of the increase in employment during the first half of the decade. The Exchange Equalization Account, established in April 1932 with £175 million – an amount that was twice increased by £200 million – had the same effect on foreign exchange rates. It counteracted divergences on the market by purchasing and selling. The British government also introduced measures against competition and in favor of cartels: the Coal Mines Act of 1930, for example, made a cartel scheme compulsory; the Traffic Commissioners restricted competition in road transportation in 1930 and 1933; the Herring Industry Board and the Spindles Board of 1934 and 1936, respectively, restricted competition and employed subsidies. Similar interventions were especially successful in supporting sugar beet production and civil aviation.

In the course of the 1930s, the State thus played an active part in the cartelization of industry and it intervened directly to provide a monopolistic framework where firms were too weak or too scattered, as in the old staples of coal, cotton, iron and steel, shipbuilding and agriculture. (Pollard, 1983: 106)

State intervention in Britain was most extensive in the agricultural sector. Between the mid-1920s and the mid-1930s, the British Sugar Subsidy Act granted roughly £40 million to subsidize sugar beet production and processing, resulting in 32,000 new jobs. The government also merged eighteen factories into the British Sugar Corporation Ltd. The Wheat Act and the Import Duties Act of 1932 provided direct subsidies and established standard prices. The Agricultural Marketing Act of 1931 and 1933 organized marketing for two-thirds of the producers and introduced compulsory controls over output and prices. The Potato Marketing Board (1934) controlled production by imposing penalties for excess acreage. A Milk Marketing Board (1933) controlled sales and set uniform prices. The Bacon and Pig Marketing Board (1933) and the Cattle Industry Act (1934) paid large subsidies to encourage domestic production. The annual cost of agricultural subsidies during the 1930s amounted to between £30 million and £40 million. Laissez-faire was dead, indeed, in British agriculture (Pollard, 1983: 145–53).

France went much further than Britain. Between 1931 and 1935, protectionism was accompanied by bilateralization of trade. The government used tax relief to subsidize industries until 1931 and rescued ailing companies thereafter. The Banque National de Crédit was safeguarded. The state became a shareholder of certain companies, such as the Société Air-France, Compagnie Générale Transatlantique, and Société Nationale des Chemins de Fer. The state also began organizing the market and controlling prices. The latter step was taken in 1933 when the government introduced price controls on corn. The following year, it also placed limits on output. Prices of cereals, wine, and sugar were heavily subsidized. In 1935, the Laval government enacted the *décrets-lois* on the silk, milling and shoe industries to limit production by prohibiting new factories. Thus, compulsory state-regulated cartelization took hold in French industry. The Popular Front government went even further in May 1936 by initiating a policy to increase consumer demand. In June 1936, the Popular Front government announced an important package of reform:

From the beginning of the next week, we shall bring before the Chamber a group of bills ... These bills will deal with ... the forty-hour week; collective bargaining contracts; paid vacations; a public works program to provide facilities for public health, science, sports and tourism; the nationalization of armament production; a wheat office that will serve as a model price support system for other agricultural products ... (*Journal Officiel*, 1936: 1315–16)

The government's argument was entirely unorthodox: they did not believe in market equilibrium or in Jean Baptiste Say's famous liberal principle that every supply creates its demand. Theirs was a demand-side economic approach. Wage increases and job-creating public works had to "restore," as the government phrased it, the purchasing power of the population, and increased demand could offer an exit from the crisis. Then in the spring of 1938, the Daladier government adopted a policy of investment stimulation and a kind of planning, combined with increased military expenditure.

The severe financial and banking crisis led, in 1934, to the introduction of legal controls over private banking, when deposit activities and investment business were separated. A new Banking Regulation Act, which provided significant tax reductions, was put into effect. The entire banking sector was also made subordinate to the Commission Bancaire. The Belgian National Unity government of van Zeeland established the Office National du Redressement Economique in March 1935 to organize economic recovery. Between 1935 and 1939, a moderate public works program was realized with nearly 3 billion francs. Credit organizations were also founded for agriculture and smallholders. "The economic crisis of the 1930s made clear that state intervention in the economy had become urgent" (Mommen, 1994: 32).

Several of the continent's peripheral countries went so far with state intervention as to found state-owned companies and introduce state planning. The Polish government created the Fundusz Bezrobocia, renamed in 1933 as Fundusz Pracy (Unemployment Fund and Labor Fund, respectively) to finance public works. By 1936, state planning had become decisive: a six-year Defense Expansion Plan (1936–42), and a four-year Investment Plan (1936–40), introduced widespread planning. More than 100,000 jobs were created. As one of the central goals of military preparation, a significant effort was made to industrialize the country by creating the Centralny Okreg Przemysłowy (Central Industrial Area), the Warsaw-Krakow-Lwow triangle, in a four-year industrialization plan. By the end of 1938, Vice-Premier Eugeniusz Kwiatkowski sought to make such planning permanent by preparing three five-year plans (Kostrowicka et al., 1966: 340–1).

The Hungarian government initiated a five-year plan in March 1938 as well. The state invested 1 billion pengő into the economy, more than 20% of which was spent on improving transportation, while 60% supported military developments. Sixty percent of these investments were covered by a special property tax, 40% by internal loans. Both, however, were refinanced by the state, and at the end, covered by inflationary financing. In February 1939, the Supreme Military Council ordered the realization of the five-year plan in two years, and then, in 1941, the investment for the program was increased to 2.6 billion pengő. At the same time, a 1 billion pengő Ten-Year Agricultural Plan (1942–51) was enacted (Schweng, 1951: 4). Currency in circulation jumped from less than 500 million to nearly 900 million pengő in 1938. In 1938–9, budgetary expenditures reached one-third of the country's national income (Berend and Ránki, 1958: 299–300, 377–8).

By the mid-1930s, state intervention and regulation had increased along with preparations for war. The revelation of Hitler's aggressive plans and his Four-Year Plan of war preparation generated an answer from both allies and enemies of Nazi Germany. In 1936, Britain initiated a large naval program to cope with its three potential antagonists, Germany, Japan, and Italy. Britain also wanted to match Germany in the air and began a huge investment program in the air force, including the development of a long-range bomber fleet. Construction of 8,000 planes was projected within three years. Britain concentrated on technological superiority in these programs. To extend the capacity of armament industries, the number of state-owned factories, the so-called Royal Ordnance Factories, was increased. By the spring of 1938, five plants had been put into operation and ten new ones were on the books. With state financial contributions, private factories such as Austin, Vickers, the Nuffield Organization, and the English Electric Company also increased their capacities (Ránki, 1993: 24–5). Figure 2.1 charts industrial recovery in the decade to 1938.

State ownership spread in the peripheral countries as well. The Yugoslav state-owned mines provided 35% of the country's coal and 90% of its iron ore output. By 1939, the number of state-owned companies was fifty-two. In Romania, 70% and 80% of metallurgical and coal output, respectively, was produced by state-owned mines and factories. Armament, aircraft, and transportation equipment industries were also partly state owned. By the end of the 1930s, the Polish state owned 95% and 93% of merchant shipping and the railways, respectively. It also owned roughly 100 industrial firms, among them the entire armaments industry, 80%, 50%, and 40% of the chemical, metal, and iron industries, respectively. State-owned banks also played the leading role in the banking industry. The Bank Akceptacyjny, founded by the state in 1933, monopolized all short-term crediting. Besides transportation, state ownership was mostly characteristic of armaments and other strategic sectors in Europe, and the share of state companies rarely surpassed more than 5–7% of industrial output (Ránki and Tomaszewski, 1986: 37–9).

Military expenditures in France between 1933 and 1938 were even higher than in Britain in proportion to national income, and increased by more than 40% during the second half of the 1930s. Armaments expenditures, in real value, increased sharply all over Europe: 470% in Germany, 250% in Britain, 370% in the Soviet Union, 130% in Czechoslovakia, 115% in Denmark, 112% in Austria, 98% in Sweden, 92% in Holland, nearly 60% in Italy and Poland, and nearly 50% in Hungary (Milward, 1979: 39, 40, 44, 47).

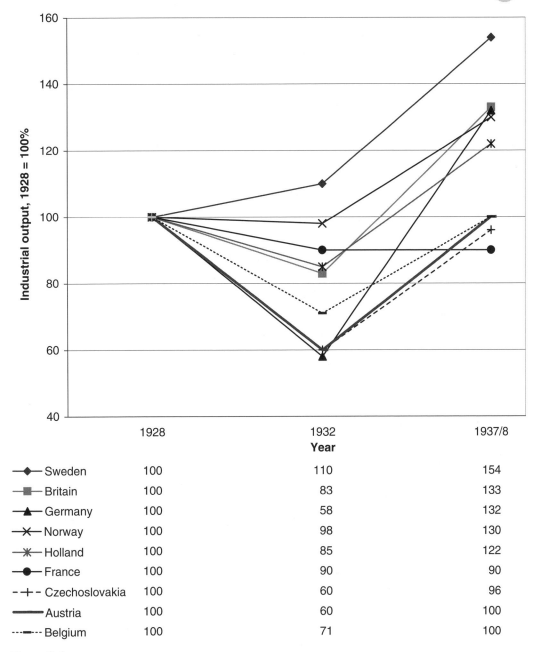

Year	1928	1932	1937/8
Sweden	100	110	154
Britain	100	83	133
Germany	100	58	132
Norway	100	98	130
Holland	100	85	122
France	100	90	90
Czechoslovakia	100	60	96
Austria	100	60	100
Belgium	100	71	100

Figure 2.1
Industrial recovery,
1928–37/8

The state greatly expanded its role as regulator, financier, and buyer of an ever-increasing part of output, and also as owner of large segments of the economy. Increasingly throughout the interwar decades, laissez-faire was negated and replaced by protectionism and a regulated market economy with an important role for the state. The era ended when the "market [was] the only organizing power in the economic sphere" (Polanyi, 1964: 68–9). In these troubled times, society, as a matter of natural self-defense, according to Karl Polanyi, re-absorbed the economic system into the social system. The institutional separation of society into an economic and political sphere ended and the economic order became again a function of social and political considerations. For Polanyi, it was a return to normalcy after the "complete reversal of the [historical] trend of development," which characterized the entire nineteenth century (Polyani, 1964: 68).

The theory of the regulated market

This new experience soon led to the emergence of a new economic theory challenging the blind belief in market rules and the balancing role of an "invisible hand," as formulated by Adam Smith and popularized by Jean Baptiste Say with his famous law that each supply creates its own demand because production provides the income to buy the products. Say's Law, however, apparently stopped working.

A variety of new insights began to challenge this traditional concept. The Swede Johan G. K. Wicksell was among the first to question the validity of Say's Law and supply-side economics. In his view, economic depression was a consequence of monetary disequilibria. He advocated new money creation to satisfy demand and rejected the traditional view that cheap money generates nothing but inflation. His theory of money and interest paved the way for a new economics. The Cambridge economist R. F. Kahn explained the "multiplier" effect of any increment to the circulating purchasing power. According to his interpretation, an additional increment in purchasing power will be multiplied by various "leakages," since the money circulating generates additional buying and selling at every step. This happens because each recipient of the circulating money buys additional goods, thereby supporting additional suppliers. If the leakage is one-third of the total amount, according to Kahn, original payments will be multiplied three times.

A new approach was in the making to replace the traditional laissez-faire theory. The real breakthrough arrived with the works of a British economist, John Maynard Keynes. He criticized the classical theory of the mechanism of market equilibrium as early as 1924. In an open letter to Franklin D. Roosevelt published in the *New York Times* at the end of 1933, he clearly outlined his new idea: "I lay overwhelming emphasis on the increase of national purchasing power resulting from governmental expenditure which is financed by loans" (Keynes, 1933). The "Keynesian Revolution" was crowned by his *General Theory of Employment, Interest and Money,* published in 1936. Keynes rejected the existence of market automatism by proving that income from production will not appear entirely as demand. Individuals and firms save more from income because they do not find investment profitable. Moreover, "when real income increases . . . the community will wish to consume a gradually diminishing proportion of it." Savings, in other words, are not mere prerequisites of investments. When savings surpass investments, they have a deflationary impact and withhold output at a lower level of demand. According to Keynes, it is therefore not the supply that creates its demand but rather the demand that determines supply.

Keynes also questioned the concept of the automatic recovery of the labor market:

The outstanding faults of the economic society in which we live, are its failure to provide for full employment and its arbitrary and inequitable distribution of wealth and incomes . . . I believe that there is social and psychological justification for significant inequalities of incomes and wealth, but not for such large disparities as exist today. (Keynes, 1936: 84)

J. M. Keynes arrived at a revolutionary new principle: supply and demand are not balanced in the market; one must consider consumption, savings, investment, and the liquidity of capital (which is also influenced by interest rates) together. As a consequence, economic growth might be generated by additional employment in certain sectors of the economy and by increasing consumption through state intervention, which would create additional demand and, in the end, generate additional supply. Money, in his view, is not merely a "neutral" intermediary in the market; it has an independent role. Reducing the rate of interest itself may stimulate investments, but there are limits since investments do not automatically and necessarily respond to rate cuts. "It seems unlikely that . . . policy on the rate of interest will be sufficient by itself to determine an optimum rate of investment." By printing additional money and financing public works, the state may have a more positive impact: it can create jobs and generate additional demand. Moreover, generalizing from the multiplier theory, Keynes maintained that any addition to purchasing power generates a multiplied effect, and both investments and employment increase many times more than the original additional investment and employment generated by the state. The additional investment and job creation will increase income and people will consume more. He concluded that it was necessary to create additional purchasing power and more jobs through public investment and moderate inflationary financing. In this way, state intervention could pave the way out of economic depression (Keynes, 1936: 27, 117, 211, 372, 374, 378).

Although it is true that "the virtual break-up of laissez-faire as a body of doctrine . . . has followed, and not preceded, the decline of laissez-faire in the real world" (Dobb, 1964: 188), the Keynesian theory formulated from the experience and lessons of the real world during the interwar decades itself influenced economic policy and market relations. Keynes won over the governments. From instinctive defensive reflexes, deliberate economic policy measures and consistent and complex state interventionism were born. Michael Kalecki, the leading Polish economist, told his students that the head of the military junta that ruled Poland during the second half of the 1930s invited him to his office and asked for an understandable explanation of the Keynesian concept. Theory, indeed, turned out to be practice and strongly influenced economic activities for three to four decades to come. A new war and war economy made this theory triumphant.

War economy, 1939–45

The war exploded in the early fall of 1939 and then culminated with Germany's attack on the Soviet Union in the summer of 1941. War production, which had increased during the 1930s, burgeoned in the belligerent countries of Europe after 1939 and 1941. The main players at this point were Germany, Britain, and the Soviet Union, as continental Western countries were defeated and occupied by Hitler within a few months. Germany, which did not mobilize its economy for a long and total war prior to 1941 because of its *Blitzkrieg* economic strategy, easily won a series of battles until the summer of that year. After that time, however, total war mobilization followed and the war effort multiplied. Consumer expenditure dropped from 55% to 38% of GNP. Basic industries and armaments production increased from 30% of industrial output in 1939 to 45% in 1942 and 61% in 1944. After the *Blitzkrieg* collapsed, German armaments production nearly tripled within two-and-a-half years (Ránki, 1993: 175–7).

With the exception of Britain, the Soviet Union, and traditionally neutral Switzerland and Sweden, Nazi Germany occupied most of the European continent and harnessed it into a war economy. By December 1941, the bulk of the European half of the Soviet Union was also occupied. The stage for a "New European Order" was set. "The economies of occupied Europe could be divided into three major zones, where the form and shape of exploitation were different, but the function, role, and finally the results were the same:" a) the satellite countries of Central and Southern Europe, including the fascist Slovakian and Croatian puppet states; b) occupied Western Europe; and c) the conquered and absorbed territories of Austria, the

Czech lands, Poland, Serbia, and the Soviet Union (Ránki, 1993: 318). Germany ruled 3.3 million square kilometers of territory with a population of 238 million. Nazi Germany looted and exploited Europe and recruited and enslaved millions: in 1944 more than 9.3 million foreign workers labored in Germany. They represented 30% of the industrial workforce and 35% of the labor force in the armaments industry. The occupied West European territories contributed significantly to German war production. They provided 20% of Germany's coke, 25% of electro-steel and steel sheet production, 20–25% of trucks, 40% of clothing, and 25% of work shoes (Milward, 1970: 132, 165, 238). The neutral countries also increased their production for Germany. The value of Swedish trade with Germany doubled between 1938 and 1941. Between 1941 and 1944, exports to Germany increased from 17% to 42% of total Swedish exports (Milward, 1977: 323–5). Between 1938 and 1945, war prosperity led to an 18% and 21% increase of per capita GDP in Sweden and Switzerland, respectively.

Total war required the utmost economic effort from all participating countries. The Soviet Union, which carried the heaviest burden of the war and lost its most developed Western territories, engaged in superhuman efforts to survive. Stalin's industrialization policy was already serving war preparations during the 1930s (see Figure 2.2). The armaments industries got absolute preference from 1940 on and increased output by two-and-a-half times between 1940 and 1944. The production of consumer goods, however, fell from nearly 40% to roughly 20–22% of all industrial output. The production of tanks and armored vehicles increased nearly sevenfold, and combat aircraft production more than fourfold (Harrison, 1985).

British economic achievements were also impressive. Iron ore and aluminum production increased by 37% and 55%, respectively, during the war years. The number of aircraft produced in 1938 was only 2,827, but already 26,461 by 1944. The latter figure included specialized bomber aircraft production, which increased more than tenfold. Tanks and self-propelled artillery production grew from less than 700 a year to nearly 9,000 by 1942. Naval and landing craft production rose more than sixfold between 1941 and 1943. In response to military requirements, the production of radio valves also increased threefold. The war consumed only 15% of the national product in 1939, but by 1943 its share increased to 56% (Pollard, 1983: 203, 214).

The war efforts required a far more sophisticated war economic system than ever before. Regulated markets became the rule in spite of the differences between political and social systems. The main characteristics of the wartime regulated market system were similar across the entire

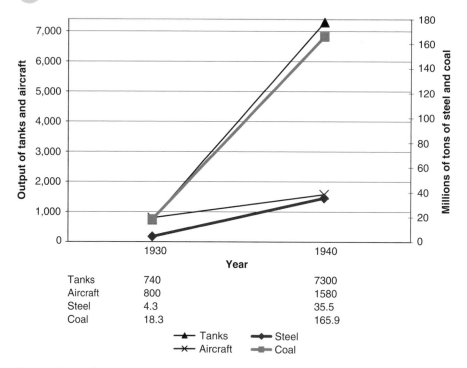

Tanks	740	7300
Aircraft	800	1580
Steel	4.3	35.5
Coal	18.3	165.9

Figure 2.2 Soviet industrialization and war preparations in the 1930s

continent. Free market prices were replaced by a controlled and regulated price system, which was subordinated to resource allocation. Financial policy, which had been the main vehicle of state economic policy, ceased to be the main determinant. Physical controls dominated. The war effort demanded a strict priority system based on centralization of information, decision-making, and execution of those decisions. It required a strong administrative organization. Alan Milward describes the British system, which emerged in January 1941 when the so-called Lord President's Committee developed into a kind of parallel cabinet with authority over the war economy and the House of Commons practically lost its role. "What emerged was almost as far from democracy as the government of Germany or Italy" (Milward, 1979: 111).

A huge administrative apparatus was built up: the Ministry of Food, founded in April 1940 with 3,500 employees, employed 39,000 people by 1943. A whole set of ministries ran the British economy. The establishment of the Ministry of Economic Warfare in September 1939 was followed by the formation of the Ministerial Priority Committee and the Principal Supply Officers Committee. In 1940, under the Churchill cabinet, the Ministry of Supply, the Ministry for Aircraft Production, and a special Airplane Production Council were also formed. The entire population was registered and the control of labor hiring was introduced in order to minimize labor mobility and to shift labor to essential areas of war production. Between April and November 1941, 200,000 women were transferred from civilian industrial sectors into the munitions industry. The Employment of Women Order in early 1942 went further and ordered all women between the ages of twenty and thirty (this increased to forty from 1943) to obtain a job through the Employment Exchanges.

Production and material supply were directed by the state apparatus. Various kinds of planning were responsible for meeting the demands of the war effort. In January 1940, the Harrogate Programme set a goal to produce 2,500 aircraft per month. This was superseded by the Hennessy Programme, which called for faster output, and then by the Bomber Programme of December 1941, which shifted priority to the production of heavy bombers. In early 1942, special committees directed shipping, raw materials, and munitions production. In the summer of that year, a Ministry of Fuel and Power was created with authority under the Emergency Powers Bill to intervene in the private sector. "The government had gained almost unlimited economic authority over all British citizens and their property" (Ránki, 1993: 124). The state took drastic measures, ordering a 25% cut in household consumption and cutbacks on consumer industries. As a result of restrictions on civilian consumption, clothing production declined by 37% and output of household goods by 57% during the war.

State intervention in agriculture, in an effort to secure an acceptable food supply, was a crucial arena for wartime regulation all over Europe. In Britain, however, it became even more important, since the country had relied on agricultural imports. Before the war, 70% of domestic food consumption was met by imports. As of 1939, the government initiated a drive toward self-sufficiency as much as possible, especially in grain. It paid £2 per acre for plowed pastureland. The government invested more than £700 million in food subsidies during the war. Using a complex pricing and regulatory system, the main goal of shifting from a livestock to a crop economy was successful: cereal output doubled, as did the calorie production of British agriculture. Food imports were cut by half. "This increase in production in a free economy could not have been achieved" (Ránki, 1993: 251).

State regulation, subsidization, planning, and increased war production were costly and required a special financial policy, which was introduced by the Churchill cabinet. In order to fight runaway inflation, strict rationing of consumer goods and price controls were introduced covering 90% of an average household's expenditures, with the aim of suppressing consumer spending and transferring resources to armaments. But it also controlled inflation: while from 1939 to 1940 wholesale prices jumped by

43%, afterwards they slowed down and increased rather moderately, closing at the end of the war in 1945 at levels only 77% higher than those of 1939. The cost of living increased by only 34%, while wages increased by 44%.

Wartime expenditures skyrocketed, increasing sixfold between 1938–9 and 1944, mainly down to four times more tax revenue and nearly twenty times more borrowing. Tax revenues met more than half of the accessed war expenditures, even during 1943–5. Borrowing, disinvestments abroad (withdrawal of previously invested capital), and credits from the Commonwealth and from the United States provided the required financial resources (Hancock and Gowing, 1949).

In many respects the British war economy did not differ much from others, though British and German labor policy and economic relations with other countries contrasted sharply. After 1941, nearly the entire continent was under German rule and subordinated to the Nazi war economic system. The occupied territories in the West and East alike in essence became part of the German economy, run by a Nazi administration according to the requirements of the German war machine. The allied countries were also incorporated into the German war economy, but under their own administrations. The Hungarian government, for example, introduced programs to produce munitions, tanks, and aircraft. From 1941, direct German orders and joint programs subordinated the Hungarian economy to that of Germany. The joint Messerschmitt aircraft program of 3 billion pengő, connected to an ambitious bauxite-aluminum program and an oil extraction project, was partially controlled by the Hungarian government, but later controlled directly by a German agency, the Deutsche Industrie Kommission in Ungarn.

Free markets for products were practically closed. Raw material and engineering output was almost entirely bought by the Hungarian state and delivered to Germany. By 1942, 90% of the capacity of the Hungarian cotton industry and nearly 80% of the woolen industry was given over to state orders. Raw material and energy supplies were controlled by the state as well. From 1939, various committees directed supply, but in 1942 a Central Raw Material Office was founded to distribute important raw materials. Various restrictions, standards, and recycling orders were introduced to conserve raw materials and substitute artificial ones where possible. In 1943, private construction works were banned. Energy restrictions and rationing became two of the most important tools of state control.

During the war years, Hungarian agricultural deliveries to Germany were also increased under a harsh requisition system. Estates and farms were required to deliver a fixed amount of product calculated against the net income of each acre of arable land. Within the country rationing was introduced for all important food products, such as bread, flour, fats, milk, butter, and potatoes. In August 1939, the government fixed all prices and a special institution, a Price Control Office, was established. War expenditures required that the state play a central role in financing the war economy. This role assumed added importance because the bulk of the deliveries to Germany were left unpaid (Hungarian National Archive, 1942). Between 1938–9 and 1944, war expenditures increased from 12% to 44%, and budgetary expenditures jumped from 33% to 72% of the Hungarian national income. The only way to cover these huge expenses was inflationary financing. The number of banknotes in circulation increased fourteenfold during the war. The situation was analogous in Romania and Bulgaria. In Central and Eastern Europe, the market economy ceased to exist.

During the first half of the twentieth century, generated by two major wars, the most tragic depression in economic history, and the disappointing and humiliating failure of modernization and industrialization in the European peripheries, a new economic model emerged: the regulated market system. Free trade, the gold standard, and a self-regulating market system ceased to exist. Newly invented methods of intervention served to counterbalance cyclical trends and achieve special economic goals such as self-sufficiency and extreme war production. In other words, intervention supported economic growth. The successes of the new experience had a long-lasting impact on Europe, inspiring further experiments. More accurately, the war economy during the first and second world wars was a seedbed for all twentieth-century economic regimes. The extreme war efforts and their requirements were more or less well handled by centralized, state-run, and strictly regulated market systems. It became clear that a self-regulating, free market system would be unable to deal with all these tasks.

The impact of the regulated market economy: European economic performance

Two major world wars and a devastating Great Depression made the period between 1914 and 1944 a deeply troubled dark age. Regulations and state intervention served crisis management and helped the national economies to cope with the immense difficulties. In the final analysis, the European economy, as well as the world economy, registered the slowest growth in its modern history (see Table 2.3). Europe's GDP increased by 70%, but on a per capita basis the increase was only 37%, somewhat smaller than the growth of the world economy.

In spite of the generally slow economic growth, some important modern structural changes did occur in Europe, especially in the West and

Table 2.3 GDP and GDP per capita in Europe and the world, 1900–50 (based on Maddison, 1995a; 227–8)

| Year | Europe | | | | World | | | | Europe in % of world |
	GDP	1913 = 100%	GDP/ capita	1913 = 100%	GDP	1913 = 100%	GDP/ capita	1913 = 100%	
1900	908,455	73	2,012	85	1,976,876	73	1,263	82	159
1913	1,241,635	100	2,381	100	2,726,065	100	1,539	100	155
1929	1,514,923	122	2,757	116	3,696,156	136	1,806	117	153
1950	2,116,057	170	3,259	137	5,372,330	197	2,138	139	152

Figure 2.3
Economic growth (GDP per capita) 1900–50

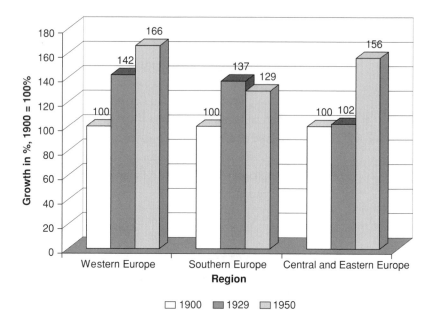

Scandinavia. There was a significant shift from agriculture to industry. The contribution of agriculture to income in Denmark declined from 30% to 21%, while the share contributed by industry increased from 24% to 36% between 1910 and 1950. The Norwegian economy underwent a similar structural change: the contribution of agriculture declined from 24% to 14%, while that of industry, especially the steel, engineering, and chemical industries, increased from 26% to 36% in the same period (Jörberg, 1976:

Table 2.4 Output of electric energy of 23
European countries (based
on Mitchell, 1998: 562–5)

Year	Gigawatt hours	%
1925	80.36	100
1950	388.40	483

415, 424, 427). Agricultural employment in Norway declined to between 10% and 20% of total employment, and to 25% in Scandinavia as a whole.

Services experienced the largest gain, and the so-called tertiary sector became the largest sector of the economy, employing 35–50% of the active population in the West by 1950.

In both the West and Scandinavia, average growth was a result of the combined rate of the declining old and rising new industries. Britain presents a clear example. The country's traditional staple industries, most of all the textile industry, gradually but permanently lost ground: their combined share of net industrial output was 37% in 1924, but only 28% by 1935. Cotton and cotton products, the leading export items of nineteenth-century Britain, decreased by half and 60%, respectively, between 1912 and 1938 (see Figure 2.4). The cotton industry's labor force and machinery declined by one-third. This was partly the consequence of the industrialization drive of less developed countries, which began supplying their own consumer goods, partly a shift in the more advanced countries toward new sectors based on new technology. By contrast the production of electricity, electrical goods, and automobiles doubled between 1929 and 1938. Aircraft and rayon production increased fivefold. Investments in older staple industries declined by more than 20%, while new rising industries increased their share by 21% (Pollard, 1983: 54–5, 73).

France's technological–structural modernization can be seen in the decline of coal and iron output (by 13% and 42%, respectively) and the increase of electricity and artificial fiber production (by 33% and 73%, respectively) between 1929 and 1938 (see Figure 2.5). In the Netherlands, the share of employees in the textile and clothing industries declined from 25% to 19%, but increased in the engineering and chemical industries from 17% to 30% (Jansen and Smidt, 1974: 36).

These changes were made manifest by the triumph of electricity. In 1919, only a small number of houses in Britain were connected, but by

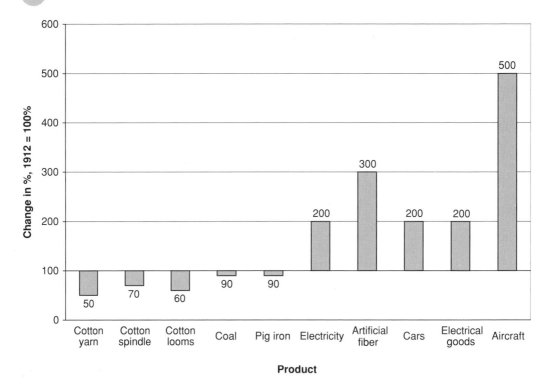

Figure 2.4

Restructuring of
British industry,
1912–38

1939 already two-thirds were served by electricity (Luckin, 1990: 52–3, 57, 73–5, 172). Electrification topped the agenda throughout Europe and advanced steadily (see Table 2.4).

The historical importance of the rise of electricity in Europe is well illustrated by the fact that electricity use jumped 400% during the interwar years, while energy consumption overall climbed only 25%. Increased consumption was linked to public use, industrial use, and the spread of household machines. Some of these new electric machines, however, appeared exclusively in bourgeois households. In 1932, 1,750 electric irons, 500 heaters, and 460 stoves were used per 10,000 households in Switzerland. These figures were higher than in the United States. In France only 850 electric irons, 85 electric heaters, 8 electric stoves, and 120 vacuum cleaners existed in each 10,000 households (Landes, 1969: 435, 439, 440). Certain electrical appliances immediately conquered a large market, assisted by the decline of electricity prices.

The telephone and radio spread swiftly in Europe (see Table 2.5), giving rise to a large service sector as well. The triumphant conquest of the radio began almost immediately after World War I, and during the first half of the 1920s virtually all European countries established regular broadcasting: Holland in 1920, Britain in 1922, Germany in 1923, Hungary in 1924.

Table 2.5 The spread of telephone and radio in 21 European countries
(in 1,000s based on Mitchell, 1998: 765–72, 775–9)

Year	Telephone*	1950 = 100%	Radio**	1950 = 100%
1900	650	2.9	–	0.5
1913	5,305	24.0	270***	5.2
1950	22,146	100	51,532	100

* line in use; ** receiving licenses; *** 1925

Figure 2.5
Restructuring of
French industry,
1929–38

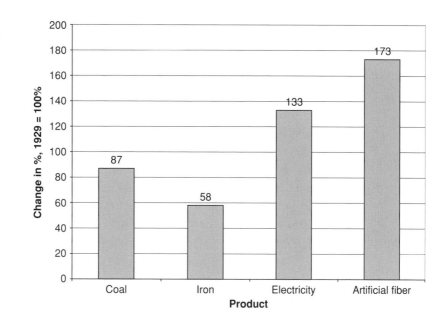

The car industry, in its infancy at the turn of the century, gained impetus
during the war (see Table 2.6). Soldiers used trucks and cars during World
War I and "the war popularized a product that had heretofore been viewed
as elitist." The automobile projected the aggressive image of speed and
modernity. A typical 1920s driver looked like a fighter pilot (Möser, 1998:
203, 206–7, 210–11). The spread of motor vehicles was unstoppable. Mechanization of agriculture also became a major force of economic growth in
Europe, with the first tractors appearing at the beginning of the century. In
Western Europe, mechanization gained momentum in the interwar years.

Table 2.6 Number of motor vehicles in Europe
(based on Mitchell, 1998: 735–42)

Year	Number in 1,000	1950 = 100%
1913	431	4.7
1950	9,229	100

By 1950, in the area of the Council of Europe, 839, 600 tractors were being used in agriculture.

After World War I, aviation blossomed in the West. As early as the fall of 1919, one of the first airlines was founded, the Koninklijke Luchtvaart Maatschappij voor Nederland en Koloniën, or KLM Royal Dutch Airlines, and bought airplanes from Fokker (Dierikx, 1995: 221–2). The British, French, Belgian, Spanish, Polish, Swiss, Hungarian, Soviet, German, Finnish, and Czech airlines were founded between 1920 and 1924 (Taylor and Mondey, 1983: 70–9). A new infrastructure was created as well. Military airfields were transformed, and in the 1920s Croydon (a military airfield, rebuilt and reopened in 1928) and Le Bourget served London and Paris, respectively, while Johannisthal emerged as Berlin's main airport. In 1923, Tempelhof Airport opened and from 1926 became the home of Lufthansa (Higham, 1995: 21–3; Braun, 1995: 45–6). Between 1934 and 1944, several airports were opened in Britain, among them Gatwick (1936). The construction of Heathrow Airport began in 1944.

The real breakthrough in aviation was connected with World War II. Heavy bomber and fighter planes became deadly weapons. Mass production became a must: Germany, Britain, and the Soviet Union produced roughly 118,000, 132,000, and 158,000 airplanes, respectively (Ránki, 1993: 175). The war resulted in huge industrial capacity and a new impetus toward faster air transportation.

New technology began influencing old-technology sectors. Diesel and electric locomotives modernized railroads, though progress was rather slow. In the territory of the Council of Europe, steam locomotives still represented 78% of the total locomotive stock in the 1950s (*Council of Europe*, 1959: 268).

New products based on new technology spread across Europe, though with a sharp disparity, stimulating mostly the western half of the continent (including Scandinavia). While the advanced core adjusted better, the less developed peripheries declined to a prolonged crisis and could not find a way forward.

Box 2.2 KLM

KLM, or Koninklijke Luchtvaart Maatschappij voor Nederland en Koloniën, was established in October 1919 as one of the world's first airlines. The "Flying Dutchman," well known from when Holland became the first modern naval power with the largest commercial navy, turned toward the new form of travel and transport. Albert Plesman, a thirty-year-old entrepreneur, recognized the potential of the new business and opened the company's first business route between Amsterdam and London in the spring of 1920. A few months later services began to Copenhagen and Hamburg. In the first year, 345 passengers and 15 tonnes of cargo and mail were transported. Although at the beginning KLM used chartered British planes, it soon turned to Dutch-made Fokker planes, the four-, five-, and then seven-seater F-2 and F-3, and F-7.

The ambitious Plesman, a hard-nosed manager, enlarged the business and established the first intercontinental flights in October 1924 to the Dutch East Indies (Indonesia) and in 1929 to the Far East. By 1931, regular passenger services carried four passengers from Amsterdam to Batavia (Jakarta). The trip took ten days, with more than eighty-one hours' flying time. Around that time, instead of the Fokker aircraft, which reached speeds of about 200 kilometers per hour, Plesman became the first in Europe to buy American Douglas aircraft, the DC-2 and then the DC-3. Services were set up to Australia, India, Egypt, South America, and the Caribbean. By 1930 KLM was carrying 18,000 passengers, a number which had swollen to 160,000 by 1939, making KLM the fourth biggest airline in Europe.

World War II and the Nazi occupation of the country almost ended the company, but in April 1945, KLM reopened its business and a new chapter of its history. In the fall of that year the Far East service was in regular operation, and by May 1946 the company opened Europe's first regular service to the United States. During the years of revolutionized air travel and burgeoning tourist business, KLM realized an extraordinary expansion – in the 1998–9 business year, the company carried more than 15 million passengers and 578,000 tonnes of cargo and mail on its 117 modern aircraft. The network connected six continents, 90 countries, and 500 cities.

Structural changes in employment, particularly the decline of agricultural employment, had a tremendous impact on economic performance due to the marked differences in labor productivity between various sectors. The productivity gap was enormous, even in less developed countries. In

Table 2.7 Labor productivity in Western Europe and Scandinavia*
(Maddison, 1995a: 249)

Country	1913	1938	1950	1950 as % of 1913
Britain	4.40	5.98	7.86	179
France	2.85	5.35	5.65	198
Germany	3.50	4.84	4.37	125
Netherlands	4.01	6.26	6.50	162
Belgium	3.60	5.27	6.06	168
Denmark	3.40	5.31	5.85	172
Sweden	2.58	4.27	7.08	274
Norway	2.19	4.30	5.41	247
Switzerland	3.25	5.90	8.75	269

* GDP in 1990 ppp dollar/work-hours

1950, an average Spanish agricultural worker produced $320 value of product, while in non-agricultural sectors the value of worker output reached $1,582. In Yugoslavia, the difference was similar: $140 compared with $1,751. Productivity, one of the best parameters of technological modernization, thus increased much faster in countries that were able to make crucial structural changes (see Table 2.7). Western European labor productivity (the value of produced GDP per work-hour) increased at a rate comparable to that of the previous half century – between 1870 and 1913 by 194%; between 1913 and 1950, by 191%.

Between 1913 and 1950, productivity in France nearly doubled, while in Sweden, Norway, and Switzerland it increased by more than two-and-a-half times. Even the best European performance, however, was not enough to catch up with American productivity levels. Moreover, relative to American productivity gains, European productivity experienced a constant decline (see Figure 2.6). In 1870, Western European productivity represented 70% of the American level, by 1913, 59%, and by 1950, only 46% of it. Peripheral productivity was much lower. In the southern and eastern regions it did not reach half of the West European productivity level and was more than half a century behind.

Growth performance thus varied among the regions of Europe. Mancur Olson correctly states that "conventional economic models have not succeeded in explaining the great difference in economic performance

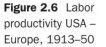

Figure 2.6 Labor productivity USA – Europe, 1913–50

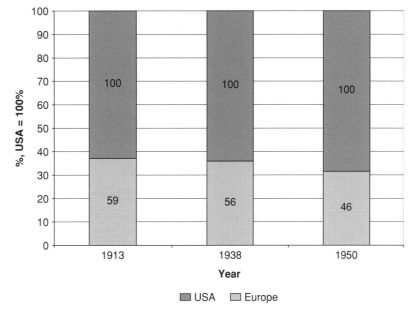

in different countries or historical periods" (Olson, 1994: 73). However, his explanation that well-established special interest groups in "consolidated," well-developed countries decreased productivity by influencing policy making, does not offer a convincing explanation of performance disparities in the first half of the century. Certain growth theories are more convincing when positing that less developed countries may grow faster by adopting the advanced countries' technology and productivity. However, even this did not happen in most of the backward peripheries of Europe in the first half of the century. Disparity in performance was striking. Instead of the moderate 37% European increase, the three Scandinavian countries more than doubled their per capita income level between 1913 and 1950. On the other hand, Ireland grew by a disappointing 29%, Central and Eastern Europe (without Russia) by 26% (see Table 2.8).

The Central and East European countries lagged further behind after World War II than before World War I (see Table 2.9). A latecomer, Scandinavia exhibited a catching-up process, and by the mid-century moved into the most advanced core of Europe.

The huge disparities in economic performance (see Figure 2.7) are rooted in a complex set of causes. In the Scandinavian case, the spectacular catching-up process between 1900 and 1950 was the product of several factors: a social capability to absorb and adapt advanced technology, a high level of education, stable institutions and social peace based on rising welfare institutions, consistent export orientation, and, accordingly,

Table 2.8 GDP per capita in three European regions, 1913 and 1950 (1913 = 100%) (based on Maddison, 1995a)

Year	Western Europe*		Scandinavia**		East–Central Europe***	
1900	3,456	86	2,408	79	1,450	85
1913	4,013	100	3,045	100	1,701	100
1929	4,960	124	3,970	130	1,889	111
1938	4,990	124	4,738	156	1,989	117
1950	5,745	143	6,130	201	2,135	126

* Seven leading countries; ** three countries; *** six countries

Table 2.9 Regional income disparities within Europe, 1900–50 (Western Europe = 100%) (based on Maddison, 1995a)

Year	Western Europe	Scandinavia	East–Central Europe
1900	100	70	42
1913	100	76	42
1929	100	80	38
1950	100	107	37

specialization of production. The peripheries lacked social capability, used import-substitution policies counterproductive for their small countries, remained backward in education and social mobility, and preserved their obsolete class society and inequality. In some cases, new state borders and state formation also created severe transitory obstacles. Consequently, they could not enjoy the "advantage of backwardness" and lagged further behind than before.

Most of the peripheral countries retained their traditional agricultural structure – between 50% and 75% of total employment remained in agriculture. Industrial employment somewhat increased (from 20% to 30% in Central Europe, and from 10% to 15% in the Balkans). The service sector remained backward. The division between the industrial West and agricultural South and East did not change much at all.

An indication of the disparity in technological–structural modernization between Western Europe and the peripheries can be found in statistics

Figure 2.7
Regional disparities, 1900–50 (GDP per capita) (Western Europe = 100%)

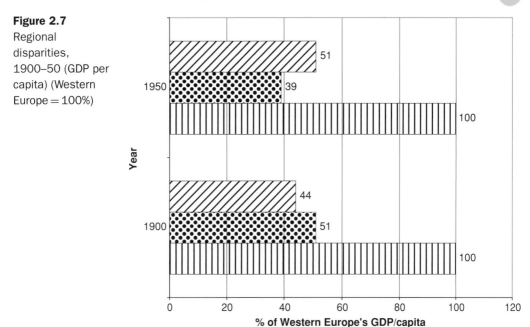

% of Western Europe's GDP/capita

▨ Central and Eastern Europe   ⬡ Southern Europe   ⬚ Western Europe

on the spread of the automobile and telephones. For example, by 1950 the per capita number of telephones in the peripheries was only 7–9% that of the Western level (see Table 2.10).

Europe's deteriorating role in the world

As a consequence of the relatively slow West European growth and the preservation of the relative backwardness in the peripheries, Europe's leading economic position in the world economy, which began to slip in the early twentieth century, continued its relative decline during the first half of the twentieth century. The demise of colonialism was one indication. All the main colonial empires were weakened during World War II, and the colonies became less controllable and more determined to regain their independence. Britain left India in 1947, which opened the gates to independence in other colonies as well. Colonial possessions after World War II became a heavy burden, forced military interventions, and the colonies ultimately gained independence.

The United States and other former white colonies continued their rise and surpassed Europe in many fields. The gap first appeared before World War I, and widened after World War II. The U.S. income level rose to three times that of the European average; per capita GDP of the most advanced

Table 2.10 Number of cars and telephone lines per 1,000 inhabitants (based on Fischer, 1978: 143, 150)

| Year | Car | | Telephone | |
	8 core**	6 peripheral***	8 core**	6 peripheral***
	Countries		Countries	
1914/1920*	9	1	247	12
1929	120	14	434	33
1939	217	17	623	63
1949	204	14	899	79

* Car = 1914; Telephone = 1920; **Britain, France, Germany (in 1949, West Germany), Belgium, Holland, Denmark, Sweden, Switzerland ***Italy, Portugal, Greece, Hungary, Poland, Yugoslavia

Western European countries stood at only 74% of the American level in 1950. In 1913, Europe produced more than one-third of the world's total GDP; by 1950, slightly more than one-quarter of it. In contrast, the United States, Canada, Australia, and New Zealand increased their share from more than one-fifth to nearly one-third. The United States became the world's first consumer society. The number of passenger cars increased from 1.1 million to 40 million between 1913 and 1950. The value of the stock of machinery and equipment per employed person in the United States surpassed the combined levels of France, Germany, Britain, and the Netherlands. After World War II, the number of scientific workers in American manufacturing industry per 1,000 wage earners was five times higher than in Britain. British productivity declined from 86% to 62% of that of the United States between 1913 and 1950. The Dutch level dropped from 78% to 51%, and the Western European level as a whole fell from 59% to 46%. Mediterranean and Central and Eastern European productivity did not reach one-quarter of the American levels. A decimated Europe saw an average annual population growth of 0.6% between 1913 and 1950, while population growth in the United States doubled that, increasing the number of inhabitants by 50%. Europe's share in the world population declined from 28% to 23%. Its share of world exports declined from 60% to 41% between 1913 and 1950. Intra-European trade made up 58% of European imports and 69% of exports in 1913, but this dropped to 37%

and 55%, respectively, by 1947. In 1913 Europe delivered nearly 82% of the world traded manufactured goods; by 1937, it contributed little more than two-thirds.

Europe, the world's banker for nearly a century, gradually lost this position, while the United States emerged as a major lender country after World War I. World War II led to a radical change: in the framework of the wartime Lend-Lease program the United States sent nearly $44 billion in goods, materials, and services to its allies. Immediately after the war, a $3 billion first-aid package followed. From 1948, the Marshall Plan added $13 billion. Europe, shocked and severely weakened, had lost its leading role in the world economy.

CHAPTER 3

Economic dirigisme in authoritarian–fascist regimes

A decades-old debate persists over the existence of a "fascist economic regime." Alan Milward, more than a quarter of a century ago, argued

> Most economic historians have so far adopted the convention of treating "the fascist economies" as an entity in the inter-war period . . . Was there a distinct political economy of fascism? And how did it differ from that of other political groupings? The more research that is published, the less do existing theories of the political economy of fascism carry conviction . . . [Regarding] Italian and German economic policies in the fascist period . . . differences will be seen as more important . . . than the similarities. (Milward, 1977: 379, 412)

Besides the debate over the similarities and differences between the Italian and German systems, debate persisted over fascism itself. From the perspective of this economic history analysis, it is not relevant whether Italian fascism and German National Socialism may be generalized as fascist regimes, nor is there a need to differentiate them or establish that "nazism [is] a distinctive branch grafted on the fascist tree." It is not relevant here whether a narrower definition of fascism excludes "the royal military–bureaucratic–oligarchic dictatorships," including regimes led by political forces such as Primo de Rivera's Unión Patriótica and later Franco's Movimiento Nacional in Spain, or Salazar's União Nacional in Portugal (Linz, 1976: 9, 11). General John Metaxas's dictatorship in Greece had no party backing at all. His "Fourth of August Regime" rejected party organizations. "Those of you who in the past have belonged to parties," stated Metaxas in his declaration, "are now under the obligation of forgetting them utterly; there are no more parties in Greece" (Stavrianos, 1963: 627).

Regulated market systems in nationalist regimes were widespread in interwar Europe, and they were all based on protectionism and state interventionism. In this chapter I am making an effort to generalize an extreme version of this political–economic regime, characteristic of various kinds of oppressive, non-parliamentarian, one-party, dictatorial–military–fascist political systems (not only fascism), and constituting a clearly distinctive type of economy, which I call *economic dirigisme*.

Dictatorial political regimes all paired extreme economic nationalism with absolute control of trade and finances. State interventionism was excessive and uncontrolled, often combined with the creation of state-owned sectors of the economy. The requirements of war economy were also built in to the regime and played a consistent role in it. The state gained an upper hand by violently abolishing opposition, banning all but government parties, "nationalizing" unions, and creating "national movements" – sometimes only youth movements but always using the army as a base – which all served the absolute power of a "leader," *Duce, Führer, Caudillo*, or *Archigos*. Authoritarian nationalist regimes aimed at "economic independence," meaning self-sufficiency, and strove for modern, strong economies, often in the service of an efficient military strength to fulfill the goal of internal stability and/or expansion. To gain legitimization and popularity, economic dirigisme introduced welfare institutions and leisure-time programs. These distinctive features appeared together in similar economic systems in a number of countries and regions.

Fascism may well have served "big capital," or the interests of the middle class, or an independent party bureaucracy, as various interpretations emphasize. Regardless of whether it was the dictatorship of the bourgeoisie, a "third way" between capitalism and socialism, a counter-revolutionary right-wing system, or a mixture of Right and Left populism, economic dirigisme was an inherent aspect. It combined state supremacy and private entrepreneurial interest with oppression of the masses. The regimes, nevertheless, gained mass popularity by introducing full employment policy, organization of leisure time, various institutions reflecting the "collectivist" concept of national (racial) solidarity and unity, and last but not least, populist welfare measures. Mussolini captured this idea in his statement "intelligent capitalists do not concern themselves only with wages but also with housing, schools, hospitals, and recreation for their workers" (Sarti, 1971: 93). The systems of "warfare" and "welfare" were thus not isolated from each other but combined in state economic dirigisme.

The Janus face of authoritarian regimes is revealed by their approach to genuine workers' organizations: free trade unions were destroyed and robbed of their ability to represent workers' interests. At the same time formal workers' representation was institutionalized from above. Furthermore, although the regimes may have served the big corporations, the corporations also had to serve the "supreme national interests" defined by the "leader" and the party–state bureaucracy.

There is one aspect of the old debate on fascism which is impossible to avoid. Economic dirigisme emerged mostly in less industrialized, partially modernized countries in the southern periphery of Europe. On this point I am in agreement with William Welk, who observed the correlation between the rise of fascism and the attempt to modernize. As Welk described the attractiveness of the regime of modernization, after its first years of accomplishments:

Dirt, thievery, the *mafia*, the *lazzaroni*, the old-time *dolce far niente* tended to disappear, and cleanliness, order, and efficiency were established . . . Industry and trade were expanded, splendid new roads built, millions of square miles of marshland reclaimed, and . . . the fastest liner afloat was made to carry the Italian flag. (Welk, 1938: 245)

James Gregor had the same view:

Fascism is here construed as a developmental dictatorship appropriate to partially developed or underdeveloped, and consequently status deprived, national communities in a period of intense international competition for place and status. Fascism was, in fact . . . strongest and succeeded to power in the Latin countries of Europe where the gross national product and the per capita income were lowest, and in countries marginally industrialized . . . (Gregor, 1969: xiii).

The case of German National Socialism, however, suggests, as Alan Milward stated, "that this is a very insufficient interpretation of fascism," since Germany had "a highly developed economy" (Milward, 1976: 380). While most of the regimes of economic dirigisme were indeed – using a post-World War II expression – "modernization dictatorships" in the Mediterranean region, Germany definitely did not belong to this category. Germany, however, also introduced economic dirigisme during the 1930s. Why? The first part of the answer might be the recall of the political–economic–national trauma of 1918 and the postwar humiliation, the feeling of degradation and decline, an unacceptable loss to rival powers in the race to be number one in Europe. One may not forget the poisonous remark of Comte de Mirabeau in his *Monarchie prussienne*: "Prussia is not a state with an army but an army with a state." For Prussian-led Germany the loss of face which accompanied the military defeat was devastating. In a decade, a second blow, the Great Depression with its unparalleled mass unemployment and the halving of the country's industrial output, knocked Germany out. The driving force of the status-deprived country was national pride, urge for revenge against the victors, and thirst to realize the failed expansionist imperial dream. German experience during World War I taught the lesson that wartime economic dirigisme was the key to the utmost military and economic accomplishments. The war generation, which bore this conviction, played a leading role in radical movements to revitalize Germany. Warlike economic dirigisme consequently prevailed even though the per capita GDP in 1933 was twice as high in Germany as in Italy, and even higher than that in Spain.

Nazi Germany thus introduced a regime which combined the well-known system of war economy with an excessively dictatorial, monolithic party–state power. Economic dirigisme in Germany had different origins and goals from those in Italy, Spain, or Portugal. It also had several different features. Nonetheless, it was economic dirigisme.

Important elements and characteristics of economic dirigisme were exhibited in some of the Central and Eastern European countries as well. Poland under the military junta, Horthy's Hungary, and the so-called royal dictatorships of the Balkans during the 1930s became unquestionably authoritarian regimes. These countries, like those in the Mediterranean, shared agrarian backwardness, disappointment over their prewar performance, and determination to modernize and industrialize. Postwar economic chaos and the tragedy of the Great Depression pushed them toward protectionism and state interventionism. While these countries displayed several characteristics of economic dirigisme during the 1930s, especially since they were partly integrated into fascist–Nazi economic blocs, many others remained absent. There were no significant state sectors or any form of corporatism and populist welfare system. In certain respects, Central and Eastern Europe introduced more a regulated market system than an authoritarian economic dirigisme, or experienced a hybrid of the two.

The origins and characteristics of economic dirigisme

To understand the origins of this economic system, it is important to stress again the role of World War I. Like the regulated market system, economic dirigisme was closely connected to the experience of the war economy. Quoting again John Maynard Keynes:

War experience in the organization of socialized production, has left some near observers optimistically anxious to repeat it in peace conditions. War socialism unquestionably achieved a production of wealth on a scale far greater than we ever knew in Peace. (Keynes, 1927: 5, 35, 39, 47–9, 52–3)

Disappointed countries, which failed to catch up during the laissez-faire era and desperately wanted to change their destiny, naturally looked to the war economic system as a new opportunity to realize their goals. Postwar regulations taught them how to apply wartime measures in peace.

Moreover, they looked for a more radical, more mandatory, more controlled economic system. Such an economic regime would be incomprehensible without the dictatorial political systems which introduced it – even though they often differed from each other and had different historical backgrounds.

The roots of Italian fascism went back to the late unification of the country. As a latecomer, Italy remained far behind the advanced West. It preserved ancient, obsolete socio-economic elements in its southern provinces, and was too weak to participate in the ongoing race for building colonial empires. The Italian new Right, which emerged to political prominence during the first two decades of the century, advocated total national unity and undertook the mission to lead Italy from international submissiveness to imperial greatness. The Italian elite enthusiastically joined the war, hoping to realize the national dream. The results of World War I, nevertheless, were disappointing. The country slipped into economic chaos, hit by hyperinflation and a $3 billion debt. War efforts led to a 32% increase of per capita GDP between 1913 and 1918, but this was followed by a 25% decline by 1921, below the prewar level. Shortage and starvation were accompanied by deep disappointment: Italian nationalists felt cheated and aspired to gain additional territories on the east side of the Adriatic Sea, as well as colonies in North Africa.

The postwar situation generated a revolutionary disorder. As in many other countries of Europe, the Bolshevik Revolution also had a mobilizing effect, especially during the "Red Biennium" of 1920–1. To restore law and order, as well as to re-establish national pride and ensure a place in the sun for Italy, a "preventive counter-revolution" took place. Benito Mussolini emerged as a charismatic leader. A former radical Leftist, he subsequently embodied the merging of extreme Right and extreme Left. Mussolini borrowed the genuinely proto-fascist concepts of the Italian Nationalist Party, which later was absorbed by his Fascist Party. The towering Nationalist Party leader Enrico Corradini conceived a synthesis of nationalism and syndicalism. His doctrine of the "nation as the greatest unit of collective life, as [a] truly and literally greater individual being," the need for "internal peace for the sake of external war," and most of all his reinterpretation of the Marxian class struggle as the struggle between the "proletarian nations and the European plutocracy" paved the way for a genuine fascist concept. The other Nationalist leader, Alfredo Rocco, who later became Mussolini's cabinet minister and official theorist of fascism, went further and became more programmatic. The Nationalist Party congress in Milan in 1914 accepted his view that nationalism and liberalism are incompatible in both political and economic doctrines. The party turned toward protectionism. At the 1919 party congress, Rocco introduced the idea of "integral syndicalism," or a corporative system in which workers' syndicates and employer organizations cooperated and the corporations replaced existing political institutions as directing organs of the state (Saladino, 1974: 234–5, 242–3, 250). The regime was not totalitarian at the beginning, but this evolved from the mid-1920s.

Italy's example served as a model for Spain. The declining former colonial great power, though neutral in the Great War, suffered a disastrous defeat in Morocco in 1921. The country declined into a deep and permanent political crisis. The *trienio bolchevista* followed: agitation in rural *latifundio* zones, virtual civil war in Catalonia, organized mass strikes, lockouts, hired assassins, an anarcho-syndicalist movement, and fears of social revolution. The middle class and peasantry demanded law and order and an authoritarian nationalist rule (Harrison, 1985). In September 1923, General Miguel Primo de Rivera led a successful coup which ended constitutional governance. Political parties were banned and workers were forced into corporative organizations. The military regime, however, had neither ideology nor party, and the foundation of a Patriotic Union could not replace a fascist type of mass movement. Social protests and resistance led to the overthrow of Primo de Rivera in 1931 (Payne, 1974: 186–7). After five years of constitutional government, when an abortive military coup, general strikes, and separatist movements made the country ungovernable, the left-wing Frente Popular won the elections of February 1936. General Francisco Franco launched a second military coup in July. A bloody civil war, killing around 1 million people, paralyzed the country for three years. The dictatorial regime went on to triumph in Barcelona, Madrid, and the entire country in the first half of 1939. It was backed by the fascist Falanga Española and the right-wing coalition of Acción Popular, assisted by Mussolini and Hitler. Franco's nationalist–military dictatorship was born in one of the longest civil wars of the century.

Portugal underwent a similar experience. The army's revolt in 1917 led to the dictatorship of Major Sidónio Pais and, following his assassination in 1918, political chaos. Within fifteen years, forty cabinets had been formed, there had been revolts by monarchists and the army, and a successful military coup in May 1926 and the dictatorship of General António Carmona. Carmona followed the example of Mussolini and Primo de Rivera, banning political parties, which were replaced by the União Nacional. Carmona's reign was succeeded by the long-lasting dictatorship of António de Oliveira Salazar.

Greece, a less typical case of authoritarian economic dirigisme, lost a reckless adventure against Turkey to "liberate" Greeks in Asia Minor in 1921. As a consequence, nearly 1.5 million Greek refugees, equal to one-quarter of the population, flooded the country. Political chaos, repeated military coups in 1925, 1926, 1933, and 1935, and border conflicts with Italy and Bulgaria followed. In the poor country where two-thirds of the population depended on agriculture but half of them were hidden unemployed, social unrest was permanent. During the 1930s there were hundreds of strikes and demonstrations, and the Communist Party became part of a victorious coalition, a kind of a popular front in the 1936 elections. As General Metaxas stated in his first declaration: "I took . . . power necessary to face the communist danger . . . [and will keep it] until the country is cleared of communism . . ." (Stavrianos, 1963: 672).

The Metaxas dictatorship was much shorter than its Spanish and Portuguese counterparts, but after two civil wars in 1944 and 1947–9, various dictatorial regimes and military juntas ruled the country. The last dictatorship, the junta of colonels led by Georgios Papadopoulos, held power between 1967 and 1974. The European peripheries sought new roads to development: Mediterranean Europe was ruled by right-wing authoritarian dictatorships and fascist regimes.

The German Nazi movement's deepest roots went back to the late unification of the country. Germany, a latecomer like Italy, underwent successful industrialization and economic modernization. Its economic success, however, was not accompanied by successful establishment of an empire. It generated a militant right-wing, expansionist, *völkisch* pan-German movement, and the rise of the right–populist–racist German Workers Party. The movement made a distinction between Jewish *raffendes* (usury) *Kapital* and Aryan *schaffendes* (creative) *Kapital*. It declared the Jews *volksfremde* (alien from the nation) and millions of Central and East European Germans in Poland, the Czech lands, Hungary, and Romania *staatsfremde*, alien from the states they lived in. German right-wing movements were genuinely expansionist. World War I offered the possibility of realizing the expansionist dreams of a colonial German empire; the defeat was more than devastating. The victors humiliated Germany, occupied the Ruhr valley, then demanded unrealistically high reparations. Defeat, war exhaustion, starvation, and the beginning of world history's highest hyperinflation generated a revolutionary wave in Kiel, Bavaria, and Berlin. Revenge-thirsty nationalism feeding on right-wing efforts to establish law and order led to the formation of military units, the *Freikorps*, which suppressed revolutionary attempts and murdered revolutionary leaders. Adolf Hitler wanted to go further, but his attempted *putsch* in Munich in November 1923 failed at the *Feldherrnhalle*. The Weimar Republic was established in 1919. Ten years later history's most devastating depression hit Germany the hardest, cut industrial output by half, and put 6 million people out of work. Hitler and his Nazi apparatus established themselves by exploiting the parliamentary rules of the Weimar Republic in the desperation of crisis, and then swiftly introducing a totalitarian system.

All of these regimes began with a political doctrine, though these were often confused and altered once in power. They nevertheless lacked a consistent economic doctrine and program before they took over. They were fundamentally nationalist, militant, violent, and unhesitant about using brute power, since all of them were highly hierarchical and elitist, and all adhered to the *Führer Prinzip* rejecting parliamentary pluralism and democratic principles. They moved to establish "order" and national greatness based on a strong and unchallengeable – in some cases expansionist – state. The almighty state and its domination in every sphere of life stood at the heart of these regimes. The state assumed responsibility for the collective life of the population and the economy, which in turn had to serve national goals.

Mussolini's *Marcia su Roma* ended with the foundation of the first fascist regime in Europe in October 1922. War, expansion, the absolute role of a totalitarian state as the embodiment of national interest – all became the key words of fascist rule.

War alone keys up all human energies to their maximum tension and sets the seal of nobility on those peoples who have the courage to face it . . . Life [is] elevation [and] conquest. [The Fascist state is the] keystone of the fascist doctrine. If the nineteenth century was the century of the individual . . . [the twentieth century] is the collective century, and therefore the century of the State. [The totalitarian state is also] an economic organization of the nation . . . The importance of the state is rapidly growing . . . The Fascist State lays claim to rule in the economic field no less than in others . . . and all the political, economic, and spiritual forces of the nation . . . circulate within the State. (Mussolini, 1935: 26–31)

In more pragmatic terms, Italian fascism, which declared war on liberalism and laissez-faire, also sought to establish a colonial empire, mechanize agriculture, and establish huge industrial complexes, thus becoming a modernization dictatorship.

Economic dirigisme emerged between the two world wars and developed its peculiar regimes most characteristically in Italy, Germany, Spain, and Portugal, and in a more limited way in Greece.

When Benito Mussolini founded his *Fasci di combattimento* in Milan in 1919, and even during his *Marcia su Roma* in 1922, he did not have a clear idea about the fascist regime, let alone its economic philosophy and institutional structure. "Fascism in its beginnings," stated Hans Kohn, "was not a doctrine and had no clearly elaborated program." Mussolini, indeed, declared in 1922:

Our program is simple: we wish to govern Italy. They ask us for programs, but there are already too many. It is not the programs that are wanting for the salvation of Italy but men and will power. (Kohn, 1966: 148–9)

In Milan, when his one hundred followers accepted the program of Fasci, the main economic points were the least original, borrowed from the Left: introduction of progressive taxation, expropriatory taxes on war profits, minimum wage, nationalization of the munitions industries, and workers' participation in industrial management.

The situation was strikingly similar in Germany. The first "unalterable twenty-five points" of the economic program of Gottfried Feder's German Workers Party, the embryonic Nazi Party, in 1920 were more or less the same as the first fascist program, borrowed from the Left, stressing the preference of public interest (*Gemeinnutz*) before self-interest (*Eigennutz*). The main points included the confiscation of war profits, the demand for the death penalty for profiteers and usurers, abolition of land rents, nationalization of trusts, communalization of department stores, and profit sharing in big corporations.

The authoritative regimes, nevertheless, gradually developed their own economic programs. Mussolini's concept in the very first years contained rather alien, even liberal elements. It took time before it became consistently fascist. The 1921 party program, for example, declared the goal of the "reduction of the state to its essential functions of a political and juridical order." Mussolini stated: "I am for the individual and against the state," "down with the state in all its forms and permutations." He also announced, "we will not accept dictatorship." During the first years of fascist rule, the old-fashioned liberal economist-turned-cabinet minister De Stefani ran the Italian economic policy and implemented decontrols and anti-statist practices. He withdrew government subsidies and privatized the telephone system. Tariffs were liberalized and the high tariffs of 1921 lowered. Italy returned to strong protectionism only in 1925, after the dismissal of De Stefani and the appointment of Count Volpi (Mack Smith, 1959: 377–8; Gregor, 1969: 145, 151, 158–61, 174).

Having absorbed opinions from various sources, Mussolini gradually developed his own ideas. In his speech in March 1919, he repeated Corradini's view that the world is divided into "rich nations and proletarian nations [and the latter are] demanding a place in the world to which they have a right." He accepted the idea of Vilfredo Pareto that Italy, as a proletarian nation, must expand its industrial capacities rather than redistribute goods and ownership of the means of production. Mussolini dropped his earlier Marxist concept on class and class struggle. "Classes do not exist, the class struggle does not exist." He became an ardent nationalist and *statalist*, who identified society with the nation and the nation with the state:

The Fascist conception of life stresses the importance of the State and accepts the individual only in so far as his interests coincide with those of the State . . . Fascism stands for liberty, and for the only liberty worth having, the liberty of the State . . . Outside of it no human or spiritual values can exist. (Mussolini, 1935: 10–11)

Economic activity, according to Mussolini, was an integral part of political activity, and economic programs were subordinate to political goals. The fascist program called for the state to undertake a complex "plan of public works to meet the new economic, technical, and military necessities of the nation." Electrification of railways, road construction, and the development of hydroelectric power generation were central to this program. The fascist state and economy, like the entire nation, however, "must be militarized . . . I consider the Italian nation," announced Mussolini, "in a permanent state of war" (Kohn, 1966: 149–50).

A fascist economic program gradually took shape. The *Duce*, step by step but basically from the mid-1920s, established a strong dictatorial regime. The law of January 1926 granted Mussolini the power to issue decrees having force of law. From that time on, more than 100,000 decree-laws were issued. Elections became a mockery: the list of candidates was suggested by the corporative bodies (described later), selected and finalized by the Gran Consiglio, and the voters had the right to approve or reject. During the 1929 "elections," only 134,000 votes were cast against the official candidates. That number dropped to 15,000 in the 1934 elections (Mack Smith, 1959: 389–90). Mussolini also used the well-organized Fascist Party to mobilize the population in various campaigns. He initiated his "Battle of Birth," a program to boost the birthrate. In 1927 he stated:

The fundamental aspect of the political power of a nation . . . is its demographic strength . . . What are 40 million Italians [in the face of hundreds of millions of Germans, Slavs, and colonial people]? In order to count something in the world, Italy must greet the second half of this century with no fewer than 60 million inhabitants. (Livi Bacci, 2000: 175)

Indeed, from the late 1920s Italy banned contraceptives and introduced a bachelor tax, reduced taxes for large families, and gave no-interest family loans with progressive debt cancellation with each childbirth.

Mussolini's most successful campaign was the "Battle of Grain," a project of agricultural self-sufficiency, which heralded a new political and economic era. Populist policies made the regime popular and, in certain fields, efficient. As it emerged during the 1920s and 1930s, Italy became a model for various authoritarian regimes, regardless of the historical differences underlying the rise to dictatorial power of each regime.

The political systems of General Metaxas's and Colonel Papadopoulos's Greece, or Primo de Rivera's and then Franco's Spain, and Salazar's Portugal were different from Mussolini's Italy or Hitler's Germany. Regardless of the historical evaluation of whether these regimes were fascist or nationalist–militarist–conservative–authoritarian, they all introduced some version of economic dirigisme. Austria and Poland, together with other Central and Eastern European countries, also borrowed several elements of Italian economic dirigisme.

Hitler himself, however, declared in the early 1920s: "The basic feature of our economic theory is that we have no theory at all" (Braun, 1990: 78). As with Italian fascism, however, the almighty role of the state was also a central element of Nazism. In *Mein Kampf* Hitler speaks about the

subordination of the interests and life of the individual to the community . . . The state is a means to an end. Its end lies in the preservation and advancement of a community . . . assembling and preserving the most valuable stocks of basic racial elements . . . [and] slowly and surely of raising them to a dominant position. [In the folkish state] decisions will be made by one man . . . authority downward and responsibility upward. (Hitler, [1936] 1971: 299, 393, 398, 449–50)

Functions and programs of the state

After the murder of the socialist deputy, Giacomo Matteotti, in the summer of 1924, Italian fascism abolished the parliamentary system and turned to totalitarianism. Economic dirigisme, however, emerged gradually. During the 1920s, the only clear sign of a state interventionist attitude was an aggressive agricultural policy. The December 1923 Act of Land Reclamation dealt with irrigation, energy production, river navigation, and road construction. Mussolini's ambitious agricultural self-sufficiency plan led to the increase of the area under wheat cultivation by 15% in the south, and yields per hectare grew by 20% nationwide during the second half of the 1920s. The electro-irrigation plan and the *Bonifica Integrale*, a large land-reclamation program, the growing use of tractors, and an increase in the application of artificial fertilizers by 55%, together generated an increase in agricultural output. In 1925, Mussolini established his Wheat

Committee and launched the "battle" for self-sufficiency in wheat production, the *Battaglia del Grano*. The Integral Land Reclamation Law of December 1928 allocated 6.5 million lire for agriculture, nearly four times the amount spent from 1870 to 1922. By the mid-1930s, 4.7 million hectares were reclaimed, showcased by the Pontine Marshes land-reclamation project.

Land reclamation and the first autostrada construction in the mid-1920s were the first major job-creating programs. Modern highways linked principal towns in north Italy: railroads were electrified – roughly 5,000 kilometers by 1939; in 1929–30, 33,000 workers were employed for these projects, a number which grew to 71,000 in 1933–4. Between 1928 and 1942 the number of tractors in use increased from 18.2 thousand to 50.8 thousand, and of other machinery from 2.9 thousand to 43.0 thousand. "In 1935 under a system of compulsory pools, the State took over complete control of the wheat market as regards both prices and quantities" (Ricossa, 1976: 285).

The Battle for Grain was a success. Annual output was 57 million quintals in 1913, but it had fallen to 40 million by the war's end. Under Mussolini's campaign, output rose steadily to 80 million quintals by 1937, and made imports unnecessary. From 1936–40, food imports dropped from 30% to 15% of total imports. Before World War I, Italy, though basically an agricultural country, ran a deficit in food trade in which food exports covered only 90% of food imports; by 1936–40 exports surpassed imports by 180%. Agricultural interventionism was successful and the government declared the "Victory of Wheat" by 1933 (Zamagni, 1993: 258–64; Florinsky, 1936: 165–70). The entire campaign, however, was a typical "success" in the framework of self-sufficiency in an era of worldwide agricultural overproduction.

Import substituting and protectionist economic policies also energized industry. Italian industrial output increased by 25% overall between 1923 and 1929, but outputs for the metallurgy and chemical industries grew by nearly 50%, output of iron, steel, and artificial dyes each grew by roughly 85%, electricity production doubled, and gas and car production trebled between 1923 and 1929. Italy produced seven times more aluminum and twenty-two times more petroleum in 1929 than it had in 1923 (Zamagni, 1993: 273, 277).

State interventionism followed a similar pattern in Spain. The policy of self-sufficiency favored inefficient wheat farmers rather than the potential export-oriented fruit economy in País Valenciano, although this policy was not unknown in non-dirigist countries. The Primo de Rivera dictatorship in 1926 enacted two decrees and initiated a twenty-year irrigation and public work project, as well as a program of better utilization of water resources.

Box 3.1 The autobahn

The autobahn (autostrada, freeway) changed modern traffic and transportation in the twentieth century. The idea to build freeways was born before the advent of heavy auto traffic. The concept called for two lanes of divided traffic in either direction, engineered without curves or crossings, accessed by special entrance and exit lanes, and equipped with rest places integrated in the highway design. In Germany, a private company, the Automobil-Verkehrs- und Übungs-Strasse, was established in 1909 to build a ten-kilometer-long autobahn between Charlottenburg and Wannsee in Berlin. This road was completed only after the war. In the mid-1920s, several countries showed interest in the invention, but Italy was the first to open an autostrada, from Milan to the north Italian lakes in 1924. By 1935, a road of nearly 500 kilometers was in operation.

Meanwhile, various German companies prepared plans for autobahn networks, but they were considered too expensive. The Ministry of Defense even warned about the danger of a possible fast French offensive using the autobahns. Consequently, the plans, except for the 20-kilometer-long Köln–Bonn road that opened in 1932, were not realized. In December 1932, Fritz Todt, a Nazi engineer, presented his *Braune Denkschrift*, a memorandum on the network plans, to Hitler. Hitler recognized the huge potential of autobahn construction and one of his first actions after the *Machtergreifung* was to establish the Gesellschaft Reichsautobahnen in the summer of 1933. Newly appointed Reichsbank president Hjalmar Schacht guaranteed finance. Todt was appointed general inspector, responsible for the realization of the project. Construction began simultaneously in fifteen locations with 15,000 workers in the spring of 1934. "Strassen des Führers" – Hitler turned the first spade – served both job creation and war preparation. The first 22-kilometer stretch between Frankfurt and Darmstadt was ceremonially opened in May 1935, followed by the 25-kilometer München–Holzkirchen, and 61-kilometer Darmstadt–Heidelberg segments. By the fall of 1936, the first 1,000 kilometers of autobahn were completed. In 1938, in the first *Autobahn Jahr*, forty-two short road stretches were opened, and by the end of 1941, with 6.5 billion marks invested, nearly 4,000 kilometers were in operation. The modern freeway network, with its 9,000 bridges, became a model for the world.

The tactical concept for the serial opening of short stretches of road, almost always in the symbolic propagandistic presence of Hitler, offered a permanent self-cultivating opportunity. Hitler presented himself as "Father of the Autobahn." Josef Thorak, the celebrated sculptor, built a

17-meter-high heroic statue to celebrate the creation of the autobahn. Dozens of statues were erected along the roads. Autobahn propaganda films were produced and screened (altogether around fifty of them, each 10–15 minutes long). Between 1933 and 1936, special autobahn paintings were commissioned. The freeways were celebrated as the "Pyramids of the Third Reich." In 1936 an exhibition entitled "Die Strassen Adolf Hitlers in der Kunst" was opened. Ernst Huber exhibited 200 aquarelles, and dozens of others presented their documentary paintings depicting the construction. The autobahn network became the secular church architecture of Nazi Germany.

Under the control of the Energy Council, regionally based Confederaciones Hidrográficas were established to build dams and canals. The most successful, Confederation of the Ebro, opened more than 74,000 hectares to irrigation in four years. An act of 1927 started a colonization program and settled thousands of peasants in newly improved agricultural land. The Franco government intensified this program after the civil war: major irrigation works in Badajoz and Jaén preceded colonization of small farmers, and then a program of consolidation of *minifundia* from 1952 (Harrison, 1985: 56–9; Anderson, 1970: 44).

After Hitler gained power, an intensification of the previous job-creation programs of the Brüning government followed: in June 1933, the so-called First Reinhardt Program of 1 billion marks initiated waterway, public building, and most of all an ambitious *Reichsautobahn* construction program. In September, the Second Reinhardt Program provided 0.5 billion marks in subsidies and 0.4 billion marks in tax privileges for rural construction works and urban housing projects. During the first two years of the regime, 4% of the annual GDP was spent on public works. The housing program led to the construction of more than 1.8 million new apartments between 1933 and 1939 (Hardach, 1976: 58–60). Although the largest share of public expenditure, 28%, was spent on housing projects, the second largest, 21%, was earmarked for road construction. Rearmament, consuming only 2–5% of expenditure during the first years, became the single most important item, first 10% of total public expenditure after 1936 and then 17% by 1938 (Overy, 1982: 50).

Like Mussolini, Hitler initiated a program for population growth. Already in *Mein Kampf*, Hitler had declared the *Pflicht der Erhaltung der Rasse* (the responsibility of maintaining the race) which demanded the subordination of personal freedom and interest. Early marriage was advocated not as a purpose in itself but to serve the great goal of *Vermehrung . . . der arischen Rasse* (multiplying the Aryan race) (Hitler, [1936] 1971: 275, 279). The authors of a work on the new Nazi German marriage law in 1938 used an even harsher rhetoric: "The marriage, first of all, serves not personal happiness, but the fulfillment of the obligation to the national community (*Volksgemeinschaft*)." Hitler went further than Mussolini and sought to double the German population by pressing for the four-children family pattern, instead of the existing two-children family practice. Besides various strict measures and laws, a massive propaganda apparatus worked on the realization of the plan. Exhibitions were organized, such as *Die Frau*, and *Das Wunder des Lebens*, and an honor medal (*Ehrenkreuz der deutschen Mutter*) was introduced in 1938 for women with more than three children (the gold medal being awarded for eight children) (Mühlfeld and Schönweiss, 1989: 50, 126, 168, 176).

A new institutional feature of economic dirigisme in Italy was the creation of the corporate state. The corporative system was the populist concept of replacing parliamentary democracy by corporative bodies, a joint institution for employers, employees, and the state, under state tutelage. Soon after gaining power in December 1923 Mussolini presided over a meeting with representatives of employers and workers. In October 1925, the agreement of the Palazzo Vidoni created the Fascist Confederation of Workers as the only legal worker representation, while the Confederation of Italian Industries became the sole representative of employers. These associations were organized by occupation at a communal level. A pyramid of bureaucracy was built: provincial and inter-provincial associations, then federations and, at the top, national confederations. By 1934, eight workers' and employers' confederations encompassed industry, agriculture, commerce, banking and insurance, with a ninth for liberal professions and arts. The state, formally a mediator, made executive decisions about the entire activity via the Ministry of Corporations. In 1926, a law introduced the fascist Labor Courts to hear labor disputes; between 1926 and 1933 nearly 150,000 cases were submitted to the courts. In the same year, the National Council of Corporations was established with the participation of high officials of the Fascist Party and government, and from 1930 Mussolini presided over the Council. It is fair to say that the state subordinated the labor organization but gave more autonomy to the employers:

In practice the labor syndicates were run as extensions of the state bureaucracy by party-appointed officials while employer associations enjoyed effective autonomy under their own officials . . . who were responsible to their own constituents. (Sarti, 1971: 80)

The corporative system, however, was more of a façade than reality until 1934:

> Until 1934, Italy was a Corporate State without corporations. It was only by the law of February 5, 1934, that the corporations were officially established. In the summer of 1935 they were still in an embryonic stage. (Florinsky, 1936: 83)

By that year, the entire institution was ready to regulate "economic relations and the unitary discipline of production," as the Charter of Labor stated. Instead of the large National Council of Corporations, the real decision-making body became the much smaller, newly established Central Corporative Committee, in effect directed by cabinet members and the secretary of the Fascist Party. The corporative system created a new institutional framework, replaced the parliament, and nationalized the trade unions. Strikes were banned. Mussolini triumphantly announced: "Corporativism supersedes Socialism and supersedes liberalism: it creates a new synthesis" (Florinsky, 1936: 87–96). In reality, it was, as noted at the time,

> completely dominated by the Fascist party and the Fascist government . . . [so] that everywhere the party's and government's plans and wishes are bound to prevail . . . The Fascist corporate state has been limited almost exclusively to putting a stamp of approval upon whatever measures the Fascist government has chosen to propose. (Welk, 1938: 83, 152, 250)

The Great Depression generated new initiatives. In May 1932, Ugo Spirito, professor of philosophy at the University of Rome, with the approval of Mussolini, delivered a communication at a highly publicized conference in Ferrara in which he announced that the corporative system possessed its own dynamism and requisite stages,

> a hybrid form that would ultimately divest itself of residual capitalist elements to become an "integral corporativism" in which private property would no longer constitute loci of particular interest independent of, and conceivably opposed to, the interest of the state . . . Proprietary corporations would assume full responsibility for production, thereby putting an end once and for all to the historical conflict between private and public interest. (Sarti, 1971: 96)

In November 1933, in his *Discorso per lo Stato Corporativo*, Mussolini maintained that depression was not a crisis within the system of capitalism but the crisis of the system itself. He declared a need for "complete organic and totalitarian regulation of production," a burial of capitalism. In 1934, he went even further by stating that fascist economy was to be based not on individual profit but on collective interest. As the Charter of Labor, accepted by the Fascist Grand Council in 1927, expressed, "management was ultimately responsible to the state, which could regulate production whenever the public interest required it to do so" (Sarti, 1971: 95).

The idea and institutional practicality of the corporate state became extremely attractive in other dictatorial countries. General Primo de Rivera "promoted though imperfectly implemented, a corporate scheme for political economic organization." For Francisco Franco

the corporate form of representation and the principles of authority and community . . . were deemed to be the classic way of doing politics in Spain, temporarily perverted by inappropriate flirtation with foreign liberal models. (Anderson, 1970: 58–9)

In the highly centralized and authoritarian Franco regime, where the government was responsible to the head of state with power to issue decree laws, a corporative reorganization was carried out. Following the Italian model, Franco combined management and labor in a single organization, closely connected with the National Movement, or party. Membership was compulsory. In 1964, roughly 9 million workers (in the so-called "social" section) and 3.3 million employers (in the "economic" section), 92% of the labor force, belonged to the syndical organization. It had local branches, and twenty-six vertical organizations in various economic activities such as banking, farming, and textiles. All top-level syndicate leaders were appointed, most of them by Franco. Syndical organizations appointed one-quarter to one-third of members of the Cortes, or Parliament, the least powerful government body. Workers and employers were required to agree by negotiating to avoid "anarchy" and class conflict. Independent workers' representation, unions, and strikes were banned (Anderson, 1970: 66–9).

Although a corporate state was not established in Greece, strikes and trade unions were not only banned but also replaced by the terms of the Compulsory Arbitration Act, which gave the leading role to the Ministry of Labor for resolving labor disputes. The state also introduced a collective wage bargaining and agreement system, which defined workdays, wages, and vacation times. In the first two years of Metaxas's dictatorship, nearly 45,000 disputes were settled in this way.

The corporative idea played an important role in early Nazi rhetoric. Reorganization of the state according to estates (*Stände*) had already found voice in Feder's program as well as Hitler's early speeches, and in the 1930 work of Hans Buchner of the *Völkischer Beobachter*, the Nazi daily. The formation of the Reichsnährstand or agricultural estate, and then the Reichskulturkammer in 1933, signaled the first steps toward a corporative system. Development of the idea, nevertheless, was put on hold soon after the *Machtergreifung*. The law of "organic reconstruction" of German business in early 1934 established an openly statist concept and subordinated the economy to the Ministry of Economy. Associations were formed in all trades, with appointed leaders and obligatory membership for firms. All industrial and trade activities were organized into twelve groups, seven for the main industries and five for commerce and minor industries. The Reichswirtschaftskammer, or Chamber of Economics, was established in November 1934 as a state-directed authority for business. The law of 1934 introduced the Arbeitsfront, the Nazi labor organization, ostensibly as a substitute organization for the unions, which virtually merged into the Arbeitsfront. The *Führer Prinzip* was also introduced in the economic sphere: the owner of an enterprise became *Betriebsführer* (company leader) and the employees the *Gefolgschaft* (followers) and they "worked together for the furtherance of the purpose of the enterprise, and for the benefit of the Nation and the State in general" (Florinsky, 1936: 105).

Although entrepreneurs had independence on investing, decisions about products, research and development, and other fields of company management, the state set strict limits, regulating prices and distribution, and influencing and often ordering investment decisions. Important goals of the state bureaucracy were realized by state-owned companies and the compulsory cooperation between state-owned and private firms.

Self-sufficiency, planning, and the populist welfare system

With the years of the Great Depression, state intervention reached a new phase in Italy. In June 1932, a law was enacted on *consorzi obbligatori* (compulsory cartels) to regulate competition, prices, and production, an idea that Mussolini's influential brother Arnaldo had been advocating. The cotton cartel, formed in the summer of 1932 and authorized by the government, made decisions for private business for thousands of producers and dealers, distributed raw materials by fixed quotas, regulated the quantity of output for each company, and fixed prices. Compulsory cartels were eventually the arms of the government.

In March 1936, Mussolini announced a plan for autarchic development of the Italian economy. An organized mass movement advertised the slogan *Preferite il Prodotto Italiano* (buy Italian products). International trade controls were introduced, including a system of import permits. The International Trade and Currency Supervisory Office, later the Under-Secretariat, was also established. Planning agencies and a Foreign Exchange Office began operations. Licensing for imports, a broad price-fixing scheme, and a Price Control Committee were introduced. As Mussolini stated:

November 18, 1935, marks the starting point of a new chapter in Italian history . . . [which] will be determined by this postulate: to secure within the briefest time possible the greatest possible measure of economic independence. (Carr, 1964: 124)

Self-sufficiency became a necessity and generated further radical measures during the Great Depression and the second half of the 1930s after Mussolini's Ethiopian adventure. The League of Nations voted for a boycott, and fifty-two countries joined: Italy became isolated. Mussolini continued his modernization drive for self-sufficiency even harder. The aggressive fascist modernization dictatorship and the regime of economic dirigisme with its extreme state interventionist economic policies were strengthened during the years of the Great Depression: public expenditure was increased from less than 20% to more than 33% of GDP between 1929 and 1936, and ambitious state investment served both economic modernization and counter-cycle policy. Due to the policy of self-sufficiency, Mussolini's agricultural program doubled the number of tractors during the 1930s. Hydroelectric power generation and electricity output also increased by 50% during the depression years. The electrification of railroads doubled and accounted for 56% of total railroad traffic by 1939. Industrial output declined temporarily by one-quarter, but the Italian economy suffered only a minor setback: per capita GDP declined by only 6% between 1929 and 1933, but by 1935 surpassed the pre-depression level by 7% (Zamagni, 1993: 246, 265, 269–73). By 1938, the Italian economy had recovered and the country was making impressive strides toward industrialization. In the early postwar years Italy achieved one of the highest rates of growth in Europe: by 1921, it had matched prewar levels and by 1929 these were exceeded by 31%, and by 1939 62% (Maddison, 1995a: 180–1).

The state gained an upper hand in Nazi Germany almost immediately after the *Machtergreifung*. The 1934 law declared that the owner of a business might be removed if he "abuses his authority." The minister of the economy gained the right to prevent planned expansion of companies and also to order entry into compulsory cartels or other industrial combinations. The *Gesetz zur Errichtung von Zwangskartellen* (a law on the establishment of compulsory cartels) (July 1933) was an effective way of controlling investments. Prices were controlled by the Reichskommissar für die Preisbildung (October 1933), and wages were frozen in 1933. A capital stock law of December 1934 restricted dividend payments to 6%. In the spring of 1936, the Rohstoff- und Devisenstab, under the direction of Hermann Göring, introduced a strictly controlled raw material and foreign exchange distribution policy. A price freeze was introduced in November 1936. A new rearmament-financing scheme was introduced between 1934 and 1936: formally the expenditures were financed from loans (*Mefo-Wechsel*) from the Metallurgische Forschungs-GmbH, a front company for the biggest German corporations. In reality, the Mefo-bills were discounted by the Reichsbank, enabling the bank to finance military expenditure in a hidden inflationary way.

The free labor market was eliminated. Both "labor passports" and obligatory labor service, *Reichsarbeitsdienst*, were inaugurated, followed by compulsory labor conscription. Some of the strictest controls were placed on foreign economic connections, trade, and finance.

Although Hitler [had] been in power for a much shorter period than Mussolini, the German methods of control and state intervention [were] probably more far-reaching and rigid than they [were] in Italy. The whole structure of business control was really patterned after the army ... The whole organization depend[ed] ... on the Party, which [was] just as much the mainstay of the economic system as it [was] the pillar of the political regime. (Florinsky, 1936: 115)

The Metaxas dictatorship also initiated extensive public work programs, road, and government building construction. High protective tariffs between 20% and 150% *ad valorem* were introduced in the 1920s, and intensified during the 1930s. They promoted job creation and industrial development. Industrial output increased sharply: compared with 1921, it had risen by 38% by 1929, and then during the next decade by another 50%, i.e. more than doubled in interwar Greece. The country practically became part of the Nazi economic bloc: Greek exports to Germany increased from less than 20% of the total before 1933 to 43% by 1938.

State intervention had already been initiated in Spain by Primo de Rivera in the 1920s. The dictator introduced the highest tariffs in Europe, and assisted the development of the metallurgy, cement, construction, and locomotive industries. A decree of July 1926 sanctioned the investment of 3.539 billion pesetas on "productive areas" for ten years. As one of the consequences, steel output increased by more than 60% between 1926 and 1929. A comprehensive program of railway and road construction was launched by the newly established Consejo Superior Ferroviario and the Patronato del Circuito Nacional de Firmes Especiales. Another element of the regime's infrastructure policy was the development of electricity production: between 1925 and 1930, output increased from 1,725 million to 2,800 million kWh. During the late 1920s, public investments surpassed private ones. The government also initiated a "Buy Spanish" campaign in 1927, and the economy became more isolated and autarchic (Harrison, 1985: 60–4). Spain was the only one "among the civilized countries," as the Spanish economist Román Perpiñá stated in 1936, "with a complex and significantly autarkic economy" (Harrison, 1985: 84). Exports declined sharply so that little more than one-quarter of pre-depression export levels were achieved by 1935. Although agricultural unemployment remained traditionally high – nearly 60% of total unemployment – less than 13% of the insured population was unemployed in the early 1930s.

Spain, allied under the Franco regime with Hitler and Mussolini, went further and economic isolation became more severe. Spain was excommunicated by the democratic world, and an economic boycott of the country was among the first steps taken by the newly established United Nations in 1946. Economic self-sufficiency, combined with industrialization, became a necessity in Spain. The Law of National Interest Industries enacted a 50% tax reduction for affected industries and guaranteed 4% interest on invested capital. It reduced tariffs on imports for national industries and, in critical situations, authorized forced expropriation by the state. The Franco regime also introduced import licensing and quotas for products from certain countries. From 1948, introducing a method used broadly during the Great Depression, it adopted multiple exchange rates as directed by the Instituto Español de Moneda Extranjera.

In 1941, Franco nationalized the broad-gauged railroads and began a program for construction of dams and roads. The Instituto Nacional de Vivienda directed public funding of a rent-controlled housing program from 1939 and 16,000 units were built each year until 1954. Between 1956 and 1960, the ambitious First National Housing Plan targeted the construction of 550,000 units and actually built 77% of them. The Franco regime introduced strict price controls from the very beginning, especially for energy, raw materials, and building materials. The Charter of the Rights of Labor and the Ministry of Labor regulated labor relations and centrally set wages until 1954.

Controls were conceived to be part of the systemic structure of the relation of state and economy, a normal and expected part of public regulation . . . Market forces were a residual rather than an intentional policy mechanism. (Anderson, 1970: 53, 55)

The Franco regime's *Ordenación de inversions* (the investment regulation program) became virtually a one-year planning enterprise in 1959–60, before being followed by a series of state directives from the fall of 1962. Finally the First Development Plan of 1964–7 was introduced, a Planning Commission was established, and the French type of macroeconomic planning was reproduced in Spain. After 1953–9, as the cold war brought Spain into *de facto* alignment with the West, the regime gave up economic dirigisme and adjusted to the neo-liberal West (Anderson, 1970: 162–73).

Box 3.2 Hjalmar Schacht

Hjalmar Schacht was one of the most talented financiers and managers of the twentieth century. He could have been the banker of President Roosevelt and the manager of the New Deal. It happened that he worked for Hitler and managed his war preparations.

Schacht's parents emigrated to the United States from Schleswig-Holstein in 1871 and remained enthusiastic Americans throughout their lives. The family, nevertheless, failed financially and returned to Germany in 1876 and the next year Hjalmar Horace Greeley Schacht was born. (Horace Greely was the admired American liberal journalist.) Young Schacht received a good though eclectic education; he enrolled at five universities and studied medicine, literature, journalism, French, sociology, and a great deal of economics, and earned his Ph.D. in Philosophy in 1899. Schacht started his career as an economic journalist, but was soon employed by the Dresdner Bank. He achieved his major international success in 1923 as the national currency commissioner, father of the anti-inflationary policy which halted the world's most severe runaway inflation. As a consequence, he was appointed president of the Reichsbank that year for the first time.

On one hand, Schacht was a cosmopolitan, a committed free trader and Freemason, one of the founders of the Deutsche Demokratische Partei in 1918, friend of the head of the Bank of England, who met with President Teddy Roosevelt and, thirty years later, with Franklin D. Roosevelt. On the other hand, he was a German nationalist, one of the sharpest critics of Western policy against Germany, and a believer in the need for German rearmament.

In 1930, Schacht resigned from the Reichsbank and began a courtship with the Nazis. In December 1930, he participated at a dinner party at Hermann Göring's apartment. In a few weeks, again at Göring's home, he met Adolf Hitler. In August 1932, Schacht offered his services to Hitler in a letter. A few weeks after Hitler gained power, he offered the Reichsbank presidency to Schacht, who accepted it on the spot. His most important task was to finance the economic recovery program combined with an economic war preparation. That was the essence of his *Neuer Plan*, announced in September 1934, which established a Nazi-led self-sufficient regional bloc in Central and Eastern Europe, Hitler's *Grossraumwirtschaft*.

In 1934, Hitler offered him the economics ministry and plenipotentiary of war economics in addition to Schacht's bank presidency. As "economy tsar" he built up the institutions of state control, invented the mechanism of hidden inflationary financing, and created a system of economic dirigisme. He did not join the Nazi party itself, but received the Golden Party Badge in 1937. Why did he join Hitler? "To fight for right and justice wherever I had the chance to do so," as he stated, or, as he wrote in his postwar memoirs, to "fight against the excesses of the regime from inside"? Or simply because of his love of power, bottomless ambition, and self-confidence?

From 1936, however, Schacht's star began to fade. Miscalculating his influence, he started a rivalry with Göring and lost. Göring took over the war preparations and became the plenipotentiary of war economy. By 1937, Schacht had been dismissed as economics ministry, though he remained minister without portfolio. In two years, he was dismissed from the Reichsbank. The disappointed, self-admiring Schacht distanced himself from Hitler, and was even arrested after the assassination attempt on Hitler in 1944. He spent four years in prison but was acquitted at the Nuremberg trials. From the 1950s he re-emerged as financial advisor for the Indonesian, Egyptian, Iranian, and other governments, and opened his own bank in Düsseldorf. In 1970, he died at the age of ninety-three.

Salazar's Portugal introduced the legal basis for state planning in 1933, and launched the first fifteen-year reconstruction plan in 1935. Between 1953 and 1958 a new plan gave priority to infrastructural and industrial investments. During 1959–64, 1965–7, and 1968–73, further plans followed. All these plans served *orgulhosamente sós* (economic isolation) (Thomas, 1987: 996).

Planning became an organic part of Nazi Germany's economic system as early as September 1934, when Hjalmar Schacht, president of the Reichsbank, introduced his *Neuer Plan*, a combined plan to overcome foreign trade difficulties, and to begin war preparations in the arena of international economic relations. The new system established full control of foreign trade and international payments. Trade relations were reorganized and based on bilateral barter agreements. The quantity of imports was strictly limited and currency payments were replaced by payments in kind. These measures were rather widespread during the Great Depression and not specifically the product of economic dirigisme. The *Neuer Plan*, however, was the beginning of a German *Grossraumwirtschaft* (a large economic space) for Germany to import food and raw materials from nearby countries of *Südosteuropa*. A series of bilateral trade agreements between 1934 and 1939 methodically created a safe, ground transportation-based German economic sphere, which included Hungary, Bulgaria, Romania, and Yugoslavia.

This kind of planning, nevertheless, was followed by a strict state plan for war preparation. The Reich Defense Law of May 1935 created a post "to put all economic forces in the service of carrying on the war" and Schacht was appointed as Plenipotentiary-General in peacetime. In October 1936, the Nazi government went further and by decree initiated the Four Year Plan with the explicit goal of making the German economy "in the event of war . . . able to withstand a blockade to the greatest extent possible." Hermann Göring, the number two in the Nazi hierarchy, became the new economic tsar and head of planning. Rearmament and economic preparation were the focus of the plan. The Four Year Plan Office was, accordingly, divided into six departments: production of raw materials; distribution of raw materials; utilization of labor; agricultural production; price control; and foreign currency control. One of the most important elements of the plan was the development of substitute materials: synthetic gasoline from lignite, synthetic rubber (buna) from lignite and calk, synthetic fiber, and methods for exploiting low-quality iron ore. Some of these industries emerged in the newly established state-owned Reichswerke Hermann Göring.

During the war, state planning developed further. In April 1942 Zentrale Planung, a central planning board, was established. It held meetings every other week, and gained the upper hand in the coordination of economic administration. The German economy was strictly centralized and directed by a huge party-state bureaucracy that was often reorganized. The two main institutions were the Ministry of Economics and the Four Year Plan Office, which continued its work in the framework of the so-called second Four Year Plan period during the war. A huge network of institutions directed the Nazi economy. Albert Speer headed the Ministry of Armaments and Munitions, renamed in 1943 as the Ministry of War Production and employing 6,000 staff. The Heereswaffenamt employed nearly 3,000 employees, gave orders to industry, and supervised industrial performance, deliveries, and financing. The Oberkommando der Wehrmacht, and its Wirtschafts-und Rüstungsamt – which was incorporated into the Ministry of Armament in May 1942 – also ran a huge bureaucratic organization for war production. The extreme state centralization of the Nazi war economy was most clearly expressed by the institution of Führer Forderungen, Hitler's supreme decision-making body on the war economy and production. Its decisions were unquestionable. The Nazi economic system was a combination of an extreme economic nationalistic, state interventionist dirigisme and a centralized war economy (Zilbert, 1972; Milward, 1977).

The system of economic dirigisme expanded state interventionism to the extreme and in most cases led to the creation of a strong state-owned sector in the economy. Mixed economy was not an invention of fascism, "but fascism took the unusual step of trying to institutionalize the relationship between public and private power and . . . followed a path different from that of the Western democracies" (Sarti, 1971: 79). One of the first major steps in Italy, motivated by the attempt to achieve self-sufficiency, was the foundation in 1926 of Azienda Generale Italiana Petroli (AGIP) for the exploration and production of oil. The public company supplied nearly 29% of domestic oil and oil products by 1939. State ownership, however, proved most influential in the banking sector. The 1926 Banking Act transformed the Banca Napoli and the Banca Sicilia into public institutions, and granted to the Bank of Italy power to control all other banks. A mixed banking system was introduced. The Instituto Mobiliare Italiano (IMI), founded in 1931, became a major force for the reorganization of the Italian banking system and enjoyed significant state participation. The creation of the Institute for the Economic Development of Southern Italy in 1938, and of the Industrial Financing Institute in 1939, further strengthened the state's role in banking.

The most important breakthrough for the creation of a mixed economy was the foundation of the Istituto per la Riconstruzione Industriale (IRI), a giant company which took a controlling share in several companies, including the Banca di Roma, Banca Commerciale, and the Credito Italiano, the country's three main banks. IRI was a major shareholder in companies, representing 42% of total joint-stock capital of the country. At the beginning, it was regarded as a temporary institution of reorganization, but in 1937 it was transformed into a permanent holding company. IRI's assets were scattered over ten sectors, but were concentrated in areas less attractive for private investors. It controlled most of the telephone companies, 100% of steel, arms, and coal production, 90% of shipyards, 80% of shipping and locomotive building companies, 30% of electricity output, and several engineering firms, including Alfa-Romeo and most of the old wartime companies such as Ansaldo, Terni, Breda, and others. The year 1933 saw the establishment of the STET (for the telephone sector), in 1936 came the FINMARE (to control shipping), and in 1937 FINSIDER (to run the iron and steel industries). IRI, a fully state-owned, public law corporation, enjoyed broad legal and financial autonomy. The same was true for other state-owned or mixed companies such as the Azienda Nazionale Idrogenazione Combustibili (ANIC) (1936), in partnership with Montecatini and AGIP, for refining, processing, and marketing oil products.

During the 1930s, the fascist government established new industrial development zones such as Bolzano and Ferrara by providing subsidies, tax exemption, and infrastructure. The state's ultimate move to dominate

the Italian economy was the Banking Act of March 1936, which nationalized the Bank of Italy and established control over the entire banking sector. Separation of short-term credit from medium- and long-term credit
was sanctioned. Long-term credit transactions for industry became a state
monopoly of IMI (Zamagni, 1993: 279, 293–7, 300–2; Posner and Woolf,
1967: 22–6).

The market economy was in fact overwhelmed by semi-planning, which manifested itself in various ways, and in peculiar, from 1933, in the law on new
industrial plants, in other words by State control of the most important private
investments. (Ricossa, 1976: 287)

Public and private companies worked in close cooperation.

The 1930s were marked . . . by a growing confusion between the roles of private
enterprise and the state. The result was a mixed economy, whose direction was
not in the main determined either by central planning or by market forces,
but by agreement between powerful oligopolistic groups, some of them under
public control. (Lyttelton, 1976: 141)

The final stage of the radicalization of fascist economic doctrine and the
amalgamation of an even larger state sector of the economy came in the
very last chapter of the history of Italian fascism after the coup of July
1943, when Mussolini was arrested and Italy announced unconditional
capitulation to the Allies. SS troops liberated Mussolini, who reorganized
his power and established his Fascist Republic in North Italy. The Program
Manifesto of the reorganized Partito Fascista Repubblicano in November
1943 announced the goal: a European community based on the principle
of "the abolition of the capitalist system; the struggle against the world
plutocracies." The program guaranteed private property, but also stated
that "exploiting labor" was prohibited, and that "in the national economy,
everything that, in scope or function, goes beyond private interest . . .
comes within the State's sphere of action." The Fundamental Premises for
the Creation of a New Structure for the Italian Economy in January 1944
announced a broad nationalization program

of those industries that control sectors vital to the economic and political
independence of the nation, including those enterprises that furnish primary
materials and energy and other indispensable services for the development of
the economic life of the nation . . . [In February 1944] companies with a share
capital exceeding one million lire or employing one hundred workers were all
nationalized. (Gregor, 1969: 288–9, 293–4, 299, 300, 388–9)

This program was not realized. Hitler lost the war, and Mussolini was captured and lynched by the partisans.

Following the Italian pattern of the IRI, Franco's Spain also established a gigantic state-owned holding company, the Instituto Nacional de Industria (INI), in 1941. This institution was responsible for promoting import substitution, especially in branches which were less attractive for private investors. Accordingly, INI invested in steel, hydroelectric power generation, shipbuilding, agricultural chemicals, aluminum, and communications. Between 1943 and 1960, INI owned twelve companies and had majority or minority shares in nearly fifty others. Its share in investments represented roughly 15% of total investments in the country. Seven of the twenty most important Spanish companies, among them Ensidesa, Iberia, Seat, Enpetrol, and Hunosa, were closely connected to INI, which controlled the production of 48% of refined oil, 46% of shipbuilding, 40% of fertilizer, 50% of automobiles, 58% of aluminum, 36% of coal, 25% of steel, and 20% of electricity. By the late 1970s, INI owned more than sixty companies and had shares in 200, altogether employing more than 200,000 people (Bernecker, 1987: 971).

Hitler was also ready to establish state-owned industrial sectors. The most telling illustration is the foundation of the Volkswagen Werke. In January 1934, the outstanding Austrian-born German car designer Ferdinand Porsche sent a report to the newly established Nazi government on building a German Economy Car and offered his design. That May, Hitler received him in his Kaiserhof headquarters to discuss the potential of the Volkswagen model. Hitler demanded a cheap car costing less than 1,000 marks ($400). In 1936, Hitler decided to invest and build an independent Volkswagen factory under government supervision to start operation in 1938, and set the target to produce 400,000–500,000 cars a year. Populist propaganda also advocated *Volksschlepper* (people's tractor) and the Hitler Jugend's *Volksjäger* ("people's hunter," a fighter aircraft), which pushed motorization ahead (Möser, 1998: 219–21). The idea of producing cheap people's cars appeared soon and forcefully, led by populist regimes. In Mussolini's Italy, the extremely small Balilla car served this goal.

Almost entirely in connection with military preparation, but also with new scientific research initiated by the Nazi state, the Air Ministry began rocket and space programs in 1935. June 1939 saw the first test flight of the Heinkel-176, the world's first rocket aircraft, and ten weeks later the test flight of the Heinkel-178, the world's first turbojet airplane. By 1944, Messerschmitt was producing jet fighters, which entered combat. The first V-2 ballistic missiles were used against Britain during World War II (Neufeld, 1999: 207–11).

Box 3.3 Volkswagen

The "Beetle" became the greatest success in the history of the automobile industry, and Volkswagen (VW) one of the world's greatest multinational giants. The VW was a product of two Austrian–Germans: an engineering genius, Ferdinand Porsche, and an evil political genius, Adolf Hitler. In 1931, Porsche made his first designs for the Beetle and worked on the technological solution of a people's car. Hitler, having gained power in January 1933, opened the Berlin Auto Show in April and announced his program to motorize the masses. Porsche looked for connections, got an audience, visited Hitler within a few weeks, and sold his cheap idea to the auto-lover Hitler. A contract was signed, tests completed, and Hitler announced the start of production in 1938 and laid down the cornerstone of a factory, financed by the Nazi state. A new settlement, named after the Nazi organization, *Kraft durch Freude Stadt* (Strength Through Joy City), was considered the "mother town of National Socialism." Production of the Kraft durch Freude cars began in April 1939 with 3,000 workers.

However, civilian production was immediately replaced by production for the army. During World War II the highly inventive Porsche created various types of vehicle – Kuebel cars, four-wheel drive Kommandeur cars, pick-up versions, and even an amphibious car. The war proved a unique occasion for experimentation: expenses did not matter; production was for the benefit of the war effort. At the end of 1944, however, Allied bombing destroyed two-thirds of the factory.

After the war the Nazi model town was renamed Wolfsburg, Ferdinand Porsche and his son, Ferry, were jailed for two years by the French authorities, and Major Ivan Hirst, the British commander of the factory, arranged a repair shop and until 1948 even built 20,000 cars, called Volkswagen from the end of 1945.

From January 1948, Heinz Nordhoff, a mechanical engineer, was appointed top manager in the state-owned company, back in German hands. He created the Volkswagen Werke as it is known today. His almost monomaniac "one-model policy," building Beetles, remained unchanged for the entire twenty years of his rule. It proved an unparalleled success. Why? Partly because of the bold experiment: the unchanged model; nobody felt they were driving an obsolete car. Partly because of the outstanding quality: it was normal to drive a VW for 20–30 years. The company offered the best possible service network as well, and the car remained relatively cheap.

By 1959, daily production increased to 3,000 cars and annual output to 500,000. VW had 50,000 workers, and the three-millionth Beetle was produced. Wolfsburg's population quadrupled during this decade. The company, meanwhile, constantly improved the model: during the 1950s, 200 changes were made. They enlarged the windows and motor, introduced turbo-charging and water-cooling, and changed the transmission, but basically did not alter the model. By 1972, when the company employed 200,000 people, VW Beetle sales surpassed the record set by the Ford Model T. In 1977, after forty-three years of producing the same model, the last Beetle car rolled off the assembly line in Germany. More than 16 million Beetles had been sold.

Volkswagen underwent expansion and soon became a multinational empire. During the 1950s and 1960s, new plants were built in Hanover and Braunschweig. VW purchased the Bavarian Audi in Ingolstadt, and the NSU in Baden-Würtemberg. By the mid-1970s, VW had eight huge factories in Germany. International expansion went hand in hand: in 1953, VW opened its plant in São Paulo, Brazil, which became the most active overseas operation; in 1962, another factory was opened in Puebla, Mexico. Plants were established in South Africa, Indonesia, Uruguay, Nigeria, New Zealand, Belgium, the Philippines, Ireland, Yugoslavia, Australia, and even in the United States. In the early 1990s, VW bought a huge part of the Czech Škoda firm. Exploiting the opportunity of China's opening and market transformation, Volkswagen established a factory in China and by the end of the century was the main player in the country's skyrocketing car market.

By 1958 the company's products had reached 123 countries. By 1980, VW plants abroad employed four times more workers than the mother plant did. At that time, one VW was produced somewhere in the world every thirty seconds, but a buyer still had to wait six months to get one.

After the oil crisis, which rocked the car market, VW soon recovered. New models were developed. The Golf (Rabbit) replaced the Beetle, though the Brazilian and Mexican factories continued producing the old model. The new middle-class car, the Audi 100, and then the Audi 80, Passat, Scirocco, and Polo met success on the world market. In 1979, at the Frankfurt Auto Show, the new Jetta was introduced. During the 1970s, VW produced seventy-two varieties of car and at the turn of the century VWs became the best-sold cars in the American market.

Ferdinand Porsche died in 1951. His son and grandson, however, returned to Wolfsburg. The latter designed the renewed the Volkswagen Beetle, which was introduced at the Detroit Auto Show in 1998. The circle was closed: the VW story began and returned to Porsche and the Beetles (Sloniger, 1980).

Box 3.4 Radar and the ballistic rocket

The British radar and the German ballistic rocket have parallel histories illustrating the connection between World War II and the development of technology. As a consequence of Hitler's rise to power, preparation for war accelerated during the 1930s. In 1934, the Director of Scientific Research at the British Air Ministry, Henry Wimperis, urged the formation of a scientific committee to conduct research on the possibilities of air defense. At the end of that year, a research team was formed under the chairmanship of Henry Tizard, Rector of Imperial College. Wimperis invited Robert Watson-Watt, a descendant of James Watt and head of the Radio Research Station of the National Physical Laboratory. Wimperis asked him about the possibility of a "death ray," a damaging radiation device targeting enemy aircraft. Watson-Watt, who, during World War I measured atmospheric reflection and worked on using radio to locate thunderstorms, was the leading radio scientist in the country. His team rejected the idea of radio destruction, but recommended research in a five-page memorandum on radio detection of aircraft, using ultra short-wave transmission.

In 1935, Watson-Watt received immediate funding to work on the details and build a prototype of the detection device. The first successful experiment at Daventry in February proved that electromagnetic energy indeed could be reflected from aircraft and prove useful for detection. Between the spring of 1935 and 1938, but even afterwards, hundreds of scientific and technological problems were solved. A series of inventions led to the development of the cavity magnetron, which generated microwave radiation a hundred times more powerful than that of previous test devices, and became the key element of radio direction finding, or as it was named after 1943, radar. Before the war, a chain of radar stations was built along the seashores of Britain. The radar, signaling approaching aircraft and locating them, helped to defend the country against the most devastating German air attacks. Britain won the Battle of Britain in 1940. The radar became indispensable to the air transportation boom after the war.

The story of the ballistic rocket began with a few German rocket enthusiasts, including a student who completed his engineering studies in Zürich in 1931. The son of a Prussian aristocrat, Wernher von Braun began working to develop a rocket in Raketenflugplatz Berlin in the fall of 1930. Having worked together for a short while, his team sent a memorandum to the Reichswehr about the possibility of long-range artillery. After the *Machtergreifung*, Hitler and Göring began preparing for war, and sought to build a strong air force. In connection with these efforts, under the leadership of Colonel Dornberger, a prototype aircraft rocket engine fueled by alcohol and liquid oxygen was tested in Kummersdorf in 1935. Dornberger also dreamed about building a bombardment rocket with a tonne of explosives and a 160-mile target range. Von Braun began working on the project. The army and air force financed the establishment of a rocket research base on Usedom Island, at Peenemünde, with about ninety staff members. By 1937, the Dornberger team, led by von Braun, produced the first experimental A-3 rocket. This experiment, and a few more that followed, failed. The work progressed rather slowly. Hitler did not have faith in the success of rocket weapons. He expected more from another project: the Luftwaffe's pilotless flying bomb, the Vergeltungswaffen-1, or Vengeance Weapon-1 (V-1). The latter was launched against London in June 1944.

Von Braun's new 14-tonne, 41-meter-tall rocket, the A-4, was launched in the presence of Albert Speer, but failed again in June 1942. In October, however, the improved model turned out to be a success. Von Braun was awarded the War Merit Cross, First Class. His career advanced apace. He joined the SS in 1933, and the Luftwaffe in 1936, became a member of the Nazi party in 1939, an SS second lieutenant in 1940, lieutenant in 1941, captain in 1942, and major in 1943.

In July 1943, Hitler received Dornberger, who by that time had become a General, and von Braun at his headquarters. His *Blitzkrieg* dreams had evaporated, his army was in retreat. The film footage of successful rocket experiments as well as von Braun's explanations impressed him. He thought he had the dreamed-of wonder weapon at hand. He wanted to launch a rocket war immediately and demanded the mass production (2,000 per year) of the world's first ballistic rocket, the A-4, or, as it was soon called, the V-2. Hitler awarded a titular professorship to the thirty-one-year-old von Braun, and apologized – as he said, the second time in his life – for not having believed in the success of rockets.

Mass production, however, was delayed because of two devastating allied bombardments of Peenemünde, and the construction of the subterranean rocket factory, Mittelwerk, in the Harz Mountains. Slave labor from concentration camps in inhuman conditions provided the bulk of the labor force. Von Braun's first V-2 exploded near Waterloo Station in London in September 1944. Another 263 rockets followed.

In May 1945, the rocket team was surrounded by the American army. Thanks to the logic of the emerging cold war, and regardless of membership of the Nazi party and the SS, as well as war crimes, members of the team became American citizens in ten years. In 1950, Wernher von

Braun became Director of Research at the Army Guided Missile Center in Alabama, and then Director of the Marshall Space Flight Center of NASA, and built the Jupiter C and Saturn V boosters. The latter carried the American astronauts to the moon (Zimmerman, 2001; Piszkiewicz, 1995).

Authoritarian dirigisme also expanded state intervention into social affairs. Regimes sought to offset centralized oppressive rule with welfare measures to earn mass support. This policy played a central role in legitimizing the regime. Welfare measures appeared in post-World War I Italy: the foundation of a social security institution, the Cassa Nazionale per le Assicurazioni Sociali (CNAS), in April 1919, introduced compulsory unemployment insurance and national insurance contribution to pensions. The fascist government took over these institutions and broadened their social policy. In 1925, L'Opera Nazionale Maternità e Infanza (ONMI), a maternity and child welfare organization, was added and provided health care for around 700,000 and later 1 million mothers and children.

The major progress in welfare policy accompanied the Great Depression. In a speech in Milan in October 1934, Mussolini announced the year of "social justice." Complex measures were taken against rapidly increasing unemployment, which rose from 0.2 million in the summer of 1929 to 1.6 million in January 1934. The state forced an agreement between the workers' and employers' confederations and introduced the forty-hour work week. Extensive programs of public works followed. Land reclamation, housing construction, road building, electrification projects, and even archeological excavations translated into 86 million workdays and employment for 289,000 people in 1934. By July 1935, unemployment declined to 0.6 million people. Social security institutions were reorganized in 1933 with the foundation of the Istituto Nazionale Fascista della Previdenza Sociale (INFPS), which incorporated the former CNAS, the maternity fund, unemployment insurance, and some health insurance schemes (anti-tuberculosis insurance). Family allowances were introduced in 1934 to supplement wages for families with one wage earner. Social insurance expenditures, which reached 300–400 billion lire annually during the second half of the 1920s, increased by 1–1.5 billion lire in the mid-1930s. Old age and invalidity insurance was paid for 60,000–70,000 people in the early 1920s, but for nearly 500,000 by the mid-1930s. Health insurance policy was centralized through the foundation of a national health organization, the Istituto per l'Assistenza di Malattia (INAM), in 1943.

One of the most successful welfare institutions of fascist Italy was the Dopolavoro, or leisure time organization, enacted in May 1925. Membership rose from 0.3 million at the beginning to 3.2 million by 1937. The large and overly politicized organization offered cultural and sports programs and reduced-price tickets, maintained libraries and sports facilities, and organized recreation activities. Opera Balilla, the fascist youth organization, aimed at youth indoctrination, also offered rich programs for its members (4.3 million in 1934), including regular two-week summer vacations in seashore and mountain camps. Although all these institutions served fascist propaganda to legitimize the regime, they also positively influenced the everyday life of the population (Welk, 1938: 102–3; Zamagni, 1993: 315–17; Florinsky, 1936: 130–3).

Nazi Germany also initiated welfare policy, though to a lesser extent. There were extensive housing projects, and the Nazi Arbeitsfront organized vacations: already in 1934–5, 200,000 workers participated in cheap, organized vacations. Working conditions were inspected and improved: by 1940, 18,000 new factory cafeterias, 24,000 new locker rooms, and 3,000 sports facilities were established. Similar to the Italian Dopolavoro organization, the Kraft durch Freude (Strength Through Joy) movement brought together millions of workers and provided sports, cultural and leisure time activities. In 1934, 2 million workers participated in organized holiday trips. The Hitlerjugend movement mobilized 6 million young people between the ages of ten and eighteen in 1934 and also provided various activities and summer camps.

The Metaxas regime, besides arresting and deporting union leaders, banning strikes, and repressing the population, introduced labor legislation, guaranteeing minimum wages, and paid annual two weeks' vacation. Public health legislation established medical clinics for workers, medical care for working mothers, and financial assistance at childbirth.

Dictated regional economic integration

Economic dirigisme was a self-sufficient system *par excellence*. But was it possible to achieve self-sufficiency in relatively small European countries with one-sided energy and raw material resources? Of course not. The system thus required regional cooperation. Fascist Italy, while announcing the era of autarchy, simultaneously set to work on a regional agreement system to create a customs union with Austria and Hungary. Close economic connections were established among the three countries in 1931 in the framework of the so-called Brocchi system, which provided hidden customs reductions for the three. In the fall of 1933, a triple agreement system was finalized, and in March 1934, Mussolini, Dollfuss, and Gömbös, the three countries' premiers, signed an alliance treaty. In May, the Protocol of Rome added an economic chapter to the agreement. As a leading Hungarian economic journal interpreted:

This economic alliance reflects the rise of an Italian-led, economically based Central European political formation, which will be able to replace the strength and function of the former Austro-Hungarian Monarchy. (*Pesti Tőzsde*, 1934)

The agreement guaranteed Hungarian grain and animal exports to Italy and Austria, with significant subsidies. Italy agreed to import 1 million quintals of Hungarian grain and to pay 56 lire in subsidies per quintal above market price. For the next 1 million quintals, 23 lire subsidies were approved. In 1934–5, the Italian government paid 76 million lire in subsidies to Hungary. The Austrian government agreed to annual purchases of Hungarian cattle (12,000 head per year), pigs (132,000), and poultry (5,000 tonnes). While total Hungarian exports increased by only 12% in 1935, the exports to Italy increased by 80%. Hungary guaranteed the importation of Italian and Austrian industrial products (Berend and Szuhay, 1978: 251).

The Italian-led cooperation system was, however, strongly limited and it eventually collapsed. Nazi Germany created a larger regional agreement system under its own leadership and made an aggressive diplomatic effort to undermine the Italian plan. On January 17, 1934, at a Berlin meeting, the Nazi cabinet agreed:

As we well know, the Italian government is trying to establish an Italian–Austrian–Hungarian custom union. It is in our interest, in establishing strong political positions in Hungary, to counterbalance these attempts. (Documents, 1950: 372)

German government authorities decided in January: "It is the intention of Germany to link the Hungarian economy closely and inseparably to the German economy by agreements" (Deutsches Zentral Archiv, 1934: 41288). The Nazi *putsch* attempt in Austria, and then the *Anschluss* in March 1938, finally ended the Italian efforts to create a regional economic bloc with neighboring Central European countries.

Mussolini was somewhat more successful in realizing his ambitions to build a colonial empire by absorbing large North African and Balkan territories. "We have a right to empire," stated Mussolini, and he undertook colonial adventures in Libya and Ethiopia. Italian settlers were sent to populate a North African colony. In 1936 the proclamation of the Empire followed by a new Ministry of Italian Africa signaled the ambitious goal. In reality, as Denis Mack Smith said, it was a "parody of an empire" (Mack Smith, 1959: 452). Penetration into the Balkans was more successful, especially in Albania, which was closely connected by economic ties and then, in April 1939, by occupation, and the creation of a customs union and the unification of the Albanian franc with the Italian lira. A long-term colonization project was prepared to bring 2 million Italian settlers to outnumber the local population. Albania, "the fifth coastline of Italy," nevertheless was only a bridgehead for planned further Balkan expansion. The incorporation of southern Slovenia, the Dalmatian seashore, Montenegro, and a part of Macedonia was realized only during the war (Radice, 1986: 311, 352, 446).

The German plan, actually a part of Schacht's *Neuer Plan*, was aggressive economic expansion and led to the creation of a German *Grossraumwirtschaft*. State Secretary Hans Ernst Posse recounted:

Since the readjustment of the interior German economic space . . . had been accomplished, it was time to consider it as the most essential task of economic policy to fit the German economy in the Grossraumwirtschaft, which was taking shape. (Posse, 1934: 83)

The year 1934, indeed, saw a crucial breakthrough for Nazi Germany. In January and February, negotiations led to a new trade agreement between Germany and Hungary. Similar agreements followed with Bulgaria, Yugoslavia, and Romania. In this regional system, built on a set of bilateral agreements, export quotas were granted to the agricultural and raw-material-providing Southeast European countries, and Germany, using its funds frozen in the area, paid higher than world market prices. All the transactions were based on barter and clearing systems. Germany thus paid for its imports with industrial products, and the settlements were closed at the end of the year. Ten percent of the value of the exports to Germany went to a so-called *conto ordinario* and served for purchasing goods available only for hard currencies. The countries of the region also opened their markets to German industrial goods (see Table 3.1). The region's share of German foreign trade increased from 3–4% to 10%, but more than one-third in basic food staples such as wheat and meat, and two-thirds in tobacco and bauxite between 1929 and 1937 (Basch, 1944: 181, 192).

Germany gained important economic positions and became economically dominant in the region. After the *Anschluss* and the occupation of the Czech lands, Germany made investments in key sectors of these countries. At the end of the 1930s, Hitler was able to dictate conditions and exact total subordination from clients, thanks to Germany's economic superiority combined with political pressure, and, in some cases, the promise of challenging the borders created by the Versailles Treaty. Building a large economic zone of "controlled cooperation," or German-led integration, was combined with the creation of "a sphere of political influence" (Carr, 1964: 127–8).

Table 3.1 German share in foreign trade in % (Berend and Ránki, 1974: 281–2)

	Exports to Germany, % of total		Imports from Germany, % of total	
Country	1933	1939	1933	1939
Bulgaria	36.0	71.1	38.2	69.5
Hungary	11.2	52.4	19.6	52.5
Romania	16.6	43.1	18.6	56.1
Yugoslavia	13.9	45.9	13.2	53.2

At the new German–Hungarian trade talks in February 1939, the head of the Hungarian delegation described the German attitude toward Hungary in his confidential report in the following way: "In general the tendency became obvious that Hungary was to be degraded to the level of a raw material base." Prime Minister Pál Teleki wrote in a personal letter: "The German Empire possesses such vast and widespread interests in our country, that she can control and . . . influence all of Hungary's economic life" (Hungarian National Archive, 1939: Res. 30; 358). Nazi Germany subordinated the region as an *Ergänzungswirtschaft*, or complementary economy for the German war economy. Moreover, Walther Funk, Nazi economic minister, stated in 1940:

Germany now had the opportunity to politically achieve a continental European *Grossraumwirtschaft* under German leadership. Whoever had political power in Europe had the right to establish a new economic order, and the other countries had to adjust their economies to our demands. (quoted in Ránki, 1993: 67)

In the spring of 1941, the interim Hungarian *chargé d'affaires* in Berlin sent a confidential report to the Ministry of Foreign Affairs summarizing information given by a spokesman of the Nazi minister of foreign affairs on Nazi economic policy plans in a reorganized Europe. According to German plans, the Southeast European nations had "to conform to their natural circumstances."

[Industrialization] was incompatible with the agricultural character of these countries . . . [They] must also conform their economies to the demands of the continental economy . . . Their agricultural production should be directed by the needs of the other parts of the continent; the main products are to be cereals and oil-seeds . . . agricultural industry may develop . . . The production of raw materials will be supplemented by their local processing into semi-finished products . . . Lastly, they will prevent the establishment of industries inconvenient from the German point of view. (Hungarian National Archive, 1941: Res. 466)

From 1940–1, when virtually the entire continent was under German rule, the over-ambitious Nazi program focused not only on a traditional self-sufficient *Grossraumwirtschaft* east of Germany but also on a *Kontinentaleuropäische Grossraumwirtschaft* with three zones of Europe. Each of these zones – the satellite Southeastern Europe, the occupied Western Europe, and the conquered Poland, Czech lands, and the Soviet Union – had special functions in the dictated cooperation.

Southeastern Europe would play the traditional role of agricultural and raw material supplier, but in a new way, by a "controlled cooperation," adjusted to the German requirements. Indeed, the region became a complementary part of the Nazi war economy and three-quarters of its foreign trade linked it to Germany in the 1940s.

Occupied Western Europe was incorporated into the German economic system as an industrial supplier, adjusted to German requirements. In the war years, the Belgian industry worked for Germany: three-quarters of its metalworking capacities were used for German contracts and deliveries. In occupied Norway German authorities decided to build a large aluminum industry to serve German aircraft production. In January 1943, a decree of the Nazi Four Year Plan Office gave the right of unified control of the armament economies of all occupied territories to the Ministry of War Production. "After March the French and Belgian economies were treated for all purposes of production planning as part of Germany" (Milward, 1977: 151).

In a letter to Funk on August 17, 1940, Göring conceptualized a postwar program of integrating German and West European economies:

Before the end of the war as intensive as possible a penetration of, in the first place, the Dutch and Belgian, but also the Norwegian and Danish economies, should be attempted by German capital on a very wide basis . . . [to create] in the shortest time common economic links and connections of interest between Germany and these countries. (Quoted in Milward, 1977: 162)

The Polish and Russian territories, however, would be ruthlessly robbed. "Was für England Indien war, wird für uns der Ostraum sein" ("what India was for England, the East will be for us") said Hitler during one of his "table talks" (Radice quoted in Picker, 1965: 143). Regarding Poland, a detailed *Verorderungsblatt für das Generalgouvernement* of Hermann Göring ordered in 1940:

All raw material, scrap, machinery, and so forth which can be used in the German war economy must be removed from the territory. Enterprises which are not absolutely essential for the maintenance at a low level of the bare existence of the inhabitants must be transferred to Germany. (Quoted in Radice, 1986: 341)

From the spring of 1942, extreme efforts were made to transport millions of virtual slave workers from the conquered territories. Fritz Sauckel was appointed Generalbevollmächtige für den Arbeitseinsatz (Plenipotentiary for Labor). He presided over the transport of 1.5 million Poles (out of a planned 4 million) to Germany. The so-called Göring Plan detailed procedures to exploit the Caucasian oil, the iron of Krivoy Rog, and the Ukrainian black soil area as a breadbasket for Germany.

In certain parts of the occupied territories, in the Protectorate of Bohemia-Moravia, Western Poland, which became a new *Gau* (province of the Reich) of Danzig-Westpreussen and Wartheland, *Volksdeutsche* settlers were recruited from the Baltic States, Romania, and elsewhere to Germanize these incorporated territories.

Conquering, subordinating, looting, and exploiting the entire European continent was integral to Nazi war efforts and served the dream of victory over Britain and the United States and establishment of an integrated, German-led Europe and German world domination. Economic dirigisme, the most aggressive growth-oriented system, which did not hesitate to employ dictatorial measures domestically, also forced economic collaboration of subordinated countries internationally. The realization of self-sufficiency, impossible in a national framework, was targeted in an enlarged, politically allied and subordinated region. A large area of controlled cooperation, a regional or all-European dictated economic integration, belonged to the plans and partly to the practice of genuinely expansionist authoritarian regimes.

Economic results

Economic dirigisme had a major impact on the economy of the authoritarian countries. The German economy had a much better growth performance than most West European countries. During the 1920s, German economic growth was moderate; by 1929, it surpassed prewar levels by only 13%. The Great Depression, however, eliminated all the advances in growth and in 1932 per capita GDP reached only 85% of the 1913 level. However,

Table 3.2 GDP per capita in Southern Europe in 1990 ppp dollars and % (Maddison, 1995a: 194–8, 200–12)

Year	Italy		Spain		Portugal		Greece		South Europe*	
1913	2,507	100	2,255	100	1,354	100	1,621	100	1,934	100
1929	3,026	121	2,947	131	1,536	113	2,386	147	2,474	128
1938	3,244	129	2,022	79	1,707	126	2,727	168	2,425	125
1950	3,425	137	2,397	106	2,132	158	1,951	120	2,476	128

* Four countries

the Nazi economic regime brought about a rapid recovery, mostly because of the immediate war preparation and the creation of a self-sufficient German economy, and by 1938 the income level surpassed the 1932 nadir by 57% and the 1913 level by 34%. The tremendous war effort after 1941 generated a rapid growth: per capita GDP increased by 22% between 1938 and 1944, and surpassed the 1913 level by 63%. After the extremely heavy war devastation, the German income level in 1946 was less than half of the 1938 level, but eliminating bottlenecks and rebuilding capacities led to speedy reconstruction, and the German income level by 1950 was only 16% lower than in 1938, but still 12% higher than in 1913.

While the Nazi German economic performance was a result of the war economy, some of the South European authoritarian countries, most of all Italy, Greece, and Portugal, had an even more impressive achievement up until World War II. Spain, however, was devastated by the civil war. Greece, first occupied and then civil war-ridden during the 1940s, dropped back sharply (see Table 3.2).

Most of the Mediterranean countries, nevertheless, reflected the typical characteristics of the economic nationalist policy in peripheral countries, the most important being the absence of technological–structural adjustment of the age within their self-sufficient economic framework. Consequently, most of them preserved their obsolete economic structure. The Spanish, Portuguese, and Greek economies maintained their largely agricultural character, with nearly half of the population in the latter two countries working in agriculture. Moreover, the agricultural population expanded during the 1930s from 48% to 50% in Portugal, and from 46% to 51% of the total labor force in Spain, while industrial employment declined by 5% during the 1930s (see Figure 3.1).

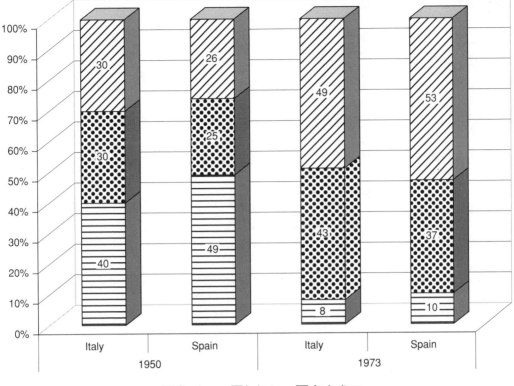

Figure 3.1 Changes in sectoral employment, Italy and Spain, 1950–73

In 1930 illiteracy remained at 40% in Greece and 60% in Portugal, although it decreased during the 1930s – in the case of Greece to 27% by 1940. The lack of successful modernization was also indicated by the fact that by 1930 55% of Greek exports still consisted of tobacco, and 72% of industrial workers in Portugal worked in mostly small-scale and old industrial branches such as textile, leather, wood, and food-processing industries (Fischer, 1978: 992).

The European peripheries, in spite of their achievements, were unable to change their economies radically or alter their relative backwardness in relation to Western Europe: in 1913, the four Mediterranean countries' income level reached 52% that of Western Europe. By 1950, their level declined to 48% of the West. The dirigist regimes in Spain and Portugal survived World War II. One was re-established in postwar Greece and lasted until the 1970s. During the postwar decades these regimes, especially in Spain, gradually transformed from economic dirigisme toward West European mixed economy. The Spanish economic regime shifted from the Mussolini type toward a postwar French system. The Iberian countries became unofficial members of the European Economic Community. Free

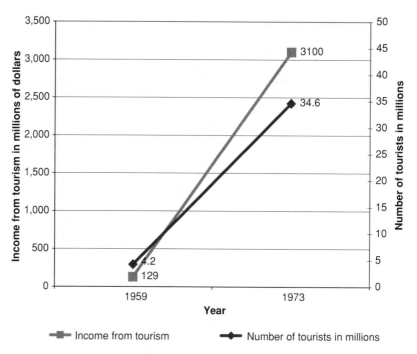

Figure 3.2 Rise of tourism: Spain

trade policy gradually replaced import substitution, and Western tourists flooded the countries (see Figure 3.2).

Due to the cold war confrontation, Greece also became part of the Western alliance. The Truman doctrine of 1947 introduced Western assistance to the country, which became a member of NATO in 1952, and in a decade began preparing cooperation with the European Economic Community. The economic performance of these countries was no longer representative of economic dirigisme.

CHAPTER 4

The centrally planned economic system

If economic dirigisme was an extreme version of the regulated market economy, the centrally planned system was the most extreme version of economic dirigisme. It was equally statist and interventionist. If economic dirigisme was strongly growth-oriented in an autarchic way, and served war preparation, the centrally planned economy was a special system to achieve a forced maximum economic growth and self-sufficiency. It was a "child" of the German war economy, and also served, with an extraordinary radicalism, the modernization and war preparation of economically less developed countries. The state socialist planned economy abolished private ownership, the market mechanism, the role of market prices, and the role of supply and demand. Unlike all the other systems, this first non-market economic regime was, at least partly, born from a theory.

Marxist theoretical legacy, Lenin and the Bolshevik program

Karl Marx was an extraordinary product of his time: the philosophy of Enlightenment and passionate Romanticism. A renaissance scholar, Marx, as his later disciples maintained, combined German philosophy, English political economy, and French socialism, and made important contributions to philosophy, economics, and history. As a radical journalist he left Germany and emigrated to Britain after the 1848 Revolution and became a student of contemporary British capitalism. According to Marx, capitalism historically opened the road toward a stormy development of productive forces, technology, and organization, but meanwhile led to a polarization of society. Marx believed that economically interpreted history and political economy were the master sciences to understand and influence social development. He used the Hegelian dialectic and shared a teleological concept of history, believing, as all the children of the age, in progress as a law of nature. As expressed in the foreword of *Das Kapital*, historical progress, though unilinear, is realized by class struggle and revolutions. Social harmony is a natural law, but attainable only through continual struggle – beyond capitalism.

Marx's point of departure was Ricardo's labor theory of value, but he transformed it by distinguishing between the labor value of the *product* of labor and the value of the workers' *labor power*. In his powerful concept, labor was a special commodity, which produced more labor value than required for its reproduction. In other words, workers were working only part of the workday for themselves while the other part of the workday was unpaid and produced a surplus value. Consequently, the wealth accumulated in the hands of a small layer of the bourgeoisie, which expropriated the surplus value. Capitalist economy consequently led to a permanent concentration of capital and the destruction of small-scale independent enterprise. The accumulation of wealth generated the proletarization of the population, and the accumulation of poverty among the proletariat.

Marxian analysis and critique of capitalism produced an extraordinary impact, opening a new chapter in history and influencing the entire 150 years that followed. The Marxian theory offered a political program for the workers' movement. Although Marx and his comrade-in-arms and frequent co-author, Friedrich Engels, sought to avoid utopian dreaming about a coming perfect society, they still drew some basic conclusions for the future from their analysis of capitalism. These conclusions, though based on a most scholarly analysis, nevertheless were a kind of daydreaming, no less utopian than Plato's, Thomas More's, or Rousseau's. They shared a common belief with Rousseau that private ownership was a sin and the source of all manner of crimes. Capitalist society, in this interpretation, would bear the seeds of its own destruction and create its own "grave-diggers," the proletariat. Since history was driven by class struggle, the proletariat would launch a revolution, and, in the place of capitalism, a transitory dictatorship of the proletariat would expropriate the expropriators and introduce a new, just, and humane society, socialism. The basic contradiction of capitalism, collective production and private expropriation, constituted an obstacle for further development. Private ownership would thus be replaced by collective public ownership. In their landmark *Communist Manifesto*, Marx and Engels stated in 1848:

The first step in the revolution by the working class is to raise the proletariat to the position of ruling class . . . The proletariat will . . . centralize all instruments of production in the hands of the state, i.e., of the proletariat organized as the ruling class; and increase the total productive forces as rapidly as possible. (Marx, 2000: 261)

The *Communist Manifesto*, however, did not offer a blueprint for peasant agriculture.

> There is no need to abolish . . . petty-artisan and small peasant ownership, the development of industry has to a great extent already destroyed it, and is still destroying it daily. (Marx, 2000: 256)

This view was based on the British historical experience. Small farming indeed gradually disappeared in Britain and the peasantry diminished to roughly one-tenth of the population before World War I. Britain's present, suggested Marx, is the future of all mankind. The peasant of today, consequently, would become the worker of tomorrow. In the long run Marx was certainly right. However, in Germany, France, and all over Europe, the peasantry remained a significant layer of society around the turn of the century and the socialist movement had to face existing reality. German social democracy was forced to turn to the peasant question and address it. Karl Kautsky, Marx's best pupil and leading theoretician of the German Social Democratic Party, was the first to undertake this task and suggested the cooperative reorganization of agriculture as a consistent policy. He asked the old Friedrich Engels to participate in the debate about the peasant question, which generated Engels's work on the *Peasant Question in France and Germany* (1894).

> What, then, is our attitude toward the small peasantry? How shall we have to deal with it . . . [after] our accession to power? We shall not even think of forcibly expropriating the small peasants (. . . with or without compensation) . . . Our task . . . [is] a transition of his private enterprise and private possession to co-operative ones, not forcibly but . . . [by] example and . . . social assistance . . . we shall not interfere in his property relations by force, against his will. We shall . . . facilitate his transition to the co-operative should he decide to do so, and even make it possible for him to remain on his small holding for a protracted length of time to think the matter over . . . [Regarding] big and middle peasants, [the solution is] the pooling of farms to form co-operative enterprises . . . Most likely we shall be able to abstain . . . [from] forcible expropriation . . . Only the big landed estates [will be simply expropriated]. (Marx and Engels, 1955: 433–8)

Marx, in *The Civil War in France* (1871), also introduced the idea of planning: "[u]nited cooperative societies are to regulate national production upon a common plan . . . putting an end to the constant anarchy . . . of capitalist production" (Marx, 2000: 593). Capitalism, in Marx's analysis, creates a high degree of organization within the firms, but anarchy characterizes the relations among the firms in a chaotic market. Planning, based on collective ownership, will eliminate this "contradiction" and anarchy of capitalism.

Collectivist socialism also transforms distribution and introduces an egalitarian system. Marx offered a perfect utopian program, very attractive for poor masses in nineteenth-century class society. At the first stage of the new society, socialism, he stated in his *Critique of the Gotha Program* of the German Social Democracy, proper equality is not yet possible because society is not rich enough for that: everybody works according to his ability, and receives his share according to the amount of labor performed. Marx here forecast a moneyless economy:

the individual labor time of the individual producer is the part of the social working day contributed by him, his share in it. He receives a certificate from society that he has furnished ... such an amount of labor ... and he draws from the social stock of means of consumption as much as costs the same amount of labour. The same amount of labour which he gives to society in one form he receives back in another. (Marx, 2000: 614–15)

Since socialism eliminates the obstacles to further development of productive forces, which were created by capitalism in its later stage of development, the material base for an equal and just society will be created. Consequently, at the higher stage of classless society, communism, a genuinely equal society will realize the principle "from each according to his ability, to each according to his needs." At that stage, a self-governing civil society forms the political superstructure of communism.

Marx and Engels thus developed a concept of future socialism and communism which would be based on the nationalization of the means of production and collectivization of peasant agriculture. They also developed the concept of planning in a society where nothing would disturb the rapid growth of productive forces. Finally, they developed the basic principles of egalitarian distribution and self-governing organization.

They maintained in their early and unfinished work *German Ideology* (1847) that "communism is for us not a state of affairs which is to be established, an ideal to which reality will have to adjust itself," but a development emerging from existing circumstances (Marx, 2000: 187). In reality they produced a blueprint for future socialism. It became a mobilizing program for Marxist socialist movements.

Facing the realities of a transforming capitalism, however, turn-of-the-century socialist movements began revising Marx. The Marxian forecast of an ever-polarizing society heading for revolution did not materialize in advanced Europe. Around the time of Karl Marx's death the rapid rise of the middle class became the leading trend in West European societies.

In the wealthy countries, the *Communist Manifesto's* powerful slogan that the proletariat has nothing to lose but its chains was no longer true. A marked polarization developed between the industrializing Western core and the Southern and Eastern peripheries of the continent.

Two types of revisionism emerged simultaneously. In the West the Right-revisionism of Eduard Bernstein and his followers, most of all German and Austrian socialists, gained ground. In the East the Left-revisionism of Vladimir I. Lenin and his Russian Bolshevik followers became dominant. Right-revisionism led to the concept of "organized capitalism" via parliamentary reforms, social legislation, and "socialism in distribution." The Right-revisionists rejected proletarian revolution and the "expropriation of expropriators." Western socialism radically transformed.

Left-revisionism, however, preserved the Marxian idea of proletarian revolution, but rejected and revised some other basic assumptions and ideas of Marx and Engels, who wrote in their *German Ideology* that socialism would emerge only in the most advanced countries, "as the common action of the leading nations." Socialism thus may emerge on the material base of advanced capitalism and the division of labor of advanced countries. If a communist revolution won in a backward country, they prophesied "only poverty would be distributed and the struggle for necessities would start again...communism would be a local phenomenon," and the development of the world economy automatically "would destroy local communism" (Marx and Engels, 1970).

Left-revisionism, which emerged in Russia, rejected the main concept of Western Right-revisionism on parliamentary reformism. In Russia, as in the backward peripheries of Europe, autocratic regimes did not even have a parliamentary system, and the socialist movement was banned and persecuted. Left-revisionists also rejected Marx's presumption on the possibility of socialist revolution only in advanced countries acting together. Lenin and Trotsky argued that peasant Russia, where capitalism was emerging and a relatively small but strongly concentrated working class was in the making in big cities, had become the hotbed of proletarian revolution. Leon Trotsky revised Marx in his *Itogi i perspektivy* (*Results and Prospects*) of 1906. He introduced the concept of permanent revolution and argued that backwardness was the prerequisite for proletarian revolution, and that Russian workers would be forced to carry out a revolution and might gain power more easily than their counterparts in the advanced countries. A successful Russian revolution then would destroy conservative inertia in the West and ignite the proletarian revolution there (Wistrich, 1982: 51, 58). Lenin argued similarly, maintaining that in the imperialist world system, the "final stage of capitalism," the victory of the proletarian revolution, is possible only in backward or semi-developed countries, the "weakest links in the chain of imperialism."

Both Lenin and Trotsky, nevertheless, preserved the Marxian concept that backward, peasant Russia, though the cradle of revolution, would prove unable to build a socialist society but would have begun the process of change: "The ice has been broken; the road is open." They believed the West would follow. As Nikolai Bukharin, the young talented Bolshevik economist who studied in Vienna, explained in his *Economics of the Transformation Period* in 1920, the revolution became victorious in backward Russia because

here the state machinery was organized the most weakly . . . The state apparatus proved to be so unstable that it could be relatively easily overthrown by the proletariat in the large urban centers. But, on the other hand, the causes of the easy victory were dialectically transformed after the victory of the proletariat into causes of the greatest difficulties. The economic backwardness of the country . . . presents enormous obstacles. (Bukharin, 1971: 166)

The revolution, Lenin and Trotsky repeatedly argued, would spread to advanced countries, first of all Germany, and the advanced nations would "complete this process" (Lenin, 1971: 650). As Trotsky maintained, there was "no escape from the contradictions of backwardness within the framework of a national revolution." The only way was for revolutionary Russia to "unite its forces with those of the socialist proletariat of Western Europe. Only in this way will its temporary revolutionary hegemony become the prologue to socialist dictatorship." Trotsky, a consistent thinker and theoretician, posed the question, however, of the outcome of a socialist revolution in Russia if revolution failed to spread and conquer advanced countries. His answer was definite and prophetic: the Russian revolution either would be destroyed by a conservative Europe, or would be eroded by the primitive economic, social, and cultural conditions (Wistrich, 1982: 62; Trotsky, 1973: 333).

Although the state socialist regime was born from theory, its exact realization was also closely connected to Germany's war economy. Vladimir I. Lenin, debating with his Left opposition in *The Immediate Tasks of the Soviet Government* (April 1918), advocated the use of the "last word of capitalism" and the introduction of the "best system of accounting and control." The following month he published his *"Left-Wing" Childishness and the Petty-Bourgeois Mentality*, outlining his idea:

[T]ake the most concrete example of state capitalism . . . It is Germany. Here we have "the last word" in modern large-scale capitalist engineering and planned organization, *subordinated to Junker-bourgeois imperialism.* Cross out the words in italics, and in place of the militarist Junker, bourgeois, imperialist *state* put *also a state*, but a different social type . . . a *Soviet* state . . . and you will have the *sum total* of the conditions necessary for socialism. (Lenin, 1971: 417, 443)

In the Soviet type of economic regime, "state capitalism" was indeed replaced by state socialism, originating with the most sophisticated German war economic system and taken to extremes by the Stalinist command economy. From its beginning, state socialism was both a modernization dictatorship and a totally isolated war economy.

The Bolsheviks, though utopian in several respects, had to be pragmatic as well. Until the mid-1920s, during Lenin's life they continued rope dancing to both revise and preserve Marx's theory on socialism. In 1924, the rising new leader, a non-theoretical-minded but smart and cunning organizer, Josif V. Stalin, in his *Foundation of Leninism*, just repeated the traditional Marxist view, that "the forces of only one country" would not prove enough for the final victory of socialism, and that peasant Russia could not be a "self-sufficient entity" of socialism (Stalin, 1972: 120).

The Bolsheviks, for a decade after their October revolution, waited for a world revolution, first in Europe and then in China. After the victory of the revolution the Bolsheviks were not even aiming for the immediate realization of the basic requirements of a socialist transformation. Instead, they stabilized their power by distributing nationalized land among the peasants and created millions of new peasant farms. They nationalized only the "commanding heights" of the economy and allowed private business, although controlled from above by the state and from below by workers' factory committees. Up until June 1918, as a consequence of an "elemental-chaotic proletarian nationalization from below," only individual firms were nationalized, altogether 487 of them, two-thirds of which were in shambles. In January 1918, a decree flatly banned nationalization without specific central authorization. "The evidence," concluded Alec Nove, "is still consistent with the intention to maintain a mixed economy for a considerable period." Only the June 1918 decree introduced a comprehensive nationalization (Nove, 1992: 46–7).

In the desperate post-revolution situation of civil war, hunger, and total chaos, the Russian economy nearly collapsed: gross output of industry dropped to less than one-third of the 1913 level, coal output and electricity generation fell to less than one-quarter, and agricultural production declined by 40%. In this situation, however, a utopian modernization plan was presented to the Bolshevik Party Congress in 1920. Electricity, as all over Europe, became the symbol of modernization. This was clearly expressed by Vladimir I. Lenin's obsession with the electrification of backward Russia. The Soviet political system combined with electrification of the country were the key factors for entering the Promised Land: communism. Alec Nove describes the presentation of the world's first long-term development plan:

[Krzhizhanovsky] illustrated the plan with a vast map of Russia in which electric light bulbs showed the electrification of the future. Such was the state of Moscow's electricity supply at the time that it was necessary to cut off almost all the city in order to ensure that these lights on the map would not cause overstrain at the power station. (Nove, 1992: 64–5)

The GOELRO Plan, as it was called, aimed to create the technological base for the overall modernization of Russia.

Large-scale industry based on the latest achievements of technology and capable of reorganizing agriculture, implies the electrification of the whole country . . . The execution of the first part of the electrification scheme is estimated to take ten years. (Lenin, 1974: 642)

Reality, nevertheless, was a devastating hyperinflation, which made the currency practically valueless. Cautious gradualism soon was abandoned. Extraordinary measures were needed and the new leaders did not hesitate to introduce them. These measures, however, were mere consequences not only of a dramatic economic catastrophe but also of utopian ideological dreaming, which made a virtue of the necessity. The Bolsheviks enthusiastically welcomed the "introduction" of communism. As Nikolai Bukharin and Evgeny Preobrazhensky stated: "The increasing depreciation of the currency is, essentially, an expression of the annulment of monetary values" (Bukharin and Preobrazhensky, 1969: 391). The Supreme Economic Council resolved:

State industrial enterprises should deliver their products to other state enterprises . . . on the instruction of the appropriate organs . . . without payment . . . [Railroads and the merchant fleet] should transport gratis the goods of all state enterprises . . . The Congress expressed the desire to see the final elimination of any influence of money upon the relations of economic units. (Nove, 1992: 71)

Utopian dreams gained ground: "Introduction of communism seemed to be the answer to the desperate situation." In the draft of the party program of 1919, Lenin spoke about the will "for the most rapid carrying out of the most radical measures preparing [for] the abolition of money." Wages were paid in kind, and public transportation and municipal services were provided gratis. Private trade was made illegal, and in April 1919, firms employing five or more persons were nationalized. By August 1920, 37,000 enterprises became state-owned; 5,000 of them employed only one person (Nove, 1992: 57–9, 63). A "food dictatorship" was introduced: armed detachments seized food from the peasants, and the *prodrazverstka*, a compulsory delivery system, was born. A militarized system, called War Communism, was introduced.

A new Party Program was adopted in March 1919, which advocated the "transforming [of] private ownership of the means of production and distribution into social ownership." The program also stated the goal of "the maximum centralization of production." The section on agriculture announced the goal of "founding Soviet farms, that is to say, large-scale socialist economies," and to "support . . . the communal cultivation of the land." Instead of trade, a nationally organized distributive system was targeted, based on "the organization of the whole population into an integral network of consumers' communes" (Program, 1969: 431, 446, 450, 452).

A few months after the new program was adopted, two theoreticians of the party, Bukharin and Preobrazhensky, published an exhaustive commentary on the program. In their interpretation, agricultural productivity would be increased by communal, large-scale agriculture, which would require tractors, electricity, and a modern crop-rotation system, which would in turn reduce the agricultural labor force "to one-half or one-third." Rational argumentation was mixed with utopian ventures, such as communal kitchens: instead "of preparing 100 meals in separate kitchens, we prepare one dinner . . . in the kitchen of the village commune." A similar utopian goal was expressed concerning distribution. Bukharin and Preobrazhensky spoke about the abolition of private trade and the introduction of "class rationing," and "the payment of the workers in kind" (Bukharin and Preobrazhensky, 1969: 311, 352–5, 377–9, 391).

War Communism, however, undermined the Russian economy even more, and the system failed. The economic situation in 1921 grew tragic. At the Seventh Party Congress complaints were made about the "disintegration" of the proletariat. Peasant revolts engulfed the countryside and in February 1921, even the bedrock of Soviet power, the sailors of Kronstadt, revolted. Doctrinal enthusiasm for "introducing communism" withered away.

Prodrazverstka, the confiscation of peasant "surpluses," was condemned. Lenin evolved from a utopian revolutionary to a pragmatic statesman and announced the retreat: "[w]e must say to the small farmers: . . . produce food and the state will take a minimum tax . . . Only agreement with the peasantry can save the socialist revolution in Russia" (Lenin, 1947:

117, 120–2). In 1921 the *Novaya economicheskaya politika* (NEP), a New Economic Policy, was introduced:

> We presumed to be able to organize the state production and . . . distribution . . . on communist lines in a small-peasant country directly ordered by the proletarian state . . . We were wrong . . . A number of transitional stages were necessary . . . [We have to build on] personal interest, personal incentive and business principles . . . We must first set to work . . . state capitalism. (Lenin 1971: 651)

The new tax in 1921 was hardly more than half of the quantity of food confiscated in 1920. In two years, tax in kind reached only 10% of output; in 1924, tax in kind was replaced by taxes in money. The peasants were allowed to market their products and hire labor. Grain production increased from 38 million tonnes to 77 million tonnes between 1921 and 1926, approaching the prewar level of 80 million tonnes. In May, a decree legalized small-scale private industry. In the food-processing and leather industries alone, 7,000 state-owned firms were leased out to private entrepreneurs. Militarization of labor ceased and a free labor market was reintroduced. A decree denounced "all kinds of equalization." Trade became overwhelmingly private, amounting to 78% of all retail turnovers in 1922–3. The ideal of an economy without money or gold was shelved and sarcastically shifted to a faraway future: "When we are victorious on a world scale," wrote Lenin, "we shall use gold for the purpose of building public lavatories in the street" (Lenin, 1971: 656). Meanwhile, in the present, Gosbank, the national bank, reopened and issued a new stable currency, the chervonets, with 25% gold reserve. The NEP, noted Lenin, was intended "seriously and for a long time." He probably thought about a generation-long policy when he spoke about twenty-five years as a bit of a pessimistic forecast. Bukharin explicitly mentioned a "generation, at least." It was not the case. The retreat of the retreat occurred in the very same decade.

Forced industrialization and central planning: "socialism in one country"

The positive economic consequences of the introduction of the NEP were unquestionable. Industrial output doubled between 1921 and 1923, and doubled again by 1925. The next year, it surpassed the prewar level by 10%. The Bolsheviks, however, worried about the destiny of the revolution and the restoration of capitalism, and attacked compromises. Lenin, himself seemingly confused or overly tactful, announced as early as November 1921, a few months after the introduction of the NEP, that "we retreated to state capitalism, but we did not retreat too far . . . There are visible signs that the retreat is coming to an end . . . in the not too distant future" (Lenin, 1971: 659).

A Left opposition emerged. At the Twelfth Party Congress in April 1923, Trotsky launched a harsh attack against the NEP and spoke about its liquidation. He avowed that the coming years would have to be the period of "primitive socialist accumulation" (Carr, 1952: 379). The "Left opposition," the Trotsky-led "Group of 46," openly condemned the NEP in a declaration in *Pravda* in October 1923 and demanded the introduction of a centrally planned "dictatorship of industry."

A fierce debate erupted linked to the struggle to replace Lenin, who fell ill in the fall of 1923 and died in January 1924. Trotsky, the actual leader of the revolution, was an evident successor. The main architect of the new economic concept was an ally of Trotsky and one of the most talented Bolshevik economists, Evgeny Preobrazhensky. Alexander Erlich, the historian of the industrialization debate in Russia, explains:

The left-wing Communists wanted to solve the harrowing problems of a socialist regime in a backward Russia, faced with advanced capitalist countries, by aiming at a resumption of all-out revolutionary action in the West and at the rapid growth of the industrial proletariat at home. The less chance the first part of the blueprint had in the immediate future, the stronger was the emphasis put on the second . . . The task consisted in stating the case not in terms of wishful thinking . . . but in the language of present-day realities . . . This was precisely what Preobrazhensky attempted to do. (Erlich, 1967: 31–2)

Preobrazhensky explained the concept of the recommended policy in 1924, in a lecture series, and later, in 1926, in a book, *Novaya Ekonomika* (*The New Economics*). His point of departure was that after the revolution, in a transitory period,

the socialist system is not yet in a condition to develop all its organic advantages, but it inevitably abolishes at the same time a number of the economic advantages . . . of a developed capitalist system . . . How to pass as quickly as possible through this [critical transitory] period . . . is a question of life and death for the socialist state. (Preobrazhensky, 1965: 89)

The central problem was, he explained, to achieve a high rate of capital accumulation and investments, generate a most rapid economic growth, and reach a high level of growth. But how to achieve a high level of accumulation in a poor, low-income country? History and economic theory did not provide an appropriate model for that. An exit from the poverty circle – low income level begets low level of capital accumulation and investment begets slow growth rate – had not yet been found. The nationalized part of the Russian economy, the small industrial sector, could not supply the required resources. Neither could the rather primitive, mostly subsistence peasant economy. In a backward peasant country, suggested Preobrazhensky, the only way to increase accumulation was the exploitation of the peasantry, the bulk of the population, by a forced "accumulation in the hands of the state of material resources mainly . . . from sources lying outside the complex of state economy." He called that the period of "primitive" (or preliminary) socialist accumulation, a period of the creation of the material prerequisites for socialist production. This theory was based on Marx's famous concept of "primitive accumulation" in Britain, explained in Chapter 24 of *Das Kapital*, "a prolonged exploitation of petty production" to develop modern industrial capitalism. The same introductory period was needed for socialism, the argument continued. Preobrazhensky argued that it would be possible to siphon resources from the private peasant economy to the state's accumulation fund for industrial investments through the mechanism of a price "scissors" of artificially low agricultural prices coupled with artificially high industrial prices set by the state. Additionally, a high protectionism, based on the monopoly of foreign trade, would serve as extra taxation of the population. An inflationary policy would also reduce the income of the population, including the wages of workers in the state sector (Preobrazhensky, 1965: 91, 111).

This system required the destruction of the market and market prices and their replacement by a centrally planned and state-directed economy. The program, which was discussed with shocking openness and brutal clarity, offered a policy of forced capital accumulation and industrialization, a consistent, long-term economic policy for non-industrialized, backward countries. A dramatically new economic model was invented, a non-market economic system, a road to catching up with the industrialized West. Economic theory had not offered anything like that before.

For the post-Lenin old Bolshevik rivals such as Lev B. Kamanev and Grigori E. Zinoviev as well as Nikolai Bukharin, but most of all for Josif V. Stalin, Trotsky's leadership was not acceptable. They formed an alliance, took up the gauntlet, and rejected the Left opposition by denouncing "ultra-industrialization." Bukharin offered an alternative and argued that the realization of Trotsky's and Preobrazhensky's concept would "destroy the domestic market." In his *Zametki ekonomista* (*Notes of an Economist*), he explained:

In their naiveté the ideologists of Trotskyism suggest that a maximum yearly transfusion from the peasant economy into industry will generally ensure a maximum rate of industrial development. But that is clearly not the case. The highest rate can be *sustained* only . . . on the basis of a rapidly growing agriculture . . . [T]he development of industry depends on the development of agriculture. (Bukharin, 1982: 310)

He argued consistently in defense of the market, market prices, and profit incentives. Stalin joined the criticism of Trotsky and Preobrazhensky at the Moscow Party Conference of January 1925, using Bukharin's ideas that industry is to "rest on the home market, the peasant market," thus the government has to exercise "special attention and special care to the peasantry" (Stalin, 1972: 190–1). Even in 1927, he argued in the same way against the "political rupture with the peasantry," and against "the disruption of equilibrium in the whole economic system" (Stalin, 1949: 299–313).

The political infighting spawned an important theoretical debate, which yielded distinct policy alternatives. Certain politicians and economists, among others Grigori Sokolnikov, recommended a focus on agricultural development and exports:

Only by stimulating agricultural exports, can we obtain during the next years an amount of foreign currency which will enable us to finance the importation of equipment as well as of raw materials for our industry and to accomplish re-equipment and expansion. (Erlich, 1967: 28)

Others, such as Bukharin, recommended a more balanced policy, an "optimal combination" with a solid, moderate beginning of industrialization. All of these policy recommendations were combined with arguments for using the market mechanism. Another leading economist, Vladimir A. Bazarov, stated:

[Only the market mechanism] makes it possible, under present circumstances, to provide an automatic check of the correctness of all action . . . I firmly believe that . . . the existence of market and economic accounting is the necessary prerequisite of any possible planning, whether there will be a world revolution or not. (Bazarov quoted by Erlich, 1967: 73)

The economic debate, however, was not decided by economic arguments but by political power. In the harsh struggle for succession in the year of Lenin's death, 1924, a pragmatic, cynical, and cunning Stalin offered *his* original revision of Marx and the previous Bolshevik concept. He dropped the traditional view on the final victory of socialism as the concerted action of the advanced European countries, an idea he himself had repeated a few months earlier. Instead, he announced his own popular political platform:

not only the revolution but also the building of socialism would be possible in backward, peasant Russia. In his *Problems of Leninism* at the end of 1924, Stalin declared:

We can build socialism . . . [because] we possess . . . all that is needed to build a complete socialist society, overcoming all internal difficulties . . . by our own efforts . . . without the preliminary victory of the proletarian revolution in other countries . . . It is no use engaging in building socialism without being sure that we can build it completely . . . that the technical backwardness of our country is not an insuperable obstacle to the building of a complete socialist society. (Stalin, 1976: 211–12)

The concept of "socialism in one country," though without a theoretical argumentation, was a powerful slogan. Bolshevism was combined with nationalism, and the destiny of the revolution was left in the hands of Russia. Stalin offered his leadership to its realization. In the mid-1920s, especially after 1927, European and Chinese revolutionary attempts were all defeated. Russia, indeed, remained alone. Stalin's "socialism in one country" was attractive for many, but lacked a practical program for its realization. The only program available for reaching rapid industrialization and catching up with the West was, paradoxically enough, the one of his rivals and the opposition, Trotsky and Preobrazhensky. The unscrupulous Stalin eliminated his rivals and expelled the Left opposition from the party. He forced them to emigrate (Trotsky), sent them to prison (Preobrazhensky), and, in the end, ordered their murder. Achieving his goal, he cynically "borrowed" the program of the Left opposition and "nationalized the revolution."

The practical realization of "socialism in one country" was forced capital accumulation, industrialization, and the destruction of the market economy. The private economy, which was partly rehabilitated with the reconstitution of a mixed economy during the NEP years, was again eliminated at the end of the 1920s. From 1925, a "quiet" strangulation of the private sector began: the supply of raw materials was strictly limited, and surcharges on transportation (50–100%) were introduced for private traders and entrepreneurs, while an amendment to the criminal code (Article 107) brought in severe punishments for "evil-intentioned" price increases. Private trade declined from 42% of the total commerce in 1925–6 to 5.6% by 1930. In that year, private trade was banned and became the "crime of speculation." Employment of labor also became illegal. The role of the private sector in the Soviet economy declined from 54% to 9% between 1925–6 and 1932 (Nove, 1992: 33–4).

Box 4.1 Dnieprostroi

Dnieprostroi, the construction of a gigantic hydroelectric station on the river Dniepr between 1928 and 1933, was a turning point in Soviet history. During the debates in the mid-1920s, Trotsky and the Left opposition urged rapid industrialization, but Stalin and the majority of the Bolshevik Party rejected it and advocated a more gradual and balanced economic development policy. Around the end of the 1920s, however, Stalin changed his mind. Having eliminated his Left opposition, he took over and imposed policy in the most ruthless way. The starting signal of Stalin's industrialization drive was the construction of the Dniepr Dam.

It was, actually, not a new idea: the concept was first floated in 1905. Soon after the Bolshevik Revolution, Lenin initiated an ambitious plan of electrification of the country, the GOELRO Plan. In Lenin's interpretation, electrification would create the technological base for modernization. Planning began in 1920. In 1925–6, Trotsky headed the Dniepr Dam planning commission, and already dreamed about an industrial complex connected with the new energy resource. The first scheme was accomplished by 1926. The construction of the dam required an investment of roughly 200 million rubles and was expected to create a hydroelectric power station with a capacity of 230,000 kilowatts and an annual production of 1.2–1.3 billion kilowatt-hours. American experts, headed by Colonel Hugh Cooper, builder of the Wilson Dam and power station, were invited, and at last the Central Committee of the Communist Party made a positive decision in November 1926. By the summer of 1927, more than 10,000 people were at the gigantic construction working in parallel on both sides of the river. The entire country watched and followed the news of progress on the project. It became a symbol of modernization and economic independence. It was the first time that American technology was introduced in peasant Russia.

During the construction, the planned capacity of the power station was increased to 530,000 kilowatts, more than twice the original plan. The Fifteenth Party Congress and then the Planning Office discussed the use of cheap electricity in 1928–9 and decided to build a huge iron and steel works in Zaporozhye and Krivoy Rog, as well as an aluminum works and a chemical complex. The power station was connected with the Donbass, a rich coal and iron field, and became the main vehicle of forced industrialization during the first Five-Year Plan. In five years the gigantic power station and the new industrial complex were in operation.

The construction heralded a new age, especially since parallel gigantic construction projects were initiated: the Trans-Siberian railway, connecting Russia with undeveloped Central Asia, Kazakhstan and Western Siberia, a prerequisite for the industrialization of Siberia; and the Volga-Don Canal, serving transportation and irrigation of huge areas. The country of illiterate *muzhiks* emerged as an industrial giant. Meanwhile, a forced, brutal collectivization of agriculture uprooted millions of peasants and led to the imprisonment and murder of millions. Many peasants worked at the great construction works as slave labor. Stalin, nevertheless, proudly declared in the early 1930s that his country, due to the "great construction works of communism," had become industrialized. Economic preparation for the coming war began.

Stalin began his industrialization drive in 1927–8. In the spring of 1927, groundbreaking for the enormous Dniepr hydroelectric project signaled a new era of rapid industrialization. The old, influential Bolshevik leaders, Stalin's former allies against Trotsky, rejected the about-face: the majority of the Fifteenth Party Congress voted down the program of rapid industrialization. In the spring of 1929 Bukharin denounced "the policy of the feudal-military exploitation of the peasantry."

Stalin did not hesitate to turn against his former allies, now dubbed the Right opposition. They were dismissed from the party leadership and soon accused of fictitious crimes, including treason. Finally, in the hell of purges and show trials, they were all killed in the 1930s. Stalin, fifty years old in December 1929, became the unchallenged ruler of Bolshevik Russia at the head of the new political economic system. Between 1928 and 1934 Stalin realized his "second revolution," an unprecedented terror regime. The so-called Shakhty show trial of 1928 against "bourgeois industrial specialists" and those which followed between 1934 and 1938 were only the tip of the iceberg: the terror destroyed the entire well-to-do peasantry. The "liquidation of *kulaks* as a class" physically eliminated around 10 million people. Even more were uprooted from the countryside and enrolled in gigantic industrial investment projects. The Soviet Union became a despotic police state and behind the shield of dictatorship and terror, the collectivization of agriculture and "ultra-industrialization" campaigns were launched. Private peasant farmers were forced into collective farms: in 1928, private farmers cultivated 97% of the land; by 1930, more than half of them were pushed into collectives; and by 1936, 90% of peasant households were collectivized. The central goal of the Stalinist economic regime combined rapid catching up with the advanced West and preparation for war. Stalin summarized this in February 1931:

One feature of the history of old Russia was the continual beatings she suffered because of her backwardness. She was beaten by the Mongol khans . . . by the Turkish beys . . . by the Swedish feudal lords . . . by the Polish and Lithuanian gentry . . . by the British and French capitalists . . . All beat her because of her backwardness . . . We are 50 or 100 years behind the advanced countries. We must make good this distance in 10 years. Either we do it, or we shall go under. [In 1933, he added:] We could not know just when the imperialists might attack us at any moment . . . The Party could not afford to wait . . . It had to pursue the policy of accelerating development to the utmost. (Stalin, 1976: 528–9, 599–60)

From December 1927, the First Five-Year Plan was under constant preparation. Several drafts were prepared and the targets always increased. At last, in the spring of 1929, the Five-Year Plan of National Economic Construction of the USSR, a three-volume document of 1,700 pages, was accepted. The astonishing plan projected an increase of industrial output by nearly two-and-a-half times by 1932. The production of investment good branches increased by nearly four times. Three new industrial centers were created in Central Asia, Siberia, and the Far East. The industrial labor force and urban population doubled. Russia marched toward the realization of the goal of self-sufficiency, as *Pravda* declared in September 1927, the "absolutely right policy, guaranteeing us economic independence" (Carr and Davies, 1974: 867).

Forced, planned industrialization policy was a deformed bastard of the Enlightenment: while it rejected and defamed the humanistic essence of Enlightenment, it inherited a belief in changing history for the good through social action. Economic growth, regardless of its cost, became the absolute value and goal. History's most ruthless and in many respects most effective modernization dictatorship was established. Economic nationalism became dominant in its most extreme form. The world's first non-market economy was created. Central planning was introduced to realize the dream of a high rate of capital accumulation in a poor peasant country; agriculture and the entire population were exploited; and Russia was industrialized at a frenzied tempo.

A triumphant Stalin reported to the Seventeenth Party Congress in January 1934 that the Soviet Union had eliminated "backwardness and medievalism. From an agrarian country it has become an industrial country" (Stalin, 1976: 672). During the 1930s, as a consequence of planned, forced industrialization policy, the Soviet Union increased its per capita GDP by a unique 61% in a period when Western Europe's growth was only 8% and the world average was only 2%. Over the entire period between

Table 4.1 Catching-up process of the Soviet Union, 1900–50 (based on Maddison, 1995a)

Year	GDP/capita	%	Soviet Union in % of West
1900	1,218	82	35
1913	1,488	100	37
1929	1,386	93	28
1938	2,150	144	43
1950	2,834	191	49

1913 and 1950, instead of the moderate (37%) European increase, the disappointing Mediterranean (28%) and Central and East European (26%) growth, the Soviet Union, as with the miraculous Scandinavian performance, almost doubled its per capita income level. The world admired what happened there. While the Mediterranean and Central and East European countries lagged more after World War II than before World War I, a very backward Russia exhibited a catching-up process (see Table 4.1). Russia trebled its industrial output, while Central and Eastern Europe increased industrial output by only 35%, and the Southern European countries declined by 10% (see Figure 4.1).

In the case of Soviet Russia, the miraculous growth from the early 1930s on was the result of concentrated efforts, based on a regime of modernization dictatorship, which forced capital accumulation and social mobility, educational revolution, central planning, and war preparation – in other words, a consistent policy and institutions of rapid growth.

From an isolated Soviet system to the Soviet bloc

In the summer of 1941, Hitler attacked the Soviet Union and in a few months nearly conquered the European half of it. That winter, however, the Nazi *Blitzkrieg* collapsed at the door of Moscow. In a year, the Wehrmacht suffered a devastating defeat at Stalingrad. The Soviet army began its counter-offensive, liberated the occupied Soviet territories, and, in the summer of 1944, reached the borders of neighboring Central and Eastern European countries, partly occupied by and partly allied with Nazi Germany. Between the summer of 1944 and the spring of 1945, Poland, Czechoslovakia, Romania, Hungary, and the entire Balkans were liberated from German and local fascist rule. In some cases, such as Yugoslavia,

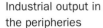

Figure 4.1

Industrial output in the peripheries

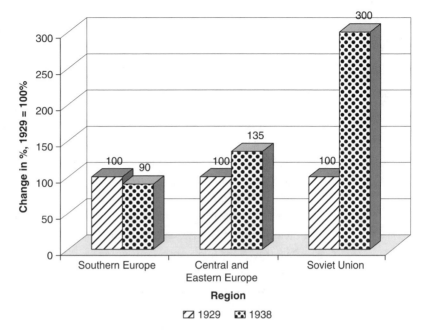

Albania, and Greece, countries outside or at the edge of the main frontlines of the war, local communist partisan forces liberated the countries when the German grip was loosened by Allied victories. In Romania, a *coup d'état* assisted liberation. In most other places heavy fighting led to the withdrawal of German and local Nazi forces, and the collapse of collaborating regimes.

In the liberated Central and Eastern Europe, especially in Poland and Yugoslavia, the population was decimated. The two most important minorities of the region, Jews and Germans, were killed and expelled respectively. Most of the prewar regimes were compromised and collapsed. Historical continuity was strongly disrupted. The region could not return to normalcy.

The international situation also changed radically. The victorious great powers sought to guarantee their own and international security and to maintain the wartime alliance. These proved to be conflicting goals. The United States cautiously kept the secret of the atomic bomb and established air and naval bases on different continents. The Soviet Union ruthlessly began building a security buffer zone along its Western border, demanding "friendly" governments in Poland and the Balkans. Britain, after Churchill's offer of a sphere of interest (the "percentage") agreement to Stalin in October 1944, bloodily suppressed the Greek anti-German communist partisan forces to safeguard its Mediterranean positions (Fontaine, 1970). When the war ended, no one was ready for further compromise. As a self-confident

President Truman said in December 1945: "I do not think we should play compromise any longer . . . I am tired of babying the Soviets" (Truman, 1955–6: 552).

However, the prestige of the Soviet Union and the communists, as a consequence of their heroic fight against fascism, reached its zenith throughout Europe. The French, Italian, and Belgian communists took part in post-war coalition governments. The Soviet Union was not an isolated country any longer but emerged from the war as a superpower. In Yugoslavia and Albania, genuine communist takeovers followed the self-liberation of the countries by communist-led partisan armies. In Czechoslovakia the Communist Party emerged strongest from the first free elections in 1946.

A self-generating cold war emerged between 1944 and 1948. Fear, suspicion, and misunderstanding generated mutual fears, suspicions, and misunderstandings, and, consequently, aggressiveness. In the cases of Yugoslavia and Albania, liberation by local communist partisan armies was immediately followed by communist takeover. In Greece, the communist forces were defeated by British troops, and then, when fighting was renewed, in a civil war. Before the end of 1945, on the strength of an agreement between Stalin and Churchill (in October 1944), Romania and Bulgaria were forced by Stalin to establish communist fellow-traveler governments. Poland, strategically important for the Soviet Union, shared this fate and the communist-led pseudo-government, the Lublin Committee, became the transitional government of the country, with the participation of some members of the former Polish government in exile. In the words of Hugh Seton-Watson, "bogus coalitions" took over a great part of the region. Only Czechoslovakia and Hungary preserved genuine coalition governments comprised various Christian, peasant, liberal, social democratic, and communist parties for a few more years (Seton-Watson, 1952).

In May 1946, Winston Churchill addressed the American public: "From Stettin to Trieste an iron curtain has descended across the continent. [Behind that] the Communist parties . . . are seeking everywhere to obtain totalitarian control" (Churchill, 1974: 7290–1). The cold war made it more important to the United States to include Germany in a united and economically flourishing camp of the West. The original plan of the Roosevelt administration in 1944–5 aimed for harsh punishment and the de-industrialization of Germany. The so-called Morgenthau Plan, prepared by the U.S. Treasury Secretary and presented to Winston Churchill during his meeting with President Roosevelt in Quebec, envisioned a postwar Germany that was "primarily agricultural and pastoral in its character" (Kimball, 1984: 317). This plan, however, was replaced by assistance and rehabilitation. In 1946, Secretary of State James F. Byrnes stated in his Stuttgart speech: "The American people want to help the German people to win their way back to an honorable place [in the world]" (Truman, 1968: 238). Because of the logic of the cold war, Germany became an important part of the Western alliance system.

In March 1947, the Truman Doctrine established the so-called containment policy by "supporting free peoples who resist attempted subjugation by armed minorities or by outside pressures." At the end of that year the Marshall Plan was officially announced. It aimed at furthering European economic reconstruction, but most of all, "to develop a bloc of states which would share similar political, social, economic and cultural values to those which the United States . . . uphold." It also aimed to force the European nations to accept and integrate Germany into this bloc (Milward, 1984: 114, 123).

On the opposite side, an opposing bloc, the Cominform, was established in October 1947 "to coordinate the activities of the communist parties" and fight "imperialist expansionism." A sneaking confrontation led to the brink of armed conflict. The victorious powers became unable to agree on the solution of the German question and each side undertook unilateral action. The Western powers created "Trizonia" from the three occupation zones, and introduced a new currency in June 1948. The Soviet Army closed the roads between Trizonia and the Western zone of Berlin. An American airlift fed 2 million West Berliners for months. Germany was separated into two states. Stalin informed his satellites: "World War III is inevitable in three to four years" (Berend, 1996: 36). In 1950, the Korean War led, indeed, to the brink of World War III.

Although a third world war was avoided, the harsh confrontation of a cold war and an hysterical arms race characterized the postwar decades until 1963, and then, in a milder form and lower intensity until the 1980s. Postwar generations, as Günter Grass noted in his fictitious twentieth-century German diary, felt themselves living in war: in 1945 his hero was skeptical: "What is peace, anyway? For us war never ends." In 1999, his hero concluded: "What I remember most is war, war with breaks in between" (Grass, 2000: 116, 273).

Europe, as well as Germany at its center, was divided and the two parts for a while were hermetically isolated. Competing East and West organizations were established: NATO versus Warsaw Pact, European Economic Community versus the Council of Mutual Economic Aid (CMEA, or Comecon). These basic political trends penetrated national policy, social, political, and economic affairs throughout Europe. Paradoxically enough, the cold war era proved to be a long period of stability and peace in Europe.

A creeping cold war and a rising conflict between the victorious allies became manifest in 1947–8. Stalin did not hesitate to "sovietize" the entire Central and Eastern European region, including the Soviet occupation zone of Germany. A Soviet bloc was created east of the river Elbe. The countries of the region were ruled by satellite communist parties, subordinated to Stalin. Comecon, a bilateral bloc-wide economic organization, and then the military alliance organization, the Warsaw Pact, hammered out the bloc as a uniform sovietized zone. Yugoslavia and Albania deliberately introduced Soviet-type regimes and non-market economies in a most orthodox way. Other countries, under the close watch of the Soviet Union and assisted by its army and agents, copied and implemented the Soviet system. Communist leaders who believed in an independent Polish or Romanian road toward socialism, such as Władisław Gomułka and Lucrețiu Patrașcanu, were eliminated. Those who acted independently and refused to subordinate themselves to Stalin, but whom he was unable to destroy, such as Josip Broz Tito of Yugoslavia and later Enver Hoxha of Albania, were excommunicated and isolated. Show trials, assisted by the Soviet secret police and realized by local Stalinist leaders, publicly confirmed the ruthless Stalinist dictatorship.

The satellite communist parties and governments obediently followed the Soviet *ukaz* (mandatory order), and in 1947–8 they introduced the same non-market, centrally planned economic regime that Stalin had arranged twenty years before. Nationalization of nearly the entire economy was realized between 1946 and 1948. It happened either in consecutive steps, such as nationalizing certain industries first followed by others, or in one swift stroke by nationalizing all companies that employed fifty or one hundred people. In 1946 Poland nationalized all enterprises employing more than fifty people. At the end of that year, nearly 90% of Albanian industry was state owned. Bulgaria carried out a general nationalization in December 1947, which created a state sector including 95% of industry. Romania accomplished the same in June 1948. In most countries, a second wave of nationalization combined with administrative state measures of over-taxation, strict restrictions, etc. eliminated small-scale private ownership as well. In Hungary, after nationalization of all companies that employed 100 employees in March 1948, a second wave expropriated small-scale companies with ten or more workers in December 1949. The non-agricultural sectors in the entire region became state owned between 1948 and 1952.

Yugoslavia introduced five-year planning first in 1947. Most of the other countries, after short-term reconstruction plans during the late 1940s, turned toward Soviet-type planning from 1949–50. The first five-year plans implemented forced accumulation and industrialization. With preferences for heavy industries, all the first five-year plans served military preparation.

Box 4.2 The Danube–Black Sea Canal

The Danube–Black Sea Canal was one of the biggest construction works in the history of Romania. The idea of building it arose in 1948 when the communist regime was introduced, and construction began the following year. During the first three years, however, altogether three kilometers of earthworks were completed. Little progress was made even though twenty-five canal administrators were tried and several were sentenced to death for "sabotage." In 1953, with only four kilometers completed, the project was canceled. It was a tremendous failure. Backward Romania did not have the technological background for the project, which used mostly slave labor and imprisoned "*kulaks*" and "enemies" of the regime.

After twenty years of silence, a megalomaniac party boss, Nicolae Ceauşescu, reinitiated the project. The Communist Party decided in June 1973 to create a hydropower and transport system across Dobrogea at the narrowest point between the Danube (Cernavodă) and the Black Sea (Constanţa). The canal shortened the route toward the Black Sea by 400 kilometers. The enterprise took on a symbolic meaning: it was advertised as the road to the future, a hallmark of modernization.

The importance of the canal was manifold, first of all for Nicolae Ceauşescu, who enjoyed the height of his power and popularity in the early 1970s. He posed as the initiator and planner, who often inspected the progress of the work, and played the role of the modernizing national hero. Meanwhile, the canal also served electrification, development of transportation, and irrigation of huge landed areas in Dobrogea. The government decided to produce domestically all the machinery and equipment needed for construction and operation. Huge excavators were produced in Brăila and began working in 1975; different kinds of heavy earthmoving machines were delivered from Braşov, locks and servomotors from Constanţa Shipyard and Reşiţa.

Probably most importantly, Ceauşescu distanced himself and Romania from the Soviet Union. He combined the most orthodox Stalinism with burning nationalism and gained popularity both at home and in the West. The canal, in this respect, played an important role. The Danube had become internationalized in the late nineteenth century. Except for the war years, this situation remained unchanged until the end of World War II. The Belgrade Convention in August 1948, dominated by Andrey Vyshinsky, deputy to Minister of Foreign Affairs Vyacheslav Molotov, nullified the 1921 international agreement which put the Danube under international control, excluded the Western powers, and took the entire Lower Danube under Soviet control. The Danube was the border river in that area between the Soviet Union and Romania, but most of the Delta belonged to Romania. At the entrance to the Delta, the old Danube port city, Galaţi, was the traditional Romanian trade and export center. Ceauşescu sought to assert Romanian control with a new waterway from the Danube to the sea, before Galaţi, avoiding the Delta area.

It took ten years to build the canal, locks, and four bridges – 300 million cubic meters of earth and rock were excavated, 3.6 million cubic meters of concrete were used to lay the concrete bed for the more than 64-kilometer-long and 7-meter-deep and 70–120-meter-wide canal. In October 1983, the Cernavodă lock opened to let water into the canal. In April 1984, the last section was also filled. Unfortunately, severe technological mistakes and bad-quality work did not allow it to be properly opened for quite a while. Nevertheless, a Romanian canal was accomplished to demonstrate modernization ([The] Blue Waterway, 1984).

That was the real meaning of putting 83–84% of industrial investments into these branches in Bulgaria and Romania. Half of the investments of the first years of the plan in Hungary directly served military purposes. "We prepared for the war," stated Mátyás Rákosi, Hungary's Stalinist leader in 1953 (Berend, 1996: 80–1).

Although the uniform plans, copying the Soviet model, aimed to reach full collectivization within five years after 1948, they failed because of the strong resistance of the peasantry. Many farmers had owned land only since 1944–5 when land reforms parceled out the big estates. Driving them into collective farms was a difficult job. Yugoslavia became independent from and even hostile to the Soviet Union in 1948–9, and terminated collectivization after 1953. After Stalin's death, a brief period of de-collectivization took place all over the region. At the end of 1958, however, Moscow ordered the resumption of collectivization. Poland refused, but the other countries complied. With the exception of Yugoslavia and Poland, collectivization of agriculture was concluded in 1960–1.

The classic Soviet institutional system of planning was also introduced. The Soviet policy of industrialization, gigantic construction works, and collectivization was subserviently copied. Until the end of World War II the Soviet economic regime was an isolated system; no other countries followed in its footsteps. After the war, the Soviet economic regime became uniform throughout the bloc. The first purges in Poland and Romania, and the split with Yugoslavia in 1948, made it clear that the Soviet Union would not tolerate any kind of independent road, such as Josip Broz Tito's independent policy and Władisław Gomułka's "Polish road to socialism."

The characteristics of the centrally planned economic system

The regulated market economy practiced state interventionism. Economic dirigisme went further and built up huge state-owned economic sectors. The Soviet-type non-market system was based on state (or state-run, so-called cooperative) ownership of the entire economy. The private sector represented not more than 3–4% of the national economy. Foreign trade became the monopoly of the state; foreign and domestic trade were separated. Producers did not have the right to sell their products abroad, but specialized foreign trade companies were created and directed by special ministries.

Although most of the agricultural enterprises were not formally state owned, collectivization created the *kolkhoz*, formally a cooperative farm with elected management and a chairman. In the first period, basically one village formed a *kolkhoz*. By the mid-1970s, the average size of a *kolkhoz* in the Soviet Union had increased fivefold to 6,000 hectares of land with about 500 member families. In reality, the *kolkhoz* was only a pseudo-cooperative with almost no independence. Management, contrary to the bylaws, was "recommended," but in practical terms appointed by party organizations. The members did not have the right to choose the form of cooperation, but had to follow the centrally decided model, the so-called *artel* type (92% of collective farms were *artel* types in 1931). A decree of July 1932 regulated the payment system for members by introducing the *trudoden* or workday unit, according to the quantity and nature of work performed. A model charter of 1935 regulated the entire *kolkhoz* management.

The most important element of state control and direction, however, was the compulsory delivery system, the quota of compulsory "sale" to the state, introduced by the decree of January 1933. Since it was not a trade procedure but a compulsory obligation, the state did not have to pay "real" market prices, but a very low price, sometimes even below the cost of production. For example, in 1932 Zagotzerno, the Soviet grain procurement organization, paid 5.7 rubles for a centner of rye, and sold it for 84 rubles. The price system was planned to exploit the peasantry: the state sold kerosene for 18 kopeks per liter in towns, but for 30 kopeks, and later 38 kopeks, in the countryside. In that year, the sugar price was increased by 95% in towns, but by 163% in villages (Nove, 1992: 207, 213).

The state procurement organizations controlled the production activity of the *kolkhoz*. *Kolkhozes* were prohibited from owning heavy machinery. Contracting with the state-owned Machine Tractor Stations (established in 1929 and abolished in 1958) was mandatory. In exchange for performing machine work, payments were made in kind. The Machine Stations also had a political supervisory role upon a *kolkhoz*. Local party and state authorities decided the sowing plans, based upon calculations by central authorities. In other words, the *kolkhoz* did not have even the right to decide its own performance. Collectivized agriculture, if formally cooperative, practically was state run.

The essence of the state-directed *kolkhoz* system was to serve state accumulation, the exploitation of peasantry, and to restructure the labor force from agriculture to construction work and industry. It faced certain limitations. The extremely low agricultural prices endangered the existence of the peasants. Low prices thus were partially compensated. Regulations were amended to provide each member family with a small private plot (0.25 hectares at the outset). The land belonged to the *kolkhoz*, but was cultivated privately, mostly using medieval farming methods. These small plots supplied families with milk, meat, lard, potatoes, and vegetables. A decree of May 1932 allowed, however, the free sale of *kolkhoz* grain, and other farm products from the private plots if procurements were fulfilled. The role of the tiny private plots, 3% of the sown area, was tremendous: they produced 40% of meat and nearly 70% of eggs, providing 45% of the income of member families, and altogether 25% of total agricultural output in the 1960s.

Collective farms in Central and Eastern Europe had to adopt the Soviet pattern during the 1950s. When collectivization was accomplished in the early 1960s, strict Stalinism was already undermined, and collective farms gained more independence. The relationship between state and collective farms was more commercialized. In some countries, as in post-1956 Hungary, compulsory delivery was abolished and the state bought the products from cooperatives. Private plots, representing roughly 10–12% of landed area, became legally commercialized and market oriented, and produced one-third of Hungarian agricultural output. Animal stock was not collectivized and half of the stock remained in private hands.

A certain part of the land belonged directly to the state as *sovkhoz*, or state farms. During the Stalinist period, their importance was limited, since the emphasis was on low-cost agriculture for the state. In 1953, state farms occupied only 10% of the sown area. After Stalin's death, and with the new agricultural policy of Nikita Khrushchev, state farms gained great importance and were expanded. Several *kolkhozes* became state farms and by 1983 they cultivated 53% of the sown area. In Central and Eastern Europe, state farms played a more important role from the beginning and owned one-fifth to one-quarter of the landed area. Most of them became experimental farms, and introduced modern methods, industrialized chicken "factories," and high-yield crops.

Based on state or collective ownership, the entire economy was subordinated to and directed by a central plan and a hierarchical Soviet state bureaucracy. The First Five-Year Plan of 1928 introduced strict central planning in the Soviet Union. In Central and Eastern Europe that happened mostly from the late 1940s and early 1950s. Yugoslavia began its first five-year plan in 1947. Czechoslovakia and Bulgaria followed in 1949, Poland and Hungary in 1950, Romania and Albania in 1951.

Formally independent legal–economic units, the state-owned companies had no freedom to perform independently, and did not act according to market laws. The Soviet planning institutions treated each company like a branch unit of a gigantic mega-trust, the state-owned national economy. The "headquarters" of the mega-trust planned and directed each branch and the branch units delivered to each other accordingly, without selling and buying. The "headquarters," in this case, was a central planning office, along with various economic ministries, which directed and controlled the economy. The companies were required to fulfill centrally set plans, produce what they were ordered to produce, deliver the products to another state-owned trade company which actually distributed the products among the consumers, including export firms, and, via the state-owned retail network, to the population. In other words, producers had no connection whatsoever with the market and were totally dependent on central orders regarding the assortment, technological parameters, and quality of their products. The same was true regarding the input: state companies did not buy on the market, but were supplied with raw material, energy, and labor according to their production plans. Input and output, all addressed by the central plan, consequently were independent of the market. State companies did not "sell" their products, and consequently did not gain profit from their activity. Their only incentive was the fulfillment and over-fulfillment of the plan, which was honored by progressively increasing bonuses for the managerial staff and also for workers. State companies also received investment funds from the state budget, based on their plans for expanding and modernizing.

The banking system was centralized and the national bank became practically the only banking institution for providing credits and controlling firms' accounts. Commercial banking was abolished, although a few specialized banks assisted the central bank. An investment bank and foreign trade bank served central planning in special areas. A network of savings banks for population savings and credit was established.

Central authorities distributed labor the way they distributed investments, raw materials, energy, and other production factors. The labor market, like all other markets, was abolished. Obligatory registration, offices of "labor mobilization," the *Służba Polsce* (service to Poland), youth brigades, and "organized recruitment" for priority sectors in Czechoslovakia created an institutional network of labor administration. Work was mandatory, and workers were not allowed to change work places. Trade unions lost their genuine function and became a "transmission" organization of the party.

The market was replaced by central distribution. This did not mean, however, that prices and money were abolished. Market prices, influenced by supply and demand, disappeared of course. All prices were fixed and changed by central authorities according to policy requirements. Wholesale or factory prices served only accounting and controlling functions. Although plan directives for a producer contained physical parameters and required the production in tonnes, square meters, pieces, etc., each product had an artificial price, set by an office. State companies (and most of them produced not just one but several products) thus had a "global production plan," which was expressed in money terms by simply adding together the "value" (or price) of various produced products.

Money and prices had a limited market function between the state and the population to regulate consumption. This sphere of "market prices," nevertheless, was also fixed. Prices were not influenced by supply and demand but regulated by central authorities, which set prices according to policy goals. Prices for staple food products, such as bread, butter, and milk, were fixed low, often lower than the cost of production. This policy made basic supply and consumption affordable for the population. The same was true for transportation, rents, baby clothing, etc. Textiles, home appliances, and other consumer goods, however, had an artificially high price, often three to four times above the cost of production to limit and curb consumption. Yet price policy was not the only way to control population consumption – central distribution was equally, if not more, important. Housing was not on the market at all, and apartments were distributed by city councils, based on applications and politically considered (even categorized) preferences and decisions. If needed, staple food products and clothing could also be rationed.

The five-year time period was short enough for planning and realizing certain central targets, and a roughly equal number of good and bad harvests could be assumed. This medium-term plan was not operational, it was supposed to translate the economic goals of the party–state into an aggregate plan. The five-year plan, then, was broken down to operational annual plans (and, for practical reasons, to quarterly, monthly, and even ten-day units). Various chapters of the plan, closely related to each other, covered the entire national economy. First a detailed production plan prescribed total production, dividing this aggregate into main sectors of production, but also listing thousands of the most important priority products. Quantities were given mostly in physical units: the number of tractors to produce, apartments to build, tonnes of coal to extract, steel to produce. The operational plan, furthermore, ordered the distribution of materials and products so that production and distribution (or "rationing" plans) were also connected.

Production and distribution were planned by the method of physical "balances" where sources and uses had to be balanced. That was the heart of central planning. These balances considered all the sources such as domestic production and imports, and uses such as input to production, exports, and population consumption. The two sides had to be balanced. To mention a rather simple example, the quantity of coal output plus imports had to cover the requirements of the energy industry, other companies (including chemical firms) which used coal as raw material, and last but not least, population consumption for heating.

The central plan also distributed labor, in numbers and wage funds, and calculated the demand of existing branches of the economy and the planned expansion in certain areas. The same was true regarding investments. An aggregate investment sum, calculated on the basis of accumulation potential and savings, was broken down according to planned development targets: how much investment was required for construction, industry, transportation, etc. Furthermore, certain high-priority projects were given a special place in these plans. Investment plans and development plans had to be in balance, not only in general terms but in terms of a time dimension: investments in the energy sector had to precede investments in processing branches; and transportation capacities had to be enlarged to be able to deliver the increased output of other sectors. Investment plans were part of a broad budgetary plan, which had to cover all the financial requirements of the various plan directives, or orders.

The central plan also detailed the exact targets for technological development, the kind of new technologies and the fields in which they would be introduced, and the sectors responsible for their production. Exports and imports required a special section in the central plan to cover domestic unavailability or shortage, and to order increased output of certain export products to be able to import others.

All the plan orders were expressed in plan indicators, strictly addressed, and compulsory for the addressees. Breaking down or disaggregating the central plan resulted in several million plan indexes, addressed to economic branches, and, at the final stage, companies. Since the fulfillment of the plan and each plan index had to be closely controlled, and corrected if necessary, this type of material planning required a huge administrative network and bureaucracy. Although administrative arrangements often changed, only the backbone of the administrative hierarchy should be described here. At the top of the hierarchy stood the party, or more specifically, its leading bodies, the Politburo and Central Committee, together with their "executive branch," the government. In the economic arena, government consisted of a set of institutions. At the top stood the political decision-making body of the Supreme Economic Council, and the Central Planning Office. This office prepared the five-year plan and the constituent yearly operational plans. The Planning Office also disaggregated the national plan for each sector of the economy – industry, agriculture, transportation, services – as well as for the main branches of each (Nove, 1977).

At that level, branch ministries assumed responsibility. Each sector of the economy was directed and controlled by a ministry. Their number and scope often changed, but separate ministries directed the energy sector, iron and steel, chemical, engineering, and textile production. Separate ministries presided over consumer goods industries, transportation, construction, agriculture, domestic trade, and foreign trade. In some countries as many as two or three dozen branch ministries received their plan, broken down from the aggregate national plan by the Planning Office. It was their responsibility to continue to divide the ministerial plan into sectors. The Ministry of Light Industry, for example, broke down its plan for the various branches under its control: textiles, leather, clothing industries, etc. In certain periods, under the ministerial branch organization, specialized sub-divisions, or directorates, were also established, and continued to dis-aggregate the plan for each of "their" factories. Finally, the central plan was addressed to each single firm. A compulsory annual plan for a larger firm often contained several thousands of compulsory plan indexes. "The plan," concluded János Kornai, "is a monumental piece of bureaucratic coordination" (Kornai, 1992: 112–14).

State companies received their plan and the required resources from above and were free from concerns about marketability, cost, quality, or whether their products were up to date. Their only incentive was to fulfill the plan. This was first of all compulsory, but also profitable because wages and bonuses were dependent on plan fulfillment. In practice, the basis for bonuses was only a single plan index, the so-called global production plan, which expressed the fulfillment of the aggregate plan in money terms. Bonuses for the managerial staff were progressive due to the fulfillment and over-fulfillment of the plan, based on the central policy goal of maximum rate of growth. Bonuses often reached one-third or even half of an annual salary. Hundreds of other compulsory plan indexes, such as the assortment and quality of production, input of labor, energy, and material, were not calculated in global plan fulfillment.

Plan indexes, which specified quality, raw material content, and assortments to be produced, were also important, especially because fulfilling and over-fulfilling the global production plan was easier if they were ignored. Companies could produce more "efficiently" by neglecting the plan regarding the variety of assortments and quality, and by using more energy and other inputs in production. The incentive system, however, was based solely on the global production index, without regard for the effect on other plan indexes. Running the economy, nevertheless, required a permanent control and correction mechanism. Plan indexes were provided for the companies by ministries, and companies had to report their fulfillment to the ministries. A detailed, bureaucratic control system required almost permanent reporting. Reports were processed and immediate direct intervention followed if necessary. Hundreds and even thousands of corrective central orders were given to companies to enable them to fulfill the plan. This kind of "hand-operated" central governance was an inseparable part of central planning – that was the only way to correct and modify economic activity if something went wrong. Since planning was a complicated cogwheel system, a failure in any cogwheel triggered a chain reaction. If coal output could not reach the planned quantity, intervention was needed to cover the planned quota with imports, and additional export goods for payment in kind.

The planning regime, strictly hierarchical as it was, nevertheless required the collaboration and participation of the firms in the planning procedure. If plans set targets too high for companies to fulfill, it was also a disaster for the ministerial and planning officials. Even if political decisions required the most extreme growth, planners had to be careful to make plans realistic enough to be accomplished. At certain stages of state socialism, planners and ministries sought to make a kind of bargain with directorate and company managers. It was an informal process, based on personal connections, and later on sometimes institutionalized as "counter-planning." Central planners demanded cooperation, and firm managers wanted concessions. Higher production targets were compensated by higher investment and more supply. Central planning, in the final analysis, was not as centralized as it appeared (Soós, 1986).

Central planning did not use compulsory plan indexes in planning cooperative agriculture. Compulsory sowing and delivery plans and the entire arsenal of state regulations and interference did, nevertheless, involve central planning in agriculture as well. Another sector where simple compulsory plan indexes could not work without modification was foreign trade. Trade with market economies was often badly needed, even though it was strictly limited and the main emphasis was on economic self-sufficiency. Even in the later years, the Soviet-bloc countries had to buy those products, raw materials, and investment goods which were not available on the socialist CMEA market. About one-third of total foreign trade was realized with free market economies. Fixed prices and planning for exports and imports was not possible because world market prices in the course of a five-year plan were unpredictable. Fixed domestic and free market prices were disconnected and the difference had to be compensated.

The centrally planned economic regime, consequently, had to find a "lock system" both to connect the non-market to the market economy and to isolate them from one another. The solution was a special "price equalization mechanism" by which foreign trade prices became hermetically isolated from domestic prices. Companies producing for export delivered their products to the foreign trade company, which paid the domestic price for it, and then sold the products abroad at a competitive price level. If the products were sold at a lower than domestic price, the "deficit" incurred by the foreign trade company was reimbursed by the state price-leveling fund. If the products were sold with a margin of profit, the profit had to be transferred to the same state fund. The mechanism worked in the same way in the case of imports. Even if imported products were much more expensive, they were sold to domestic firms at domestic prices and the difference, again, was compensated by the state fund. In the case of cheaper purchases, the foreign trade company transferred that difference to the state fund. The price-leveling system thus safely isolated and connected free-market and non-market systems like a lock between different water levels in waterways.

Safeguarding and attempts to legitimize the regime

Lack of market incentive in the bureaucratic planning and controlling system, besides propaganda and some financial incentive, basically required an iron discipline for the operation of the cogwheel system of central planning. The *ultima ratio* of plan fulfillment was the dictatorial regime and the criminalization of deviation from the plan. Legalized terror in the form of new legislation punished "diversion or sabotage" with criminal penalties, including death in the most serious cases. Deviation from the central plan without acceptable reason was punished, according to the seriousness of the damage it caused, by long prison terms, even capital punishment. The same was true for doing any harm to the compulsory delivery system in the countryside. High-ranking managers, ministerial officials, simple workers, and peasants could all equally fall victim to the draconian laws. Sentencing for such economic "crimes" was not an empty threat but an everyday reality in Stalinist regimes.

Dictatorship made it possible to pay extremely low salaries to workers and employees, or "prices" for the peasants for delivered products. Income level, consequently, was sometimes nearer to Third World than to Western standards. Since this policy did not change for a very long time, social dissatisfaction was practically unavoidable. Dictatorial regimes were, however, stable safeguards against any kind of resistance. Anyone who complained publicly was tried and punished, according to the criminal code's articles on "anti-state propaganda and conspiracy." The XIX/127 paragraph of the Polish criminal code, for example, declared that "weakening of people's power, generating dissatisfaction and unrest and the disturbance of the people's economy" might be penalized, according to the seriousness of the case, by sentences ranging from five years' imprisonment to death (Berend, 1996: 56). When revolts shocked some of the bloc countries, and national governments were unable to halt the masses, the Soviet army was ready to "save" the regime through military action. This happened in Hungary in 1956 and in Czechoslovakia in 1968, and was justified as the Brezhnev Doctrine.

The regime, though dictatorial, nevertheless required legitimization. Patriotic propaganda, with slogans to strengthen the country against "imperialist" attacks, helped legitimize the suffering of the population in the Soviet Union. Stalin's call in his 1931 speech for forced industrialization to cope with backwardness and to prepare for attack from the West gained credibility when Hitler attacked the Soviet Union ten years later. State socialism, however, could not be built with national and communist enthusiasm alone. Low incomes had to be compensated by various social measures made possible by the non-market system. The state paid five to ten times more subsidies than the population paid for rent, transportation, staple food items, children's clothing, movie and theater tickets. Subsidies followed the ancient principle of satisfying the people by guaranteed *panem et circenses*, i.e. extremely low expenditures for basic food items and entertainment.

Important welfare institutions were also introduced. The creation of a welfare state was a deliberate part of the Bolshevik Revolution. In commenting on the new party program in 1919, Bukharin and Preobrazhensky announced that all workers would be

exempt from any expenditure for social insurance . . . Social welfare benefits apply to all cases of loss of capacity for work and to all cases of unemployment . . . [for] members of workers' families in case of any worker's death . . . Allowances

are given at the full rate of a worker's earnings in case of illness, accident . . .
A life pension of 1,800 roubles per month is payable . . . In case of a worker's
death, the family receives a life pension ranging up to 1,200 roubles per
month . . . Social welfare benefits will be paid to all persons without exception who live by wage labour, and will be extended to home workers . . . and
peasants. (Bukharin and Preobrazhensky, 1969: 416–17)

The Soviet regime, and then Central and East European state socialist
systems, introduced an even broader welfare system, including guaranteed
full employment, free education at all levels to university, and free health
care to every citizen, though on a poor level. Families received a fixed
amount of child support per child. Extended maternity leave – three years
in Hungary and half a year with 80% salary in Albania – also became part
of the welfare package. Hungary, twentieth among the European countries
in per capita GDP, was twelfth in social insurance spending. Welfare policy,
as a consequence, somewhat counterbalanced Third World-level wages.

Regional integration system of planned economies

Centrally planned state socialist economic systems with their non-market
mechanisms were the most protectionist regimes of all. Self-sufficiency was
a central tenet of the Soviet Union, and even the small Central European
countries followed that pattern. None of these relatively small countries
could, however, realize self-sufficiency, especially in energy and raw materials. When the Soviet bloc was established, foreign trade became an important factor in planned economies as well. The regimes, however, sought to
be independent from the "capitalist world market" as much as possible.
All these factors contributed to the foundation of a regional integration
organization, Comecon, in 1949.

As usual, Stalin placed this pragmatic initiative on an ideological foundation by declaring the existence of "two separate, capitalist and socialist
world markets" in his *Economic Problems of Socialism* in the USSR in 1952.
Comecon, nevertheless, was mostly an umbrella over a set of bilateral trade
agreements that the Soviet Union and the other bloc countries signed with
each other. If national self-sufficiency was impossible, regional autarchy
was pursued. All member countries became economically dependent on
Moscow: instead of the previous 10–20% trade with each other, from the
early 1950s 60–75% of the foreign trade of these countries was realized
within the Comecon framework. About half of that share was Soviet trade.

Comecon, like the German-led *Grossraumwirtschaft* of the 1930s and
early 1940s, replaced market and money relations by trade in kind and a

clearing system of payment. Hard currency was thus basically excluded and the member countries paid each other with deliveries of goods. Accounting and control, similar to domestic "trade," required the use of money terms. Fluctuating prices, however, were inconvenient for planned economies. All of these countries were interested in adjusting foreign trade prices to fixed domestic prices. This made five-year planning easier and more reliable. As a consequence, during the extreme world market price increases in the years of the Korean War, Comecon introduced fixed prices in trade among member countries. The 1950 world market prices were fixed and used unchanged until 1957. It became easy to calculate all the required imports and exports from and to each other for the entire five-year period. In the Comecon framework, bilateral trade agreements guaranteed the energy and raw material supply for the small Central and Eastern European countries from the Soviet Union, while they mostly paid by industrial products, which helped Moscow ease the shortage of investment and consumer goods. On the other hand, industrial deliveries for the huge and undemanding Soviet market helped the rapid industrialization of the agrarian countries of the region, which were able to sell their uncompetitive, low-quality engineering and other industrial products in the Soviet market. In sum, according to various calculations, the fixed prices generated an extra gain of around $17 billion for the Soviet Union in its trade with the partner countries during the 1950s.

After Stalin's death gradual changes appeared in Comecon. In May 1956, at the Berlin session of the CMEA, new forms of economic cooperation were initiated: decisions were made to build and commonly finance oil pipeline and joint electric networks. Joint companies were established: the Polish–Hungarian Haldex in 1959, the Hungarian–Bulgarian Agromash and Intransmash in 1965. Nikita Khrushchev proposed planned division of labor and specialization among member countries to enable single countries to produce certain products for the entire Comecon market. In engineering, agreements were signed on thousands of products, and monopolies were granted to certain countries to become system-wide producers and suppliers of specialized products. Romania became the producer and supplier of diesel locomotives, Bulgaria of certain types of computers. Hungary agreed to produce 228 types of machines, and was given the monopoly in the production of 48 types for the entire Comecon market. Hungary ceased producing 3–5-tonne trucks and 5–7.5-tonne special vehicles, as well as an agricultural machinery line and freight cars, but in exchange it cornered the Comecon market on buses. The Ikarus Company became the world's sixth largest bus producer with a 6% share of the world's bus output. In December 1957 CMEA's Standing Committee for Chemical Industry initiated a long-run development program of cooperation to develop the flagging Soviet bloc chemical industry.

In the early 1960s Khrushchev suggested the establishment of a joint Comecon Central Planning Office to introduce system-wide planning. Resistance to the possibility of total Soviet economic domination resulted in the idea being rejected. Nevertheless, Comecon launched an aggressive campaign for cooperation agreements, especially in the engineering and chemical industries. The "Basic Principles of the International Socialist Division of Labor" was accepted in 1962, and the International Bank for Economic Cooperation, a multilateral clearing house, was founded in 1963. In April 1969, the Twenty-third Session of Comecon decided to prepare an integration program, which was adopted by the Twenty-fifth Session in July 1971 with the extremely long title "Complex Program for the Further Intensification and Improvement of Collaboration and Development of Socialist Economic Integration of CMEA Member Nations" (Ausch, 1972). Government authority was delegated in certain areas to business associations such as Intertextilmash (for textile machinery), Interatomenergo (for construction of atomic power stations), and many others. A joint Comecon International Investment Bank was established in 1971 to finance cooperative projects.

Several joint investment projects were also concluded. Among others, the Irkutsk cellulose plant, Siberian oil extraction, the 5.5 thousand kilometer "Friendship" Oil Pipeline, the 2.7 thousand kilometer Soyuz Gas Pipeline, the "Peace" Electric Power Network, and the Yamburg Gas Pipeline. By 1980, 130 multilateral agreements served cooperative industrial projects. Between 1970 and 1980 the percentage of traded machinery produced cooperatively rose from 20% to 40%. Unlike in the European Community, however, this kind of cooperation served only for letting the individual countries produce different products for bloc-wide selling. There was no cooperation in producing different parts for the same product in different countries.

Comecon modernized its price system in the late 1950s. Instead of unchanged fixed prices, prices were established for a five-year plan period. According to the new Bucharest Agreement in 1958, Comecon prices were adjusted every fifth year to the average of the world's market prices of the previous five years. After the oil crisis of 1973, when oil prices skyrocketed, the Soviet Union initiated a new price system: Comecon prices were adjusted annually to the previous five-year average world price level. Oil prices, consequently, followed the world market price increase, but were still cushioned from sudden fluctuation. From the 1960s on, the Comecon price system became advantageous for small member countries. The Soviet Union, according to various calculations, provided $30–$70 billion in "hidden" subsidies to the bloc countries (Marer et al., 1991). Comecon, which served regional integration and self-sufficiency but also Soviet economic domination of the bloc countries for four decades, collapsed together with state socialism and the Soviet Union in 1991.

The goal and balance sheet of the centrally planned economy

What were the goal and advantage of the non-market economic regime? The model was planned to create the possibility of forced capital accumulation. Poor agricultural countries with low income levels had a traditionally low accumulation rate. Poor economic and social conditions thus perpetuated backwardness. Some governments made efforts to increase exports and invest from the income, as well as assist development through state interventions. They also tried attracting foreign investments. There was, however, no effective model to remedy Russian-type backwardness until the Bolshevik Revolution. Behind the shield of dictatorship, the elimination of markets and market prices made "primitive socialist accumulation" possible. Low prices paid for agricultural products and high prices for goods sold to the peasants, the so-called price scissors, led to an unprecedented jump in the rate of accumulation in the poor peasant countries. Instead of the interwar accumulation rate of 6–8%, these countries accumulated 25–30% of their GDP during the 1950s, and 20–25% into the 1970s and 1980s.

Although investment efficiency was rather low, capital accumulation still generated rapid growth. According to Frederick L. Pryor, in the course of the three postwar decades an annual increase in the gross fixed capital investment of more than 8% was needed to achieve an annual 4–5% increase in the GDP in the state socialist countries (Pryor, 1985: 76).

High investment was combined with extremely high labor input for nearly two decades. The agricultural countries of Central and Eastern Europe possessed an almost unlimited labor surplus, and millions of the peasants were uprooted by collectivization and pushed into major construction works and industry. In the two decades after 1950, 40–50% of the agricultural labor force left the countryside. Between 1950 and 1973 the agricultural population witnessed some extraordinary declines, from 82% to 32% in Bulgaria, and from 53% to 24% in Hungary (see Figure 4.2). Female labor was also mobilized so that women's share in employment

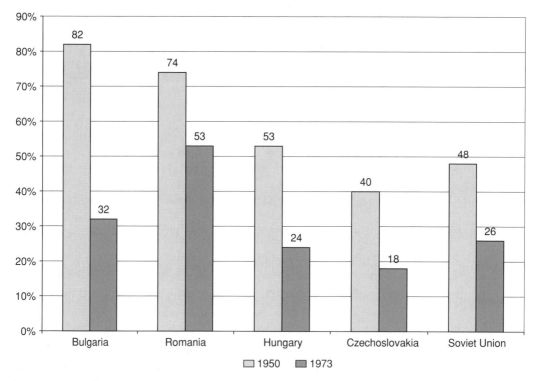

Figure 4.2 Decline of agricultural population: Central and Eastern Europe

nearly reached their percentage share in the population. As a consequence, in the 1950s the annual increase of labor input surpassed 9% in Yugoslavia, 8% in Bulgaria, and 7.4% in Hungary. Although the growth of labor input slowed down in the 1960s, it still increased by 5% annually in Bulgaria and Romania, and by about 2–3% in other countries of the region. The industrial labor force continued to grow moderately during the 1970s and 1980s (Berend, 1996: 185).

The forced investment and industrialization policy brutally and radically transformed the traditional, in most cases pre-industrial, societies of the region. Millions of uprooted peasants left the countryside and moved to urban, industrial workplaces. The previously peasant and rural societies – two-thirds to three-quarters of the population lived in the countryside before World War II – became urbanized and mostly blue-collar worker societies in the course of a single generation. For at least two decades high social mobility generated a more modern social structure. Central and Eastern Europe at last followed the Western post-Industrial Revolution social transformation.

The drastic elimination of the old elite was accompanied by a sharp economic leveling of society. The traditional hierarchical, polarized class society was replaced by a homogeneous society, which destroyed nearly caste-like social differences. Outside agriculture, 85–98% of the population became employees of a redistributive state. Income differences narrowed sharply. Although income equalization killed incentive and became a major obstacle to efficiency and effectiveness, it helped destroy the obsolete and rigid social structures and attitudes. Radical social transformation, though brutal and painful, became the most durable and, in the longer run, positive consequence of state socialist modernization dictatorship.

Industrialization, urbanization, and the social revolution from above to create a homogeneous society were assisted by the creation of a new elite, and a huge army of trained experts. This drive was later also influenced by cold war competition. Social changes thus went hand in hand with an educational revolution. The Soviet Union, which inherited one of the most backward educational systems of Europe and an illiteracy rate of two-thirds (according to some estimations 70%) of the population before World War I, gradually introduced a modern educational system. By the 1950s, the number of students attending elementary and secondary schools was three times greater than in 1914. Compulsory schooling was fixed at four years in 1930 and at seven years by 1949. Major reform in 1952 introduced a universal and compulsory ten-year education (Poignant, 1973: 91).

An extensive educational expansion characterized the Soviet Union and the Soviet bloc countries after World War II. The Soviet secondary educational system was an organic part of the ten-year-long compulsory education. In addition to the general educational system common to all students, special schools and classes served to educate gifted children in the arts and mathematics. Vocational training, after eight years of basic schooling, was elevated to the secondary school level and extended a further 3–4 years. This vocational training awarded certificates for graduates of specialized secondary schools (*tekhnikums*) and opened the door for specialized higher education. About one-quarter of the relevant age group completed this type of vocational training in 1970.

Throughout Central and Eastern Europe, as part of the building of a socialist welfare state, kindergarten and pre-school systems were established (state, community, and enterprise institutions), which absorbed more than 90% of the children between the ages of three and five years. Basic general school education lasted 8–10 years. Secondary education incorporated the gymnasium, the *tekhnikums*, and vocational training, the latter combining certain elements of basic secondary education. In a dramatic shift from the pre-World War II situation, when in the best cases about 10% of the age group attended secondary school, during the 1960s and 1970s almost the entire age group between fourteen and eighteen was enrolled. Secondary education nevertheless retained its largely practical, vocational orientation. In Czechoslovakia, 61% of the age group was enrolled in vocational schools, 20% in technical schools, and only 15% in the generally educating gymnasium in 1990 (Karsten and Majoor, 1994: 81, 124).

Higher education in Central and Eastern Europe, as in the Soviet Union, included various types of specialized *Hochschule*-type institutions for agriculture, technology, education, foreign trade, economics, etc. Evening and part-time training was introduced and became widespread. Altogether, the percentage of 18–24-year-olds enrolled in some form of higher training increased from a prewar 1–2% to 15–20%. The region began catching up with the rest of the continent in terms of numbers of young people enrolled in secondary and higher education. However, the educational system was handicapped by over-specialized, strongly practical training, which provided insufficient foundation for retraining and flexibility in further education (Berend, 1978).

Rapid growth and industrialization – reproduced backwardness

The non-market system, like the war economy, had another major advantage: it was able to realize the ambitious growth and industrialization targets. Unlike in a free market system, all the accumulation was channeled into the state's fund, and the government had the right and means to decide and invest in the fields of its preference. The entire economic history of the Soviet Union reflects this fact: agriculture was exploited, infrastructure neglected, and preference was given to industry, especially the so-called heavy industries which produced investment goods and armaments. In the early decades, more than half of total investments were channeled into industry in the Soviet Union, but even during the 1960s–1970s the figure was more than one-third. In the various Central and Eastern European countries, the interwar average of 15–18% of industrial investments was increased to 50% during the 1950s, then moderated to an average 35–40% during the 1960s and 1970s. The most reform-oriented Hungary decreased industrial investment to one-third of the total and followed a more balanced development policy from the mid-1960s (Berend, 1996). On a sixty-year average, the Soviet Union devoted 84% of industrial investment to the "heavy industries" (Kornai, 1992: 173, 175). In Central and Eastern Europe, "heavy industries" at first absorbed 75–90% of total industrial investments. That unparalleled share decreased, though it remained high, mostly above 50% until the end of the 1980s.

These, together with huge labor input, were the "secrets" of rapid industrialization, which transformed the entire agrarian Soviet Union and

Central and Eastern Europe in an historically brief period of time. Fast economic growth indeed characterized centrally planned economies. The Soviet Union and the entire Soviet bloc continued their speedy growth in history's most rapid development era after World War II. Between 1938 and 1973 Western Europe increased its per capita GDP by 260%, the Soviet bloc by 276%, and the Soviet Union alone by 282%. During the postwar quarter of a century the annual 3.9% growth of the countries with a centrally planned economy was one of the highest growth rates in history (Maddison, 1995a).

Rapid economic growth resulted in a dramatic structural change and led to historically swift industrialization. Instead of an overwhelmingly agricultural Russia where more than 70% of the labor force was occupied in agriculture, the Soviet Union emerged as an industrialized country. By 1973, only 20–25% of the gainfully occupied population worked in agriculture, while 40% worked in industry and construction. In the Soviet-bloc countries, between 40% (Czechoslovakia) and 75% (Romania) of the population was occupied in agriculture in 1950. Those figures dropped to 18% in Czechoslovakia and to 53% in Romania by 1973. In Hungary this share dropped from 53% to 24% (Berend, 1979: 243). The industrial population increased from 18% to 35% in Hungary, in some cases to 40–50%, typical for Central Europe, and from 8% to 28% in Bulgaria, typical for the Balkans. Altogether, half of the GDP was produced by industry, and only about 20% by agriculture in Central and Eastern Europe in the mid-1970s.

The "belated industrial revolution," however, suffered from devastating weaknesses. The advantages of a centrally planned economy came at a very high price. It severely lacked market information and incentives, and also entrepreneurial interests in the bureaucratically managed state economy. In the regional self-sufficient system (where three-quarters of foreign trade was conducted with other Comecon member countries) these regimes were isolated from the world market, did not have to compete in it, and were not forced to be competitive and technologically up to date.

Moreover, cold war restrictions – the so-called COCOM list of banned technology exports to Soviet bloc countries, initiated by the United States Congress in 1947 – cut off the countries from technology imports until the collapse of the regimes. At certain times export of 2,000–3,000 items, among them all the most sophisticated new technology, was banned. As a consequence, communication systems, including telephone networks, remained primitive: by the end of the 1970s only 7.4 telephone lines existed per 100 inhabitants, one-quarter of the coverage in Common Market countries, and less than one-tenth of the coverage in the U.S. The communication revolution did not arrive in the Soviet bloc. When the reform-oriented Soviet journal *Literaturnaya Gazeta* asked a few authorities' opinions in 1988 "How do you evaluate the personal computer situation prevailing here?" the reply was in unison: "It's a catastrophe . . . Our existing level of computer production varies between 1/100 and 1/1,000 of the American level." "The situation is simply parlous," stated one respondent. "The computers we produce are freaks on which nothing serious can be done." A third answer maintained: "The situation is tragic in all respects whether we look at scientific research, cultural development, or education." Computer education in the Soviet Union did not commence until 1985. Banking and other transactions were still handled manually – automatic money machines did not exist until the collapse of the regime (Judy and Clough, 1989: 6,7, 23–5, 31, 35, 47). In the late 1970s altogether 650 computers were in operation in the entire Soviet bloc.

While the centrally planned economies achieved a very high growth rate, they reproduced their inferior economic state and backwardness in a different way. State socialist countries were unable to adjust to modern world economic trends, the new technological and structural requirements of the world economy.

The Soviet Union produced pioneering technological achievements in military technology, and kept pace with the world's technology leader, the United States, in the cold war arms race for decades. In certain periods it was even ahead of the United States.

The Soviet Union exploded its first fission bomb in 1949, and the first thermonuclear fusion device in 1953. It launched its first nuclear submarine in 1958, three years after the first American nuclear submarine was ready, and years before Britain and France. During the cold war decades, the Soviet Union emerged as a main player in military technology, especially rocket and space technology. In October 1957, it launched the world's first artificial satellite, Sputnik 1, followed in 1958 by Sputnik 2, carrying a dog, Layka. The progress was breathtaking: in 1959 the Soviet Luna 2 landed on the moon and Luna 3 achieved the first circumlunar flight. In April 1961, the historic first manned space vehicle, Vostok 1, carried the first man, Yuriy Gagarin, in space. From the mid-1960s the Soviet Union initiated its Voskhod program and in April 1971 Salyut 1, the first space station, was launched, followed by five more between 1974 and 1982.

The military sector, including military technology, however, was entirely isolated from the civil economy. It functioned in a different economic regime. Salaries and various privileges (including special shops to buy otherwise non-existent goods) were incomparably better for those who worked in the military industry, which had a concentration of the best talents and experts. Cost of research and production was not an issue, and all possible resources were plowed into this sector, which spent half of the Soviet budget to compete with the United States. Military technology research and production remained an isolated enclave, which did not penetrate the civil economy. From the mid-late 1970s, because of the regime's general economic crisis, the Soviet Union was unable to remain competitive and during the 1980s it lost the arms race.

The second half of the twentieth century was characterized by a new technological, communication, and service revolution. The Soviet Union, and countries based on centrally planned economies, could not keep pace with this transformation. Industry, though it made great progress, followed the technological and structural requirements of the early twentieth century: tremendous efforts were made to build traditional iron, steel, and early twentieth-century engineering branches. In the 1960s, Czechoslovakia, the most advanced of the Central European countries, consumed three times more fuel than France and five times more than the United States per 1,000 tonnes of industrial output. To produce one tonne of pig iron, Hungary and Poland used almost 40% more coke than Sweden. The steel input per $1,000 value of engineering products was 2–4 times greater than in Germany, Austria, and Italy.

The Soviet bloc could not match the dramatic structural changes of the West: agricultural occupation, which declined to 2–4% in Western Europe by the early 1990s, remained 15–25% in the former bloc countries. Employment in industry, 25–35% in the West, preserved its roughly 40% share in Central and Eastern Europe. During these decades the so-called service revolution in the West led to a 66–75% employment of gainfully occupied people in services, while only 30–40% worked in services in the bloc countries, and only 25–30% of investments were channeled into services. Services were the fastest growing sector in the West. Although some economists debate the role of services in productivity increase, since service productivity was growing slowly, services helped productivity increase in agriculture and industry and actually contributed significantly to the increase in productivity. In Central and Eastern Europe, however, this sector was mostly sacrificed for industrialization and remained far behind (Berend, 1996: 183–98).

As a consequence of the lack of modern specialization, weak services, and relatively backward technology, productivity increase was rather moderate (see Figure 4.3). In this respect, it is interesting to compare the levels of productivity in the Western European, Mediterranean, and Central and Eastern European countries. While the former represented spectacular progress, the centrally planned economies reached only very slow development. Between

Figure 4.3 Labor productivity in the peripheries, 1950–73 (USA = 100%)

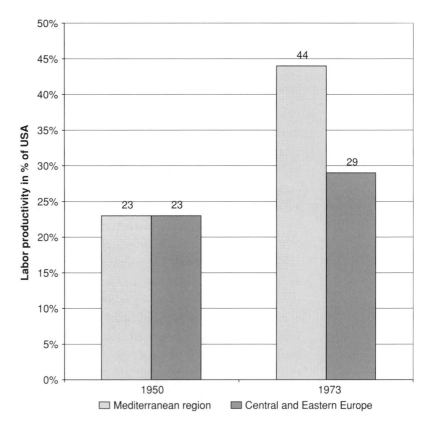

1950 and 1992, the level of labor productivity (GDP per worked hours) of the West European (4.4-fold increase) and Mediterranean countries (6.2-fold increase) was impressive, whereas the Central and Eastern European economies, including the Soviet Union (2.8-fold increase), made very little relative progress. The Mediterranean countries, roughly on the same level as Eastern Europe in 1950, surpassed it by more than two-and-a-half times by 1992 (see Table 4.2). Rapid growth thus led to the industrialization of Central and Eastern Europe, but reproduced an obsolete industrial structure, technological base, and productivity level.

The centrally planned economy was an efficient model for backward agricultural countries in the early stage of industrialization, since it offered a high rate of accumulation and rapid growth. Labor resources, however, dried up when surplus manpower shifted to the industrial sector.

Furthermore, demographic trends changed and population growth slowed down, stopped, and then decreased. During the first half of the twentieth century birth rates, though declined, remained much higher than in the West, roughly 22–24 births per 1,000 population, although in certain cases, such as Yugoslavia, the Soviet Union, and Poland, they were as

Table 4.2 Labor productivity (produced value in 1990 dollars per hour),
(Maddison, 1995a: 249)

Region	1950	1992
West Europe*	5.82	25.30
Mediterranean**	2.89	17.97
Central & Eastern Europe***	2.41	6.83

* 11 countries; ** 4 countries; *** 6 countries

high as the traditional 26–30 births per 1,000 (Mitchell, 1976: 648–54). The
average number of children per woman, however, declined from 2.5–4.0
in the early twentieth century to about 2.0–2.5 by mid-century.

From time to time the Soviet bloc countries and governments introduced harsh policy measures in an attempt to halt the decline in fertility.
In the Stalinist Soviet Union a most conservative legal and propaganda
effort sought to strengthen families with several children. Common-law
marriage, which gained legal status in 1926, was outlawed in 1944, sanctions were introduced against divorce (1935, 1944), and abortion became
a major crime (1936). Child allowances, maternity leave, and public institutions (maternity homes and kindergartens) were aimed at encouraging
more children in the family (Geiger, 1968: 69, 72, 93–5). Similar measures
were introduced in other Soviet bloc countries during the early 1950s.
Abortion was considered a major crime in Stalinist Hungary. In Nicolae
Ceauşescu's Romania, a fanatical attempt to increase the population led to
the ban of any kind of contraceptives, even condoms, during the 1970s–
1980s (Kligman, 2000).

As in some other, non-dictatorial countries, all renewed attempts to
reverse the declining birth rate failed, in spite of the crudest state interventions and the most pressing ideological advocacy.

The short-term effects [of this kind of measures] often produced great differences in the number of children born, but the long-term effects were
evaluated as modest . . . [C]ompleted family size per woman grew by . . .
0.2 children in Romania, [while in Hungary and Czechoslovakia the decline
in family size was checked, but no increase was achieved]. (Kamarás et al.,
1998: 247)

Thus, policy interventions, because of the changing, more urbanized lifestyle, severe housing shortages, and extensive recruitment of female labor, were unable to stop the population decline. By the end of the century, female employment in Central and Eastern Europe was nearly equal to the percentage of females in the population, reaching 40–50% of all employed people. In 1960, only 20–30% of married women participated in the labor force, but by 1980 their levels of participation in many countries reached 50–75%. The highest rate was found in the Soviet Union (87%) (ILO, 1980).

At the end of the century, the number of children per family in Central and Eastern Europe dropped to 1.5. By the 1990s, Russia had only 1.4 children per family. These figures were lower than reproduction levels, and this led to a population decrease during the last decades of the century. The so-called "extensive" development project based on high investments and labor input worked for only a short while. The new technological revolution also rang the death knell of the rigid bureaucratic system.

Reform attempts that failed

The only route to further development would require retooling the growth paradigm to a so-called "intensive" model of productivity growth, based on improved services and technology. Some of the ideologically less rigid regimes of the region recognized these new requirements and began reforming accordingly. The death of Stalin in March 1953 was followed by the New Course, or "Thaw," as Ilya Erenburg's short novel dubbed the process. Georgi Malenkov, the handpicked successor to Stalin, however, did not want so much to change the system as to moderate extremism in both the Soviet Union and its satellites. Accumulation and investments were slowed: from 25% to 13% of GDP in Czechoslovakia, from 28% to 21% in Poland, and from 25% to 15% in Hungary between 1953 and 1955. Mild policy corrections led to the increase of consumption from 66% to 77% of the material products in Bulgaria between 1952 and 1955. Industrial investments were moderated and agriculture and services gained. Agricultural investments nearly doubled in Albania and Hungary in the mid-1950s (Brus, 1986: 45–7). The de-Stalinization trend under Nikita Khrushchev, who replaced Malenkov, opened some small windows of opportunity. But most of all the independent Yugoslav route after the 1948 split with Stalin, and the Polish and Hungarian revolutions of 1956, marked turning points in the history of Soviet-type communism. Reforms followed and became unstoppable in some countries, the pioneer among them being Yugoslavia. The backbone of the transformation began with the introduction of the system of workers' self-management. The law of June 1950 made firms independent of central authorities, and managed by elected workers' councils. Search committees selected directors of the companies. During 1952 compulsory plan directives and physical allocation of resources were abolished. Prices were partly freed that year as well and the companies performed in a market environment. Foreign trade was also liberalized. The December 1951 Law on Planning abolished compulsory plan indexes along with de-aggregation of central plans. Collectivization of agriculture was halted and the peasants were allowed to disengage from collective farms. By 1958, less than 2% of the arable land belonged to cooperatives. The labor market was also freed; moreover, workers gained the right to go abroad to work and a reformed type of state socialist economy was introduced. An informal party–state control, however, preserved several central elements of the Soviet-type economy. Notably, the national bank was preserved as the only source of credit, and with it the low level of self-financing (only one-quarter of total investments).

A second wave of economic reforms in Yugoslavia began in 1965. Prices were further liberalized and nearly half became free market prices. Limited foreign trade liberalization was also tried. Most importantly, the banking system was reorganized: commercial banks were established and the national bank regained its role as a central bank in a market economy. Enterprises gained independence, central planning was made redundant, and annual operational plans disappeared (Brus, 1986: 170–1).

The Yugoslav alternative made a strong impact on Central and Eastern Europe. Hungary prepared a major reform after the 1956 revolution. An expert committee, appointed by the new Kádár government, recommended the marketization of the economy. The Gomułka regime radically reformed agricultural policy. Reform in the Yugoslav direction became attractive, and reform initiatives were generated by crises in other countries as well. In Czechoslovakia, for example, economic growth stopped in 1961–3 and signaled the malfunction of the system. The reform wing of the Communist Party prepared a reform plan, which was accepted in January 1965. Planning was preserved, mostly by central, state financing of major investments, but compulsory plan indexes and physical allocation of materials were replaced by market incentives. According to the new rules, firms would profit from their sales and profit would influence wages. The price system was changed so that only 15% of the prices (mostly for energy and raw materials) remained fixed, while 80% could fluctuate between certain limits. In 1967, when the reform was introduced, nearly half the investments were financed from company profit (Šik, 1968). The reform became an introduction to a bold political change, the Prague Spring of 1968, but the entire reform trend was brutally halted by the Soviet and Warsaw Pact military intervention in August that year, which drove Czechoslovakia back to anti-reform conservatism.

Under strict Soviet oversight, reforms in Central and Eastern Europe were cautious and partial. When the critical year of 1956 generated a shift toward reform, an international meeting of the communist parties in Moscow in 1957 sharply and ominously denounced the "revisionist attempts to undermine socialism by means of the market" (Brus, 1986: 99). After a successful partial reform in Hungary during the 1960s, the Soviet daily, *Pravda*, openly "forecast" that the Central Committee of the Hungarian party, at its next session in three months, "will increase the role of central planning and state control" (*Pravda*, 1972). The official Hungarian party newspaper reported the Soviet criticism in December 1973, and listed the "friendly concerns: how can there be a planned economy if there is no compulsory plan for companies? How can the role of the state be asserted if over half the investments are in companies' hands?" (*Népszabadság*, 1973). The first Hungarian and Polish reform attempts failed, and the Czechoslovak experiment was crushed.

Reform continued nevertheless and grew more successful in Hungary. The bloody 1956 revolution and the first armed revolt against Soviet domination, despite its defeat, gave more room for maneuver. Although retaliation was bloody, the regime, in the long run, could not return to Stalinist practices without risking a new political explosion. Besides, Leonid Brezhnev trusted in the subservient loyalty of János Kádár in political and international affairs, and the Soviet Union tolerated a measure of domestic economic reform in Hungary. The country could even join the General Agreement on Tariffs and Trade (GATT) in 1974, and the International Monetary Fund in the early 1980s. Although a major reform initiative of 1957 was dropped under pressure from the Soviet Union, the regime of János Kádár returned to reform in the mid-1960s.

The market-oriented reform, coded "New Economic Mechanism," was accepted in November 1965. Soviet-type planning was abolished. A resolution of the Hungarian Socialist Workers Party stated:

The system of plan indicators, the breakdown of the annual national economic plan through the ministries to the companies must be abolished. Companies themselves should draft their . . . working programs, and these need not even be endorsed. But we must at the same time cause the active role of commodity relations and of the market to unfold. (MSzMP, 1968: 306)

The price reform of January 1968 created a mixed price system: 70% of wholesale (factory) prices of raw materials and energy sources remained fixed, but 78% of the prices of finished industrial products became free market prices. At the time of the reform's introduction, half of the consumer good prices became free as well. A more radical price reform followed in 1979–80 when the so-called international competitive price system linked domestic and world market prices. Around the end of the 1980s, most of the prices were already market prices in Hungary. State companies worked in the market environment and earned profits. That became the source of investments and wages. An alternative, strictly regulated market system was cautiously in the making in Hungary between the early 1960s and late 1980s.

Marketization, which made good progress, was followed by a "hidden" privatization, especially from the early 1980s. By the mid-1980s roughly 80% of construction work, 60% of services, 35% of agricultural production, and 15% of industrial output were provided by private companies (Berend, 1990; 1996). Until 1988–9, however, even the Hungarian reforms remained the most radical half measures.

Poland, after Gomułka's return to power during the October 1956 revolution, followed the Yugoslav pattern and returned to private farming. With 3.5 million private farmers, only 58% of the labor force worked in the socialist sector of the country by 1960 and hardly more than 60% of national production came from the state sector. In a highly counterproductive way, however, the compulsory delivery system and an exploitative price scissors were preserved. Peasant farmers could not buy machinery; Polish agriculture declined into a state of semi-subsistence farming. The result was worse than collectivization (Korbonski, 1965). Some measures were introduced to decentralize the economic system. A few major industrial firms gained direct export rights, but the price equalization mechanism was preserved and excluded market interests in exports (Matejka, 1986: 263, 266). Polish reform plans proved abortive in the Gomułka era during the 1960s and then took a wrong turn under Edward Gierek in the 1970s. The country then followed the Hungarian path of reform after the dramatic political and economic crisis of the early 1980s, under the shield of a party–military regime. When Soviet control was loosened in the era of Mikhail Gorbachev's *glasnost* and *perestroika* during the second half of the 1980s, Hungarian and Polish reforms were reinvigorated.

Had a more flexible Soviet regime emerged in time, could it have accommodated more courageous experiments and reforms? The chance for reform, even if historically not excluded, was definitely missed in Central and Eastern Europe. Most of the countries of the region, post-1968 Czechoslovakia, Romania, Bulgaria, and Albania, did not even attempt reforms. The Gorbachev regime liberalized the political arena, but *perestroika* hardly touched the economic realm. These regimes rigidly maintained an only administratively corrected Stalinist model. Post-Stalinist Central and Eastern Europe preserved the basic characteristics of the non-market, centrally planned Stalinist economic system until the end of the 1980s. This led to the dramatic decline and collapse of the regime.

Crisis and collapse

The turning point in the history of the Soviet bloc occurred in 1973. The rapid growth of the previous decades ground to a halt: in 1979 and 1980, Hungary's growth rate declined to 1.6% and 0.0%, respectively. Poland, in 1981 and 1982, experienced a severe decline, −10% and −4.8%, respectively. Yugoslavia's annual growth dropped to 1.2%, 0.6%, and −1.1% in 1981–3. During the second half of the 1980s, Romania experienced an annual growth rate of 0.7%; the economies of Yugoslavia and Poland stagnated at an annual rate of 0.5% and 0.2%, respectively (*World Tables*, 1990). Growth policy on the Soviet bloc had to be changed and the economy slowed significantly – from an annual 3.9% increase of the GDP between 1950 and 1973 to 1.2% between 1973 and 1989 (Maddison, 1995b: 97).

All these changes were seemingly connected with the oil crises of 1973 and 1980. The real causes, however, lay much deeper. The reserves of the extensive import-substituting industrialization dried up around the late 1960s. The isolation of the region eased somewhat and foreign trade with market economies became more important. Most of all, during the 1970s and 1980s a new technological revolution became manifest. The appearance of the personal computer in 1974 signaled and symbolized the turning point. The old leading export branches of the world economy became obsolete. Sales of their products depended on major price reductions. Raw material prices, on the other hand, increased. The countries of import-substituting industrialization could not follow the technological revolution and experienced devastating trade deficits. In the case of the Central and Eastern European countries' terms of trade, the ratio of export to import prices declined by 20–30% in the first five years after 1973. These countries were thus required to export one-fifth to one-third more in exchange for the same amount of imports (*Statistical Yearbook 1990*). The lack of adjustment to build up new modern export sectors, based on the achievements of the technological revolution, exacerbated the crisis.

This kind of peripheral structural crisis, the inability to follow modern economic transformation, was known in economic history. It was similar in Central and Eastern Europe and in Latin America. Moreover, what happened between the 1970s and 1990s had happened in the region twice before, during the 1870s–1890s and then again in the 1920s–1930s. The Schumpeterian structural crisis (the decline of the old and the rise of the new leading sectors as a consequence of technological revolution, which generated a 1–2 decade stagnation or slow growth) of the 1970s–1980s hit the state socialist countries especially hard; they were unable to introduce competitive new technology and export sectors.

If there was no escape forward, was there no escape at all? As in the structural crises of the late nineteenth and mid-twentieth centuries, the region found a "rear" exit. Instead of restructuring their economies the countries preserved their obsolete economic branches and export sectors. Most of their export items, non-convertible to Western markets, were sold in the isolated regional Comecon market. This market was safe and had been highly protected since the 1950s. The historical pattern was familiar: escape from the structural crisis of the 1870s–1880s had been guaranteed by the strongly defended markets of the multinational Habsburg and Romanov empires. In the interwar period the regional alliance system, Hitler's *Grossraumwirtschaft*, offered the same exit possibility. In the same way, the countries of the region once again found a temporary exit from their difficult situation within the Soviet-led Comecon system. The non-competitive market, characterized by permanent shortages and fixed state-managed trade agreements, served to defend the economy of the Soviet bloc. Trade with free market countries was marginal. State socialist governments were thus slow to react to the changed international economic environment. Even reform-oriented Hungary's government stated in 1973:

that the crisis disrupting the capitalist world economy would leave Hungary and other socialist countries unaffected – that it could be halted at the frontier. Quite a long time passed before it was realized that the factors behind the crisis were not temporary or rooted in political sanctions. (Berend, 1990: 232–3)

The Polish reaction was much worse. The administration of Edward Gierek attempted to overcome economic troubles by implementing a policy of hyper-investment. During the first half of the 1970s, investments increased by 133%, and in 1975 Polish GNP increased by 29%. In other words, Poland further expanded obsolete and outdated industrial sectors of its overheated economy. The country, energy exporter before, became energy importer by the end of the 1970s (Berend, 1996: 229).

A delayed reaction, however, had the most serious consequences, due in part to the erosion of Comecon trade. An unavoidable slowing down

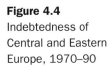

Figure 4.4
Indebtedness of
Central and Eastern
Europe, 1970–90

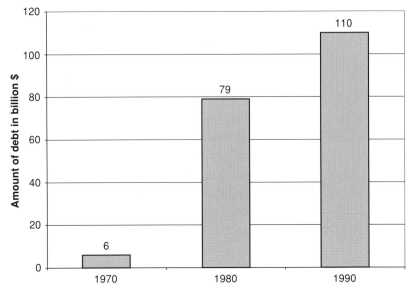

of production increased shortages and pushed countries onto the open, free trade world markets. Some of the countries of the region, looking to gain more independence from the Soviet Union, deliberately weakened economic ties and built closer connections with the West. Poland, Hungary, Romania, and Yugoslavia developed important trade relations with free market countries and reduced trade with the Soviet-led Comecon countries to 40–50%. During the second half of the 1970s, more than half of their foreign trade became free market trade. As relatively small countries, their economies were sensitive to fluctuations in foreign trade: in the mid-1970s, exports made up nearly half of the Hungarian and 20–25% of the Polish, Yugoslav, and Romanian GDP. Under such conditions, a lack of adjustment led to a rapid and dramatic further deterioration of the terms of trade (*Statistical Yearbook 1990*).

Since Comecon member countries followed the traditional fast-growth policy, they were faced with an ever-increasing trade deficit. The situation required a quick fix, which had seemed easy during the 1970s. The financial market was flooded with cheap "oil dollars," as a great portion of the tremendous extra income of the oil-exporting countries was exported. It was easy to borrow and the governments of the region did not hesitate to do so to bridge the deficit gap with loans. As a result, almost all of the region's countries fell into a trap of indebtedness. Between 1970 and 1990 the net amount of debts in the region increased from $6 billion to $110 billion (see Figure 4.4). Hungary's $20 billion debt was approximately two times greater than the value of the country's exports, but Poland's $42 billion debt was five times higher than its export income. Debt service consumed 40–75% of the hard currency income of these countries. Meanwhile, cheap credits were no longer available and interest rates rose to 14–16%. New credits, however, were needed to repay the old ones. From the $20 billion in debt incurred by Hungary, only $4–5 billion had been invested. Poland, Yugoslavia, and Bulgaria became insolvent and requested a rescheduling of their repayment. Romania tried to escape from the indebtedness trap as Nicolae Ceauşescu, the paranoid dictator, ordered repayment by cutting domestic consumption drastically. By 1985, electricity consumption had dropped to 20% of 1979 levels. The stores were empty and the cities and homes darkened. Romania, a broken and destroyed country, managed to repay its debts by 1989, a few weeks before a bloody uprising erupted and the dictator was executed (Berend, 1996: 230–2).

The crisis in Central and Eastern Europe was extremely severe. Besides the economic slowdown, quite a few Central and Eastern European countries which had fixed prices under state socialism started to lose control over inflation. In 1989, the rate of inflation in Poland reached 251%. Yugoslavia fell into a period of hyper-inflation measuring 1,269% (*Transition Report, 2001:* 61).

The temporary achievements of state socialism, such as rapid growth, full employment, and an improving standard of living, were undermined and the regime could not cope with the deepening crisis. Even the elite lost confidence that a solution could be found. Economic crisis generated a political crisis and the regimes lost their temporary legitimacy. This led to the peaceful collapse of state socialism in 1989–91.

This one-and-a-half-decade-long economic crisis did not come to an end with the collapse of the regime. In fact, it became more serious. First of all, the traditional "rear" exit from the structural crisis was no longer available. After 1989, the countries of the region lost the protective shield of the safe and non-competitive Comecon market and were forced to enter the world market and compete with advanced industrialized countries. Furthermore, the countries of Central and Eastern Europe now had to compete not only in the world market but in their own domestic markets, which in the cases of Poland and Czechoslovakia had been opened abruptly to outside competition. In Hungary, this process took three years. The crisis, in effect since 1973, not only continued but deepened further during the early 1990s.

Between 1989 and 1992–3, GDP and output across the region declined 25–30% and 30–40%, respectively. Unemployment jumped from zero to 13–20%, and in crisis-ridden Yugoslavia, in some of its successor states, to 40% and 50%. Agriculture collapsed throughout the region, in some cases falling to half pre-1989 levels (Survey, 2000: 42). Although the march toward Europe and the shift from plan to market was, in the long run, the only promising road after the failure of state socialism, the transformation itself has caused a partially unavoidable "transformational crisis." In addition, economic policy during the first part of the transition period was in many respects mistaken, especially in its unnecessarily sudden jump from a centrally planned to a laissez-faire economy, from an entirely state-owned to a privatized economy. A regulated market instead of a self-regulating market, a mixed economy with a restructured and efficient state-owned sector, at least initially, would have generated a more organic transition from plan to market. Such an approach, however, was immediately rejected.

Hyper-inflation shocked quite a few countries in the region in the early 1990s. It soared to nearly 600% in Poland in 1990, reached more than 1,000% in Estonia and Lithuania, rose to more than 1,500% and 1,200% in Russia and Ukraine, respectively, and to more than 9,000% in Yugoslavia in 1992. Bulgaria struggled with an inflation rate of more than 1,000% in 1997. Nevertheless, from 1997 to the end of the century, the average rate of inflation in the region dropped to single digits, though it remained high in several countries: more than 20% in Russia, 46% in Romania, and 60% in Belarus (Survey, 2000: 92; *Transition Report, 2001:* 61).

As a consequence, living standards declined sharply in the first half of the decade, especially for the more vulnerable layers of society. During the early 1990s, the number of people living in poverty increased from less than 3% of the population in 1987–8 to more than 25% by 1993–5 (Ellman, 2000: 126).

In Central and Eastern Europe, the sharp decline of the early 1990s was followed by a gradual recovery, which practically ended at the close of the twentieth century. In the successor countries of the Soviet Union, the decline continued until 1996. While in 1989 the Soviet GDP per capita had reached 49% of the Western level, because of the sharp decline until 1996 it reached, in 2000, only 24% of the Western level (see Figure 4.5). Due to a lack of or insufficient adjustments to current technological–structural requirements, economic decline was not halted in some of the countries of the region until the end of the century. While Central Europe started recuperating after 1993, and from less than 80% of the 1989 level reached nearly that level by 2000, the successor states of the Soviet Union continued declining from 70% of the 1989 level to hardly more than 50% of it (see Figure 4.6).

The fast economic growth thus was followed by stagnation or decline during the last quarter of the twentieth century (see Tables 4.3 and 4.4).

Figure 4.5 Per capita income in the Soviet Union (in % of Western Europe)

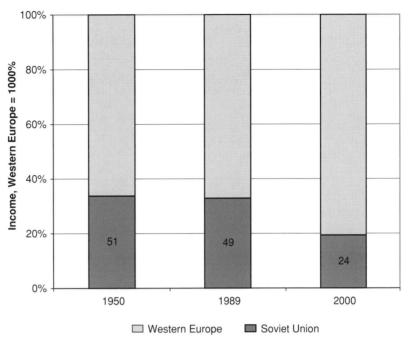

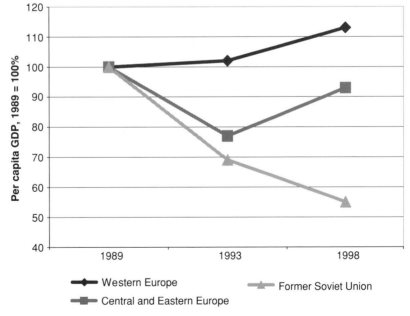

Figure 4.6 Per capita GDP in Central and Eastern Europe and the former Soviet Union, 1989–98

Table 4.3 Per capita GDP 1989–98 in million 1990 international dollars (Maddison, 2001: 330)

Year	Central–Eastern Europe		Former Soviet Union		Western Europe	
1989	5,902	100	7,078	100	15,880	100
1993	4,526	77	4,907	69	16,149	102
1998	5,461	93	3,893	55	17,921	113

Table 4.4 GDP growth rate per capita (Maddison, 2001: 186)

Region	1950–73	1973–98
Central–Eastern Europe	3.79	0.37
Soviet Union and successors	3.36	−1.75
Western & Mediterranean	4.8	1.78

Table 4.5 Per capita GDP in % of the European Union (Survey, 2000: 175)

Country	1950	1989	2000*
Albania	–	18	15
Bulgaria	29	35	24
Czechoslovakia*	69	65	56
Hungary	50	57	53
Poland	48	38	40
Romania	24	39	27
Yugoslavia*	29	45	24
Soviet Union*	51	49	24

* And successor states

The gap between Central and Eastern Europe and the West increased in that short period of time from a ratio of nearly 1:3 in 1973 to disparities of 1:4 in 1999.

The gap between East and West was wider in the early 1990s than ever before in modern history (see Table 4.5). Technological–structural modernization, imported capital and know-how, however, led to significant improvements from the early to mid-1990s. Poland and Hungary showed the highest increase in labor productivity, roughly 10% per annum from 1992 onward. The changes in post-1989 Central and Eastern Europe, in sum, triggered an adjustment process of the former centrally planned state socialist countries and they, in turn, have become closely connected with an integrated Europe. Adjustment, however, has been uneven and far from complete. The Western rim of the region, eight countries, were accepted by the European Union by 2004, while two-thirds of the region continues to lag far behind late twentieth-century economic modernization. The centrally planned economy, though transitorily rather successful, terminally failed at the end of the century.

CHAPTER 5

Mixed economy and welfare state in an integrated post-World War II Western Europe

After World War II a new, consistent economic system emerged in Western Europe. Although most of the elements of the new regime had already been "invented" and applied in one of the previously introduced economic systems, they were realized in a new combination and accomplished with various important new elements that, at last, resulted in a new economic system.

One of the most characteristic elements of the postwar Western regime was state interventionism. It was not new at all, having been a feature of the regulated market economy of the interwar decades. It became, however, more complex: besides counter-cyclical measures, subsidies, foreign trade and monetary regulations, it led to the foundation of a strong state sector of the economy, often combined with planning.

The mixed, mostly private, partly state-owned economy was not a novelty either. Economic dirigisme operated a peacetime mixed economy in interwar Italy and Spain. Postwar mixed economies, though in different ways and scope, also used state planning. This method, again, was already familiar in the interwar Soviet non-market system, and, in some way, in countries of economic dirigisme. After World War II, nevertheless, state-owned companies followed the targets of state planning and worked in an undisturbed market economy. Planning was not forced upon them but served competitiveness and the introduction of new high-technology sectors.

The most peculiar novelty of the postwar West European economic regime was the integration of all these elements of state intervention into a free trade system. State regulations, interventions, and state-owned sectors of the economy during the interwar years served self-sufficiency and were combined with protectionist measures. In contrast, in postwar Western Europe free trade policy led to the creation of an integrated market and then a European Union of countries with regulated and mixed economies, and welfare states.

Postwar mixed economies operated in a corporative social environment. The interventionist state initiated the cooperation of labor unions and employer organizations to avoid permanent conflict, wage struggles, and the emergence of a wage–price spiral. A corporative system also characterized interwar economic dirigisme, but was dictated by a fascist–authoritarian dictatorship. In postwar Western Europe it worked in a democratic system, based on deliberate cooperation of independent partners. Wage and profit moderation monitored by the state led to higher investment activity and growth. The state was not an external entity but an integrative, stabilizing factor, part of the productive and self-correcting market economy (Blaas and Foster, 1992: 1–2).

The state also played an active part in institutionalizing social peace through the creation of the welfare state. Nationalization and welfare originally belonged together in socialist programs and policies. "The socialists are marked out by their belief that the public authorities should take on the responsibility . . . by controlling production . . . and the distribution of incomes" (Clegg and Chester, 1953: 4). Welfare policy thus had a long history and was not a postwar novelty. Its roots also went back to non-socialist, paradoxically even anti-socialist politics of late-nineteenth-century Bismarckian Germany, and turn-of-the-century Scandinavia. It also belonged to interwar regulated market systems, including economic dirigisme and the centrally planned economy. All of these regimes introduced welfare institutions. Postwar Western Europe built up a welfare state by implementing and further developing welfare policy and institutions, and creating an incomparably mature and complex welfare system with a reinterpretation of citizen rights. Besides political rights, employment and social security were considered to belong to the natural rights of citizens. The West European welfare system introduced social security for the middle class, but also methods toward equalizing income distribution by counterbalancing low wages with state services. The rich Western welfare state with its redistributive mechanism, social, health care, and educational policy successfully counterbalanced sharp income disparities, promoted equal opportunity, and added an economic factor to democratic institutions. It also added a social factor to economic growth.

All these elements borrowed in some form from previous experiments, and economic regimes were reworked into a peculiar postwar synthesis of experimented European economic systems, which constituted a new model.

Postwar international regulations

The immediate postwar effort to create a stable international system resulted in a solid base for the new economic regime by transforming the international framework of the European economy. The post-World War I period was characterized by a leadership vacuum: Britain had already lost its nineteenth-century position as economic leader and the United States had more or less emerged as the successor, but neither of them recognized the new situation and continued to act according to past patterns. Britain was no longer able to control international economic processes and the United States did not attempt to do so. Consequently, the world economy fell into disorder, international cooperation disintegrated, and individual countries sought to solve problems on their own. The Great Depression and World War II, however, taught a bitter and unforgettable lesson. It had, maintained Sidney Pollard, "a decisive traumatic effect on the whole of European development thereafter." Pollard notes that European leaders showed

a determination not to repeat the mistakes . . . and deliberately set about their task of formulating an international political and economic order which carefully dealt with all the sources of conflict, instability, and grievance. (Pollard, 1986: 278, 310)

The victorious great powers, led by the United States, took steps to build a more stable, regulated international economic system before the war ended. In July 1944, forty-four nations gathered at Bretton Woods, New Hampshire to establish a stable international financial system. The International Monetary Fund (IMF) was created for a multilateral system of payments, based on convertible currencies and stable exchange rates. With a period of readjustment until 1952, member countries decided not to use exchange restrictions or discriminatory measures. They agreed to pay contributions – 25% in gold or dollars, 75% in national currency – according to a quota system, based on their GDP and role in international trade. Originally the United States had a quota of nearly $2.8 billion, Britain $1.3 billion, China $550 million, France $450 million, and India $400 million. Voting rights in the Fund's deliberations were awarded according to the amount of the contributions, which meant that the U.S. would lead. From IMF sources, member countries could get assistance in overcoming short-term balance-of-payment difficulties. In the case of long-lasting financial troubles, devaluation of local currencies was accepted.

When the international monetary system was functioning smoothly, the Fund's operations were expected to be of minor importance. On the other hand, should imbalances and other difficulties arise, the Fund was considered to possess ample reserves and sufficient powers to return the world monetary system to normalcy. (Kenwood and Lougheed, 1971: 240–2)

The Bretton Woods agreement also contained the foundation of the International Bank for Reconstruction and Development, or World Bank. Member countries raised $10 billion in loan capital, which was increased to $21 billion by 1959. The main function of the World Bank was to aid reconstruction and give loans to governments and private enterprises for development projects.

Europe's new monetary system was also strengthened by the implementation of the Marshall Plan, and the foundation of the European Payments Union and the Bank for International Settlements. They helped maintain multilateral liquidity, corrected intra-European payment imbalances, and effected automatic clearing of deficits.

The United States also championed a system of international free trade. In 1947, the U.S. government invited twenty-seven countries to Geneva for negotiations to reduce tariffs and other trade barriers, such as import quotas. When the multilateral General Agreement on Tariffs and Trade (GATT) was signed by twenty-three countries in October 1947, 123 sets of negotiations covering 50,000 items were incorporated into the agreement. Tariffs were curbed. In less than fifteen years, the number of member countries increased to seventy, which together represented 80% of world trade. As a consequence of GATT's continued efforts, especially the Dillon Round (1961) and the Kennedy Round (1967), progress was made in reducing tariffs and eliminating quantitative (quota) restrictions. Interwar protectionist economic nationalism was eliminated. In the Western half of the continent, at least, all of these international institutions knit the countries together into a system, which came to be termed "Western."

The most significant international institution building was the economic integration of Europe. It began spontaneously and immediately at the end of the war. One of its forerunners was the Benelux tariff community (established by the London Convention of the governments-in-exile in 1944) with common external tariffs from 1948. The customs union was transformed into an economic union in 1958. In the summer of 1947, France suggested a Benelux–French–Italian customs union. In March 1948, a French–Italian customs union agreement was also signed. The spontaneous European initiatives gained tremendous impetus in 1948 with the introduction of the

European Recovery Program, the Marshall Plan. The U.S. initiative and financial aid of 1% of the American GDP, or $17 billion between 1948 and 1952, received strong political motivation from the outbreak of the cold war. In 1947, a Committee of European Economic Cooperation was established with the participation of sixteen countries, followed by the formation of the Organization for European Economic Cooperation (OEEC) in April 1948. The OEEC worked out the reconstruction program for the continent and decided upon trade liberalization and the formation of a payment union. The concept of a "European organization," maintained Alan Milward, became an important step toward political and economic integration, "a West European government in embryo" (Milward, 1984: 70). One of the main accomplishments of the Marshall Plan, in addition to assisting reconstruction and the foundation of postwar prosperity, was the cultivation of a new spirit of European cooperation. In a major step forward, France, Germany, and Italy, together with the three Benelux countries, formed the European Coal and Steel Community in 1952. The six member countries went much further in 1957 in the Treaty of Rome, which laid the foundation for a European Economic Community of 160 million people. Within an American-led and assisted international institutional framework, the European governments were able to apply a number of other lessons of the Great Depression and the war. As Alan Milward stated:

Western Europe was reconstructed, not from the destructive consequences of the Second World War only, but from those of the catastrophic economic collapse of 1929–32 and . . . from the consequences of the First World War too . . . [including] the total political reconstruction of Western Europe. (Milward, 1984: 463, 466)

Capital formation, technology transfer, closing the technology gap, effective use of human capital, establishing the "social capability" to adopt efficient managerial methods – all these factors of economic growth are closely connected with policies established by international agreements and employed by national governments. This aspect is convincingly stressed by recent research:

A full understanding . . . of economic growth requires a subtle appreciation of the impact of policy and institutions on incentives to invest and obstacles to complete catching up. (Eichengreen, 1994: 32)

    The social, legal and political institutions, both international and national . . . are of paramount importance in explaining . . . growth. (Crafts and Toniolo, 1996: 22)

In twentieth-century economic growth, the importance of these factors is more than evident. The two thirty-year periods before and after World War II embodied diametrically opposed approaches to policy and institutions. World War I opened the floodgate for nationalist policy, which engulfed Europe, especially its peripheries. Protectionism, import-substitution, hostility, and economic warfare undermined economic ties and trade connections. The League of Nations proved impotent in restoring free trade. During most of these three decades, currencies were not convertible. Capital exports, except for a few years during the second half of the 1920s, were non-existent. Domestic market orientation and self-sufficiency as a central policy goal made impossible economies of scale and efficient investments. Competitiveness and efficiency lost their strategic importance, hindering technology transfer and catching up. A broad legal network served economic nationalism and isolation. Labor and capital were in sharp confrontation.

After World War II, Europe and the entire advanced world learned the real lessons and radically reoriented policy toward building new international and European institutions.

The intention was to undertake the task left unachieved by all after 1918. The inadequacy of the post-Versailles settlement was blamed for the economic collapse of 1929, for the National Socialist Party and for the Second World War. (Milward, 1984: 56–7)

The "European house" built on "national foundations" and among "national walls," was crowned by an "international roof" (Milward, 1984: 464). This "roof" nearly collapsed with the breakdown of Bretton Woods in 1971, but was strengthened by the Tokyo and Punta Del Este Rounds (1973 and 1986, respectively), the foundation of the World Trade Organization, and, in a stop-and-go process, gradual European integration.

The integration process was accompanied by a new social arrangement, introduced almost immediately after the war. In place of class warfare a *Sozialpartnerschaft* was established, a kind of corporative system, based on voluntary collaboration of labor unions and entrepreneurs, assisted and monitored by the state. The sentiment of social solidarity also led to the rapid rise of the welfare state in the entire Western half of Europe. Although welfare institutions had a long history going back to the late nineteenth century, a matured and international European welfare state was the product of postwar arrangements. Policy and institutions became decisive factors in economic growth.

As an important element of total political reconstruction and policy change, Europe gradually ended its centuries-long colonial rule. Colonies as sources of raw materials and cheap labor, as well as markets for industrial products from the rising European core, were key elements of the emergence of commercial and early industrial capitalism. If colonialism reached its zenith at the beginning of the twentieth century, the institution was fatally undermined during the interwar decades, and the crisis culminated after World War II. The fight against the zealous new empire-builders, Germany and Japan, led to the signing of the Atlantic Charter in August 1941 and the foundation of the United Nations in October 1945, both imbued with the principles of independence and freedom. During the war years, the colonies became more independent and developed nationalist self-identity. Paradoxically, Japanese conquest undermined well-established colonial regimes such as the Dutch rule in Indonesia, as did the British military victory over Italy in East Africa. Charismatic leaders such as Mahatma Gandhi, Sukarno, Ho Chi Minh, and others electrified mass movements. The cold war generated a deadly competition for allies: colonies and other dependent countries could choose to turn for assistance to one of the rival superpowers, strengthening their relative positions and opening windows of opportunity. The subordinated regions and countries also began organizing themselves: Third World conferences were held in Bandung, Indonesia, in 1955, and in Accra, Ghana, in 1958. The United Nations became a strong forum for de-colonization.

Some colonial powers collapsed soon after World War II. The Italian and centuries-old Dutch colonial empires disappeared in a few years. Ethiopia, Somalia, Libya, and Indonesia became independent. Belgium, owner of the Congo, eighty times larger than Belgium itself, offered independence to the African country a year after riots took place in 1959. British policy wisely muted its resistance to landslide independence movements, and instead sought to reorganize the empire as a Commonwealth of free countries. Hindu India and Muslim Pakistan became independent in 1947; Ceylon and Burma followed the next year. British colonies gained independence peacefully between 1957 and 1967. France tried to reorganize and modernize its colonial empire with the postwar establishment of the French Union of overseas departments, overseas territories, and associated states. The colonies, however, demanded independence and France withdrew from Syria, Lebanon, Tunisia, and Morocco. Defending national *gloire*, consecutive governments launched devastating wars in Indochina until 1954, and then in Algeria between 1954 and 1962. After a humiliating defeat France was forced to recognize Vietnam's independence. Independence for Cambodia and Laos followed. President De Gaulle offered independence to all of the colonies that did not want to join the French Community, a kind of commonwealth he established. The French colonial age ended. Between

1961 and 1964 the Portuguese colonies of Guinea-Bissau, Mozambique, and Angola revolted. The debilitating wars further impoverished Portugal and triggered a domestic revolution in 1974, which precipitated the end of Portuguese colonial rule. "In less than twenty years, from 1945 to 1965, nearly all the European possessions in Asia, Africa, and Indonesia had gained independence." The remaining colonies followed during the 1970s and 1980s, and the colonial era symbolically ended with Britain's handover of Hong Kong to China in 1999 (Jordi, 2003: 45).

The process of de-colonization was accompanied by increasing complaint among the metropolitan countries. They considered colonialism to be a major financial drain, which might hinder domestic modernization and represented more a burden than an asset. The colonies, so essential in the early history of capitalism, lost their importance. It was not only the consequence of expensive colonial wars and unavoidable investments to improve the local situation; it was basically a function of economic–technological change in postwar Europe. The new prosperity was based on a new technological regime and, consequently, a new division of labor. An ever-increasing trade connected the highly industrialized countries and led to close cooperation and division of labor among developed industries – instead of trade with developing countries, the bulk of trade connections bound the member countries of the European Community (see Chapter 6). Meanwhile, the advanced core itself became an agricultural exporter. Most of these developments took place in the 1950s and 1960s, in parallel with de-colonization, when the West European powers turned to internal modernization.

Economic integration and the rise of the European Union

Europe's development trend was closely connected to the spectacular and unparalleled economic integration process of Western Europe, which became a determining factor of inter-European economic restructuring. The renewal of the old continent was invigorated by the creation of a European Community, and then the formation of the European Union. Europe had learned from its twentieth-century tragedy, the two world wars and the killing of tens of millions of Europeans, the interwar decades of hostility, the rise of extremist regimes, and tragic economic crisis.

The creation of an organized international monetary system, state intervention, and social solidarity were the consequences of those hard lessons. Another, equally crucial lesson was provided by the counterproductive, and, at the end, economically and politically self-destructive interwar economic nationalism. The lesson was so bitter and so closely connected with the tragedy of interwar hostility and the wars that political parties and governments, the adult generations with personal experiences of the past, learned it well and determined to put an end to economic isolationism.

The need for cooperation among European nations, the dream to build free, interrelated economic and political systems to avoid bloody confrontations, was in the air after World War II. Altiero Spinelli and Ernesto Rossi, two Italian Leftist resistance fighters, in an internment camp on Ventotene Island in Italy in June 1941, wrote their manifesto about a dreamed rearrangement of postwar Europe, based on cooperation and integration:

The multiple problems which poison international life on the continent have proved to be insoluble . . . It will have to be recognized that European federation is the single conceivable guarantee . . . of peaceful cooperation . . . All matters . . . would find easy solution in the European federation. (Spinelli and Rossi, 1995: 5)

Various spontaneous movements emerged: a "United Europe Movement" in Britain, a Catholic–socialist "United States of Europe" movement in France, a "European Bund" movement in Germany. The first government agreements also signaled the transformed atmosphere: the governments of the Netherlands, Belgium, and Luxemburg, still in exile in 1944, agreed to the creation of a Benelux customs union with no internal duties and common external tariffs, introduced from 1948. The Scandinavian countries established their Joint Nordic Committee for Economic Cooperation with a similar goal. Although that was not realized, partial results such as legislative cooperation followed, and resulted in coordinated citizenship laws.

Spontaneous European movements mushroomed after the war. From 1947–8, a new initiative gained momentum: a Western alliance against the Soviet danger in cold war confrontation. In those years, the wartime alliance collapsed. The ministers of foreign affairs could no longer find a common platform. The Berlin conflict of May 1948, the unilateral Soviet decision to close the roads from the Western occupied zones of Germany to West Berlin, and the year-long U.S. air bridge to feed 2 million people in the Western occupied zones of Berlin, brought the danger of World War III within arm's reach.

Winston Churchill, in a speech at Zürich University in September 1946, warned:

We must re-create the European family in a regional structure called, it may be, the United States of Europe . . . If at first all states of Europe are not willing or able to join the union, we must nevertheless proceed to assemble and combine those who will . . . France and Germany must take the lead together. (Churchill, in Nelson and Stubb, 1998: 11)

Lord Dahrendorf, in his lecture at Harvard University in 1996, looked back to Churchill's speech with admiration: though German crimes are not forgotten, argued Churchill, "there must be an end to retribution . . . there must be . . . a blessed act of oblivion." Dahrendorf added: "Let us remember 19 September 1946, a mere sixteen months after Germany's total defeat!" (Dahrendorf, 1996: 4). In reality, Churchill was not a soft-hearted, generous elderly man, but the most foresighted first cold-warrior, who in 1946 advocated conciliation with Germany and European integration based on a French–German alliance.

The emerging new Western world leader, the United States, within a few months became the organizer of West European collaboration. The main vehicle was U.S. assistance for cold war allies, and military aid for Greece and Turkey in 1947. President Truman addressed Congress in March that year:

The seeds of totalitarian regimes are nurtured by misery and want. They reach their full growth when the hope of a people for a better life has died. We must keep that hope alive. [Economic and financial aid can assure] economic stability and orderly political process. (Truman, 1955–6: 106)

Secretary of State George Marshall, in his speech at Harvard University in 1948, announced an aid package of $13 billion, the Marshall Plan to assist European reconstruction, and the "return to normal economic health." Allen Dulles clearly stated in his contemporary booklet, *The Marshall Plan*, that it was

not a philanthropic enterprise . . . [but] the only peaceful course now open to us which may answer the communist challenge . . . The United States is the only country outside of Europe which can really help to bring the European states together in a union which will be a defensive bulwark against the advance of communism. [The idea of] a United States of Europe is not a project of mere dreamers. (Dulles, 1948: 111, 116)

Hitler's forecast, made in his bunker in 1945, came true:

With the defeat of the Reich, there will remain in the world only two Great Powers capable of confronting each other – the United States and Soviet Russia . . . [B]oth these Powers will sooner or later find it desirable to seek the support of the sole surviving great nation in Europe, the German people. (Hitler-Bormann, 1961: 107)

The U.S. administration worked diligently on bringing Western Europe together, necessitating European cooperation and joint management of the American aid. For the administration of the Marshall Plan, "the first lesson in economic cooperation" (Urwin, 1995: 43), the OEEC was established, which initiated the foundation of the European Payments Union of sixteen countries in 1950.

Western collaboration became crucial. In December 1947 an International Committee of the Movement for European Unity was formed, and in May of the next year the Congress of Europe was organized in The Hague with the representation of sixteen countries. The Treaty of Brussels in 1948 with the participation of Britain, France, and the Benelux states created the Western European Union to promote collaboration in economic, social, cultural, and defense issues. In May 1949, the Treaty of Westminster established the Council of Europe with ten member countries, increasing to eighteen by 1965. The Council formed the Consultative Assembly in Strasbourg and the Committee of Ministers with veto rights for each nation's representative. Konrad Adenauer initiated the idea of a European Army in 1949, trying to consolidate Germany's place in a cooperative military power. Jean Monnet, one of the most influential French politicians in postwar years, and later René Pleven, premier of France, suggested the formation of a European Army to counterbalance the U.S. plan of German rearmament. The so-called Pleven Plan suggested a common European minister of defense and the foundation of a European Defense Community in 1950. This plan failed, partly because of Britain's refusal to become involved, but mostly because the U.S. administration established the Western military pact, the North Atlantic Treaty Organization (NATO), in April 1949, with German and, most importantly, U.S. participation.

Although the U.S. initiative to hammer out a stable Western alliance against the Soviet bloc became one of the mainstays of postwar West European cooperation, several genuine European initiatives strengthened this process. The postwar generation of leading politicians with all of their shocking experiences, regardless of their political orientations, became the architects of collaboration. The Christian Democrat German Konrad Adenauer, the Italian Alcide de Gasperi, the Frenchman Robert Schuman, and the Belgian socialist Paul-Henri Spaak nurtured different national goals but worked together to create a safer Europe.

The French political elite's main goal was to pacify Germany, its dangerous neighbor which had attacked France three times in seventy years. A united Europe, in the French plans, could also strengthen its position as a "Third Force" between the two superpowers which emerged from the war, the United States and the Soviet Union. The French political elite's ambition was to lead in this Third Force.

Postwar Germany, defeated, humiliated, and burdened by the horrible legacy of Hitler, sought to regain dignity through rehabilitation as an equal member of the family of European nations. Germany was ready to sacrifice important elements of its sovereignty to achieve this. Italian conservatives and socialists, meanwhile, looked for European cooperation against a frightening internal danger of communist takeover. The small Benelux countries, victims of war whose neutrality had been violated, sought to find a secure, large European alliance.

In this political environment, a small practical step catalyzed huge changes. Chancellor Adenauer, aiming to avoid both occupation of the Saar region, one of Germany's industrial centers, under de facto French protectorate, and dismantling of the Thyssen Steel Works, one of the giants of the German military–industrial complex, proposed international control over certain German industries. As he suggested to French Foreign Minister Robert Schuman in August 1949, it "could become the starting point for a major international cooperative effort in the area of coal and steel, and . . . would be highly desirable in terms of Franco–German understanding." In March 1950, Adenauer publicly discussed the possibility of an economic union between France and Germany (Fontaine, 1970: 43). Probably at the same time Jean Monnet, in connection with his work on French planning, prepared a huge design, a supranational coal and steel community, and presented it to Robert Schuman. In May 1950, he took the initiative and invited Adenauer to Paris:

The gathering together of the nations of Europe requires the elimination of the age old opposition of France and Germany. [Schuman proposed to] place Franco-German production of coal and steel as a whole under a common higher authority, within the framework of an organization open to the participation of the other countries of Europe. (Weymar, 1957: 324)

In April 1951, six countries – France, Germany, Italy, and the three Benelux countries – signed an agreement (with 100 articles) and established the European Coal and Steel Community for fifty years. They agreed to eliminate tariffs, import quotas, and other discriminative measures and to provide subsidies for the coal and steel economy. They also vowed to establish by 1958 a common market with a common price policy and central regulation of production. Jean Monnet presided over a supranational High Authority of nine members, who had no right of veto. Decisions were made by (weighted) majority vote. Disputes were decided by an established Court of Justice (with seven members), which was also responsible for controlling the legality of the decisions of the High Authority. A Special Council of Ministers, however, was added to moderate supranationalism, although it was bound to the decisions of the High Authority and had no veto right

Box 5.1 Jean Monnet

Jean Monnet was a merchant, banker, financial advisor, sometime civil servant, but never a leading statesman. His fingerprints, nevertheless, are all over the modern transformation of twentieth-century Europe. He was probably the most important European statesman of the century.

Born in 1888 in the small French township of Cognac, to a peasant–merchant family, Monnet was not a promising child. He did not like academic studies, could not memorize poems, and was considered retarded. He never developed a real interest in books, and never became a good writer or speaker. At the age of sixteen he was withdrawn from school by his parents, who decided to teach him the art of making and selling cognac. How he emerged as a pan-European statesman is a miracle.

Monnet spent a few years in the family business in London and Canada. In the 1920s he joined the American Blair Investment Bank's Paris office. During the 1930s he spent five years in China establishing a Development Bank to finance railroad construction.

The turning point in Monnet's life was World War I, when his interest in Europe took hold. Monnet developed the idea that international control and supranational authority were needed to run an efficient allied war economy. He convinced the French prime minister to cooperate with Britain, and became a member of the Inter-Allied Maritime Transport Council. As a consequence of his outstanding service, after the war he was appointed undersecretary general of the newly established League of Nations. He soon learned that the League had no power to realize ideas. Monnet resigned in 1922 and went back to the family business.

This modest man, whose only passion was a long morning walk, and who told his friends that if condemned to death he would ask for a last meal of a can of sardines, French bread, and butter, seemingly had no personal ambitions. When Paul-Henri Spaak nominated him for president of the sixteen-member group of OEEC countries, he turned it down. Monnet wrote to Spaak that he would only accept a job which helped create a real Federation of the West. He told friends that he was interested in only one thing: Europe, and working for its integration.

Monnet was an interesting mix of a visionary and a man of deeds, who was able to realize his ideas. He had a special skill to reach goals through consistent effort, making friendly connections with influential people and then influencing them, but never in the foreground. In a way, he was a born *éminence grise*, but an unusual sort who did not serve others but used them to realize his ideas.

His obsession with coordinated European action, triggered during World War I, led him again to public service before and during World War II. In 1939 he sent a memorandum to the French prime minister suggesting the organization of an inter-allied coordination organization. Daladier sent the proposal to his UK counterpart Chamberlain. The British liked the idea, the Coordinating Committee was established, and Monnet received the joint French–British appointment to run it. He tried convincing Churchill to create a French–British Union and common citizenship. After the collapse of France, in 1940, Churchill sent Monnet over to the United States, strongly isolationist at the time, to press for economic mobilization in support of the war effort. With friendship and collaboration with intimate Roosevelt aides such as Harry Hopkins, he became a major contributor to Roosevelt's "Victory Program," the mobilization of the American economy, and the Lend-Lease project. According to John Maynard Keynes, Monnet shortened the war by a whole year.

After the war, Monnet was instrumental in promoting economic modernization via planning, which formed the postwar West. He convinced de Gaulle to introduce a modernization and reconstruction plan for the provisional French government. De Gaulle signed the decree in December 1945 and established the Commissariat du Plan headed by Monnet, who invented a working combination of market and plan, contributing to the successful postwar Western mixed and regulated economy.

The war strengthened Monnet's commitment to European integration. In 1950 he convinced French Foreign Minister Robert Schuman to initiate the unification of West European coal and steel industries under a supranational authority, combining the most important strategic industries of the former enemy countries. The "Schuman Plan" was realized and Monnet became the first president of the six West European countries' supranational High Authority. Some weeks later, he convinced René Pleven, French prime minister, to initiate a European Defense Community with a supranational army. The Pleven Plan proved ahead of its time, and failed. Monnet did not stop. He turned to the Dutch and Belgian foreign ministers, J. W. Beyen and Paul-Henri Spaak, to realize his two new ideas: the European Atomic Energy Community (Euratom) and more comprehensive integration of the six countries through the Common Market. He always worked behind the scenes, using his reputation and close connections with de Gaulle, Adenauer, Brandt, and Kennedy.

Monnet turned sixty-eight years old when his dream was realized and the European Community was established in Rome in 1957. Jean Monnet, the "Father of Europe," died in 1979 at the age of ninety.

either. A Common Assembly with seventy-eight members gained a kind of controlling role. The first major steps toward an economic integration of Europe were taken (Collins, 1975; Urwin, 1995).

In the early 1950s, there was serious discourse on a rapid further integration of the Coal and Steel Community. A draft of a European Political Community, presented in Strasbourg in March 1953, and discussions on the Defense Community as a foundation of a federation, promised radical further progress toward integration. The Dutch government made a new proposal to transform the Coal and Steel Community into a general common market agreement and to abolish all tariffs among the member countries in ten years. While plans for political and military integration failed, the economic integration plan gained momentum and in mid-1953 experts began working on the plan. Jean Monnet and Paul-Henri Spaak proved indefatigable shepherds of further integration. In June 1955, the foreign ministers of the six countries met in Messina, Italy, to discuss the creation of a common market. Preparations by the Intergovernmental Committee, headed by Spaak, and negotiations continued between the summer of 1955 and the spring of 1957. As a result, in May 1957, the six countries with roughly 180 million inhabitants – Britain was also invited but declined – signed the Treaty of Rome and founded the European Economic Community (EEC) and the European Atomic Energy Community (Euratom), which functioned until 1967 as a separate organization.

The agreement with its 248 articles, 4 annexes, 13 protocols, 4 conventions, and 9 declarations established a set of leading bodies: a quasi-executive Commission with nine members and the German Walter Hallstein as president. The Commission became the engine of the Community, fueled by the "constitutional" right to recommend policies and new initiatives. The Commission represented the European idea rather than individual national governments and was assisted by a huge bureaucracy in Brussels, soon consisting of twenty-three departments or Directorates General and 13,000 staff members. The Council of Ministers, meanwhile, represented governments of the member countries and had to reach unanimous decisions as each member had a right of veto. In practice, the Council became the legislative body of the Community and held specialized meetings of the ministers of foreign affairs, finance, and agriculture. The Council also had permanent representatives. From 1975, the European Council – consisting of heads of state and prime ministers – was added to the leading bodies to discuss main political trends twice a year.

The Parliamentary Assembly initially was formed with 142 members, delegated by member countries' parliaments. From 1979, assembly members were elected to 567 seats. Apart from certain controlling tasks, the Parliamentary Assembly had only a consultative role and was not a legislative body. Its only real decision-making power was over the small budget of the Community, created from 1.2% of the GDP of the member countries. From this modest budget, three funds were financed: a Social Fund, responsible for job creation, a European Investment Bank to assist economic growth, and a Development Fund assisting the associated French overseas territories. The rights of the parliament were expanded in the 1980s to include a veto and to appoint an ombudsman.

Among the leading bodies, the Court of Justice, with seven judges, acquired an important role to rule on the legality of the activity of the Community and on disputes among member countries. The Court, as a supranational institution, made far-reaching decisions. In 1964, it decided that national laws were subordinated to Community laws, and in 1979, the "Cassis de Dijon" ruling ordered the mutual recognition of national standards. Unlike the Coal and Steel Community, the European Economic Community was not a supranational institution. Each member country preserved its sovereign right to decide. Unanimous regulations, however, were binding on all member states, and "directives," "decisions," and "recommendations" also influenced government policy.

The European Community set the ambitious plan to abolish obstacles to free trade by gradual tariff and quota reductions over twelve years. The first step, in 1959, was a tariff reduction by 10% and an increase of import quotas by 20%. The unspoken dream of a federal Europe was the main motivation behind the free movement of labor and capital, assistance to backward regions, wage and market parity, a common agricultural and transportation policy – a complete economic integration in preparation for later political unification. As Hallstein declared in 1964, national sovereignty was considered an obsolete doctrine of "yesteryear."

Some governments, however, never shared the view of supranationalism and unification and did not want to go further than economic integration and close cooperation. From time to time, further progress was checked by political opposition from the member countries, such as France under Charles de Gaulle from late November 1959 when the Community was pushed back in an intergovernmental direction. The so-called Fouchet Plan presented a plan of *Europe des Patries*, as De Gaulle termed it, with permanent intergovernmental committees and summit meetings (Urwin: 1995: 103–5).

The development of the Community, nevertheless, was unstoppable and breathtaking. Various levels of integration were reached in a short period of time: by eliminating tariffs and other restrictions a free trade area was created before the deadline, in ten years; the Community also became a customs union with common tariffs against non-member countries by 1968. The elimination of restrictions on free movement of labor and capital elevated the community to the level of *economic union* during the 1970s–1980s. Trade connections among member countries multiplied: during the first thirty years of existence by twenty-three times. At the end of the 1980s, intra-industry trade in intra-Community trade of member countries varied between 57% and 83%, which illustrates how new and highly developed division of labor favored economies of scale (Swann, 1996; Apel, 1998: 95).

Additionally, in the common market of production factors such as labor and capital, trade connections were partly substituted by labor immigration and capital investment to produce goods on the spot instead of importing them from other countries. Free labor movement within the six member countries was gradually introduced after 1958, and was fully achieved after 1970, helped by mutual recognition of qualifications and diplomas and prohibition of any kind of discrimination. The number of immigrants increased from 2 million to 4.9 million between 1960 and 1973. (Counting the other West European countries – later members of the Community – the numbers increased from 3.3 million to 6.6 million.) Intra-European Community migrants represented 3%, extra-Community immigrants another 3%, of the labor force by 1973. Immigration was permanent. From the Mediterranean 4–19% of the labor force moved to the north. Labor mobility, however, soon lost that momentum (Molle 1994: 200–1).

Although in the first period labor moved toward existing jobs in richer member countries, this trend was soon reversed and jobs went to the labor force. The common market for free movement of capital encouraged this development. Although the Treaty of Rome already declared the principle of liberty of capital movement, it was only partially realized and several restrictions remained, especially regarding shares, stocks, treasury bonds, and bank accounts. The accomplishment of full liberalization of the capital market progressed during the 1970s, when internal direct investment flows became completely free, followed by the decision to eliminate all kinds of restrictions in 1988, which was realized by 1992. Article 73b of the Maastricht Treaty codified the prohibition of restrictions on capital movement among member states. Direct investments of Organization for Economic Cooperation and Development (OECD) countries increased by 13% per annum during the 1960s, at a rate equal to exports, but during the 1980s the annual growth of investments reached 30%, three times more than trade. Direct investments within the Community doubled every two years from the mid-1980s. Between 1985 and 1989 nearly 75 billion ECU were invested in the Community by member countries. As one analyst stated: "Jobs are indeed going to the people" (Molle, 1994: 227).

The spectacular "deepening" of economic integration went hand in hand with inclusion of new member countries, the "broadening" of the Community. Churchill established the British position toward "Europe" when he stated before the war: "We are with Europe, but not of it . . . We are interested and associated but not absorbed" (Urwin, 1995: 31). British policy, even after the war, still considered Britain as a world power, the center of the Commonwealth, and special ally of the United States. When Britain was invited to Messina to participate in the foundation of the European Economic Community, the invitation was refused.

Britain, nevertheless, applied for membership in 1958, and again in 1963, but the bid was vetoed by de Gaulle. In 1959 Britain initiated a rival institution, the European Free Trade Association (EFTA). Austria, Denmark, Norway, Portugal, Sweden, and Switzerland joined. "The Sevens," however, did not intend to go further and could not become an alternative to the European Community. At last, a new initiative in the early 1970s succeeded and Britain became a member of the Community in 1973. Because of the special British–Irish economic relationship and free trade agreement (since 1965), Ireland also joined, and Denmark, another close economic

---

Box 5.2 The Channel Tunnel

The Channel Tunnel, which opened in 1994 and linked Britain with the European continent, might be considered not only as a modern, fast transportation institution between the center of London and Paris but also as a symbol of European unification. It is a typical end-of-twentieth-century institution. In reality, however, the idea for a tunnel under the English Channel goes back to 1802, when the French engineer, Albert Mathieu, worked out a plan. In 1856, another Frenchman, Thomé de Gamond, presented a plan to Napoleon III. At the height of the railway boom the idea of building a tunnel was already combined with plans for railway connections between existing railroads in the two countries. In the mid-1870s, French and British Channel Tunnel companies were established, and the British parliament authorized preliminary works to begin. The invention of the rotary boring machine in 1875 provided the technology for construction. Although works began in 1882 at Shakespeare Cliff in Kent and Calais, only 1.5 kilometers were accomplished when military considerations brought work to a halt.

The initiative resurfaced a few more times, but only in 1957 was it seriously renewed with the appointment of a Channel Tunnel Study Group to begin geological studies. The group's report in the early 1960s declared the project to build a twin railway tunnel possible. Realization, nevertheless, took time. Prime Minister Harold Wilson and French President Georges Pompidou, in a joint statement, announced the construction plan in 1966. The British Channel Tunnel Company and the French Société Française du Tunnel sous la Manche were established only in 1971. In two more years, the British–French Treaty was signed.

The oil crisis of the mid-1970s and its aftermath, however, undermined the project, which was shelved until 1981, when Margaret Thatcher and François Mitterrand issued a joint statement on continuation. The new Channel Tunnel Treaty was signed and ratified in 1987. Among ten competing companies, Transmanche Link gained the concession and the work began in December. Huge, 1,000-tonne machines dug more than 400 meters of tunnel each week. According to the plans, three parallel 38-kilometer-long tunnels had to be built about 40 meters below the seabed, and 50 kilometers altogether, including their inland sections, between Shakespeare Cliff and Nord-Pas de Calais. In two tunnels a single railroad track was laid down, while the middle tunnel served for ventilation and services. On December 1, 1990, the French and British tunnel diggers met. In May 1994, the royal Rolls-Royce carrying Queen Elizabeth and President Mitterrand passed through the tunnel. At the end of the year, the service was opened to the public.

Opening the tunnel, in spite of its nineteenth-century background, was still a rather twentieth-century achievement. The European integration process and Britain's membership of the European Community were major prerequisites. The symbolic importance of the tunnel to join Europe was probably more important and definitely more shocking for the British than the fast direct railway connections. It expressed resignation from the traditional "splendid isolation" and the belief that Britain is not a part of Europe. In 1986, less than one-third of the British public was for the proposal, while half strictly rejected it. France and Europe as a whole, however, overwhelmingly supported the Channel Tunnel. Opening the tunnel created the first physical contact between the British island and the Continent and eliminated the physical and, in a way, the spiritual separation of Britain (Darian-Smith, 1999).

partner of Britain, did the same. After one-and-a-half decades, the Europe of Six became the Europe of Nine. The gates were open. After the collapse of the decades-old military dictatorships in Greece, and semi-fascist regimes of Salazar's Portugal and Franco's Spain, all three countries were admitted, Greece in 1981, Portugal and Spain in 1985. From 1986, the Community comprised twelve members.

In 1989, state socialism collapsed in Central and Eastern Europe, followed by the dissolution of the Soviet Union in 1991. The European balance of power shifted and neutrality between the blocs lost its importance for Sweden and Austria. Finland, bound by a 1948 treaty with the Soviet Union, was freed from mandatory neutrality ("Finlandization"). Consequently, all three countries applied and, in 1995, were accepted by the Community, which became the Europe of Fifteen. At that time, further enlargement was already discussed with Cyprus and a few Central European applicants, Poland, the Czech Republic, Hungary, and Slovenia. The preparation had begun and the number of candidate countries expanded to include Slovakia, Estonia, Latvia, Lithuania, and Malta. On May 1, 2004, the Union became Europe of Twenty-five. At the time of working, several other countries are knocking at the door of the Union.

The dramatic expansion of the Community did not stop the progress of more consistent integration. One of the most important new developments was the beginning of the realization of the old principle of equalizing economic levels within the Community. The Treaty of Rome in 1957 already declared the need for a "harmonious development by reducing existing differences between various regions and the backwardness of the least-favored regions." The realization of the principle, it was thought, would happen by market automatism. The acceptance of Ireland led to a dramatic change and the beginning of an interventionist approach. At the beginning, the Community wanted only to assist national regional policy, but from 1979 the Commission gained an independent role, and after 1984 regional policy became incorporated into a Community program. In 1975 a Regional Development Fund was created with the deliberate goal of assisting underdeveloped regions to catch up. A region was deemed underdeveloped if its per capita GDP was less than 75% of the Community's average. From the 1970s, most of the newly accepted member countries – first Ireland, then Greece and Portugal, plus most regions of Spain – were considered to be underdeveloped. In addition, underdeveloped areas within prosperous countries were designated: the Mezzogiorno in Italy, France's overseas departments and Corsica, Britain's declining industrial regions and Northern Ireland, the new "Länder," the former East Germany in unified

Germany. Altogether nearly one-quarter of the Community's population lived in such areas.

The cohesion policy, as it was called, sought to assist regions characterized by industrial decline, backward rural areas, regions with obsolete agricultural structure, and areas with high unemployment, especially among youth, and finally, very sparsely populated areas, such as the northern parts of the Nordic countries. Disparity between the most and least developed areas within the Community was striking. The ratio of per capita GDP between the ten most and least prosperous regions was 5:1; unemployment in the twenty-five regions with the highest rate averaged 21%, while the twenty-five regions with the lowest rate of unemployment had only 4% unemployment in 1993. Income parity and prosperity were ambitious goals.

To finance the catching-up process in backward regions, the Community reformed the Structural Fund and doubled its budget between 1987 and 1993. In 1987, the Community spent 7 billion ECU, 19% of its budget; by 1999, this had increased to more than 27 billion, 35% of the budget for financing cohesion policy (Hooghe, 1996). Massive Community assistance was accompanied by huge foreign direct investments (FDI) into newly accepted, less developed countries. Between 1986 and 1991, the gross inflow of FDI into Ireland was three times higher than European Union transfers. In the case of Greece, however, the value of European Union transfers was twice that of foreign direct investment (Tsoukalis, 1997: 203–5). All these transfers led to an exceptional growth rate in the newly accepted countries: between the late 1980s and mid-1990s, Ireland, Portugal, and Spain grew at a rate 2–4 times faster than that of the eight developed member countries. "Annual transfers through EU structural policies represent more than 3% of GNP for Greece and Portugal; and more than 2% for Ireland and Spain." More than one-third of the money transferred was used to pay for imports (Tsoukalis, 1997: 203). During the last quarter of the twentieth century, the European Union successfully assisted the catching-up process and helped elevate Ireland and the Mediterranean countries near to the level of the core.

The other, more controversial common target was the Community's agricultural policy, one of the very first joint programs, which consumed half of the Community's budget to support guaranteed market prices and export subsidies for producers.

More than 70 percent of farm output benefits from markets controlled to maintain prices at politically determined levels, especially for milk, cereals, sugar, beef, some fruits and vegetables and table wines . . . [This system is] permitting the Community to emerge as a major agricultural exporter by the mid 1980s. (Hoffman, 1990: 111)

The agricultural policy led to an overproduction of various agricultural products, but the surpluses were bought by the Community and sold – sometimes at a lower price – abroad.

The integration process picked up speed during the 1980s: the Single European Act of 1986, besides strengthening economic integration by removing the residual barriers to the free movement of goods, services, and factors of production, took a major step toward a supranational character of the Community by replacing the veto right with a majority decision principle in various fields of cooperation in the Council of Ministers. The veto right remained an exception and was used in case of "vital national interests," altogether fewer than a dozen times in fifteen years.

The preamble of the Single Act, furthermore, recalled the approval for a movement toward the introduction of a common currency, a decision made by the heads of state during their 1972 Paris summit meeting. This led to a major turning point at the Maastricht meeting of the European Council in December 1991, which resulted in a Treaty on the European Union. The most ambitious plans for a federal Europe were nurtured by the Commission, led by President Jacques Delors and supported by the French president and the German chancellor when they jointly appealed for political union in 1990. Luxemburg and the Netherlands soon added their support. Certain resistance remained, and the Maastricht Treaty failed to made direct progress toward this goal. The formation of the European Union, and the decision to create a monetary union, nevertheless, represented a dramatic new step in this direction (Swann, 1996). Germany, for example, against its direct economic interests, joined the common currency system, since, as Chancellor Helmut Kohl expressed, "economic and monetary integration is a matter of war and peace in the 21st century" (Tsoukalis, 1997: 170–1).

Monetary unification was an early goal of the federalist political forces. Actually, in opposition to the "minimalist" target of creating an exchange rate union, the Community as far back as the Hague summit of 1969 had declared the goal of a common currency. In June 1988, the European Council formed a committee, headed by Jacques Delors, to prepare for monetary unification. Delors, who was the real engine of further integration, presented a three-stage plan and the Council, at its Madrid meeting of 1989, agreed to begin implementation. Delays were unavoidable due to significant resistance, especially from Margaret Thatcher of Britain. In two years after the Maastricht Treaty, however, the European Monetary

Institute was founded in Frankfurt to coordinate national monetary policy and prepare monetary unification.

Discipline and convergence were established by the new monetary requirements: an inflation rate capped at 1.5% above the average of the three best-performing member countries; a long-term interest rate of $+/-2\%$ of the average of the best three performers; a national budget deficit not higher than 3% of GDP; public debt not higher than 60% of GDP; no devaluation of the currency in the last two transition years. While in 1991 only two of the member countries qualified, by 1998 eleven countries were eligible. From January 1999, the common currency, the euro, was introduced in principle, although national currencies were used for a few more years in practice.

A single European Central Bank (ECB) replaced the Monetary Institute, while the national banks became an integral part of it. The ECB is governed by a General Council, the president of the Bank, and an Executive Board (with six members and the governors of the national banks). Decisions are made by majority vote. The Central Bank became a note-issuing institution. It also makes open market operations, supports operations in the foreign exchange market, creates a minimum reserve, supervises banks, and participates in policymaking. On January 1, 2002 the euro was physically introduced and replaced national currencies in the eleven countries which joined the monetary union (Greece could not yet qualify and Britain, Sweden, and Denmark decided to remain outside, so that a two-tier system was introduced within the Union). The common currency and Central Bank became the most important supranational institutions of the European Union.

The economic integration process of Western Europe, which gradually incorporated almost the entire Western half of the continent, played a major role in assisting an export-led prosperity and the catching up of the Mediterranean periphery with the core. Postwar mixed economies and welfare states thus became part of an ever enlarging and deepening economic integration scheme, and are integrally connected with the European Union.

The emergence of *Sozialpartnerschaft* and the mixed economy

Within the integrating Western Europe, an economic system emerged based on social solidarity and strong state interventionism. One of the immediate postwar institutions, *Sozialpartnerschaft* (social partnership), was born from the strong feeling of social solidarity which engulfed Europe after the bloodiest and devastating war. Gunnar Myrdal stated in 1958:

The inherited liberal ideal of fair play has more and more generally and definitely been translated into the demand that wages, prices, incomes, and profits should be settled by various sorts of collective bargaining . . . It has become the responsibility of the state to provide such conditions by legislation and administration and by an umpire service . . . that just and equitable agreements will be reached. (Myrdal, 1960: 44)

What never happened before, "a cooperative equilibrium," was created in which "both workers and capitalists exercise restraint."

Long-term contracts, social pacts between labour, management and government, and statutory wage and price controls are three mechanisms that could be used to precommit unions to wage moderation and thereby to induce management to invest . . . [W]age restraint and high investment were the dual cornerstones of the postwar settlement. (Eichengreen, 1994: 44–5)

This new development was connected with a victorious Keynesian revolution in postwar Western Europe. It was a historic moment when both the political moderate Left and the conservative Right agreed on this policy and British Labour politicians, as well as French Gaullists and Christian Democrats in Germany and Italy, pursued practically the same policy. Left-wing political forces were never so influential in West European politics as after World War II. In the first postwar elections of 1945 and 1946, socialist and social democratic parties gained one-quarter to nearly one-half of the votes in France, Holland, Italy, Denmark, Sweden, Norway, Britain, and Austria. Furthermore, in some of the countries, the Communist Party became a significant political factor and joined postwar coalition governments in Italy, France, and Belgium. In a world where economic crisis and market imperfections were manifest, and war was the "normal" state of affairs, social solidarity became a leading idea. It generated a system of control of the market economy, income distribution, and welfare.

As an integral part of the new role of the state, various forms of democratic corporative systems were introduced. The state, together with the unions and entrepreneurs' organizations, established regular institutions to coordinate wage and price policies and keep inflation at bay. These institutions guaranteed a voice for the workers in economic and enterprise affairs. One of the most successful cooperations emerged in postwar Austria, due to the initiative of Julius Raab, president of the Bundeskammer. This institution, with the broad representation of the state, the unions, and entrepreneurs, fostered the first wage–price agreement in August 1947. *Sozialpartnerschaft* in Austria assured regular cooperation between the state and different interest groups and the second (September 1948), third (May 1949), fourth (September 1950), and fifth (July 1951) agreements followed (Butschek, 1985: 101–9).

In postwar Britain, the Trade Union Act of 1946 and the Wages Council Act of 1945 strengthened the unions' participation in economic affairs. Union leaders and the government met regularly to discuss economic policy and the direction of public enterprises. Collective bargaining, though it was already important in the interwar years, was institutionalized to determine wages. Sir Stafford Cripps, Chancellor of the Exchequer, gained the support of the trade unions and achieved wage and price stability between 1948 and 1950 (Pollard, 1986: 261–2; Lieberman, 1977: 76).

In France, during the early wave of nationalization, the leading political principle was the return of national wealth to the nation – and not to the government. The trade unions sought to establish direction by a "tripartite" (workers, consumers, and government) organization. Workers' representation in the tripartite was based on the "most representative" unions; consumer representatives were appointed by the government based on the recommendations of interest groups. In the early years, the Communist Party gained the upper hand in both workers' and consumers' representations. After the communists were forced from the coalition in 1947, the tripartite mechanism was virtually eliminated.

Though corporative cooperation failed, workers' representation at the company level was established in France. The preamble of the Constitution of 1946 declared: "Every worker may participate through his delegates in the collective determination of working conditions and in the management of the enterprise." The *comités d'entreprise* were established in firms with more than fifty employees. These committees, playing a consultative role, were involved with social welfare programs within the company (Baum, 1958: 181–2, 274–5). The corporative style of collaboration remained a main feature of France's "early postwar planning," as Jacques Delors pointed out:

Effective negotiation between the main partners in the system [became practice. The *Commissariat du Plan*, and] most senior managers . . . were prepared to gather around the table . . . also, the trade unions came. (Delors, 1978: 15–16)

In Germany, the British occupation administration introduced compulsory workers' participation in company leadership (*paritätische Mitbestimmung*), which was used as a model after the agreement between the unions and Chancellor Adenauer in January 1951. The law (*Betriebsverfassungs-gesetz*) of October 1952 introduced the *Betriebsräte* (company councils), which had the right of participation in decisions regarding personnel matters, work conditions, and working hours, and also the right to information about company affairs. From the late 1960s a planned income policy was introduced, and the *Konzertierte Aktion* initiated the mutual information between the representatives of the unions, entrepreneurs, the state, and the Central Bank to create guidelines for wage policy (Zinn, 1978: 99). In 1976, workers' representation was expanded. In companies with more than 2,000 employees (650 companies), workers gained equal representation on the board of directors (Weimer, 1998: 86–7, 273–4).

The Belgian *Projet d'Accord de Solidarité Sociale*, a social pact between the unions and employers, was initiated in 1944 to bind wages to productivity increase. In the 1950s and 1960s, several productivity agreements followed and stabilized wage moderation. In Norway, the full employment policy ("Work for Everybody") was connected to wage moderation, combined with government control on prices and profit to guarantee job creation by reinvestment. In the Netherlands the Publiek Rechtelijke Bedrijfsorganisatie established a corporative decision-making body on employment policy and investments (Eichengreen, 1994: 46, 48).

Sozialpartnerschaft, Mitbestimmung, and other forms of corporative elements of workers' participation in economic and company affairs helped stabilize postwar economies and, in most cases, contributed to the creation of social peace, wage and profit moderation, and higher investments. Bargaining was mostly centralized under government initiative, while unions gained a sort of public status. Worker participation in decision-making became, in most cases, a solid base of social peace, which provided protection against a "wage–price spiral" (Van der Wee, 1986). Although these systems began to falter in the late 1960s and did not survive the end of the century, they had an important effect on postwar economic and social development.

Meanwhile, the realization of social goals demanded an efficient market and a growing economy. Herman Van der Wee speaks about a "pentagon" of goals: full employment, full use of productive capacities, stable prices, increasing incomes based on increasing productivity, and balanced balance of payments. To achieve that, state assistance for economic development expanded to investments, finance for R&D, and various kinds of tax exemptions and subsidies. The German law of January 1952, the *Investitionshilfegesetz*, granted 1 billion marks for some "bottleneck industries" such as coal mining, iron and steel, electricity and railroads. A further 28 billion marks went to private companies in the form of tax exemptions between

1949 and 1957 (Braun, 1990: 179). The British Industrial Reconstruction Corporation was founded in 1966 and by 1971 was granting state loans and investments for private industries. Between 1965 and 1970, nearly £1.4 billion of state resources were transferred to private industries (Rees, 1973: 29). Public investment as a percentage of total investments in France was among the highest: it rose from 52% in 1947 to 55% in 1948 and 64% by 1949. In the early 1950s, public investment in France still represented 39% of total investments (Denton et al., 1968: 230).

West European activist states initiated economic and social programs and introduced regulations in agriculture, housing, transportation, banking, and insurance. The German *Wohnungsbaugesetz* of April 1950 ordered the building of 1.8 million apartments in six years (Weimer, 1998). Public credits and tax exemptions helped small and medium-sized firms as part of a *Mittelstandspolitik*.

Fiscal policy was extensively used to quicken capital formation and to facilitate the expansion of selected economic sectors. In the 1950s, taxation absorbed as much as 35% of the GNP. Large tax revenues allowed government to build up budgetary surpluses providing investment funds to both the public and private sectors. (Lieberman, 1977: 53)

The private sector received nearly 40 billion marks in state assistance between 1949 and 1957. The Stability Act of 1967 expressed a Keynesian approach through the role assigned to planning and speeding up public investments. Karl Schiller, minister of economic affairs, established a Special Investment Budget and spent 2.5 billion marks to stimulate the economy. This classic Keynesian multiplier-accelerator was also combined with reduced investment taxation. A Konjunkturrat, or Council for Anti-Cyclical Policy, was established along with a fund (from 3% of tax incomes) for state interventions.

The same was true for Italy. The state-created Engineering Industry Fund channeled 50 billion lire into the reorganization and modernization of Italy's private engineering industry in 1947. In addition, more than 120 billion lire were invested in state-owned industries. The share of public enterprises in total industrial investment increased from 19% to 49% between 1955 and 1961 (Lieberman, 1977: 107, 261).

In France, direct state investment represented 35% of the country's total gross investment. The public sector became the principal client of private economy. Eighty percent of heavy electrical engineering products were bought by the state-owned Electricité de France (Cohen, 1977: 25–6).

In Britain the state participated in industrial modernization during the 1960s–1970s, especially in shipbuilding, by regrouping companies and assisting the re-equipment of industry. The government's Secretary of State for Scotland and the Highlands and Islands Development Board provided grants and loans for various industries for regional development. The government assisted research and development (R&D) projects in the computer industry as well. Publicly financed research significantly helped technological modernization, and, as Merlyn Rees phrased it, "the growing mix of the two sectors [state and private] of the economy." The state also became an important buyer, especially in the aircraft industry. Altogether, however, the state bought only 5% of total manufacturing output in 1967 (Rees, 1973: 27, 30).

The state, the most important economic agent, which controlled 30–40% of the GDP during the war, continued to play an important and complex role in economic affairs. Classical Keynesian counter-cyclical policies to create additional demand and achieve full employment were implemented. State initiatives also spurred modernization and technological–structural advances by assisting research and development. The origins of this kind of state intervention go back to World War II. Major scientific efforts were made to develop efficient defensive and destructive weapons. The two world wars and the cold war made military expenditures astronomical. At the height of the cold war, for example, worldwide annual defense expenditure topped two-thirds of a trillion dollars. Governments employed and financed armies of scientists and engineers who worked on developing radar, jet aircraft, rockets, computers, the atomic and hydrogen bombs, and the space programs. Government laboratories, as well as contracted institutions and private companies, worked on military projects. In the 1960s–1970s, roughly half of the U.S. budget was spent on defense, including military R&D expenditure. This share was practically the same in Britain, while France spent one-third and Germany between one-fifth and one-tenth of their budgets on defense research and development.

Government-financed R&D represented about half of the R&D expenditures in market economies, while private companies financed the other half. In the late 1970s roughly 300,000 scientists and engineers were employed in R&D in France, Britain, and Germany combined. The total expenditure reached between 2% and 4% of the national product of these countries. The countries of the European Community, however, spent the equivalent of one-sixth of their own industrial R&D, as an average, on joint research, which internationalized technological development (OECD, 1987: 113). Industrialized research gave a tremendous boost to technological development, and brought to maturity the greatest results in technology.

State intervention, nevertheless, went much further, and the state became a major entrepreneur in postwar Europe. Partial nationalization became widespread, not to eliminate the capitalist economy but to secure state leadership for influencing technological and structural modernization. The British Labour government, after its impressive victory in 1945, introduced a massive nationalization program, proposed by the party's manifesto, *Let Us Face the Future*. The Labour program expressed a traditional socialist approach:

> to secure for the workers . . . the full fruits of their industry and the most equitable distribution thereof that may be possible, upon the basis of the common ownership of the means of production, distribution and exchange, and the best obtainable system of popular administration and control of each industry or service. (Declaration, 1945: 30)

In 1946, coal mines were nationalized and run by the National Coal Board. Internal shipping and railroads were nationalized next and managed by the British Waterways Board and Railway Board, respectively. Most of these sectors had huge deficits and were obsolete technologically. Electric power generation and distribution was nationalized in 1947 and run by the British Electricity Authority, as recommended by the Heyworth Committee, established in 1944. In 1948 the National Steel Board was established, and steel factories were nationalized. Road transportation, airports, air transportation, and, ultimately, the Bank of England were also nationalized. By 1949, a great part of the British economy was state-owned. The government continued to buy shares of private companies until major concerns such as British Petroleum, Rolls-Royce, and Upper Clyde Shipbuilders were also nationalized. The government gained an upper hand in infrastructure and the energy economy, and also owned roughly 20% of industrial capacity. The nationalization drive in Britain, the cradle of private industrial capitalism, demonstrated a radically changed mentality and principle after the war, which also influenced other countries of Europe.

As René Gendarme maintained, "in 1944, the great majority of Frenchmen were convinced of the economic, social and political superiority of nationalized industry over private industry" (Gendarme, 1950: 37). The National Resistance Council, in its statement of March 1944, called for

> the return to the nation of the great means of monopolized production, fruits of common labor, of the source of energy, the wealth of underground, the insurance companies, and the large banks . . . The national economy, at the stage at which it has arrived, can no longer accommodate enterprises which, like the insurance companies, give a higher priority to immediate profit than to the collective interest. (Baum, 1958: 175–6)

The preamble of the French Constitution of 1946 stated: "All property and all enterprises . . . shall have the character of a national public service, or a monopoly in fact must become the property of the community" (Sassoon, 1996: 164). France's coalition government under General de Gaulle, with the participation of the socialist and communist parties, launched a radical nationalization campaign immediately after the war. It was partly the consequence of De Gaulle's *étatist* and *dirigist* ideas, partly as retribution against collaborationist big industrialists such as Louis Renault, and, of course, partly inspired by the coalition partner socialist and communist parties. In November 1947, De Gaulle announced:

For reasons which are psychological as well as economic and moral there was a need after the liberation of France to pursue a nationalization policy in the area of coal, electricity, and credit. This is what I have done. (Jacquillat, 1988: 16)

A great part of energy production – electricity, coal, and gas – was nationalized. If not unanimous, the overwhelming majority of votes in the parliament reflected the public attitude toward nationalization. The nationalization of the Bank of France and the four largest banks was approved by 521 votes to 35, and only a handful of parliamentarians voted against the nationalization of insurance, gas, and electricity companies. The state-owned sector came to include Air France, the four biggest banks, thirty-two insurance companies, eighteen mining companies, and several large industrial firms (Renault, Gnôme et Rhône, Berliet), comprising one-fifth of total industrial output. By the summer of 1946, the main wave of nationalization was accomplished (Baum, 1958: 178–9). Until the early 1980s, France had a mixed economy with a strong state sector comprising 94% of energy industries, 83% of telecommunications industries, 46% of transportation, 44% of banking, and 6% of other industries.

In the early 1980s, the socialist government of France took steps to further increase the state sector. Eleven major private companies and all the remaining private banks were nationalized. The private sector practically disappeared from the energy, railroad, telecommunications, and tobacco industries. By the mid-1980s, 53% of the fixed assets of all French companies was held by public firms, which employed nearly one-quarter of the nation's workforce.

The Federal Republic of Germany, the most neo-liberal country in postwar Western Europe, also had a large state sector. It mostly originated from the Nazi regime. "During the Second World War roughly half of the capital of the German joint stock companies was, directly or indirectly, in the hands of public companies" (Fischer, 1978: 199). At the end of the war, public ownership was not only advocated by the social democrats but was part of the so-called Ahlen Program (1947) of the Christian Democratic Union, while U.S. occupying forces resisted major nationalizations. With the approval of the British and French occupying forces, a major electoral success in Hesse led to the acceptance of a new *Land* (state) constitution. Its Article 41 made possible the nationalization of 169 firms. A referendum about this article gained more than 70% backing in the state. In 1948 the Kreditanstalt für Wiederaufbau, a state-owned reconstruction bank, was founded to assist industries through long-term credits.

State ownership was mostly maintained with little expansion in traditional sectors such as transportation, communications, and in some industrial sectors. Public authorities at various levels owned and operated transportation, railroads, waterways, and airlines (Lufthansa was founded in 1953). Telephone, telegraph, postal service, radio and television, and the majority of utilities were also state owned. In the early 1950s, 90% of gas production, 70% of aluminum smelting, 60% of electricity output, 50% of the automobile industry (including Volkswagen Werke), iron ore, lead, and zinc production, and 20% of coal, coke, crude oil, pig iron, and steel production were in the hands of state-owned companies. The state also controlled several industrial firms via holding companies such as the Vereinigte Elektrizitäts- und Bergwerks AG (VEBA), and the Vereinigte Industrie-Unternehmungen AG (VIAG). Although several state-owned companies, including the Volkswagen Werke, were privatized during the 1960s and 1970s, by the late 1960s 650 companies were in full or partial (at least 25%) federal ownership (Hardach, 1976: 154–5). The largest state-owned enterprises were the Bundespost and the Bundesbahn, altogether employing nearly 900,000 people. The various German *Länder*, or states, and communal firms also employed hundreds of thousands of workers. By 1980, 2 million people – 12% of the total labor force – were employed by public companies. Germany was thus no exception to mainstream Western policy.

Austria became one of the most radically nationalizing countries in the West, with the goal of nationalizing all German-owned companies to avoid having them confiscated as war compensation under the Potsdam agreement. In 1946, the Austrian parliament passed the first nationalization act: the entire engineering and oil refinery industry, the three biggest banks, the German branches of the electricity industry, and the Danube Shipping Company were all nationalized. It pays to mention a paradoxical historical episode: it was the Soviet Union which vetoed Austrian nationalization, and the U.S. occupation forces which supported it and made radical nationalization possible. Roughly 22% of industrial output was in the hands of the state, but together with those industrial companies which were controlled by nationalized banks, this share reached 70% of industrial production by the early 1950s (Sassoon, 1996: 161).

Italian fascist and a copycat Francoist economic dirigisme, which created huge state-owned sectors long before Western Europe turned toward a mixed economy, easily adjusted to the Western model after the war. At the end of the war, the future of Istituto per la Ricostruzione Industriale (IRI) and major state holding companies such as AGIP, ANIC, STET, Finmare, Finsider, and others, founded by Mussolini, was cast in doubt. Central control collapsed, the organization of IRI was changed three times in three years, and four different commissars and two different presidents ruled the company.

Since Britain and France, the leading democratic countries and victors, also turned toward nationalization, Italy did not hesitate to keep its inherited state sector alive. The Italian constitution of 1947, in Article 42, declared: "For reason of general interest private property may be expropriated by law and with compensation." The existing large state sector consequently expanded. To the forty-five engineering firms controlled by IRI at the end of the war, five more were added. In 1959, the Cantieri Navali at Taranto was taken over. In 1956, IRI received the charge to build and operate the Milan–Naples *Autostrada del Sole*; in 1957 it incorporated the two remaining private telephone companies. New state holding companies were also founded: the Finmeccanica in 1948, which concentrated and controlled the twenty major engineering firms, including Alfa Romeo, Ansaldo San Giorgio, and Sant' Eustacchio; Finelettrica in 1952, which took over all electricity-operating companies of IRI and then was transferred into a new authority, ENEL, which controlled 650 companies and 70% of the country's electricity output in the 1960s. The Italian state sector produced one-quarter of the country's GNP (without agriculture), and invested more than one-quarter of total investments (Posner and Woolf, 1967).

The Franco regime in Spain cautiously followed the same model after the economic liberalization of the 1950s and the introduction of the Stabilization Plan from the beginning of the 1960s. The Instituto Nacional de Industria (INI), established in 1941, which had copied the fascist Italian model and served the goal of self-sufficiency, adopted a free trade system and gradually was incorporated into a mixed economy, similar to the French model. In the postwar era under the *Caudillo*, and after his death until 1984, the state sector remained dominant. The state controlled coal, electricity, transportation, shipbuilding, and telecommunications, and played an important role in the textile, chemical, and car industries (including

SEAT with 23,000 workers). Three major state-owned conglomerates controlled the commanding posts of the economy: INI had a share in 700 firms, holding a majority of shares in 250 of them and employing 210,000 workers in 1984; INH controlled the majority stocks of thirty-one companies in the energy sector; and the Dirección General del Patrimonio del Estado monopolized telephone and tobacco industries and held a strong position in textiles. In addition to the Bank of Spain, nationalized in 1962, nearly 100 banks were state owned. Roughly one-fifth of the country's assets were in the hands of the state.

Salazar's *Estado Novo* or the new Portuguese state, which built up a corporative system and a strong economic dirigisme, did not create a large state sector. Nationalization gained momentum only after the dictatorship was overthrown in the April 1974 revolution. In the summer of 1975, extensive nationalization took place: the electricity, steel, petroleum refining, transportation, brewing, pulp and paper, tobacco, fertilizer, cement, and shipbuilding industries were all nationalized. One of the most important steps was the nationalization of the Melo family's holding company, the Companhia União Fabril (CUF), which itself owned 20% of the country's industrial capital and produced 10% of the GDP. As a consequence, one-quarter of the country's value added was produced by state-owned firms in the mid-1970s (Morrison, 1981: 4, 47–8).

Most other West European countries had an important state sector, though mostly in services, transportation, and communications, and much less in industrial production. The state sector in Finland was one of the largest: 34% of the gainfully employed population worked in the public sector and produced one-quarter of marketed products in 1965. In Belgium, state-owned companies employed more than 7% of the labor force by 1980. Although the governing Swedish Social Democratic Party dropped nationalization from its program, the public sector was strong in services, transportation, and communications. Altogether 22% of the non-agricultural labor force was employed by the public sector in 1960. Norway nationalized the railways and telecommunications. The central bank and the formerly German-owned large aluminum company were also nationalized. In Greece, 86% of the financial sector was state owned, while the share of public companies in industry remained rather low, producing less than 4% of the total valued added in 1980 (Fischer, 1978: 198–201).

State-owned companies remained actors in a free market economy and acted accordingly. The British pattern was generally accepted and followed. The government or parliament appointed the board of management but they were free corporate bodies and worked without the direct control of the state. Their finances were not part of state finances. Certain branches, however, were responsible for the supply to the population, especially in energy, transportation, postal services, and telecommunications.

Planning in mixed economies

State intervention and ownership, in some cases, was combined with long-term planning. "As measures of state intervention . . . grew in volume and in complexity," explains Gunnar Myrdal, "attempts to coordinate them more rationally" led to planning. Planning, of course, was already invented by war economies: "improvised during World War I . . . [but] state planning during World War II was technically far superior to that earlier experience" (Myrdal, 1960: 22, 26). Planning, of course, became central in the state socialist economy, and was also practiced by dictatorial economic dirigisme. In mixed economies, where even state-owned companies preserved independence and acted according to market rules, planning was different from Soviet-type planning. Compulsory plan indicators did not exist. The central will was not forced upon state or private companies. State planning, which targeted full employment, economic–technological modernization, and long-term development goals, often was focused on specific branches of central importance. These goals were served by various kinds of state interventions and investments. The best example was French postwar planning, initiated by Jean Monnet in 1945. Jacques Delors underlined two main characteristics of French planning: "On the one hand, there is planning as a system of forecasting . . . and on the other hand the institution of the Plan itself as a focus of animation, influence and action" (Delors, 1978: 9–11). Economic forecasting used input–output analysis and the plan intervened to achieve better allocation of labor, material, and capital resources.

The first French four-year plan (1946–50, and then expanded to 1952) concentrated on six key sectors – coal, steel, cement, electricity, transportation, and agriculture. Later oil refinery and fertilizer production were added. The planning method was based on input–output analyses. Information was provided by the Statistical Office, and the concept of development projects was discussed by the *Comités de Modernisation* with the participation of thousands of industrial managers and trade union representatives. The final plan was prepared by the Commissariat du Plan, subordinated directly to the prime minister and assisted by the Ministry of Finance. State finances and positive discrimination, subsidies, credits, and state guarantees were used to realize the main targets, since the plan was not mandatory. Investments, though mostly private, were strongly influenced, encouraged, and assisted by the government.

Informal connections between high-level state administrators and economic managers, mostly fellow graduates of the Grande École, bound by "old college ties," contributed to the success. Planning was done by big business for big business:

The planners, the ranking civil servants and the managers of big business share the same attitudes, the same modes of thought and expression, the same outlook. They come from the same social background; they attended the same schools . . . Indeed, to an alarming extent, they are the same people. (Cohen, 1977: 65–6)

Plantouflage, or a shift from the civil service into high managerial positions in big business, was natural and characterized at least one-quarter of the inspectors of finance. Planning, nevertheless, served the renewal of France. "The Fourth republic initiated a twentieth century industrial revolution in France." Planning was considered to be the main vehicle for reconstruction and modernization (Lieberman, 1977: 4–5). The first four-year plan was fulfilled with great success. In most planned targets, the quantity of output of coal, electric power, cement, and steel was reached or neared. The Monnet Plan was thus followed by a second Hirsch Plan (1954–7), which in addition to industry covered agriculture and construction. Regional development plans were added in 1955. According to the targets, industrial output should be increased by 30%, agriculture by 20%, construction by 60%. Most of these targets, though not compulsory central orders, were over-fulfilled by 1957. The success of French planning led to a permanent continuation: the third plan (1958–61) was already based on an input–output matrix, and the fourth plan (1962–5) became the model of indicative planning. Each plan focused on competitiveness and modernization (Lieberman, 1977: 170–1). Plans of the 1970s and 1980s aimed at restructuring the French economy according to the new technological and market requirements. The main target of the sixth five-year plan (1971–5) was the creation of large, internationally competitive companies. In the chemical industry, for example, state planning, with an investment of $4.7 billion, helped create five major companies, three public and two private. These companies increased their share in output from 16% to 33% by 1977. The ninth five-year plan (1984–8) shifted the focus toward scientific education, vocational training, and R&D. Research and development expenditures over sales increased from 3.7% in 1980 to 5.4% by 1986. The plan initiated a restructuring of the chemical industry with rapid development of pharmaceuticals and fine chemicals. One of the leading companies, Rhone Poulenc, turned to specialties production. In connection with these changes, leading French chemical companies bought thirteen European and twenty-one U.S. specialty-producing firms between 1985 and 1987 (Martinelli, 1991: 20, 39, 40, 93, 95).

Spain, still under Francisco Franco, introduced the Stabilization Plan in 1959, opened the country, and began transforming the system of economic dirigisme into a modern Western type of mixed economy, modeled on French planning. The investment regulation programs of 1959–60, and then the series of directives of the fall of 1962, prepared the introduction of planning. The First Development Plan (1964–7), and then the second (1967–71) and third (1972–5) four-year plans, followed the method of *acción concertada*, a harmonized action of the companies and the state. The companies planned to achieve certain targets, such as new products, structural–technological modernization and increased productivity. The government offered financial assistance to plans it approved, including cheap credit for up to 70% of the planned investment project and fiscal advantages, for four to eight years. Government decisions were based on long-term targets and targeted branches such as shipbuilding and the iron and steel industry. Another major government goal was the assistance of backward regions. In 1964 the industrial development poles which received state assistance were Corunna, Seville, Valladolid, Zaragoza, and Vigo. The industrial promotion poles were Huelva and Burgos. During the second plan period between 1967 and 1971, five new development poles were designated for assistance: Córdoba, Granada, Oviedo, Lograño, and Villagarcía de Arosa (Harrison, 1985: 149–53).

Strict planning was not introduced in Italy, but a ten-year development plan was accepted for the modernization of the backward south in 1950. In August of that year a development fund, the Cassa per il Mezzogiorno, was established for agricultural modernization and infrastructure development. Most of Italian planning was linked to the state-owned sector and was realized via the large state holding companies. Ezio Vanoni's "Scheme for the Development of Employment and Income for the Decade 1955–1964," though not a government law, served as a blueprint for development policy to produce 4 million jobs and achieve a 5% annual growth. The *contrattazione programmatica* focused on start-up investments, mostly in chemicals and mechanical engineering in the late 1960s, and continued with "investment packages" for regional development in Battipaglia and Reggio Calabria in the early 1970s. In the mid-1970s chemical and steel sectors gained preference (Archibugi, 1978: 50–2).

British economic planning, according to the criticism of economist Thomas Balogh, "was a last-minute commitment by Labour before the 1964 elections." As the Labour prime minister, Harold Wilson, announced:

Economic planning must then be directed first to increasing investment, and to increase it purposively . . . A National Investment board should be set up to work out for each major industry, public and private, the rate of expansion needed. (Balogh, 1978: 127)

British economic planning sought to be a "target plan" with growth forecasts, rate of return targets, and recommended growth rates. The Science and Technology Act of 1965, and the Industrial Expansion Act of 1968, authorized assistance to reach economic development goals. Planning in Britain, however, remained unimportant (Van der Wee, 1986).

Several other countries had a similarly loose type of planning, or preserved the traditional fiscal and monetary policy instead. This usually took the form of some kind of counter-cyclical policy aimed at full employment and stable growth, sometimes combined with policy measures to promote structural modernization. After the war, the Centraal Planbureau was established and worked on regional development and short-term plans in the Netherlands. By 1963, the Bureau began five-year planning, mostly for infrastructural development. In Austria, following the "fashion," a planning ministry was established, but planning did not gain any real ground.

The rise of the welfare state

One of the most important new activities of the interventionist state, its welfare policy, was also rooted in the postwar concept of social solidarity:

In many countries, health, unemployment, retirement and training programmes were elaborated. Governments more aggressively pursued their commitment to politics of full employment. (Eichengreen, 1994: 52)

Even the *Ordoliberalen* of the German Freiburger Schule combined neoliberal free market economics with the concept of state regulation. Alfred Müller-Armack from the Kölner Schule coined the term *Sozial-Marktwirtschaft* (social market economy), a concept which was adopted and realized by Ludwig Erhard, first director of the "Bizonal" economic administration, then minister of economic affairs, and then chancellor of the Federal Republic of Germany, and the architect of postwar German *Wirtschaftswunder*. In 1957, Erhard wrote about an "overwhelming call for collective social security," and rejected the concept that in the welfare system *"der jeder die Hand in der Tasche des anderen hat"* ("everybody has his hand in the purse of others"). He argued for the closest interrelation between economic and social policies, and held that a competitive, efficient

Table 5.1 Public expenditures in % of gross
social product (Kohl, 1984: 315)

Country	1950	1965	1980
Belgium	23	37	52
Denmark	19	31	56
Germany	32	37	48
France	37	38	46
Holland	29	39	60
Norway	28	36	49
Sweden	23	34	62
Austria	19	34	49
Britain	35	38	46

free market combined with social policy measures must create *Wohlstand für Alle* ("well-being for all") (Erhard, 1990: 246–9).

To realize these commitments, West European states introduced a strong income redistribution policy. High taxation, concentration of an ever-growing portion of the GDP into the state budget and used for public expenditures became the most characteristic feature of West European states after World War II. Progressive taxation rates often surpassed 50% of personal income, and in some cases exceeded 70% in the highest income category. General government taxes by 1970 averaged 20–30% of GDP. Average tax rates were generally high – in Britain and Denmark around 30%; in Germany, France, Belgium, and Sweden they varied between 20% and 25% (Flora and Heidenheimer, 1981: 262). The theories suggesting a sharp increase of public spending in crisis situations such as depression and war proved to be well based; Europe had reacted to the previous crises, the Great Depression and World War II, by introducing high taxation and welfare policy.

With large tax incomes, the West European states increased their expenditures accordingly. In most before World War I, roughly 10–12% of the GDP went toward public expenditures; by 1935 this figure was 20–33%; after World War II this share increased dramatically (see Table 5.1).

An increasing part of state spending was social expenditure. In 1950, social transfers, as an average, accounted for only 6–10% of the GNP of the West European countries; by 1975 it was 15–20%. In France and the Netherlands, it reached 20% and 26%, respectively. In Norway and

Denmark spending on social programs in these years trebled. The increasingly redistributive role of the state was a consequence of the emergence of the Western welfare state.

This term itself was coined only in 1941 by Archbishop Temple in Britain who compared the Western democracies to the existing and frightening "warfare" and "power" states of the day. Later on the term was applied to the institutionalized system in postwar Western Europe. According to Asa Briggs's definition:

a welfare state is a state in which organized power is deliberately used . . . in an effort to modify the play of market forces in at least three directions – first, by guaranteeing individuals and families a minimum income irrespective of the market value of their property; second by narrowing the extent of insecurity by . . . [providing for] certain "social contingencies" (for example, sickness, old age and unemployment) . . . and third by ensuring that all citizens . . . are offered . . . a certain agreed range of social services. (Briggs, 1961: 228)

Ernest Mandel suggested a questionable stage theory of the development of capitalism: liberal capitalism of the nineteenth century was followed by imperialist capitalism from the end of the nineteenth century to the middle of the twentieth, but then was replaced from World War II by a "social capitalism" (Mandel, 1972).

Although the welfare state is very much a postwar phenomenon, its origins go back to the end of the nineteenth century, and have several "home countries" and even more sources of inspiration. The tradition of feudal paternalism penetrated the capitalist industrial system and preserved an atmosphere of company responsibility for the workers' well-being and led to a welfare orientation. Owners sought to win the loyalty of their workforce in this way. The London gas industry, for example, in a struggle against the unions, introduced profit-sharing in the late 1880s. The big gas companies, match manufacturers, and port transportation companies pioneered providing pensions, sick pay, accident benefits, and recreational and sports facilities in the late nineteenth century. In the British confectionery trade, Quaker employers encouraged cooperation between management and the workforce to arrive at policies that presaged "welfarism." British entrepreneurs believed that welfare measures earned greater loyalty and better work from their employees.

One of the most decisive pioneers of the welfare state, however, was Chancellor Bismarck, who introduced the world's first national, compulsory sickness (health) insurance scheme for all industrial workers in Germany in June 1883. A series of welfare legislation followed:

industrial accident insurance in 1884, old-age and invalidity pension insurance in 1889. These measures were limited to workers and were differentiated by income. Finances were based on regressive consumption taxes or contributions by the insured. Paradoxically, Bismarck's welfare measures were part of a campaign to undermine the socialist movement.

Bismarck's German laws had an international impact: the king of Sweden appointed a committee to study the German pattern in October 1884. Some months later, in July 1885, Denmark formed a similar committee. The idea gradually gained ground. By 1891, a pioneering old-age, non-contributory pension scheme was introduced in Denmark. Legislation guaranteed government participation in all accident, health, unemployment, and old-age insurances between 1889 and 1907. According to the Danish laws, accident insurance had to be paid by the employer, while health insurance was co-paid by the government; unemployment insurance was covered by public contribution: the state (one-third) and communes (one-sixth); old-age insurance was financed by the government (28.4%) and communes (71.6%). Denmark became the pioneer of modern welfare legislation. Norway introduced a compulsory accident insurance, which became mandatory for employers in 1896. A health insurance law was passed in 1909 and state and community participation was guaranteed. Sweden introduced accident, sickness, and old-age insurance with state contribution between 1891 and 1913 (Kudrle and Marmor, 1981: 140).

Scandinavian welfare was the fruit of the common masses' power . . . It embodied a solidarity of the entire community, including all citizens regardless of class, frequently offering them equal flat-rate benefits and relying heavily on tax-fixing to distribute burdens . . . (Baldwin, 1990: 60)

The political forces behind welfare legislation, indeed, varied broadly. According to the calculations of Robert T. Kudrle and Theodor R. Marmor, socialist, liberal, and conservative governments enacted introductory laws on unemployment insurance in four, six, and five cases, respectively; socialist, liberal, and conservative governments introduced compulsory schemes in three, two, and three cases, respectively (Kudrle and Marmor, 1981: 170). Initiatives thus were being born almost equally from different political angles. The development of mass democracies and the possibility of expressing and representing mass interests in legislation led to the spread of welfare legislation. Besides workers defending their interests, other layers of society exercised pressure on social issues. The peasantry and the middle class in the Scandinavian societies and the middle class in continental Europe often realized their interests via liberal and even conservative political parties. Nevertheless, Donald Sassoon stressed the direct and indirect influence of socialist ideas:

As the socialist parties emerged, their aristocratic and bourgeois opponents, while attempting to repress them, adopted some of their ideas . . . Even the Roman Catholic church shifted ground and, with Leo XIII's papal encyclical *Rerum Novarum* (1891), laid the foundation for what came to be known as the "social" doctrine of the church. (Sassoon, 1996: x)

Around the turn of the century, important new initiatives were taken by France, the first country to introduce a subsidized voluntary nationwide unemployment insurance scheme in 1905, although the canton of St. Gallen in Switzerland had pioneered a similar law in 1895. Britain in 1911 became the first to implement a compulsory national scheme, co-paid by workers, employers, and the state.

World War I and the revolutionary wave after it, including the birth of the Soviet Union, increased the urgency of social solidarity. The Great Depression and its political consequences, including Hitler's rise to power, made it clear that democracies had an economic responsibility toward citizens, and must compete with different types of populist dictatorial governments. As President Roosevelt said, democracies must prove that the practical operation of democratic government is equal to the task of protecting the social security of the people. Welfare policy, as a consequence, was expanded, and the first welfare state emerged in Sweden, under social democratic rule, from 1932.

The real turning point in the history of the welfare state, however, was World War II and what followed: the cold war competition between the West and the Soviet bloc. The war itself delivered a strong lesson on social solidarity. The American writer John Steinbeck, a war correspondent in London, wrote on July 16, 1943:

Common people have learned a great deal . . . They would like freedom from want. That means the little farm . . . is safe from foreclosure. That means the job . . . That means there will be schools, and . . . medicine available without savings . . . Is the country to be taken over by special interests? . . . Are fortunes being made while these men get $50 a month? Talking to many soldiers, it is the worry that comes out of them that is impressive . . . they do not want to go home to find a civil war in the making. (Steinbeck, 1958: 75–6)

Sir William Beveridge, head of the Interdepartmental Committee on Social Insurance and Allied Services from June 1941, strikingly expressed the same view:

The purpose of victory is to live into a better world than the old world . . . to win freedom from want by maintaining incomes . . . Want could have been abolished in Britain just before the present war. It can be abolished after the war.

Box 5.3 Sir William Beveridge

William Beveridge, who became known as the "Father of the Welfare State," was the son of a civil servant in Bengal. William was born in Rangpur, India in 1879. His family returned to England in 1890 where they bought a seventeen-room house. William entered Balliol College, Oxford, in 1897, where he studied mathematics and established his life-long attraction to statistics, facts, and logic. Later he also studied law.

His first job as sub-warden for Toynbee Hall in Whitechapel in 1903 connected him to social work. As he later described, he went there to discover "why, with so much wealth in Britain . . . so much poverty [exists] and how poverty can be cured." He soon became a recognized authority on unemployment and compulsory insurance, and a regular columnist for the *Morning Post*. In 1908, the year when his book on unemployment was published, he became a civil servant, employed by the Board of Trade, and worked on an unemployment insurance scheme. During the war, he joined the Munitions of War Committee, and then the Ministry of Munitions. Between 1916 and 1919, in the Ministry of Food, Beveridge became the mogul of price control and rationing. During his years in the civil service he realized the need for an enlightened, impartial state regulation to handle economy and social issues.

Beveridge had barely any private life. Surrounded by close friends, and probably a closet homosexual, he did not marry until the age of sixty-three. All his energies were invested in work. After the war, he revised some of his wartime views and returned to academia: in 1919 he became the director of the London School of Economics, a small institution which, under his leadership, became an internationally renowned center of social sciences.

During the interwar years Beveridge developed his concepts and published several studies, among them *Insurance for All and Everything* (1924), *Tariffs: the Case Examined* (1931), *Planning Under Socialism* (1936), and *Full Employment* (1944). During the Great Depression he gave up his free trade idea and returned to state interventionism, even accepting state planning, within a democratic system. Beveridge did not have strict partisan commitments. He preferred the middle road between Labour and

Conservatives, though having been given a peerage after the war he joined the Liberals in the House of Lords.

Destiny accidentally handed him the opportunity to make history. When World War II broke out, he bombarded the government with pleas to return to the civil service. In 1940, he became chairman of the Manpower Requirements Committee. Ernest Bevin, minister of labour, however, disliked him, and to get rid of him "kicked him upstairs" to become chairman of the Interdepartmental Social Insurance Committee in 1941. The coordination of insurance policy (among seven departments) was not a central question at that time. Beveridge, however, using his vast knowledge on the topic, consulted Keynes, worked on his report, and finished it in October 1942. It became the Bible of the welfare state. Although several welfare institutions were already in existence in the West, and Sweden was on the way to establishing a welfare state, the Beveridge Report was the first plan to offer a comprehensive and consistent model. It reinterpreted citizen rights to include the right to employment and social security, and advocated a non-contributory, broad welfare system and full employment. Beveridge became a national hero. The report appeared in a time of strong belief in social solidarity and burden-sharing: an atmosphere of social reforms. The concept took hold in Britain, and throughout most of Western Europe. The postwar European welfare state was born.

The Beveridge Report of 1942 indeed presented a complex social security plan that covered all citizens, and the rates of benefits were equal for men and women.

Medical treatment covering all requirements will be provided for all citizens . . . whatever medical treatment he requires, in whatever form he requires it . . . [including] dental, ophthalmic and surgical appliances, nursing and midwifery and rehabilitation after accidents . . . The service itself should be provided where needed without contribution conditions in any individual case. Restoration of a sick person to health is a duty of the State . . . [Young people below working age will receive children allowances, retired people above 60 (women) and 65 (men) receive pension. Unemployment benefit, disability benefit, and training benefit] will be at the same rate, irrespective of previous earnings. This rate will provide by itself the income necessary for subsistence in all normal cases. (Beveridge, 1942)

The recommendations of the report were rapidly realized: family allowances in 1945, the National Insurance Act and Industrial Injuries Act, as well as the National Health Service Act in 1946; they came into operation in July 1948. Social service expenditures jumped from £0.52 billion in 1938–9 to £1.01 billion and £1.41 billion by 1947–8 and 1949–50, respectively (Pollard, 1983: 266, 272).

Thomas Humphrey Marshall, in a lecture at Cambridge University in 1949, first developed the idea of *social citizenship*. In his evolutionary concept, based on British historical experience, the eighteenth century established individual freedom. Based on these civil rights, the nineteenth century introduced political freedom. These earlier stages of civil and political citizenship rights were necessary prerequisites for the rise and development of the market economy and capitalism. Capitalist markets, however, generate inequalities. As a corrective force, based on the previous stages of development, social rights became an inseparable part of twentieth-century citizenship rights: according to the concept of social citizenship, every citizen has the right to live the life of a civilized being according to the standards prevailing in the society (Marshall, 1950). Those who reject egalitarian concepts still accept the importance of social policy that guarantees the range of goods and services necessary to function in the society to avoid reproducing social exclusion (Sen, 1992).

Postwar Western Europe, indeed, rushed to adopt the concept of national solidarity as the basic principle of social security systems. This time too, various political forces were behind the movement. Strong trade unions and the social democratic parties, in some of the countries, served as the engines of this development. The German Social Democratic Party at its 1959 Bad Godesberg congress stated that the party "from being a workers' party became a party for the entire people" serving the interest of all social layers (Weimer, 1998: 138). One of the most effective driving forces, however, was the emerging cold war and the competition between capitalism and socialism. It was a complex confrontation, with a sharp arms race and space race, but with an equally sharp growth race and welfare race. Postwar capitalism sought to beat its rival regime not only by greater military strength, higher productivity, technological achievements, and economic efficiency, but also with better welfare policies and standards. Western capitalism established a new "capitalism with a human face."

Existing social insurances, consequently, were extended. In some countries, such as France, initially, in the *sécurité sociale* in 1945, "social rights were understood to a large extent as employment-related rights . . . Access to benefits was guaranteed to workers and their families." Besides the *régime général*, the main scheme which covered two-thirds of the working people, 122 *régimes spéciaux et particuliers* (special schemes) were introduced for various occupational groups. Schemes for the self-employed and farmers were also initiated during the *trente glorieuse* (three glorious decades)

between 1945 and 1975 and the French system "came close to the establishment of [welfare privileges as] de facto citizenship rights for the whole
population." In 1988, a guaranteed minimum income (RMI) was introduced for those who, as President Mitterrand phrased it, "have nothing, can
do nothing, are nothing. It is the pre-condition to their social re-insertion"
(Bussemaker, 1999: 44–6, 51).

In most countries social insurance was granted to every citizen, welfare
institutions became universal and comprehensive, and the welfare state
redefined citizenship rights. Besides political rights, the new interpretation
of citizenship rights included the right to social services and employment to
guarantee security and basic equality: a "full membership" in the national
community. After World War II, extensive reforms in several countries
(Belgium, France, Sweden, Switzerland, the United Kingdom) made the
catalogue of covered risks complete, so that by 1950 all nations had rather
comprehensive programs for the four "main risks."

All countries had compulsory pension insurance . . . eleven possessed compulsory accident insurance, nine had compulsory sickness insurance, while seven
had adopted compulsory unemployment insurance. (Flora and Heidenheimer,
1981: 54)

After 1950 social insurance was further extended to all citizens with the
introduction of universal insurance schemes. Several new services were
added: free education at all levels, including higher education, and, in
some countries, free retraining to learn new skills or professions. Maternity
(in several cases parental) leave was introduced with full or part salary,
varying between six weeks and six months. Family allowances were paid
per child up to the age of fourteen or twenty-one. Paid holiday became
general and generous: by 1955, twenty-nine days in Sweden, twenty-eight
days in Germany and Italy. During the 1960s, the average paid holiday
reached 32–35 days in Western Europe. Slum clearance and state-financed
housing projects, low-rent housing, cultural subsidies, and other welfare
institutions were also established.

Per capita social security expenditures in Western Europe increased tenfold between the 1930s and 1957. During the first postwar decade, expenditure on social services increased by fourteen times in Italy, seven times in
France, six times in Sweden, and four times in Western Europe as a whole.
As a consequence, 40–50% of the GNP went on welfare expenditure.

The European Community advocated "vigorous actions in the social
field" and worked out a Social Action Program to combat poverty. The
program was accepted by the Council of Ministers in 1974. It targeted
"chronic poverty" the "neglected minority of chronically poor, such as the

'unemployable' and their families, families on exceptionally low incomes or fatherless families," noting that "these groups find themselves trapped in an almost inescapable cycle of poverty." The program, an Irish initiative, originally targeted three years between 1975–8, but was extended by the Council's decision of December 1977 (Dennett et al., 1982: 3–5, 210). Several new European Community member countries introduced welfare measures from the 1970s. Spain, waiting for acceptance to the Community, increased transfer of social benefits from 9% to 14% of the GDP, while social expenditures jumped from 15% to 22% (Bussemaker, 1999: 101).

Although the economy's market mechanism remained basically intact, the welfare state intervened and modified outcomes of market forces (Barr, 2001: 14). The redistributive social system of the welfare state, for example, reduced income disparities. "The urge for economic equalization," said Gunnar Myrdal of the postwar European atmosphere, "is everywhere present, and it is commonly proclaimed as a principle" (Myrdal, 1960: 38). In Denmark, the income share of the top 5% of the population declined from 27% to 17% between 1939 and 1964, while the share of the bottom 60% of the population increased from 27% to 33%. Sweden had a similar equalization trend: the income share of the top 5% declined from 28% to 18%, while the share of the bottom 60% increased from 23% to 33%. In Britain the first group's share declined from 30% to 19%, and the latter's increased from 33% to 37% (Kraus, 1981: 215, 217–18). Income polarization became more moderate in the welfare states since free, or state subsidized services decreased the role of salary and income. "This means that in most countries, one-fifth to one-fourth of private consumption is financed by public budgets through social transfer payments" (Kohl, 1981: 317).

However, the welfare state is there not so much to act as a "Robin Hood" – redistributing income to reduce social exclusion and providing poverty relief using tax money from the more well-to-do layers of society – but more to serve as a "piggy bank," using Nicholas Barr's terms – to establish "a series of institutions that provide insurance and offer a mechanism for redistribution over the life cycle." According to Barr, "three broad areas" of the activity of welfare states belong to this category: insurance, pensions, and education. While pensions redistribute from middle years to later years of life, education redistributes from middle years to earlier years. The state must redistribute over the life cycle, argues Barr, because information is limited for a given individual, and uncertainty and risks are too big to be amenable to any insurance scheme except one that is publicly organized. If such insurance is considered a private responsibility, many people will exclude themselves from society. The community, however, will ultimately be responsible for dependent children of the failed uninsured, and for paying for the consequences of the health hazards of the noninsured (Barr, 2001: 1, 6, 7, 42).

The "piggy bank" role of the welfare state, in financial terms, is probably more important than the income redistributive function of taxing the wealthy to finance free services and benefits for the poor. According to Jane Falkingham and John Hills, between two-thirds and three-quarters of spending was life-cycle redistribution, and only one-third to one-quarter of spending served the "Robin Hood" activity in the British welfare state (Falkingham and Hills, 1995). One can easily postulate that more than half of welfare state spending in Western Europe was life-cycle redistribution of the "piggy bank" function.

Educational revolution

In connection with the welfare state, but also with the scientific–technological revolution, postwar Europe experienced an educational explosion. In 1913, the average years of education per person (aged fifteen to sixty-four) varied between six and nine years in the most advanced countries of Europe. By 1950, these figures had increased only to eight to eleven years, by between 22% and 33% (Maddison, 1995a: 37). In Spain in 1931, 50% of the population was still illiterate. In Portugal in 1940, the rate of illiteracy was 55%; this had declined to 34% by 1960. While elementary education in Western Europe was generally extended, secondary education remained limited until the 1950s.

As a consequence of the war, however, science and its direct application gained a huge reputation. Moreover, a new technological age dawned and breathtaking technological development characterized the entire postwar period. It went hand in hand with the rise of modern health systems, the welfare state, mass tourism, and several other new phenomena, often termed "the service revolution," that required millions of new white-collar workers. Literacy and a basic education were no longer enough; the importance of secondary and higher education was broadly recognized. The Organization for European Economic Cooperation (OEEC) organized a special conference in The Hague in 1959 on the topic of "Techniques for forecasting future requirements of scientific and technical personnel." Europe was shocked to learn that 65% of an age group were qualified to enter higher education in the United States and Canada in the late 1950s, and 32% really did so. The European percentages were only 7% and 5%, respectively (Papadopoulos, 1994: 27). Educational expenditures acquired the status of crucial investments for economic growth, and most advanced countries during the postwar quarter of a century increased those expenditures by 15% each year. The advanced countries spent 5–8% of their income on education at the end of the century, compared with 2–3% in 1950–4 (UNESCO, 1999: II-508–11). As an important welfare measure, education at all levels, including higher education, became free of charge, which opened the doors for children from the lower layers of society, who basically had been excluded before the war.

Moreover, during the same period democracy made natural the elimination of gender discrimination in education, leading to equal education opportunities for women. The legacy of male society and the "natural" division of labor between men and women haunted the European educational system until the twentieth century. In France in 1920, only 10% of the students were women, and at Swedish universities this figure was only 27% even by 1950. The fifteen member countries of the European Union reached absolute equality by the mid-1990s, when 51% of the students in tertiary education were women (European Commission, 1998–9: 115). As a consequence of these various interrelated factors, the exclusive character of secondary and higher education was replaced by mass education at both levels.

Educational legislation also increased the length and improved the level of training. Pre-schooling, though not compulsory, became widespread and enrolled the majority of children between the ages of three and five years. Compulsory education was extended, generally to nine or ten years, and included a basic education, as well as a partial secondary education, common to nearly all children. The European ministers of education, at their sixth conference in Versailles in 1969, agreed, "that the period of education should be extended to 11 or 12 years for all and that education should be based on a broad common curriculum" (Papadopoulos, 1994: 96). Thus, secondary education, at least in part, became compulsory and various measures were taken to create a more democratic and comprehensive educational system.

Some countries, such as Norway and Sweden (with their nine-year common school), Italy (*scuola media*), and France (*collèges d'enseignement secondaire*), introduced a single-stream comprehensive curriculum for the lower secondary level. In most cases, however, as an OECD report stated: "The selective nature of general education at secondary level and the great differences in content of general and vocational courses are outstanding features. Students are separated early . . ." (OECD, 1987: 72). In one way or another, vocational training, which was not a part of institutionalized education, and was followed only by a modernized version of guild-type apprenticeship, now became an organic part of secondary education.

Secondary education became mass training for those between the ages of fifteen and eighteen. Enrollments ballooned, and in the two decades after 1960 included two-thirds of the age group. In Belgium, Sweden, Switzerland, and Austria, 80–90% of the generation enrolled in secondary education. Around three-quarters of the age group enrolled in France, Denmark, Norway, and Italy by the mid-1980s. An ever-increasing part of the population completed upper secondary education. At the end of the twentieth century 70% of the population between twenty-five and twenty-nine years of age, as an average, finished that level in the fifteen member countries of the European Union (European Commission, 1998–9: 120). The possibility of entering higher education for the masses opened up.

Belgium offers one of the best examples of an educational revolution after World War II. In the 1980s, 90%, 97%, and 100% of three, four, and five year olds, respectively, attended pre-schools. The June 4, 1983 law introduced twelve years of compulsory education, from six to eighteen years of age. The student–teacher ratio was 20:1 (European Commission, 1987).

At the same time, higher education became common throughout Western and Southern Europe and included one-fifth to one-quarter of the age group between eighteen and twenty-four. In some countries, this percentage neared (Britain) or even surpassed (Sweden) one-third of the generation (OECD, 1987: 82). During the late 1990s in Western Europe "about one-quarter of the total labour force" worked in so-called high-education sectors, where more than 40% of the workers are college educated (Commission, 2000: 37).

Economic growth and structural changes

The welfare states, in most cases with their mixed economies, exhibited the best economic performance in modern history. It happened in the "Golden Age" of postwar international prosperity, which equally characterized the advanced overseas countries, quite a few Asian economies, and Europe. After a surprisingly fast postwar reconstruction, Western Europe experienced unique capital formation. Gross savings in the advanced European countries reached around 12–14% of GDP from the late nineteenth to the mid-twentieth century. After World War II, however, in spite of massive social expenditures, savings jumped significantly: in France, Germany, Holland, and Britain they reached a record level of roughly 25% of the GDP between 1950 and 1973, and never declined below 20% of it until the end of the century. On the basis of savings being twice as high as before, gross fixed domestic investment also varied between 20% and 25% of GDP (Maddison, 1995b: 185–6). The gross stock of fixed non-residential capital (i.e. excluding housing and other consumer investments) in Germany and France increased more than sevenfold during the second half of the century. In 1950, the capital stock of France, Germany, Britain, and the Netherlands amounted to only 40% of that of the United States. By 1991, the same capital stock surpassed the U.S. level by about 8%, while the U.S. level itself increased nearly fourfold. The stock of European machinery and equipment increased by thirteen times and the average age of machinery dropped to 6–7 years by 1991 (Maddison, 1995b: 144–9, 154–5).

European capital formation and investment during the second half of the twentieth century thus reached a level many times higher than ever before, introducing the most modern postwar technology and new economic sectors. The technological content of that period was the new industrial and communications revolution, which took root with the invention of the transistor, nuclear fusion, and the first computers. These inventions were mostly international scientific achievements, but their realization occurred generally in the United States. Technology transfer, however, made possible their broad application in postwar Europe, and accelerated growth in technology importer countries. Output and services were radically transformed.

A symbol of this new trend was the dawn of the nuclear age, which manifested itself in Europe, as in the United States, as a war industry producing weapons of mass destruction, and the atomic and hydrogen bombs. In the postwar decades the Soviet Union, Britain, and France also became nuclear powers. Britain initiated its nuclear program in the 1950s, and tested its first bomb in 1957. France, seeking to establish its great power position, launched a nuclear program and tested a bomb in 1968. Meanwhile, France also became an advocate of the Euratom agreement as part of the Treaties of Rome. Germany and Italy introduced their national nuclear programs in 1959 (Urwin, 1995: 77).

The new energy sources, however, were harnessed for peaceful applications and gradually became one of the most important energy sources for the European countries. "The military and peacetime nuclear research programs," stated DeLeon, "cannot be clearly separated." The commercial light water reactors partially stemmed from the Navy's nuclear submarine propulsion program (DeLeon, 1979: 11, 101). Britain's government White Paper in 1955 announced a plan to construct twelve large power-only nuclear plants by the end of 1965, providing one-quarter of the country's electricity. Britain opened the first full-scale commercial nuclear power plant in October 1956 at Calder Hall. Nuclear power plants followed in Dumfriesshire (1959), Gloucestershire and Essex (1962), Cumberland (1963), and other locations during the 1970s and 1980s. The French First

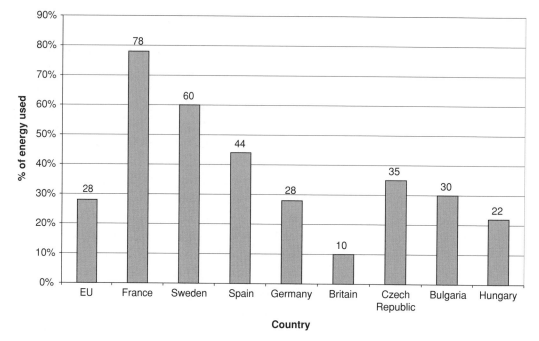

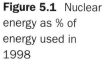

Figure 5.1 Nuclear energy as % of energy used in 1998

Five-Year Plan in 1951 contained an ambitious nuclear power program. As the State Secretary for Atomic Energy, Felix Gaillard, stated to parliament, if France "does not have [atomic power], it will appear as helpless as the most backward nations of the world today . . ." France opened the Châtillon research center in 1946, and the first nuclear electric power station in Bagnols-sur-Céze in 1956, followed by many others. Germany founded a Ministry for Atomic Energy in 1956, and opened its first reactor in Kahl, Bavaria in 1962 (DeLeon, 1979: 11, 101–3, 107, 129–30, 136–8, 154). Rapid increase of nuclear power capacity characterized Europe from the 1950s to the early 1980s; after that, nuclear programs slowed down. In the fifteen member countries of the European Union, nuclear energy production stood at one-quarter of total energy output in the late 1980s, and represented 28% of it by the end of the century. In some of the countries, nuclear energy became the most important energy source (see Figure 5.1): 78% of primary energy production is nuclear energy in France, 60% in Sweden, 44% in Spain, 27–28% in Germany and Finland, and 10% in Britain (European Commission, 1998–9: 412).

Electronics also heralded the emergence of a new epoch. The former leading sectors declined or were rejuvenated, striking structural changes occurred, and the rise of new leading sectors of a post-industrial age strengthened the position of those countries that were able to adjust. Modernization of the European economy thus led to dramatic structural changes, and a permanent shift of labor and investment from lower to higher productivity sectors.

Structural changes were helped by the renewal of infrastructure. One of the most spectacular elements was extensive motorway construction. The spread of car transportation rendered the existing road system obsolete. New fast vehicles required fast roads offered by the autobahn. At the beginning, their building was linked to war preparation, and before the war autobahn and autostrada were built only in Germany and Italy. Even in 1970, more than half of West European freeways could be found in these two countries. The real era of the European freeway began with the Geneva Declaration of 1950, which called for the construction of an international, connected European highway system of 75,000 kilometers. Italy built the *Autostrada del Sole* from Chiasso to Reggio Calabria during the 1950s and 1960s, while Switzerland began the construction of its highway system in the 1960s. An international European road network, the "E-routes," linked all countries of the continent. In 1965 the network of roads covered 46,000 kilometers; by 1975 this had been expanded to 64,000 kilometers, more than one-third of which represented the highway network in eighteen Western countries (*Basic Statistics*, 1977: 112).

A rapidly developing air transportation network was equally characteristic. Civil aviation became a major form of mass transportation in postwar Europe, kicking off in September and October 1945 when Swissair and Air France resumed operations. The Scandinavian countries collaborated to form Scandinavian Airlines System (SAS) in the summer of 1946. Faster and larger planes were produced, and regular flights connected capitals on all continents. In 1950, national airlines accomplished 700 times more passenger kilometers than before the war. Regular freight transportation was also established.

The appearance of the jetfighter near the end of the war transformed postwar aviation. Britain introduced commercial jet aviation in 1953 with the De Havilland Comet, followed by France with the SE-210 Caravelle. In the 1960s jumbo jets and supersonic aircraft were produced. The Boeing 747 made its first commercial flight with nearly 500 passengers in 1970 (Taylor and Mondey, 1983: 225).

European countries engaged in significant cooperation: the French–German agreement in 1969 led to the realization of the Airbus program. The new plane was introduced in the mid-1970s and from the 1980s conquered half of the world market in its category. The child of the French–British cooperation was the Concorde, first flown in 1969 and put into commercial use in 1976 (Béteille, 1995: 2, 7–10). Air transportation became the fastest developing branch of transportation in the second half of the century

(*Basic Statistics*, 1961: 77). By the late 1980s, 600 times more passenger kilometers and 1,200 times more freight tonne/kilometers were flown than in 1950 (Mitchell, 1998: 724–7).

The West European economies were transformed by dramatic structural changes. One of the most visible elements of restructuring was the "disappearance" of the agricultural population – its percentage share of the active population declined from 20–25% in 1950 to roughly 10% by the 1970s. In France in 1946, 36% of the population worked in agriculture, but this fell to 10% by 1975. In another 10–20 years, the percentage of French farmers fell to 2–3%. This was a consequence of the "industrialization" of agriculture. Mechanization became a major force of growth. Between 1950 and 1957, in the entire area of the Council of Europe, the number of tractors increased fourfold (*Council of Europe*, 1959: 208). During the 1970s and 1980s, virtually all aspects of farm production experienced mechanization: sowing, hoeing, and harvesting, including potatoes, sugar beets, grapes, and fruits. The use of artificial fertilizer and other chemical agents, a second major factor of industrializing agriculture, appeared around the turn of the century but made relatively slow progress during the first fifty years. After World War II, fertilizer use increased to 170 kilograms/hectare in the European Community by the mid-1960s, and 270–300 kilograms/hectare by the mid-1970s, led by the Netherlands and other highly productive agricultural economies, which used 400–500 kilograms/hectare.

As a consequence, agricultural productivity increased steeply and output shot up: in the second half of the century, annually by 2.5% in Western Europe, and about 3% in the Mediterranean countries. Britain offers a typical example: agricultural output doubled between 1950 and 1980, while employment in this sector declined by one-third. Extensive mechanization and capital investments led to a 4–5% annual increase in labor productivity. The value of food imports also declined by more than half (from 9% to 4% of GNP). In the mid-1970s, Britain supplied three-quarters of the meat and two-thirds of the wheat and cheese consumed domestically (Pollard, 1983).

In Germany, employment in agriculture declined from 5.9 million to 1.5 million people between 1949 and 1975, only 7% of the active population in the latter year. Meanwhile, the industrialization of agriculture increased labor productivity in that sector by 8.5 times. Agricultural employment declined precipitously in postwar Sweden by nearly 60%, and in Denmark by 40%, between 1946–50 and 1966–70. Meanwhile, labor productivity in agriculture, due to technological modernization, more than doubled. Significantly increased agricultural output that made Western Europe self-sufficient and even an exporter of food, however, went hand in hand with a dramatically decreasing share of agriculture in national product: in 1970–4, it varied between 3% and 10% in the Western countries, the lowest being in Germany and Britain. The contribution of agriculture to the value added dropped from 12% to less than 7% in France. This development, together with traditional American agricultural export activities, increased worldwide agricultural overproduction and hit Third World countries badly.

The share of the industrial labor force did not change much until the 1970s. A restructuring of industry nevertheless rejuvenated this sector. During the postwar quarter of a century, the old staple industries stagnated or even declined, while the application of new technology led to a spectacular rise in new sectors of the economy. In Britain during the 1960s and 1970s, the output of coal, ferrous- and non-ferrous metals dropped by 50%, while textiles declined by roughly 20%. In 1949–51, Britain was still the world's largest shipbuilder for export, and produced 38% of the world's total. By the mid-1960s, however, the country's ship exports dropped by 63% and British shipbuilding accounted for only 4% of the world's total, pushing it down to eighth place. Although the production of motor vehicles more than trebled between 1950 and 1965, Britain lost its position to international competition. By 1980, nearly 40% of domestic consumption was supplied by imports. However, output of chemicals nearly doubled and electrical engineering increased by nearly 50%.

In France, the energy sector was revolutionized. The 1946 Monnet Plan focused on this sector. Indeed, energy consumption increased by 250% between 1950 and 1970, but coal's share dropped from 74% to 17%. In the first decades, petroleum products gained ground (from 18% to 51% between 1950 and 1968). Then, after the announcement of an ambitious nuclear power program in 1955, the role of atomic energy assumed prominence. The automotive industry was also successful: the domestic market grew energetically. Car exports also rose from 26% to 44% of output. "Large-scale, dynamic industry . . . was beginning to find the French market too narrow," and a rapid internationalization began (Caron, 1979: 206–29).

In Belgium, the "opening" of the economy to increasing foreign trade contributed to the decline of the country's staple traditional industries and to the rise of new industrial sectors. Coal production fell from nearly 30 million tonnes to 13 million tonnes during the 1960s. The number of jobs in the textile industry decreased by two-thirds between 1948 and 1968. Foreign trade developed at a rate of 6% per year in one single decade, after the Treaty of Rome (1957), and Belgian exports flooded neighboring countries. Exports to France and Germany doubled. Multinational companies invested heavily, mostly in Flanders, and their role became decisive in modern sectors such as the chemical, rubber, and petroleum industries. The output of the chemical industry and of electricity more than doubled during the 1960s.

Structural changes in Scandinavian industry were dramatic. Sweden's most important traditional export goods – wood, pulp, paper, and iron ore – still represented 50% of total exports in 1947–50; by 1967–70, however, that share had declined to 27%. Meanwhile, exports of the most modern engineering products increased from 27% to 43%. In Norway, such traditional staples as fish, wood, and paper made up 24% of exports in 1946; by 1970, this share had declined to 15%. Exports of chemical products increased from 11% to 17% during the period. In Denmark, 71% of exports consisted of agricultural products and processed food in 1946–9, but by 1967–70 that share had dropped to 30%. Instead, 70% of Danish export items were industrial products.

The real engine of postwar West European prosperity, however, was Germany. Based on its strong domestic market and its integration into the European Community, Germany's economic growth also relied on an impressive structural transformation. A great part of the labor force was shifted to industry, so that the number of industrial workers increased from 8.7 million to 13.2 million between 1950 and 1965. Beginning in the mid-1960s, however, industrial employment began to decline (1975: 11.6 million), and further sectoral changes were characterized by a rapid increase of employment in the service sector. A permanent restructuring of Germany's traditionally strong and modern industry led to the relative decline of previously leading branches and the rise of the new technology sectors: industrial output in the iron, steel, textile, clothing, food, and wood industries combined declined from 42% to 32%. The mining industry lost one-quarter of its jobs. However, new, technologically advanced and research-intensive branches, such as the chemical, electrical, and precision-engineering industries, along with the business machinery and road vehicle industries increased their contribution to industrial value added from 26% to 42%.

The most striking element of structural renewal was the rapid rise of services. Employment in this sector increased at the fastest tempo, reaching roughly half and then two-thirds of the active population in what has often been called a "service revolution" (see Chapter 6). The service sector showed exceptional growth in Britain. Banking, insurance, business, professional, and scientific services employed twice as many people in 1970 as in 1950, and the share of services in GDP increased from 35% to 50% between 1950 and 1980. France's service sector employment increased from 33%

to 51% in the same period. In Norway and Sweden the contribution of the service sector to GDP increased from 50% and 47% to 58% and 53%, respectively (Krantz, 1987: 250, 254, 257, 266, 271, 274).

A revolutionary increase in labor productivity was the result of several factors: sharply increased investments; a better educated, trained, and more flexible labor force; the revolutionary technological and managerial change in the second half of the century; structural modernization, which shifted the labor force from lower to higher productivity sectors; and new national, European, and international institution building. Productivity increase became the leading factor in economic growth. In the world's six leading economies, including four European countries, labor and capital productivity increased annually by 1.74% and 0.46%, respectively, between 1913 and 1950. This relatively moderate productivity increase, however, was followed by a 4.84% and 0.73% annual increase between 1950 and 1973. Labor productivity in agriculture increased by roughly 2% per year in France and Holland in the first half of the century, but by about 6% per annum between 1950 and 1973, and as an average by 5% afterwards. Industrial productivity in France, Germany, and Holland improved only by 1–2% per year before 1950, but by 5–6% during the following quarter of a century. Labor productivity in general increased threefold in Britain, more than fourfold in Holland, more than fivefold in France, Italy, Norway, and Greece, and six-to sevenfold in Spain, Ireland, and Portugal between 1950 and the 1990s. As an average, labor productivity increased by 4.3 times in Western Europe and 6.2 times in Ireland and the Mediterranean countries. While a West European worker produced between $2 and $4 (1990 value) GDP per hour in 1913, and between $3 and $6 by 1950, he produced $25–28 GDP per hour in 1992. Figures for Southern and Eastern Europe are shown in Figure 5.2.

Compared with the technology leader, the United States, productivity in advanced European countries was indexed in 1950 at 40–60%. By the end of the century, productivity in most West European countries, especially France, Germany, and Holland, was equal to the American level (Maddison, 1995b: 70).

All of these spectacular developments were both causes and consequences of an unprecedented increase in domestic consumption. The consumption vacuum of the 1930s and 1940s produced consumption "hunger" or demand that was greater than "normal." The postwar generations suffered long from shortages of jobs, income, and consumer goods, which were from time to time rationed in several countries. It had been the case since 1914, with only a break of a few years in the later 1920s and later 1930s. Delayed and suppressed consumption became an engine of rapid postwar growth.

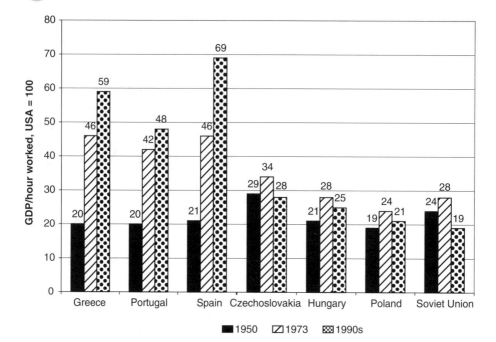

Figure 5.2 Labor productivity in Southern and Eastern Europe, 1950–90s

Consumerism was determined by rising income levels. During the 1960s and 1970s, annual household consumption in the ten most developed European countries increased, as an average, by more than 3%, while in less developed countries such as Spain, Portugal, and Greece it grew by 5% (European Commission, 1971–80: 37). Private consumption increase rose by 4–5% per year in the early 1970s in Western Europe (*Economic Survey*, 1991). Increasing income and consumption generated a shift from basics toward durables. The simple and well-proven Engel's Law expresses this consequence of income growth: the share of income spent on food and clothing decreases as consumer incomes rise. Switzerland was typical: in 1912, an average worker's household spent 61% of its income on food and clothing (see Figure 5.3); by the end of the century this expenditure dropped to 12% (*Statistisches Jahrbuch der Schweiz*, 1950, 2001). In 1950, the population of Britain, France, and Germany spent 43–45% of their income on food. In Finland this surpassed 50%, and reached 58% and 60% in Greece and Italy, respectively (Mueller, 1965: 92–3). By 1971 the ten most developed countries, as an average, spent only 27% on food. Spain and Portugal, however, still spent 34% and 52%, respectively.

This trend continued during the last third of the century, and by the mid-1990s the Belgians, Dutch, and Finns spent only 11–13%, while the fifteen best-developed European countries altogether spent about 13–14% of their incomes on food. Expenditure on clothing and footwear, standing at 15–16% in 1950, dropped to less than 7% by 1996 in the European Union

Figure 5.3

Spending on food and clothing: Switzerland, 1912–2000

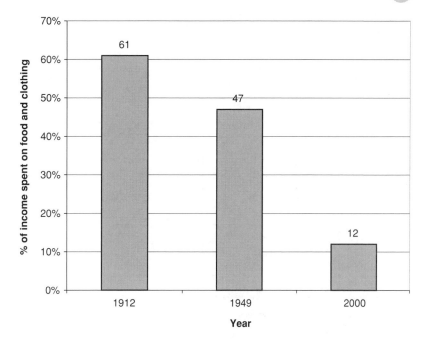

member states (European Commission, 1998–9: 164, 174). Since only one-fifth instead of nearly two-thirds of household expenditure went on food and clothing at the end of the century, compared with more than half a century before (see Figure 5.4), rising income and consumption led to a drastic change in consumption structure and the extremely rapid growth in consumption of durables and luxury goods. Postwar German journalistic jargon summed up the essence of Engel's Law in most expressive terms: while the first wave of consumption was called *Fresswelle* ("gobbling" wave) and *Kleidungswelle* (clothing wave), the uninhibited rise of consumption that followed was called *Reisewelle* (wave of travel).

The West European welfare states became consumer societies after World War II, and created an unparalleled demand-led economic upswing, which would characterize the quarter of a century between the early 1950s and the mid-1970s. Several organizational innovations helped and accelerated consumerism. One of them was the modern financing method. People opened bank accounts. The number of personal accounts doubled in Belgium, from 1.3 million to 2.6 million, in five years during the first half of the 1960s. Personal loans, mortgage loans, and the introduction of credit cards also fueled consumption.

Consumerism was also strongly assisted by modern mass distribution systems: supermarkets, unit price stores, shopping malls, various mass marketing chain stores, and consumer cooperatives spread from the second half of the 1960s. Such modern stores were rare before World War II, though

Figure 5.4

Spending on basics (food, clothing, etc.); 15 best-developed EU countries

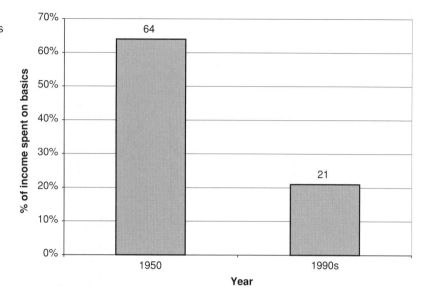

the first breakthrough of modern trade, the elegantly built department stores, the "cathedrals of consumption" (Crossick and Jaumain, 1999), began changing retail trade before the twentieth century. Their role nevertheless remained limited. Small independent shops preserved their overwhelming share of annual sales, and dominated Europe until the 1950s. American-type mass distribution, however, appeared and spread during the second half of the 1950s: the number of self-service stores in operation in Europe increased from 1,200 in 1950 to 45,500 in the early 1960s. In Germany, the number of self-service stores increased from 39 in 1951 to 53,000 by 1965.

By the early 1970s, Germany and France, as well as several smaller states including Belgium, Holland, Switzerland, and the Scandinavian countries . . . were at home with mass marketing, the supermarket, chain retailing, and the many other techniques and institutions . . . of modern commerce. (De Grazia, 1998: 59, 74, 79)

One of the very first phenomena of consumerism was the tremendous housing boom, which followed the years of reconstruction. Housing in France experienced spectacular expansion. From the 1950s to the 1970s, 26–27% of total investments were channeled into this sector. Comfortable, modern dwellings with indoor bathrooms and lavatories comprised only one-quarter of dwellings in the early 1960s; in little more than a decade, that figure had jumped to nearly two-thirds. In the early 1950s, only 21% of French households owned a car; by 1972, 60 out of 100 households did so. Refrigerators and washing machines were still rarities in the mid-1950s

Box 5.4 Marks and Spencer

Marks and Spencer, which became a limited company in 1903 in Manchester, Britain, emerged as one of the world's largest retail companies. At the end of the twentieth century, it employed 68,000 people, had 286 stores, several factories producing for the stores in Britain, and served 13 million shoppers with clothing, shoes, underwear, furniture, and various homeware items and food, including 85 million sandwiches sold weekly in 2000.

Michael Marks, the son of a Jewish tailor in Grodno, escaped from the bloody Russian pogroms of 1881, arrived in England the following year. With a borrowed £5, he became a peddler around Leeds. Since he did not speak a word of English, he put a sign on his tray: "Don't ask price, everything is a penny." This turned out to be the key to his success. In a few years, he opened his first M. Marks Penny Bazaar, and soon he had a dozen market stalls in Yorkshire and Lancashire. He looked for a partner to enable him to expand and found Tom Spencer, who invested his £300 savings into the business and became a half owner. The first Marks and Spencer Penny Bazaar store was opened in Manchester. The family lived above the store, but by 1903, when the company went public, they owned thirty-six market bazaars and shops, including three in London. In 1908, Tom Spencer had already retired, and Marks died at the age of forty-seven.

His son, Simon Marks, was nineteen years old when he joined the family business two months before his father's death. He soon found a close friend, Israel Sieff, as his partner, and in fact each married the other's sister. Simon bought up all the shares available on the market, and began running the business as joint managing director with his friend. After the war, he moved to London where he had a huge network of stores – by 1927 there were 135 stores with 10,000 employees. Next year, celebrating his father's memory, he introduced the St. Michael trademark which was used until the end of the century. The business, based on good-quality products and low prices, flourished. More than 160 stores were built or enlarged, and sales increased ten times even during the Great Depression between 1929 and 1939, when 17,000 employees worked in 234 stores. The trademark shop at the corner of London's Oxford and Orchard Streets was opened. The food and then fruit departments were introduced in the 1930s. The company pioneered ordering directly from manufacturers, avoiding wholesalers. Nothing was sold for more than 5 shillings.

Simon Marks, the son of a peddler, a bold innovator who introduced the retail revolution to Britain, was knighted during the war and received an hereditary peerage by 1961. Yet he remained a traditional, old-style merchant, visiting the Oxford Street store every day, and running the growing empire as an old family store. Nine out of fourteen directors on the board were generally family members, and Simon controlled the majority (voting) package of shares. In 1964, at the age of seventy-six, during a visit to one of the company's departments, he collapsed and died. His partner-friend, Israel Sieff, and then their sons, continued to run the enterprise.

The first non-family member chairman and manager took over only in 1984. Marks and Spencer became a modern, professionally managed company. Expansion was continuous: the company bought the People's Department Stores of Canada in 1974, and owned 227 stores in the country by 1995. Marks and Spencer bought the Brooks Brothers menswear chain in the United States in 1989, and nineteen Littlewoods stores in Britain in 1997. The company had four stores in Paris, and several in Germany, Spain, Ireland, and Hong Kong.

Marks and Spencer, a penny bazaar at the beginning of the century, had become a multinational retail chain at the end of it. Yet it was soon to experience severe financial difficulties.

(8 per 100 households), and TV barely existed at all (1 in 100 households). By 1972, 60–80% of households had all of these machines. Expenditure on food declined from half to one-third of family budgets, while expenditure on households, household equipment, health care, cultural and leisure activities increased from 23% to 44% between 1950 and 1973. "In a quarter of a century households changed from a struggle for survival to a search for personal fulfillment" (Caron, 1979: 211, 214–15). In 1950, in poorer countries such as Italy, only half of the dwellings had running water and an indoor toilet, and only 10% had a bathroom. Of 100 inhabitants, only three had telephones, fewer than eight had TVs, and less than one had a car. By the 1970s, the number of telephones and cars increased seventeen and forty times, respectively (Zamagni, 1993: 324, 376).

In postwar Britain official calculations estimated a shortage of 1.25 million houses. Although that many additional housing units had been built by 1951, the number of married households grew faster so that the housing shortage of that year was, again, estimated at between 1 million and 2 million (Pollard, 1983: 269–70). The German housing situation is best illustrated by the fact that between 1949 and the mid-1960s, 7.5 million dwellings were built and 22 million people moved into new homes (Weimer, 1998:

Table 5.2 Radio and TV licenses in Western Europe
(in 1,000s) (based on Mitchell, 1998: 775–9)

Year	Radio		TV	
1950[*]	41,884	100	177	100
1973	86,625	207	23,982	1,355

* For TV licenses, 1955; in some cases later, mostly between 1956 and 1960

144). The Scandinavian countries also experienced a "widespread acceleration in residential construction" during the 1950s and 1960s, partly as a consequence of liberalized quantitative controls on building permits, preferential treatment in credit policy, and full deduction of interest payments in taxable income (Andersen and Åkerholm, 1982: 235–6).

The consumption explosion soon reached inside the new homes. Mechanization of households became a driving force of consumption and economic growth. Energy consumption per capita of the fifteen most advanced Western countries increased by nearly 50% in the single decade between 1950 and the early 1960s. While electric household machines remained luxury goods until World War II, during the 1950s to the 1970s mechanization of West European households was almost complete. By the mid-1970s, almost every European household had a radio. The market was almost saturated (UNESCO, 1963, 1999). While television service was introduced in Britain and Germany before World War II, it did not really take off until after the war (see Table 5.2) and then in the early 1950s color TV appeared as well (UNESCO, 1963: 458–60; 1999: IV-230–6).

Although modern consumer durables spread slowly in the first half of the century, they could be found in nearly all households during the second half. Communication became much more frequent and personal. Although traditional mail correspondence in Denmark, Italy, the Netherlands, and Switzerland more than doubled between 1950 and 1975, the telephone, through a fivefold increase, became the main, everyday means of communication: during the first three postwar decades, virtually everyone (400 sets per 1,000 inhabitants) had access to the telephone in Western Europe (see Figures 5.5 and 5.6).

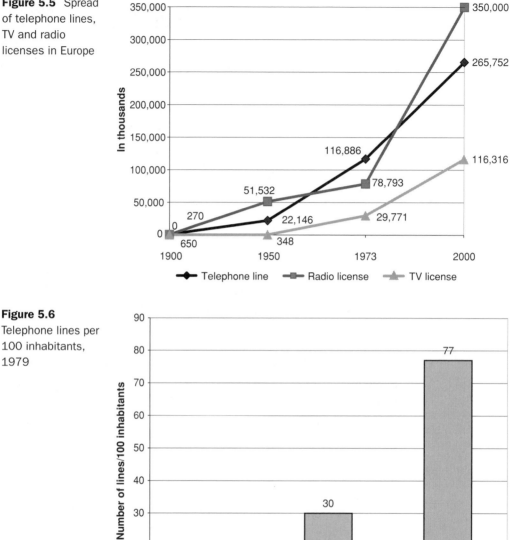

Figure 5.5 Spread of telephone lines, TV and radio licenses in Europe

Figure 5.6 Telephone lines per 100 inhabitants, 1979

When the 1928 "Home and Technology" show in Munich exhibited the mechanized household, it was only a vision of the future. More than half of German households did not even have electricity at that time, and only half of the households used an electric iron, while less than 1% had a washing machine (Reagin, 1998: 245). This situation did not change much until the end of the 1950s. In 1955, only one out of ten German households had a refrigerator. Traditional customs prevailed and three-quarters of German housewives bottled their own fruits and vegetables for winter (Wildt, 1998: 307). Neutral and flourishing Switzerland also maintained a traditional lifestyle and household.

Patterns of consumption had not changed much from the mid-nineteenth century. Most families in the 1950s lived in apartments, housework was done without technical appliances, and men went to work by bicycle or train. (Pfister, 1998: 369)

Durable goods flooded households after World War II. By 1974, as a general phenomenon in Western Europe, 59% of Belgian families had a car, 82% owned refrigerators, 88% watched TV, and 62% used washing machines (Mommen, 1994: 123–4, 148). Cultural expenditure also increased. People bought more books than before: in eleven West European countries book publication jumped more than five times during the second half of the century (UNESCO, 1999: IV-346–54).

Automobile transportation, introduced during the first half of the century, was still in its infancy in Europe. A car had been an expensive luxury before and immediately after the war. The smallest Fiat cars cost between two and two-and-a-half times the average worker's annual income (Zamagni, 1993: 314). In 1950, the number of private cars per 1,000 inhabitants was only 57 in Sweden, 46 in Britain, 20 in France, 18 in Germany, and 7.5 in Italy. After World War II, and especially during the 1970s, however, the most characteristic symbol of growing consumerism was the spectacular spread of automobiles across Western Europe. Between the 1950s and the 1970s several inexpensive models made the car accessible: the German Volkswagen Beetle, a design basically unchanged for decades, the French Citröen Deux Chevaux, and the British Morris Minor played important roles in this development. The car, even in small countries with excellent public transportation systems, became a standard and inseparable feature of Western households. Moreover, within three decades, the market had become practically saturated. Assuming an average of three people per family, the entire population owned cars by the end of the 1970s (see Figure 5.7). The number of private cars per 1,000 inhabitants in nine developed West European countries jumped to 318, a nearly twentyfold increase in Germany, and fortyfold in Italy (Fischer, 1978: 143; Mueller, 1965: 211; *Basic Statistics*, 1977: 164).

A growing modern freeway and road system with widespread car ownership reflected a significant change in lifestyle and leisure habits. Europe experienced a distinctive development trend toward shorter working weeks

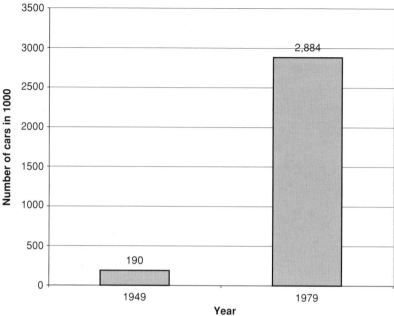

Figure 5.7 Number of cars in 10 best-developed EU countries

and longer vacations, especially compared with other rapidly developing advanced countries such as the United States and Japan. In both of the latter, the working week was longer and until the 1970s the average used vacation time in Japan was only two days. Europe, after the troubled first half of the century, was driven toward leisure. People became mobile and tourism became a mass phenomenon (Transport, 1998: 141, 144). In 1954, 73% of German tourists took trains and buses. The railroads had been revitalized and train travel increased tremendously: between the 1930s and the 1960s, the number of person-kilometers traveled by rail increased from 5.7 billion to 8.7 billion in Belgium, from 3.3 billion to 8.9 billion in Switzerland, and from 9 billion to 30.9 billion in Italy. By 1975, however, the car was the most important vehicle and more than 60% of German tourists used cars, and 12% traveled by plane. In 1965, Europeans traveled 979 billion passenger kilometers by car, but by 1975 this figure had more than doubled to 1.986 billion passenger kilometers. Air travel within Europe and between continents grew gradually and became common as well. In 1951, 0.2 million Italians traveled by plane; three decades later the number had risen to roughly 18 million. A huge industry and network of travel agencies emerged. Charter flights were organized – the first Mediterranean charter flight went to Corsica in 1950, and the Swiss Kuoni Travel Agency began organizing charter flight tours to Africa in the early 1950s. By the mid-1960s charter flights went to Bangkok and other Asian destinations.

In the 1970s, the company initiated a worldwide organizational network of subsidiaries. Millions of people visited other countries and spent vacations abroad. Spain, a most popular tourist destination, experienced a tourism explosion: in fifteen years, the number of tourists had increased more than eightfold and the income from tourism twentyfold (Harrison, 1985: 154–5).

This trend also continued during the last third of the century: the number of tourists' beds in Switzerland, one of the traditional tourist destinations, increased by more than 40% even during the last third of the century. (*Statistisches Jahrbuch der Schweiz*, 2001: 433)

In 1954, one-quarter of Germans traveled to take at least a week of holiday, 85% of them within their home country; by 1975, 56% of Germans traveled on vacation and more than half of them went abroad. Besides, instead of only one or two weeks the majority went on vacation for at least two or three weeks and secured the reputation of being the world champions of traveling.

International mass tourism became one of the most prominent signs of a new pattern of consumption. In 1950 there were 25 million travelers, but this figure grew more than 10% annually, to 160 million by 1970. Europe was the center of world tourism, since nearly three-quarters of the world's tourists visited the continent. Most of these were Europeans (Williams and Shaw, 1998: 19–20, 79, 107).

Export opportunities, which were also linked to the breathtaking consumption increases in Europe, created an even more dynamically growing export market for European countries. The postwar European economic integration process – pursued by the foundation of the European Community after 1957 – created one large (and gradually expanding) tariff-free European market. The West European countries increasingly turned toward each other and developed an export boom that made possible economies of scale for the member countries. In 1938, 53% of imports to European markets were European in origin, while 64% of exports were destined for other European countries; by 1970–2, 72–75% of European imports and exports, respectively, roughly three-quarters of European trade, originated from or was destined for other European countries.

Between 1870 and 1913, during one of the most dynamic periods of European capitalism, the value of merchandise exported from the advanced West European countries, in constant (1990) prices, increased by four times. From 1913 to 1950, however, exports stagnated and even declined by 4%. From the end of the war to 1973, European exports skyrocketed nearly six-and-a-half times (and nearly fourteenfold if two more decades

Table 5.3 Volume of exports, 1913 = 100%
(Maddison, 1989: 138)

Country	1950	1973
Austria	32	339
Belgium	112	876
Denmark	240	1,115
Finland	200	989
France	149	922
Germany	35	514
Italy	127	1,619
Netherlands	171	1,632
Norway	270	1,369
Sweden	276	1,298
Switzerland	113	676
United Kingdom	100	242

are included). Merchandise exports represented 9.4% of the aggregate GDP of Western Europe in 1950, but increased to 21% by 1973 (Maddison, 1995a: 38, 236). Altogether, in 1950 slightly more than 8% of all German manufactured goods went for exports; by 1974 roughly one-quarter of such goods were exported (Brenner, 1998: 69).

After the war West European trade experienced a rate of expansion greater than at any other time in modern history: by 1973 some West European countries had increased their volume of exports 10–15 times compared with pre-World War I levels (see Table 5.3).

The traditional trade connections in modern times linked industrial countries to those that produced food and raw materials. The exchange of industrial products for unprocessed products characterized trade among advanced core and less developed peripheral and colonial countries. After World War II, however, inter-European trade developed a new characteristic: trade among highly advanced industrialized countries. European imports from Latin America, Asia, Africa, and Oceania combined reached nearly one-third of total imports in 1938, but had dropped to 18% by 1970. The exchange of industrial products among highly developed countries became an important feature of postwar Western European trade. The industrialized European countries sold nearly one-third of their products outside the industrialized world before World War II, but only

Figure 5.8
Europe's
catching-up (GDP
per capita)
1950–73

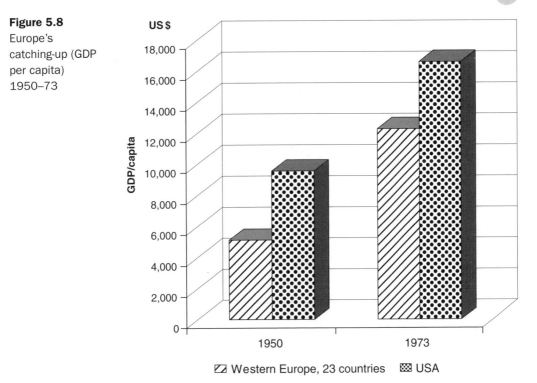

17% by 1972. More and more industrial products were produced in cooperation with other countries. Huge companies had subsidiaries in several
countries. They delivered parts and produced in specialized factories in
one of the countries and then had the goods put together on assembly lines
in another country. Postwar economic development was thus growth led
by a combination of technology, capital accumulation, structural changes,
domestic consumption, and exports.

Between 1950 and 1973, consequently, Europe experienced a breathtaking economic growth (see Figure 5.8): Britain and France, along with
Holland, had an annual growth rate 3–4 times faster than they had experienced between 1913 and 1950. Belgium's annual growth was five times
higher, while the Scandinavian countries and Switzerland increased their
growth rate by roughly 50%. As a consequence, Western Europe increased
its per capita GDP by nearly 250% in a quarter of a century. Some of the
fastest-growing countries tripled their incomes. Britain had the slowest
growth in Europe, but it was still equal to the American rate.

One of the most important new elements of Western economic development was the rapid rise and catching-up process of the previously
less developed Mediterranean and Northern countries. They experienced
many of the negative consequences of economic underdevelopment: social

polarization, and authoritarian political regimes. In the first half of the twentieth century, and to some extent even after World War II, Mussolini's Italy, Franco's Spain, Salazar's Portugal, and Greece's military junta were not *comme il faut* in the democratic West. However, during the cold war, as in the case of Germany, the United States and its Western allies put aside principles to follow pragmatic power politics. The Truman Doctrine of 1947 clearly signaled the Western political strategy toward oppressive, military regimes in the Mediterranean region. The policy of acceptance and assistance was easily adopted regarding Italy. Here, unlike in Germany, a strong resistance movement and a coup had destroyed the fascist government. An anti-fascist coalition took over and Italy joined the Allies in 1943. Rapid industrialization and economic growth followed. Agricultural employment dropped from 23% immediately after the war to 5% during postwar development. Foreign trade, which represented only 11% of GDP in 1950, jumped to roughly 20% by 1973. Italy's share of world exports more than doubled, from 2.2% to 4.6%, in two decades. Exports of manufactured products to other Western countries increased from 60% to 90% of total Italian exports between 1938 and 1963. As a consequence, Italy experienced one of the fastest rates of economic growth: instead of the average 4.7% annual growth in labor productivity among the twelve West European countries, Italy showed a 5.8% annual increase. Instead of the average 3.8% annual economic growth in Western Europe, Italy achieved 5% between 1950 and 1973.

In terms of international specialization and competitiveness, Italy gained ground in some of the modern and new technology-intensive sectors, such as electrical engineering, office, farm, and industrial machinery, electrical appliances, and cars. These sectors all became important export branches. However, the largest contribution came from such traditional sectors as the textile, clothing, shoe, and ceramics industries. Italy successfully compensated for its disadvantage in science- and scale-based industries with its huge advantage in highly specialized traditional industries. Innovative design and fashion industries, mostly small scale and based on artisan traditions, specialized and grew dominant on the international market (Zamagni, 1993; Guerrieri and Milana, 1990).

Italy experienced something of an economic miracle similar to that of Germany. Per capita GDP increased more than threefold between 1950 and 1973, approaching the GDP levels of Western Europe: income levels rose from 67% of the Western average in 1950 to 85% by 1973 (Maddison, 1995a: 195, 228).

The stabilization and economic and social revitalization of an unstable Southern Europe were also a political necessity. The logic of the cold war required that the influence of the West be strengthened as the economies of Greece, Spain, and Portugal were established, consolidated, and developed. This proved at times a hidden goal for the West, which used strong human rights rhetoric against dictatorial communism, but sought to make alliances with ruthless dictatorial regimes that ruled those countries: the Greek and Turkish military juntas and the brutal dictatorships of Franco and Salazar.

Iberia became a part of and received assistance from the West during the 1960s. In the case of Portugal, its inclusion was formalized under the highly oppressive Salazar regime. Portugal became a member of the European Free Trade Association (EFTA) initiated by Britain in 1960. Membership of the IMF, the World Bank, GATT as well as NATO followed.

The last one-and-a-half decades of Franco's dictatorship serve to illuminate this process and its importance to European prosperity. In 1953, the United States signed an agreement with Franco and established military bases in Spain. The West accepted the dictator, who had been a close ally of Hitler. In 1959, with direct Western collaboration, the Franco regime gave up isolationism and self-sufficiency. A stabilization plan was realized with contributions from the IMF, the OEEC, the assistance of the U.S. government, and leading U.S. banks. Altogether, the West contributed $420 million, which led to financial stabilization, unified exchange rates, the dismantling of trade restrictions, and the "opening" of Spain to foreign investments and the tourist industry. The World Bank sent a mission to Spain in March 1961 to prepare a development program. The next year Spain even applied for membership of the European Common Market, although the application was shelved because the Franco regime was still a political pariah. Without much fanfare, however, the European Community signed a Preferential Commercial Agreement with Spain in July 1970 with highly favorable terms. European tariffs were immediately and substantially reduced by 60%. This was significant, as 88% of Spanish industrial exports were destined for Europe. The goal was to establish completely free trade, and all quantitative restrictions against Spanish exports were removed. Even agricultural products were given a 25–100% tariff reduction. Spain, now an "external" member of the European Community, had to make only an insignificant concession: a 25% tariff reduction for European goods by 1977. Western foreign investment poured into Spain. Between 1959 and 1973 it increased twenty-sevenfold. During the 1960s, foreign capital covered 20% of Spanish industrial investments and increased capital formation by 10%. Nearly one-third of the investments came from the United States. Western tourism was initiated and increased from 4 million tourists in 1959 to nearly 35 million by 1973, and Spain's tourist industry income grew from $126 million to more than $3 billion during the same period. What emerged as a result was a Spanish economic miracle during the 1960s: exports increased fourteenfold, imports grew thirteenfold, and Spain became an industrialized country. Its agricultural population decreased from 42% in 1959 to 25% by 1973, when agriculture produced only 11% of the country's GDP (Harrison, 1985: 144–62). Economic growth reached 5.8% per year. In some years it reached 10–11%.

Other Mediterranean countries performed similarly. Greece enjoyed a 6.2% growth rate, while the annual rate of growth in Portugal measured 5.7%, in both cases much higher than the West European average. The catching-up process had begun. Rapid industrialization was taking place, the beginning of a dramatic decline of the agricultural population (from 40–50% to 8–10%) in Italy and Spain. The industrial labor force increased spectacularly from 25–30% to roughly 40%, while employment in the service sector increased from 25–30% to roughly 50%. The proportion of agriculture of the national product varied in these countries between 8% and 17%, Italy being the most similar to the West and Greece the least.

Historical circumstances prevented a number of other countries in the Western half of Europe from joining the prosperous core until World War II. Two of them, Finland and Ireland, deserve special attention. Finland developed as the border area of Sweden until the eighteenth century, and then became a border province of the Russian Empire until the Bolshevik Revolution of 1917. Independent Finland experienced a stormy political history in the first half of the twentieth century: civil war and wars with Russia during a generally disadvantageous historical period erected hurdles to economic progress. In 1950, Finland's average income stood at only about 60% of the Danish and Swedish income levels. During the postwar decades, Finland found itself with a special political status. On the one hand, it was "Finlandized" by the Soviet Union, which meant it was essentially forced to subordinate and adjust its foreign policy to Soviet requirements. Having paid that price, the country became a kind of external member of the Soviet economic bloc and could enjoy all the advantages of an enormous, though relatively backward, Soviet market. Between World War II and 1970, 13–17% of Finnish exports, almost all of its processed industrial products, were sold on the Soviet market, and 12–16% of its imports, mostly cheap energy and raw materials, originated from the Soviet Union. Postwar Soviet trade, oddly enough, was established with Finnish war reparation payments, 72% of which were engineering products. The share that this sector contributed to net industrial output increased from 19% to 31% between 1937 and 1954. On the other hand, Finland, a quasi-neutral country, also became part of the family of the Nordic countries. It joined the European free trade zone and conducted extensive foreign trade with the advanced West. About a quarter of the country's exports and 25–30% of its imports connected Finland with the West, mostly with Sweden and Britain. This unique situation gave the Finnish economy tremendous opportunity. Exports rose rapidly, by 80% between 1940–44 and 1945–50, then by another 60% between 1950–54 and 1955–9, and then again by roughly 40% between 1960–64 and 1965–9. Finnish agricultural output increased by 38% and the country became an agricultural exporter. Industrial labor productivity grew by more than two-and-a-half times and industrial output by four times between 1946–50 and 1966–70.

The growth of the Finnish export sectors mirrored trends set earlier in Scandinavia. For example, in 1951–5, timber and wood represented 41% of Finnish exports. By 1966–70, that share declined sharply to 18%. The export share of the Finnish paper industry, however, remained strong: 43% and 45% in both the early 1950s and late 1960s. The most dramatic development was the increasing role played by engineering and other industries. Their share of exports grew from 13% to 34%. Swedish investments also contributed to postwar Finnish industrialization, due to lower Finnish labor costs. Modern structural changes during this period elevated Finnish income levels close to those of the other Nordic countries. By 1973, Finland's per capita GDP matched that of Norway and equaled 80% of the GDP levels of Denmark and Sweden. By 1973, Finland had practically become part of the advanced West by reaching 88% of the average West European income level (Krantz, 1987: 281–7; Maddison, 1995a: 195,197, 228).

Non-industrialized, impoverished Ireland, a former cheap labor reserve of Britain, began to develop economically as an independent republic. Economic growth, however, remained extremely slow. "Ireland recorded the slowest growth of per-capita income between 1910 and 1970 of any European country except the United Kingdom" (Lee, 1989: 515). At the end of World War II, agriculture made a much larger contribution (37%) to the GDP than industry and mining combined (17%). By 1976, agriculture's share of GDP declined to 16%, while that of industry and mining climbed to 35%. Half of the GDP was produced by the service sector. These were all signs of a significant structural modernization. Irish investments during the same period increased from one-fifth to one-third of GDP, another important indicator of modernization. Economic growth was stable and solid, and reached more than 3% annually between 1950 and 1973 (Armengaud et al., 1987: 342, 348–9). The per capita GDP of the Republic doubled, but this development could not keep pace with the unparalleled

West European prosperity. In fact, Ireland's position relative to other West European countries declined: Irish incomes fell from 69% to 57% of the average Western income level between 1950 and 1973. During the post-war quarter century an enlarged, prosperous Western Europe, absorbing a great part of the former peripheral areas in the South and North, was in the making.

Did all these historical achievements make the welfare state stable and untouchable? Paradoxically, partly because of its achievements, in the changing world system and with rising globalization the welfare state was challenged during the last decades of the century.

CHAPTER 6

Globalization: return to laissez-faire?

Globalization and its characteristics

During the last quarter of the twentieth century, a new trend figured in the world economy: globalization. Europe became one of the main participants in this transfiguration. Several historians maintain that there is nothing new in globalization – consider an ancient form of globalization, the Christian Church (Hopkins, 2002). According to others, early modern times, and even more so the nineteenth century, marked the beginnings of globalization. In this view, globalization was successively advanced by the colonial empires, the railroads, the laissez-faire system, and the international gold standard. From late medieval times long-distance trade and cashless payment networks began internationalizing the European economy. Worldwide trade networks emerged during the early modern centuries. All these, however, were only the beginning of a long historical trend that led to globalization.

[T]he really big leap to more globally integrated commodity and factor markets took place in the second half of the nineteenth century. By 1914, there was hardly a village or town anywhere on the globe whose prices were not influenced by distant foreign markets, whose infrastructures were not financed by foreign capital, whose engineering . . . and even business skills were not imported from abroad, or whose labor markets were not influenced by [emigration or immigration] . . . [However, because of a strong backlash] the world economy had lost all of its globalization achievements in three decades, between 1914 and 1945. In the half century since then, it has won them back . . . (O'Rourke and Williamson: 1999, 2)

O'Rourke and Williamson speak about a "first globalization" from the second half of the nineteenth century, and, after a third of a century backlash in the interwar world economy, a second wave of globalization after World War II. All of these interpretations may have a rationale. Late nineteenth- and late twentieth-century globalization have several common features, and even a real connection. Economic interactions between various countries and continents – trade, migration, capital investment, establishment of subsidiaries, production abroad, and financial transactions – all existed before and characterized modern capitalism. A permanent increase in the quantity and value of trade and foreign investments occurred in the nineteenth and twentieth centuries.

In the last quarter of the twentieth century, however, a further dramatic quantitative change in these interactions, combined with a qualitative change in the international division of labor, transformed the world economy, and we indeed may speak about a new chapter in its history. The previous internationalization trends were more limited compared with the late twentieth-century phenomenon. The term globalization not coincidentally appeared in *Webster's Dictionary* only in the early 1960s. It expresses a set of new characteristics.

What are they? Economic interactions between various countries, trade, capital investment, portfolio investment, establishment of subsidiaries, and a new type of division of labor increased dramatically as globalization spread.

Trade developed by leaps and bounds. Transactions were pushed by international agreements. The post-World War II General Agreement on Tariffs and Trade, with its multilateral, non-discriminatory character, played a role in increasing postwar trade. Protectionism, however, reappeared during the difficult times of the 1970s–1980s. Against resurgent protectionism, the Western powers launched a major campaign for opening markets: the Tokyo Round, concluded in 1979, and most of all the Uruguay Round, launched in 1986, and its preparatory talks from the early 1980s, led to the Punta del Este Declaration, which paved the way for the foundation of the World Trade Organization (WTO), and drastic further market openings.

International trade was also helped by the sharply declining cost of transportation and communication. The cost of a three-minute London– New York telephone call decreased from $5.3 in 1950 to $3.2 by 1970, and to $0.9 by 2000. The cost of an air transport passenger mile was $0.30 in 1950, $0.16 by 1970, and $0.11 by 1990. Communication entered a new era as a consequence of the computer revolution, especially through the invention of the Internet and the World Wide Web.

World exports skyrocketed – from $0.3 trillion in 1950, and $1.7 trillion in 1973, to $5.8 trillion by the end of the century. Europe's exports increased

Box 6.1 The World Wide Web

The World Wide Web (WWW) became the flagship of the communication revolution at the end of the twentieth century. It was invented in 1993 by a young Englishman, Tim Berners-Lee, at the joint European research institution, CERN (Conseil Européen pour la Recherche Nucléaire), in Geneva, Switzerland.

Sitting in front of our computer and looking at an old book on eBay seems like an activity difficult to break down into parts. In reality, however, a whole series of inventions led to making it possible: the realization of computer networks, the invention of the personal computer, the use of hypertexts, and the development of the World Wide Web were all milestones on the road to our ordinary activity. The Web and the Internet, though often confused by many, are not the same. If the Internet is a freeway system – a system of connected networks – the Web is a truck service with a great number of loaded trucks carrying information. Before the WWW, there were networks of computers, ways to store and send information, but the Web became the easiest way to access them.

The story goes back to World War II, and the work of hundreds and thousands of talented inventors. Networks connecting computer systems were established continuously, first for military and then for research purposes: Joint Academic Network (JANET), ARPANET, CSNET, NSFNET (a network of networks). The first European Informatics Network was created by 1975, the achievement of CERN, and the realization of the initiative of Luis de Broglie, the Nobel laureate French physicist. CERN embarked on computer networking, and developed its independent network, CERNET. By the end of the 1980s, however, the Internet managed to connect the different networks and became the world standard. It was first used in Europe (in London and Oslo) to monitor Soviet nuclear tests. In 1990, 30,000 Internet sites existed in Europe, but two years later another 500,000 were already up and running, and the number increased exponentially during the 1990s.

Two other basic developments behind the WWW deserve special attention. First came the invention of the personal computer. The first microprocessor-based computer in the 1970s was French, while in the early 1980s Britain had the highest per capita ownership of computers. Then Apple and IBM, both based in the United States, took over. The second was the development of hypertext systems such as Xanadu, which as early as the 1960s produced computerized writing and storage systems. Various hypertext systems followed: HES and then FRESS; CERN itself produced a system, CERNDOC, to store thousands of documents.

The Optical Reception of Announcements by Coded Line Electronics (ORACLE) paved the way for downloading information if somebody had a telephone line and a TV set. Britain launched Teletext, and France Télétel, which became known as Minitel (after the name of a mini-terminal they used). It was offered free, and by 1989 5 million Minitels were in use and France became the most wired country in the world. All the elements for the Web were around, just not yet connected.

There were several attempts to make information easily available on the Internet but the breakthrough was Tim Berners-Lee's World Wide Web. The 25-year-old Oxford graduate was first employed by CERN for six months, but later returned with a fellowship in 1983 and soon got a tenure. He submitted a plan, "Information Management: a Proposal," to create the Web in 1989. Instead of a hierarchical storage system, he offered a link which worked as free association: every time one clicked on a link, a new window opened up, making it possible to keep several texts and images in-line.

In November 1990, Berners-Lee's detailed proposal described the combination of hypertext and the Internet. The new system, which streamlined access to information, was ready at the end of 1991. The following year it offered a regular service for CERN. Several new and even more practical web servers were created (Viola, Cello, Samba, Mosaic, and Gopher), and by 1993 CERN offered the Web free to the public. Web traffic increased by ten times every few months, and in 1994 the Web carried information at a rate of 400,000 bytes/second, the equivalent of a novel each second. Commercial use began and CommerceNet (later Amazon.com) started operating in 1994.

After a long fight that stemmed from CERN's unwillingness to house a project so out of its profile, as well as financial considerations, the WWW became a European–American shared enterprise. INRIA, a French research organization, and the American Massachusetts Institute of Technology (MIT) led the project in a consortium, and the European Union and the United States became co-sponsors of the system. In 1994, 10,000 Web servers were in operation globally; by 1999, this number stood at 10 million, and nearly 150 million people were connected. The WWW was established as a prime mover in the communication revolution (Gillies and Cailliau, 2000).

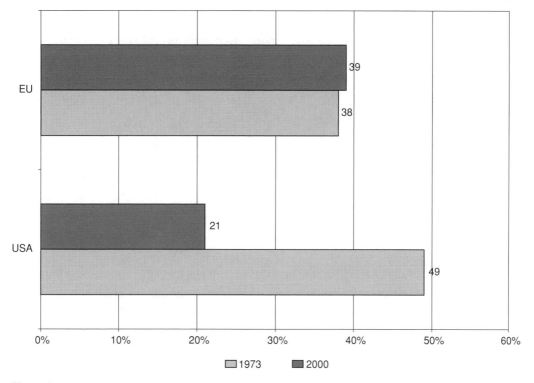

Figure 6.1 Share in the world's foreign direct investment, 1973–2000

equally dramatically – by nearly twenty times – during the second half of the century: in 1950 they totaled $0.14 trillion, in 1973 $0.90 trillion, and by the end of the century $2.73 trillion. Exports played an ever-increasing role in economic performance in Europe. The value of merchandise exports, which stood at less than 9% of West European GDP in 1950, increased to nearly 19% by 1973, and jumped to roughly 36% at the end of the century. The ratio of European exports compared with GDP was twice the world average, by far the highest level compared with all other countries or regions of the world (Maddison, 2001: 127, 362).

Foreign direct investment (FDI), a phenomenon well known since the second half of the nineteenth century, also increased in an unparalleled way (see Figure 6.1). While foreign investment amounted to $107 billion per annum in 1980, this more than doubled in fifteen years, and grew four times faster than foreign trade. It reached 6% of domestic capital accumulation, three times more than in 1970.

Foreign exchange transactions, $15 billion a day in 1973, reached $1.3 trillion daily by 1995 (see Figure 6.2), which was ten times more than in 1979, and fifty times the total value of world trade. More than 200,000 currency traders now operate around the world. Cross-border transactions of bonds and equities reached 10% of the aggregate GDP of the most

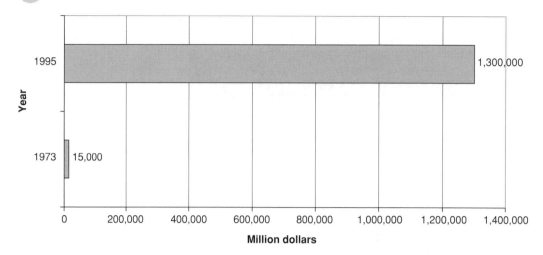

Figure 6.2 Daily foreign exchange transactions globally, 1973–95

advanced G-7 countries in 1980; fifteen years later it accounted for 140%. According to certain evaluations, less than one-fifth of foreign exchange transactions support international trade and/or investment; more than four-fifths is speculation (Rupert, 2000: 79). This was clearly signaled by the collapse of currencies and the eruption of regional crises.

International bank loans also increased and became closely connected to economic activities. In 1964, net international bank loans reached only 0.7% of world output; by the early 1990s they surpassed 16%. Foreign assets in French and German banks doubled between 1970 and 1990 from 16% to 37% and from 9% to 16% of totals, respectively (Helleiner, 2000; Perraton et al., 1997; Higgott and Payne, 2000). It was, noted Philip Cerny, "the global financial tail increasingly wagging the 'real economy' dog" (Cerny, 2000: 41).

Behind all of these tremendously increased transactions, multinational companies emerged as the dominant players in the world economy. According to the broadly used definition, multinationals are those companies which have operations in two or more countries. The origins of multinational companies go back to late nineteenth-century American business development, an automatic adjustment to the technological challenge of modern mass production. According to Alfred Chandler's pioneering works, big companies encouraged a vertical integration to minimize cost and dependence on other companies. For a secure and undisturbed flow of goods many of them preferred a "backward" integration to incorporate raw material extraction and output into the same company's framework. In various new industries where distribution was not yet established, installation, services, and later repair also became part of producers' activity. These led to a "forward" integration of transportation and distribution networks, including retail chains and service branches. The modern industrial enterprise integrated mass production with mass distribution "within a single business firm" (Chandler, 1977: 285). Integration advanced mostly through mergers of existing companies. From the 1890s in the United States, a "merger mania" permeated the economy and led to an impressive increase in company size. By 1917, one-quarter of American industrial output was produced by vertically integrated, centrally administered giant companies. This growth of firms led to changes in ownership structure as well. Family management became inappropriate for governing the more complex firms and activities. Owners began employing skilled experts, engineers, economists of all kinds, advertisement and transportation specialists. Centralized administration and a uniform accounting and statistical system were introduced (Chandler, 1977: 416). At a later stage owners withdrew from governance, and salaried managers took over. Chandler speaks about a "three-pronged investment," first in production facilities to exploit the advantage of scale and scope; second in a marketing and distributive network to keep pace with mass production; and third in management to govern the enlarged, complex business activities (Chandler, 1990: 8).

The giant, complex, multi-divisional and functional firm, argued Chandler, logically led to the maximization of scale and scope, to backward and forward integration over borders and countries, and thus to the creation of multinational companies. Multinationals represented a logical next step in expansion and many giant companies took this step as early as the late nineteenth century. By World War I, twenty-three American companies had two or more factories in Britain, and thirty-seven companies had subsidiaries in Europe as a whole (Wilkins, 1970: 212–13). The leading role of multinationals with large international networks and company empires, however, wasn't common until the last third of the twentieth century (Chandler, 1984, 1986).

In the early 1970s, multinationals numbered around 7,000; at the end of the century, there were 44,000 in operation with nearly 300,000 foreign subsidiaries, employing 12 million people and producing one-quarter to one-third of total world output. Their global sales reached nearly $7 trillion by the mid-1990s and represented 40% of world trade (about a quarter of world trade is conducted between branches of the same multinational companies), and 75% of manufactured goods. "While only a portion of multinationals are truly global, the 500 largest account for about 80% of all foreign production . . ." (Eden, 2000: 341). The 100 largest truly global multinationals control roughly 20% of total foreign assets, employ 6 million people, and sell nearly one-third of total multinational sales.

Figure 6.3 German investments abroad, 1961 and 1990

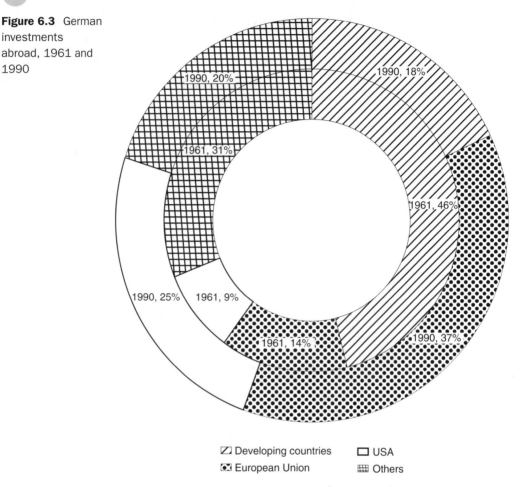

Seventy-five of the world's top 100 companies are originally German, Japanese, and American; eleven are British, while other West European countries have no more than five each. The quantitative development of global economic transactions indeed created a new quality of economic interactions.

The role of multinational companies strongly contributed to the development of a new type of international division of labor. Multinationals established subsidiaries in other advanced countries. The geographical destination of German foreign direct investments is characteristic: in 1961, 46% was channeled to developing or less developed countries; by 1990, less than 20% of investments went to these areas. The typical pre-globalization investment destination of developing, agricultural, and raw material producing areas was changed and investments were more and more directed to other highly developed countries. In 1990, only 2% of German FDI was channeled into mining industries, while nearly 40% went to trade, banking, and the insurance business, and another one-third to the chemical, electrical, machine building, and car industries. In 1961, only 14% of German investments went to other European Union countries; by 1990 this was already 37% (see Figure 6.3). Investments to the United States also largely increased. Swedish multinationals established subsidiaries in eighty-three other advanced countries, but in only seventeen developing Latin American, Asian, and African countries (Olsson, 1993). Altogether, three-quarters of the world's FDI is located in advanced countries.

During the rapid restructuring between 1985 and 1987, leading German, French, British, Italian, and Dutch chemical companies bought 116 small specialty-producing firms in other European countries, and 126 firms in the United States (Martinelli, 1991: 39). Intra-regional trade became dominant within Western Europe: in 1958, only 30% of the region's trade was channeled within the region; by 1989, this trade nearly doubled to almost 60% (Busch and Milner, 1994: 261).

In the early 1990s the world's fourth largest telecommunications multinational, the Ericsson Group, employed more than 13,000 people in Norway, Denmark, Holland, France, and Italy, but only 4,500 workers in Brazil, Mexico, Venezuela, Argentina, and Columbia (Jones and Schröter, 1993: 36, 41, 110, 116). The Finnish Nokia Company, an old but renewed firm, emerged to world dominance by changing its profile, entering the mobile phone business at the right time, and building a global network of production and distribution. Multinational chemical companies produced an increasing part of their exports in other countries: the British ICI produced 22% of its export products outside Britain, for instance, while the German Hoechst and Bayer firms produced 34% and 37%, respectively (Martinelli, 1991: 21–2). Globalized production also characterized clothing manufacture. The products of Liz Claiborne are manufactured in more than 40 countries by more than 300 independent suppliers. The Italian Benetton company, founded in 1965 with a single retail shop, by the late 1990s coordinated 250 outside suppliers, owned 5,000 retail outlets in 60 countries, and had established its own financial organization and investment bank. The automobile and electronics industries adopted an international pattern of organization. One of Ford's "world cars," the Escort, is produced and assembled in fifteen countries on three continents. "Today, most of the 40 million or so vehicles that roll off production lines each year are made by just 10 global corporations" (Knox and Agnew, 1998: 196, 206, 209). Multinationals were selling and buying components and products. Intra-industry trade became dominant. The import content of finished manufactures increased dramatically: from 4% to 29% in Britain, from 7% to 27% in France, from 4% to 26% in Germany, and from 12% to 46% in Sweden between 1950 and 1985.

Box 6.2   Nokia

Nokia's star rose high in Finland and it became the symbol of late twentieth-century communication revolution, industrial success, and globalization. Nokia grew up from three roots. A paper works, established in 1865, soon moved next to the Nokia river and was named Nokia Aktiebolaget. Between 1918 and 1922 two companies, a rubber works and a cable works, became part of the Nokia Group. The three companies formally merged as Oy Nokia Ab in 1966. Until World War II, they produced paper, rubber shoes, and cables, mostly for the domestic market.

The rise of the company began, strangely enough, after World War II in connection with Finland's war reparation burdens to the Soviet Union. Nearly 6% of reparation payments were paid in cable products. After the payments were fulfilled, cable exports continued to the Soviet Union. The Soviet markets were lucrative, stable, and predictable; exports doubled during the 1970s, and Nokia began exporting cable machinery, electronic instruments, multi-channel analyzers, then, during the 1980s, telephone exchange systems, which developed in response to Soviet orders. At the same time deregulation and European integration opened Western markets and the impressively growing company set its sights beyond the limited Finnish domestic market.

The groundwork in electronics was laid with the establishment of an electronics department during the 1960s. Sales of computers opened a new field but by 1967 represented only 3% of total sales. In 1971, Nokia developed its own computers, and also entered into the mobile phone and digital telephone exchange business, using French technology.

At the beginning of the 1980s, Nokia launched an aggressive acquisition campaign: it bought Televa, Solara, Luxor Ab, Océanic, Sonolor, and Televisso. The company became the third largest producer of color television sets in Europe. It grew into a giant: annual sales reached US $5 billion by 1987. Two-thirds of sales came from electronics, 70% of sales were exports, and more than half of the workforce worked abroad. Consumer electronics, primarily television set production, became Nokia's biggest business at the end of the 1980s.

The new focus and expansion, however, turned out to be a grave miscalculation. Several Asian countries entered the market and soon saturated it. Companies which were not pioneers in consumer electronics technology grew unprofitable. Nokia almost collapsed. One of its top managers, Timo Koski, suffered a stroke and died; Kari Kairamo, Chief Executive Officer, committed suicide in 1988.

Parallel with the collapse of state socialism, Nokia's main Soviet bloc markets also collapsed: in the first months of 1991 only 2% of planned Eastern exports were realized. Radical market reorientation was needed immediately and the company was forced westward. A real breakthrough became possible only with new, cutting-edge technology products.

Restructuring and reorganization were unavoidable. In a crucial board of directors meeting in 1994, the new Chief Executive Officer, Jorma Ollila, an outstanding mathematician who had headed the mobile phone division since 1990, convinced the company's leadership to close all the old branches – consumer electronics, paper, cable, and cable machinery production – and focus entirely on a single new product: mobile phones. The board decided to change the official language of its minutes from Finnish to English – another step toward globalization – and the company got a listing on the New York Stock Exchange. The decision was also made to close down and sell plants, including the TV set-producing branches. Practically all the old branches were closed and sold out by 1995.

Nokia, a technology follower, began developing its own research and development activities. In 1983, only 900 employees out of nearly 24,000 worked in R&D; during the 1990s, Nokia established fifty-four research centers in fourteen countries, and 35% of the company's workforce – nearly 19,000 people – worked in R&D by 2000. A 30–50% annual growth signaled the great change.

The mobile phone conquered the world during the 1990s. Nokia's sales practically doubled every year or two. Its first success was Model 101, followed by a whole series of successful new models. The life cycle of mobile phones was two years maximum; the market was seemingly limitless.

In the 1990s, the ownership structure of the company transformed radically. The role of Finnish banks and investors decreased, while foreign share reached 70% by 1997. The rise of Nokia as a global champion of mobile phones became unstoppable. The company delivered 4% and 12% of total Finnish exports in 1980 and 1990, respectively, but increased its share to one-third of the country's exports by 2000. It established sixty subsidiaries in Europe. Sharp competition with Motorola, the American world leader in mobile phones, resulted in Nokia's triumph: by 1998 the company had conquered 36% of even the American markets, while Motorola's share dropped from 37% to 26% (Martti, 2002).

Box 6.3 Benetton

Benetton became one of the most well-known clothing producers and retail networks at the end of the twentieth century, a giant multinational company with 8,000 shops throughout the world and $8 billion turnover.

Benetton, unlike most multinationals, has had a rather short history. Luciano Benetton was born in 1936 into a poor Italian family. His father had tried making money in Ethiopia with trucking but failed. He had a small business, a bicycle rental in Treviso, but died in 1945, when Luciano, the oldest son, was only ten years old. Luciano began working before and after school, sold newspapers at the station, but could not continue in secondary school. Instead, he became a full-time sales assistant in a clothing store. From the money he saved, he bought a knitting machine for $200, and his younger sister, Giuliana, knitted sweaters at night after her daily job. Their mother assembled and ironed the sweaters and the first "collection" of twenty pieces in yellow, green, and pale blue colors was ready by the mid-1950s. Luciano went door to door and sold the collection after his daily work in the store. The combination of Giuliana's good taste and Luciano's diligence and entrepreneurial attitude led to success: the products gradually gained acceptance, and the brother and sister started working full-time for themselves. They bought new machines and employed young girls to operate them. The entire family worked in the business. By 1960, in a rented warehouse, they were producing sweaters in thirty-six shades. Shops began buying the products and the business gradually enlarged.

In 1964, a stranger, Piero Marchiorello, knocked on their door and offered to open a shop, selling only the *Très Jolie* trademark products of the family factory. The following year, Luciano opened a new factory in Ponzano. The three brothers, Luciano, Gilberto, and Carlo, became responsible for certain parts of the business while Giuliana ran the design. They started buying factories in nearby villages, but less than a third of their workers were employed in their own factories. The Benettons preferred a decentralized production system and two-thirds of the people who worked for them were employed by sub-contractors. The family name became the new trademark, and the united colors the logo.

These years represented the greatest prosperity in Italian history, and the period when Italian design and fashion clothing conquered the world. In 1966, the Benettons opened a store in elegant Cortina d'Ampezzo, and then in Padua, and by the early 1970s, they owned 800 shops in Italy. By 1969, the first store was opened abroad, in Paris, and in 3–4 years, they had 100 shops in France, Germany, and Belgium.

After some difficulties in the mid 1970s, the company's expansion continued: by 1979, 280 Benetton shops were in operation in France, 250 in Germany, 100 in Britain, and 25 each in Holland and Belgium; altogether there were 1,700 shops throughout Europe. During the 1980s, following the first shop in New York in 1979, the conquest of America followed. In ten years, Benetton had 2,700 shops. Locations included Eastern Europe, Japan, and Latin America. The Benetton empire, via its holding company, had an interest in several businesses: sheep and cattle ranches in Argentina, a supermarket network, the Autogrill highway restaurant chain, olive oil-making companies, hotels, and many other businesses.

By the end of the century, the company that had been started in the 1950s by two orphans as an after-work home knitting and door-to-door selling enterprise had become a multinational giant of 8,000 shops globally, directed by fifteen members of the enlarged family (Mantle, 1999).

Globalization of the laissez-faire ideology and system

Globalization unquestionably represents a new era, in large part because from the early 1970s it was accompanied by a set of changes that comprise what UCLA Professor Perry Anderson called a "conservative revolution." Globalization went hand in hand with the emergence of neo-liberal economics, laissez-faire individualism, and postmodern cultural nihilism. In connection with the latter, an irrational, anti-Enlightenment intellectual trend emerged in social sciences and humanities. The strong belief in the possibility of understanding history and human action in order to form historical trends and pave the way toward progress – a *Zeitgeist* since the Enlightenment – disappeared.

Was this an integral part of globalized free trade and capital flow? On one hand the nature of international economic interactions indeed revitalized laissez-faire ideology. On the other hand, however, the new environment could be construed to be accompanied by control and regulation, and strictly limited to the economic arena. That was not the case. The new phenomenon globalized the ideological concept of "market fundamentalism." Under the banner of freedom and free market prescriptions, suggested by the Austrian–English Friedrich Hayek, the American Milton Friedman, and other members of the neo-liberal school in the mid-1970s, came a frontal attack against regulations, state interventions, state ownership, and the welfare state as the only solutions in cutthroat global competition in a free society.

According to Hayek, the role of the government was to protect individual freedom, free markets, free competition, and nothing more. Price and wage control policy, he argued, led to unemployment and, instead of stabilizing the economy, would create a more extreme fluctuation. State interventionism was *The Road to Serfdom* (Hayek, 1944) – the title of his book obviously expressed his view. When it appeared in 1960, his *The Constitution of Liberty* (Hayek, 1960) made him the last Mohican of classical economic liberalism. When Keynes failed in the 1970s, however, Friedrich Hayek became one of the most influential economists again, signaled by his Nobel Prize in 1974.

Milton Friedman was another central figure in the rebirth of economic liberalism, an advocate of the free, self-regulated market. He attacked expanding the regulatory state, including welfare state policy, and in his 1955 lecture series, published as *Capitalism and Freedom* (1962), recommended the privatization of the various governmental functions. According to him and the neo-liberal theory, the self-regulated market is the best source of human welfare, and the market is able to provide health care, pensions, and various kinds of insurance, while state intervention in these fields undermines competition and creates higher cost and lower efficiency. According to Friedman, instead of fiscal policy, monetary policy can guarantee the undisturbed operation of the market. His prescription called for central bank control of the quantity of money in circulation, and a slower increase of the amount of money than the growth of the real value of output, thus increasing the value of money and taming inflation. In his various works on inflation, monetary stability, and taxation (Friedman, 1959, 1963, 1969), Friedman became the front-runner of the "monetarist counter-revolution" (a term he coined in 1970). His Nobel award in 1976 crowned the legitimation of monetarism.

Friedman's popular writings, his role as the economic advisor for President Nixon, and the popularization of his views over the airwaves made him extremely influential. He renewed the argument that state intervention led to serfdom. In a lecture at Pepperdine University in 1977, he denounced American policy since the Great Depression:

Today total government spending at all levels amounts to 40% of the national income . . . federal government spending has moved in less than fifty years from 3% to over 25% – total government spending from 10% to 40% . . . The question is, will we keep trying to continue on this path until we lose our freedom and turn our lives over to an all-powerful government in Washington, or will we stop? . . . [The welfare institutions are brutal intervention in personal freedom:] you cannot do good with other people's money . . . So that force – sending a policeman to take the money from somebody's pocket – is fundamentally at the basis of the philosophy of the welfare state. (Friedman, 1978: 1–3, 7)

Instead, Friedman recommended a radical tax cut – "I think, a flat rate of around 16%" – and slashing government expenditure by privatizing nearly everything. Friedman recommended making families and individuals responsible for their schooling, health, and pension schemes. The best way for this, he suggested, is introducing a voucher system in education, health care, and pensions, to create

a free, competitive, private-market educational system . . . If you have a people committed to getting back to a free society it seems to me that is one of the great virtues of using vouchers. The same thing goes for housing vouchers or medical vouchers. [Attacking full employment policy, he argued that] a highly static rigid economy may have a fixed place for everyone whereas a dynamic, highly progressive economy, which offers ever changing opportunities . . . may have a high natural rate of unemployment. (Friedman, 1978: 75, 79, 91)

The neo-liberal school provided its prescription and program in a highly ideological form, which became popular.

The image of a free market system that is almighty and is the ultimate key of economic success, as well as the fact that it had indeed worked in some of the "core" countries and proved to embody an impressive potential for flexibility and an ability to react, influenced policy-makers, governments and international institutions to a great degree, creating an atmosphere of an almost dogmatic or religious belief in a single valid, uniform and universal model of an idealized laissez-faire system . . . (Berend, 1994: 19, 21)

Globalization ended the era of postwar restrictions and regulations. The Bretton Woods agreement was a response to World War II and the lesson of previous economic instabilities. John Maynard Keynes, one of the main architects of the postwar economic system, emphasized that under the Bretton Woods system "every member government [gained] the explicit right to control all capital movements . . . Not merely as a feature of the transition but as a permanent arrangement." Henry Morgenthau, U.S. Treasury Secretary, used a biblical term to characterize the goal of the system: to "drive the usurious moneylenders from the temple of international finance" (Helleiner, 1994: 164).

Postwar arrangements, however, were destroyed during the 1970s and 1980s. The first policy changes were initiated by the U.S. and British governments in the 1960s in the form of a regulation-free "offshore" Eurodollar market in London. The road was opened wide by President Nixon in 1971 when, following the advice of Milton Friedman, he closed the fixed exchange rate era of Bretton Woods and introduced the floating exchange rate for the dollar. In 1974 the U.S. administration abolished its own capital controls and pushed other countries to follow. Britain actually did so in 1979 by eliminating its forty-year-old capital control system. The New York Stock Exchange was deregulated in 1975; the London Stock Exchange followed in 1986. A "competitive deregulation race" began: Australia, New Zealand, France, and Germany, and then, by 1988, practically the entire European Community followed. By 1990 the Mediterranean and Scandinavian countries also abolished capital controls (Helleiner, 1994: 168–70). The Western world turned toward self-regulating, uncontrolled market and monetarist policy. Globalization, stated George Soros, placed "financial capital in the driver's seat" (Soros, 1998). This policy was advocated and enforced according to the principles of the so-called Washington Consensus, described by former World Bank chief economist Joseph Stiglitz as:

a consensus between the IMF, the World Bank, and the U.S. Treasury about the "right" policies for developing countries . . . Fiscal austerity, privatization, and market liberalization were the three pillars of Washington consensus advised throughout the 1980s and 1990s. (Stiglitz, 2002: 16–17)

When a deep peripheral crisis, stagnation, indebtedness, and mass unemployment hit Latin America and state socialist Central and Eastern Europe, a "one-size-fits-all" prescription of the Washington Consensus was made mandatory under IMF "conditions" for assistance. This policy, explains Stiglitz, was inappropriate for developing and transforming countries.

[The advanced countries] had built up their economies by wisely and selectively protecting some of their industries until they were strong enough to compete with foreign companies . . . Forcing a developing country to open itself up to imported products . . . can have disastrous consequences – socially and economically . . . [The advanced countries] did not attempt capital market liberalization until late in their development – European nations waited until the 1970s to get rid of their capital market controls – the developing nations have been encouraged to do so quickly. (Stiglitz, 2002: 34, 53, 65)

The impact of globalization on Europe

The new chapter of economic development, rapid globalization, was accompanied by the end of a politically divided Europe, and the collapse of authoritarian dictatorships in the Southern and Eastern peripheries. This was triggered partly by accidental events, such as the fall and fatal coma of the Portuguese dictator, António Salazar, at the end of the 1960s; and the death of the Spanish dictator Francisco Franco in November 1975. What followed was not accidental at all. The May 1974 revolution in Portugal ousted the Salazar–Caetano regime. A Falangist coup collapsed in Spain in 1981. Both countries, together with Greece (in 1974), which had been ruled by military juntas, progressed toward democracy, introduced a competitive market system in the framework of the European Community, and began catching up with Western Europe.

The mid-1970s represented a turning point in the history of Central and Eastern Europe as well. The spectacular progress of the West undermined communism. In Moscow for the November 1977 celebration of the sixtieth anniversary of the Bolshevik Revolution, Italian Communist Party chief Enrico Berlinguer said that his party would accept pluralist, multiparty democracy and membership of the European Community. "Eurocommunism" practically ended Western communism and led to a speedy social-democratization and then erosion of the leading communist parties.

Central and Eastern Europe declined into deepening economic crisis after 1973. Neither the Soviet Union nor its satellites were able to adjust to the new technological requirements during the structural crisis of the 1970s and 1980s. Their growth significantly slowed and even stopped. Inflation took off and most of the countries of the region walked into an indebtedness trap (see Chapter 4). The erosion of the regime undermined its transitory legitimacy. Political turmoil shocked Poland. A spontaneous workers' uprising in 1976 led to merger of the workers' movement with the intellectual dissidents, which led to the formation of the Workers' Defense Committee (KOR), and then Solidarity in 1980. The military takeover and introduction of martial law in December 1981 could not consolidate the regime and suppress resistance. In February 1989, a roundtable agreement led to partially free elections in the summer and a total defeat of the regime. Economic reforms were accelerated in Hungary to resolve the deepening crisis. A social-democratized party opposition removed the old leadership of János Kádár in May 1988 and in February 1989 the Central Committee of the party decided to hold free, multiparty elections in a year.

A last wave of a renewed cold war generated an untenable arms race, and Soviet expansionism met its Waterloo in Afghanistan in the first half of the 1980s. Accidental events again sped up the process: the death first of Leonid Brezhnev, and then of two ailing newly elected party leaders, Yuri Andropov and Konstantin Chernenko, within two years, which led to the election of Mikhail Gorbachev as head of the Soviet Union, in 1985.

His courage to withdraw from Afghanistan and denounce the infamous "Brezhnev Doctrine" of intervention in satellite countries, together with the policy of *glasnost* or openness, and *perestroika* or restructuring within the Soviet Union, finished the process of erosion. The regime first collapsed in Poland and Hungary, and then in four more countries within six weeks. At the end of 1989, East European communism was dead. In two more years it collapsed in the Soviet Union as well. The map of the region was redrawn again. Instead of eight states, in 1989, twenty-six independent states came into existence.

All these transformations eliminated authoritarian regimes in the Southern and Eastern peripheries during the last third of the century, together with their economic dirigisme or centrally planned economic systems. Europe in the 1990s became a homogeneous landscape of multi-party democracies with private-market economies. An enlarged European Union created a new framework for economic performance.

The new chapter of European economic history, which opened in 1973, reflected a deep crisis. The seemingly "endless" prosperity came to an abrupt halt. From that time onward, nothing worked as usual. Economic growth stopped, prices and unemployment sharply increased, and Keynesian demand-side economics could not cure the stagnation and decline; in fact, it generated even higher inflation. The Philips curve, the classic "law" describing the inverse relationship between inflation and unemployment, also stopped working as inflation and unemployment rose together. What followed was a sudden slowdown and decline accompanied by high inflation and unemployment (see Figure 6.4). This odd pairing of stagnation and inflation led to the introduction of a new economic term: stagflation.

Why did Keynesian economics, which worked for 30–40 years, fail? It was assisted by outside, non-economic factors, which confused usual trends. The change, in reality, was not so abrupt. As Andrea Boltho stated:

The year 1973 represented a watershed . . . a very sudden break with the past, but the trend toward a deteriorating performance had already set in earlier. In a way, the success of the 1950s and 1960s had laid the preconditions for at least some of the failures of the 1970s. (Boltho, 1982: 28)

Clouds, indeed, began gathering during the boom years. From the late 1960s, especially around 1968, corporative cooperation ended and the rising political turmoil – a mini-revolution in France in 1968, social disturbances in Germany, and the "hot autumn" in Italy in 1969 – in an overheated economy led to wage explosion in several countries. An inflationary spiral became clearly visible between 1968 and 1970.

Figure 6.4
Unemployment rate,
1950–90s

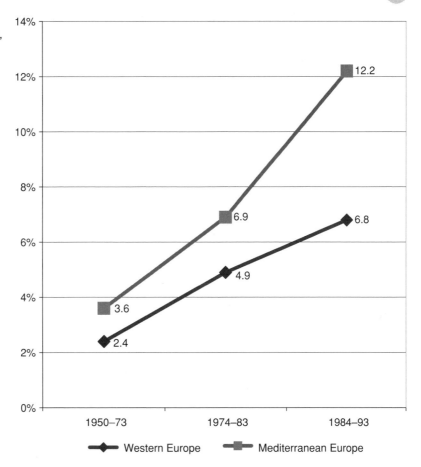

As early as the mid-1960s, it was evident that a slowdown of growth did not bring about any appreciable slowdown in price rises. . . . The rise in oil prices at the end of 1973 only hastened a phenomenon that was already emerging more and more clearly . . . (Caron, 1979: 322)

The international monetary system had already been shaken. The United States' balance of payments deficit had increased significantly, inflation had jumped to 6% in 1970, and the Nixon administration practically ended dollar convertibility in August 1971. The Bretton Woods agreement collapsed:

Not just inflation but the business cycle grew increasingly volatile . . . With the commitment to par values removed, agents had no reason to regard an acceleration of inflation as temporary. When governments stimulated demand in the effort to offset a recession, this provoked compensating wage increase; aggregate demand policies therefore elicited inflation rather than stabilizing output. (Eichengreen, 1994: 61)

All of these happened in an overheated Western economy. The gross capital stock per employee (in 1990 value) in France, Germany, the Netherlands, and Britain increased by nearly three times between 1950 and 1973.

Tremendous over-investment in the traditional industrial sectors of the modern consumption economy during the 1960s . . . [caused] massive overcapacity. This over-investment and overcapacity in the West was accentuated by the industrialization process in the Eastern bloc and the Third World, a process which was often concentrated in identical sectors . . . [T]he enormous investment in the secondary and tertiary sectors, held out the prospect of a shortage of foodstuffs, raw materials and energy. The turning of the terms of trade in favour of primary producers from the beginning of the 1970s came as a result of this growing imbalance. (Van der Wee, 1986: 90)

The entire 1970s and even the early 1980s became a period of high, often two-digit inflation in the world economy. After a quarter of a century of exceptional boom and full employment, a decade of instability, slower growth, and occasional setbacks followed. Based on ninety-four countries with 98% of the world population, the average rate of growth of 3.4% between 1950 and 1973 dropped to –0.1% between 1973 and 1987. In the same period the terms of trade of the advanced countries declined by 20% (Maddison, 1985: 13); industrial output had declined by 13%. The leading economic powers were no longer the engines of European economic prosperity.

Between 1950–73 and 1973–83, the rate of consumer price increases in the leading Western economies more than doubled (from an average annual 4.2% to 9.4%), while in the Mediterranean region they more than quadrupled (from 4.0% to 18.4%). Unemployment, which had been extremely low, averaging 2–4% in Western and Mediterranean Europe between 1950–73, jumped to 5–12% by 1984–93 (Maddison, 1995b: 84). While growth slowed down, unemployment increased (see Table 6.1). Exports, previously one of the most important driving forces of economic growth, were hit hard (see Table 6.2).

After decades of fluctuation-free growth, these developments were a shock. Investments in twelve European Union member countries fell from an annual increase of 5.6% between 1960 and 1973 to only 0.3% in the later 1970s and to –0.6% between 1980–5. The same trend characterized real GDP development: it dropped from 4.8% to 2.2%, and then to 0.5% between 1973–80 and 1980–5, respectively (Commission, 1989: 111).

Counterbalancing the harsh impacts of structural crisis and the collapse of certain traditional branches of the economy, European governments

Table 6.1 Rate of growth in constant prices and unemployment (Maddison, 1985: 19; 1995b: 361, 370)

Country	Growth 1960–73	Growth 1974–83	Unemployment 1973	Unemployment July 1983
France	5.6	2.2	2.6	8.1
Germany	4.5	1.6	0.8	7.7
Netherlands	5.0	1.4	2.3	13.7
Britain	3.1	1.0	3.2	12.6

Table 6.2 From peak to trough: fluctuation in foreign trade between 1973 and 1983 – maximum percentage peak to trough fall or smallest rise per annum (Maddison, 1985: 47)

Country	Volume of exports	Volume of imports
France	−3.0	−7.1
Germany	−11.5	−5.0
Netherlands	−4.9	−8.8
Britain	−2.2	−8.6

reacted to the new challenge in an old, traditional way. They made "defensive investments" by subsidizing ailing industries to lower the cost of production and slow their decline (Lamfalussy, 1961). The British government increased its aid to steel, mining, and shipbuilding from less than 8% of total industrial assistance before 1973 to one-quarter of that total by 1982–3. German federal aid to industry more than doubled during the decade after 1973, and aid to shipbuilding and the steel industry rose from 23% to 50% of total federal industrial subsidies. The same two industries received one-quarter of government aid in France during the same decade (OECD, 1987: 231).

European governments also increased tariffs and restrictions in an effort to defend domestic markets. The European Economic Community raised the proportion of restricted imports from 11% to 15% of total imports of manufactured goods. Restrictions on imported goods from Japan and the newly industrialized countries of Asia increased from 15% to as much as 30% by the early 1980s. To keep the economy afloat, the European countries also increased their export assistance. France paid export credits, which amounted to 5–6% of the value of capital goods exports between 1970 and 1978, but increased this amount to 10% by 1981–3. Some countries, such as Germany, gave tax relief to certain industries. Denmark, Sweden, and Holland increased export assistance from 2% to 28%, from 1% to 10%, and from 3% to 8%, respectively, between the mid-1970s and the early 1980s (OECD, 1987: 229–31).

The West European core, as an OECD analysis stated in 1987, suffered from structural rigidities that slowed application of innovative technology. Europe's position in research and development-intensive branches worsened after 1973 because of its inability to make necessary adjustments more quickly (OECD, 1987). This slow rate of structural–technological adjustment was clearly evident as Europe lost ground to international competition in technology-intensive products. European companies held only a 9% share of the world market in computer and data-processing products, 10% in software, 13% in satellites and launchers, and 29% in data-transmission services (OECD, 1987: 213). Between 1965 and 1984 the United States and Japan increased their combined share of world trade in the products of research and development-intensive branches of industry from more than 30% to more than 45%, while the share of France, Germany, and Britain combined decreased from 36% to 31% (Duchene and Shepherd, 1987: 36). In the mid-1980s, American and Japanese output of information technology was valued at $250 billion, while the output of seven leading European countries together was valued at only $66 billion. Although Europe lost ground in the production of high-tech products, and the EEC dropped from 88% to 75% of the average output of the OECD countries between 1970 and 1985, the Community did gain ground in low R&D-intensive branches of industry. Its level of production in this area increased from 98% to 115% of the OECD average (OECD, 1987: 214, 254).

What at first glance appeared as a temporary consequence of a political conflict, the oil crisis, soon turned out to be an organic part of the economic process, with deep internal roots. As a decisive new element of the changing economic environment, the globalization of the world economy gained tremendous impetus. The protectionist reflex, acting according to the pattern of the 1930s, was only transitory. In the age of globalization it would not work well. "Defensive investments" gave some breathing time for Western Europe to reconsider economic strategy and reorient policy. By the

Table 6.3 Annual R&D spending in the European Union, early 1990s (Kipping, 1997: 496)

	Germany	France	Britain	EU 12
Domestic R&D (in million ECU)	37,578	23,790	17,800	104,225
As % of GDP	2.53	2.36	2.12	1.96
Financed by companies (in %)	59.5	42.5	49.7	–
Government expenditure (in million ECU)	15,265	14,634	6,803	49,914
Financed by public budget (in %)	4.31	5.99	3.01	3.26

mid-1980s, the European governments began revising their policies. State interventionism declined and returned to previous levels. Special subsidies were canceled and deregulation and privatization became predominant. Major efforts were made to adjust to the technological revolution. The real engine of economic growth, research and – its practical application – development, was concentrated in the hands of multinationals. British, French, and German multinational companies increased their R&D spending by 1.5–4.5% annually during the 1980s–1990s (see Table 6.3). In particular areas such as fine chemical products, the highly science-based chemical companies invested 10–15% of their sales income in R&D. These leading companies accounted for three-quarters of total R&D expenditure of the advanced (OECD) countries. Governments and the European Union itself also invested in R&D.

The generally weak European Union activity in industrial policy eventually centered on R&D, but mostly by assisting European multinationals. In the early 1980s, to close the gap with American and Japanese competitors, the European Strategic Programme for Research and Development (ESPRIT) was prepared, being launched with 750 million ECUs in 1985. Further programs followed to inspire the development of communication and other new industrial technologies (RACE and BRITE), which eventually were united in a single Research and Technology Development program in 1987. From 1987 to 1991, 5.4 billion ECUs were invested in this program. Investment stood at 5.7 billion ECUs in 1990–4 and rose to 12.3 billion ECU by 1994–8. The European Union initiative under the

ESPRIT program established close cooperation among leading multinationals Siemens, AEG, Bull, Thomson, Olivetti, Philips, and six other companies which received 70% of the financing in the first stage of the program. Several European "showpieces" such as the Airbus program targeted inter-firm and inter-governmental enterprises (Béteille, 1995; Kipping, 1997: 492–5, 497).

As a consequence, R&D activity gained momentum. In one-and-a-half decades from 1980 employment in this sector increased by more than 400,000 people, or 34%. In the mid-1990s, Western Europe employed 1.6 million people in R&D (UNESCO, 1999: III-23–6).

Technology's share of manufacturing output, as a consequence, grew somewhat. Modernization and renewal of traditionally strong industries with moderate levels of R&D were more successful. The leading country in this case was Germany. German output in these branches – motor vehicles, engineering, and the chemical industry – increased from 32% to 41% of total industrial output. In France, it increased from 29% to 34%, in Holland from 20% to 25%, and in Belgium from 30% to 37% (OECD, 1987: 254). Through renewed technology, product differentiation, and specialization, these branches lowered the costs of production and penetrated markets that were less saturated and less competitive. These sectors of moderate intensity of R&D increased their exports significantly (OECD, 1987: 215).

Germany was less successful in strengthening its capital goods sector. The export/import ratio of this sector, which had improved tremendously in Japan, declined in Germany. Britain also experienced some decline, while Italy and France improved, indicating an improved comparative advantage of their products in this sector (OECD, 1987: 216). In a clear sign of structural adjustment, investment and output in information and communication technology made considerable progress: the share of income attributable to this sector tripled between 1980 and 1996.

In 1980, European income from the information and communication technology sector stood at only one-third of U.S. levels; by 1996 it had climbed to one-half. This had an important impact on output growth: during the first half of the 1990s, information technology accounted for less than one-third of output growth, but during the second half of the decade it constituted one-half of this growth. This latter contribution was equal to the contribution made by the same sector in the United States during the first half of the 1990s, indicating that Europe lagged only about five years behind the United States in terms of the diffusion of modern technology. Investment shares in these branches came close to U.S. levels in Sweden, Holland, Finland, and Britain. The fifteen countries of the

European Union, however, counted only 60 personal computers per 100 white-collar workers, compared with 118 in the United States. In 1998, there were an average of 20 personal computers per 100 inhabitants in the European Union, compared with 51 in the United States. Huge gaps also existed among member countries: Ireland and Sweden had 93 personal business computers per 100 white-collar workers, whereas Portugal had only 27. On the other hand, there were 60 mobile phones per 100 people in Finland and Sweden, nearly twice as many as in the United States (34). Denmark and France counted only 19 and 22 mobile phones per 100 people, respectively.

Output from the information and communication technology sector in Western Europe reached 4.2% of GDP. Only Ireland (7.6%), Sweden, and Finland (nearly 6% each) registered outputs comparable to the American level of 6.8% of GDP. Although job creation was generally slow during the 1990s, 75% of the net job creation in the second half of the decade occurred in high-tech sectors, in which at least 40% of the workforce had tertiary education. This was another clear sign of modern structural changes. Although somewhat behind America, Europe followed technological and structural changes closely (Commission, 2000: 37, 108–9, 115, 117).

Besides the growth of the new sectors, it became increasingly difficult to differentiate between old and new industries, due to the renewal and revitalization – or "hybridization" – that took place in several old sectors with the introduction of new technologies. Certain sectors of engineering, for example, became closely connected with electronics. Innovations resulted from further inter-sectoral technological links between mechanical engineering, precision engineering, electrical engineering, electronics, and communication. The merging of these four fields became known as "mechatronics."

Certain labor-intensive processes were relocated in countries with cheaper labor costs. Dutch multinationals already employed three-quarters of their labor force abroad in the 1970s (Jones and Schröter, 1993: 25). A strong trend of de-industrialization characterized the most advanced countries, which turned toward most modern technology sectors and services. During the last third of the century, the share of the labor force employed in manufacturing declined: in Britain from 48% to 20%, in the Netherlands from 42% to 16%, in Italy from 40% to 21%, and in Sweden from 45% to 18% (see Figure 6.5).

Western Europe, profiting from free factor movement, technology transfer, and export possibilities on an integrated European and globalized world market, belonged to the world's most internationalized–globalized

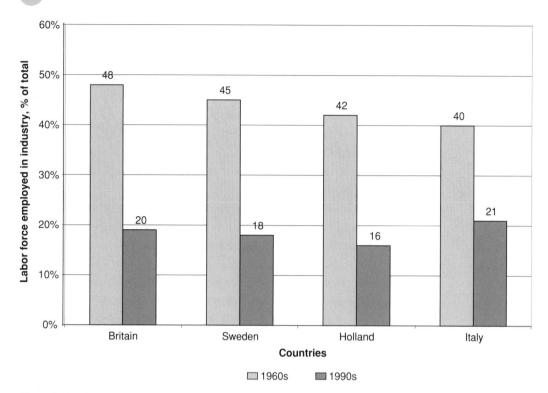

Figure 6.5
De-industrialization
of Western Europe,
1960s–90s

region. According to the globalization and internationalization indexes of
A. T. Kearney, besides the United States, mostly European countries such
as Britain, Ireland, Belgium, Holland, Switzerland, Finland, Denmark, and
Austria belonged to the global top ten countries, while Hungary and Poland
belonged to those which made the best advancement toward this category
in the second half of the 1990s (Kearney, 2000). Western Europe, consequently, was able to cope with structural crisis. Consumer price inflation,
which had reached roughly 10–14% per year, dropped to 3–5% in the second half of the 1980s. That period represented an increasing adjustment
of the Western European economy to the international requirements of
the communication–computer revolution. The surprising reversal of the
movement of oil prices on the world market played an important role in the
containment of prices: from $36 a barrel in 1981, the price of oil dropped
to $11 a barrel by early 1986.

Private consumption gradually recovered. Residential construction,
a leader during the early stage of consumer-led prosperity in Europe,
regained momentum: in the fifteen countries of the European Union,
it had fallen from 5.4% per year during the early 1970s to −1.2% and
0.3% between 1973 and 1979–80, respectively, but increased by nearly

Table 6.4 Average annual percentage change in private consumption (*Economic Survey*, 1991)

Region	1980–4 annual average	1985–90 annual average
Western Europe	1.3	3.3
Southern Europe	0.7	4.2
Total Europe	1.2	3.4

2% per annum again during the 1980s. In Germany and Austria, after the decline or stagnation that lasted from 1973 through to the end of the 1980s, residential construction increased by nearly 4% per year during the 1990s (OECD, 2000: 57). As one of the clearest signals of regained consumer vitality, the car market also recuperated. Between 1975 and 1985 the number of passenger cars in the advanced twelve countries of the West increased by only 5%; by the mid-1990s, however, the number of cars surpassed the mid-1980s level by 78%. Tourism regained momentum as well. International tourism, one of the most dynamically emerging sectors of mass consumption, increased by more than 10% annually during the 1950s–1960s. It slowed to a 3.8% rate of growth between 1975–82, then recovered during the second half of the 1980s, reaching an annual 5–7% increase. In 1970, 160 million tourists traveled the world; by 1993, they numbered 500 million, a more than threefold increase (Transport, 1998: 105, 146; Williams and Shaw, 1998: 19). Private consumption thus increased rapidly again from the second half of the 1980s. Instead of the little more than 1% annual increase during the first half of the 1980s, private consumption grew by 3–4% annually from the second half of the decade (see Table 6.4).

The other central element of postwar prosperity, exports, also recovered. Western European exports grew by nearly 8% annually before the oil crisis, but dropped to 3.3% per annum during the first half of the 1980s. The second half of the decade, however, saw a nearly 5% increase per annum. Foreign trade regained strength. Although it did not grow at the rate that was typical of the postwar quarter of a century, it picked up after 1973 (see Figure 6.6). Exports began to play a more important role in West European economies than elsewhere, and more than ever before (see Table 6.5).

Increasing exports and changing price trends stabilized current account balances as well. Before the oil crisis, Western Europe had surpluses of $2.2 billion, $5.0 billion, and $6.7 billion in 1970, 1971, 1972, respectively.

Table 6.5 Merchandise exports as % of GDP in 1990 prices (Maddison, 2001: 363)

Country	1950	1973	1998
France	7.6	15.2	28.7
Germany	6.2	23.8	38.9
Netherlands	12.2	40.7	61.2
Britain	11.3	14.0	25.0
World average	5.5	10.5	17.2

Figure 6.6

Europe's exports, 1950–2000

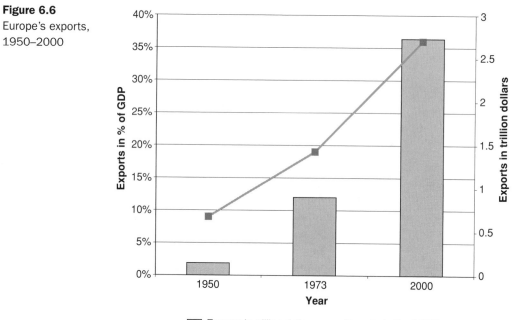

After 1973 huge current account deficits emerged. From a $4.4 billion surplus in 1974, a $12.3 billion deficit accumulated in 1974. In 1980, the deficit reached nearly $38 billion. After that, however, current account deficits began to dwindle and were eventually replaced by huge surpluses that averaged more than $23 billion annually over eight years (*Economic Survey*, 1991).

Fixed capital formation and investments regained the pre-oil shock dynamism of 5.7% annual increase after several years of negative figures. The annual growth rate also increased to 3.1% in Western Europe by the

Table 6.6 Service revolution: value added in services
as % of total value added (OECD, 2000: 63)

Country	1970–3	1999
France	55.3	72.8
Germany	50.0	68.9
Netherlands	55.7	71.3
Sweden	58.3	69.6
Belgium	52.1	72.1
Britain	63.5	73.2
Total EU 15	52.2	69.6

late 1980s. The exceptional growth of the Golden Age, however, did not re-emerge: the twelve most advanced countries of Western Europe enjoyed a growth rate of 3.9% between 1950 and 1973, but only 1.7% between 1973 and 1998 (*Economic Survey*, 1991).

Globalization brought a new impetus for continued and more rapid structural change. The "disappearance" of the agricultural population, de-industrialization, and the service revolution, which had all begun during previous decades, gained full speed. The agricultural population of the fifteen countries of the EU decreased from 13.5% in 1970 to 4.6% by 1999. The industrial population also fell during the last three decades of the century, from 41.1% to 29.1%. All of these countries experienced a full-scale "service revolution" during those decades (see Figure 6.7 and Table 6.6): employment in that sector increased from 45.0% to 66.4% (OECD, 2000: 40–1).

The growing importance of services, which employed between 50% and 70% of the active population and produced about 70% of the GDP in Western Europe, requires some explanation. Several aspects of agricultural and industrial performance, which in previous decades were integral elements of agriculture, gained a certain independence and became services during the second half of the century. For example, trucking and drying the harvest, as well as elements of cultivation and plant protection, were taken on by independent service companies. While agriculture employs only 2–3% of the gainfully employed population, services for agriculture employ another 10–15%. The decline of manufacturing employment is also connected with the separation of production and services within the industrial sector. Modern industrial firms excluded previously central service

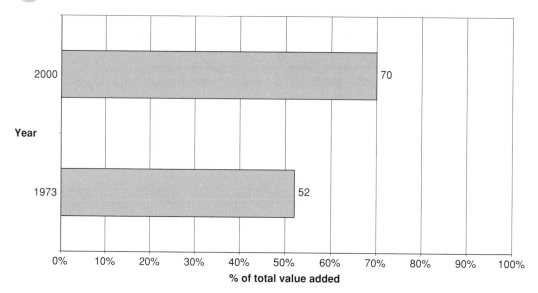

Figure 6.7 Service revolution: services in the European Union (15 countries) in % of total value added

activities such as accounting and information, and in several cases even research and development. Regional service centers were created and offered these services for industrial companies. As an OECD report phrased it:

Technological progress is transforming the nature of the relationship between manufacturing industry and the service sector, as a result of which they are becoming increasingly complementary. Indeed, it is one major cause of the growing service content of manufactured goods, sometimes referred to as the "dematerialization of products;" at the same time it promotes the "industrialization" of services. (OECD, 1987: 256)

In the advanced West, services became the key sector of the economy during the last quarter of the century. Specialized services increased efficiency and productivity. A burgeoning service sector and employment thus reflect increasing specialization and a new combination of agriculture, industry, and services (see Figure 6.8).

Structural changes contributed greatly to the increase in labor productivity because of the higher value of the outputs in the emerging sectors, while the drastically decreased agricultural and industrial labor force also produced much more than before. The most advanced countries of the West increased labor productivity by nearly three times between 1950 and 1973, and by another 76% during the last quarter of the century (see Figure 6.9 and Table 6.7).

Globalization and the enlargement and integration process of the European Union opened a window of opportunity for former peripheral countries in Southern Europe and some of the Nordic countries to be an equal

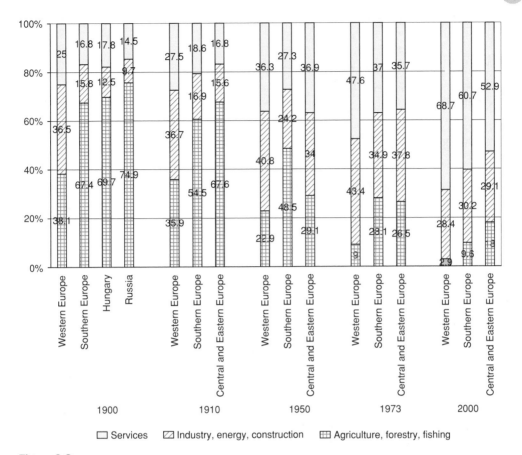

Figure 6.8
Employment
structure by sectors
of economy,
1900–2000

part of the European economic recovery, and to accomplish the catching-up process with Western Europe which began during the second half of the century.

The former Southern and Northern peripheral countries – Spain, Portugal, Greece, Ireland, and Finland – though hit by both the oil crisis and the worldwide structural crisis, did not experience the same desperation that took hold of Central and Eastern Europe (see Chapter 4). Instead, they were able to emerge from that crisis after a short period of deep economic trouble, and prosperity continued as the area integrated into the European Community. No doubt, the first impact of the oil crisis and the changing world economy shocked the Spanish economy. Nearly three-quarters of the country's energy consumption depended on oil, most of it imported. Expenditure on oil imports leapt from 13% of total import expenditure in 1973 to more than 42% – equal to two-thirds of the total value of Spanish exports.

Table 6.7 Labor productivity, GDP per hour at international 1990 dollar (Maddison, 2001: 351)

Country	1913	1950	1973	1998
France	2.88	5.82	18.02	33.72
Germany	3.03	3.99	14.76	26.56
Britain	4.31	7.93	15.97	27.45
Western Europe (12 countries average)	3.12	5.54	16.21	28.53

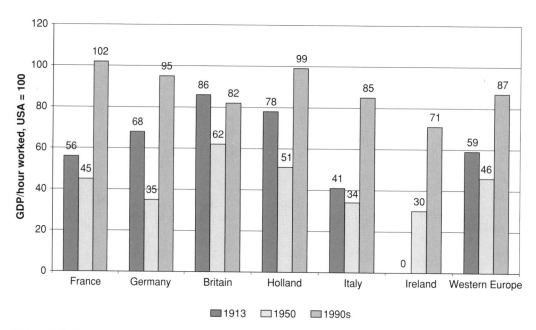

Figure 6.9 Labor productivity in Western Europe, 1913–90s

By the end of 1974, the oil crisis put an end to 15 years' economic progress. In the following year, the rate of growth of GNP fell from 5.4% to 1.1%. Over the period 1976–8, growth rates recovered slightly, averaging 2.8% a year. Nevertheless, these figures represented only one-third of the growth level of the "miracle" years and one-half of the prevailing rate in the European Economic Community countries. (Harrison, 1985: 175)

After a period of rapid expansion, investments decreased by 2–4% annually between 1975 and 1978. The number of unemployed jumped from less than 3% to more than 17% between 1974 and 1982. Sudden high inflation caused prices to increase at a rate of 37% in the summer of 1977, up from 6.4% annually between 1965 and 1972.

Despite the dramatic economic shift, Spain did not sink into a peripheral structural crisis. After the death of Francisco Franco in November 1975, Spain underwent a democratic transformation. A hidden ally of the West during the cold war years, Spain became a partner of the West, and soon a part of it. By 1978, the country had begun to respond positively to the challenge of the structural crisis. Direct foreign investments also played a central role in the recovery. Multinational companies established modern sectors and built up competitive export capacities. Industrial labor productivity increased by 76% between 1970 and 1980. Spanish labor productivity had lagged 14% behind British productivity in 1970; by 1980 Spain led by 14%. Industrial output during the troubled 1970s increased by nearly two-thirds. Agriculture was also modernized. Following the European pattern Spain increased agricultural subsidies more than eightfold during the 1970s. The number of tractors more than doubled. Labor productivity increased by six-and-a-half times, and agricultural output by nearly four times in a single decade during the 1970s (Nadal et al., 1987: 271, 274, 292–3, 308).

The Adolfo Suárez government took new steps toward the European Community. By 1978, nearly half of Spanish exports and 72% of industrial exports went to the Community. During the decade from 1976–85, exports grew by 7.9% per year. The number of foreign tourists also grew by one-third, and the income from tourism more than doubled between 1974 and 1979. The *Pacto de la Moncloa* of October 1977 between the government and the left-wing opposition parties led to the introduction of a wage ceiling, which helped the country cope with inflation. Consumer price increases, which varied between 15% and 25% per year, slowed to single digits from 1985. Meanwhile, the devaluation of the peseta by 20% increased Spain's export competitiveness (*Economic Survey*, 1991; Harrison, 1985).

Due to the *Plan Energético Nacional*, the entire energy system was modernized. After the oil crisis, Spanish oil consumption continued to increase by more than one-quarter until 1980, but then declined at that same rate until the mid-1980s, following the Western pattern. In contrast, coal, natural gas, hydroelectric power, and most of all nuclear energy consumption increased (Nadal et al., 1987: 358).

Portugal's history parallels that of Spain in many respects. However, the recession of 1973–5 probably hit Portugal more severely because it coincided with a political revolution. The colonial empire also collapsed. The *retornado*, a huge wave of about half a million refugees from the former colonies, led to a population increase of around 8% during 1973–5. In addition, previous emigration from Portugal to Western Europe, which had reached an annual figure of 120,000 people, declined sharply. Unemployment jumped from 5.5% to 14%. A transitory political chaos, mass meetings and demonstrations, sharply rising wages, nationalizations, and the uncertainty of the future accompanied the aftermath of the oil crisis and revolution. The price of imported wheat, sugar, and oil doubled, trebled, and quadrupled, respectively. Prices soared at a rate of 38% in 1974, and grew roughly 25% per year throughout the decade. In the first eight months of 1974, Portugal's trade deficit doubled, climbing to $2 billion. By July 1976, foreign exchange reserves had melted to 14% of April 1974 levels. In 1975, both industrial output and GDP declined by 5.4% and 3.7%, respectively. Investments dropped by one-fifth. "In 1976–1977, it seemed that a total collapse of the Portuguese economy was imminent" (Morrison, 1981: 111).

This did not happen. The dramatic decline was soon halted. The Western world stepped in to assist a peaceful transformation, push back the communist threat, and incorporate Portugal into the Western camp. In September 1975, the Consultative Committee of EFTA made it clear that if a pluralistic political democracy in Portugal took hold, and if communists and left-wing trade unions were curbed, it would assist the transformation process. Indeed, this is exactly what happened in November 1975. Portugal was given special status: while the EFTA market became duty free for its products, the country was given additional time – until 1985 – to eliminate tariffs and other import restrictions. Additionally, an EFTA loan for "the development and restructuring of Portuguese industry" was granted in November 1975, which financed 40% of the investments of private borrower companies. Moreover, since EFTA made an agreement with the European Common Market in 1973, Portugal became an external member of the European Community as well. Beginning in 1976 Portuguese industrial products entered the Community market without duty and soon accounted for half of the country's exports. The Council of Ministers also agreed to provide financial assistance. "The support given by Europe to Portuguese democracy," stated the Commission, "must be expressed in a spectacular manner." Portugal applied for full membership in 1977, but had to wait until its economy was consolidated. The European Investment Bank, the West German and American governments, the Swiss Central Bank, the European Council of Ministers, and the IMF showered Portugal with aid and loans: roughly $2 billion between 1975 and 1977. Capital inflow continued and by 1979 the amount of imported capital reached $6 billion. The Portuguese economy increased by an annual 25%. Enjoying all the advantages of the free market, Portugal became an equal member of the European Union in 1986 (Morrison, 1981).

Modern structural changes followed. Electrical engineering, motor vehicles, and others increased their share of the total value added of manufacturing from 18% to 29%, while traditional engineering, food, tobacco, and metal production declined from 35% to 21% during the decade following 1988 (Commission, 2000: 195). Industrial output increased an impressive 5.5% per year between 1977 and 1990. Exports, which had suffered a sharp decline between 1974 and 1976, recovered and then soared in the second half of the 1980s, in some years by 14–16% (*Economic Survey*, 1991).

Greece, meanwhile, could not cope with the shock of the mid–late 1970s, and experienced a slowing down and near stagnation. Between 1960 and 1979, the country nearly trebled its per capita income; after having joined the European Union, however, between 1980 and 1998, Greece's per capita income level increased by only 26%, slower than that of the European Union. Instead of catching up with the more advanced West, Greece's relative position declined.

Ireland, too, was hard hit by the economic crisis of 1973. Retail sales declined by 10% during the 1970s. The foreign trade deficit grew as Ireland's terms of trade fell by 26% between 1973 and 1981. Real income, which increased at an average annual growth rate of 4.4% during the 1960s, dropped to 1.1% between 1973 and 1981. The country, however, did not suffer a major decline, largely because it joined the European Community in the year of the oil crisis, 1973. By the early 1980s, foreign capital inflow exceeded net national savings. Multinational companies were instrumental in creating modern, export-oriented sectors: by 1980, fifty-five large foreign firms produced nearly one-fifth of Ireland's industrial output, but delivered nearly two-thirds of Irish industrial exports. Industrial exports, only 6% of the total in the late 1950s, jumped to 60% of the country's exports by 1980. The rate of growth of exports, averaging 8.5% per year between 1975 and 1990, was second fastest in the world behind Japan. Gross output grew by 4% per year during the 1970s (Cullen, 1987: 187–90).

Irish exports were geographically reoriented toward Europe. Britain, which received three-quarters of Irish exports before 1973, now received only one-third. The export performance of Ireland was based on marked structural changes in manufacturing. The output of modern sectors such as medical, precision, and optical instruments, electrical machinery, communication equipment, and chemicals increased from 30% to 48% of total value added between 1988 and 1998, while traditional sectors of

Figure 6.10
Ireland's per capita
income level,
1973–2000

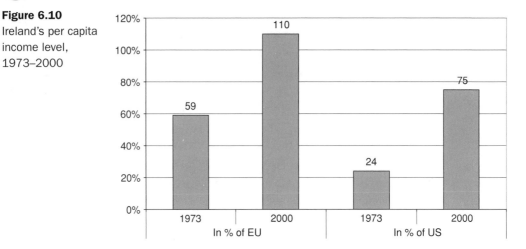

engineering, food, tobacco, and metal production declined from 49% to 34% (Commission, 2000: 195).

During the 1990s, the Irish economy grew at an average rate of 6.6% per year. This resulted in an impressive catching-up process: in 1973, the average income in Ireland was only 59% of the average EEC income level; by 1998, it had surpassed the EEC average, and reached 75% of U.S. levels (see Figure 6.10). The country held nineteenth place among the OECD countries in terms of per capita GDP in 1960, but had risen to tenth place by 1998, with only five European countries showing higher income levels (Survey, 2000: 170; OECD, 2000: 42, 57, 63).

After the collapse of the Soviet Union, a severe economic crisis curbed Finnish development and required a radical restructuring of the country's export and production. Instead of relying on the Soviet market, which had been the most important destination for Finnish exports since World War II, Finland now had to develop industries that could compete in Western markets. This led to a difficult period of transformation. Between 1989 and 1993, Finland's per capita GDP fell by 14%. During the second half of the decade, however, Finland, having built on its postwar achievements, renewed its technology and economic structure. The country became one of the technology leaders of Europe in certain high-tech industries and surpassed Swedish income levels by the late 1990s. At the end of the century, according to the World Economic Forum's Growth and Competitiveness indexes, which consider levels of technological development, macroeconomic parameters, the efficiency of public institutions, and the microeconomic environment, Finland earned the number one position, ahead of the United States, Canada, Germany, Holland, and Switzerland. The

Finnish economic miracle was one of the most spectacular in Europe: in 1913 the level of economic development in Finland matched that of Ireland, Spain, and Hungary, so that it belonged to the less developed countries of the continent. It gradually strengthened its position, however, and had already advanced according to the Scandinavian pattern of industrialization during the interwar decades. The per capita GDP of the country doubled between 1913 and 1950, and increased again by two-and-a-half times between 1950 and 1973. Finland, through a spectacular restructuring in the 1990s, became one of the economic leaders of Europe.

These once relatively backward peripheral countries of Europe accelerated their economic development through massive foreign investment, the participation of public and private multinational institutions, and the advantages of the European Common Market. Globalization contributed to a further narrowing of the technological gap, especially because multinational companies used these countries during the second half of the 1980s as a platform for entrance into the planned European Single Market. Investments in electronics and other high-tech sectors played a determinant role in structural modernization and rapid growth. During the decades of structural crisis, these countries regained their vitality and achieved export-led growth through much of the 1980s. While West European exports, in constant prices, increased by 113% between 1973 and 1992, Spanish exports jumped by 330%. Unemployment, however, remained high: 20% in Spain, and 12% in Ireland during the 1990s. Inflation also remained high and consumer prices increased annually by 15–20%, but private consumption growth kept a rapid pace of 4–5% a year. Irish and Spanish labor productivity, less than two-thirds of the British in 1973, reached 90% of the British level by 1992.

The Mediterranean countries also followed the pattern of Western structural transformation. The sharp decline of agricultural (to 5–10% of total) and industrial employment (to 25–35%), and the impressive increase of service employment, were similar to the trends in the West (Mitchell, 1998: 929–34). Services, which produced half of the GDP in 1970, contributed more than two-thirds of it in Spain, Portugal, and Greece by the end of the century (Mitchell, 1998: 929–34). The growth rate in the countries of these regions exceeded the West European average. In Ireland the growth rate was three times greater. While Finland and Ireland surpassed the West European average (see Table 6.8), Spain and Portugal reached nearly 80% and almost three-quarters of the EU average per capita GDP, respectively, by 1998 (see Table 6.9). Greece represented the only exception: the catching-up process, which was impressive between 1950 and 1973, was followed

Table 6.8 Leaders in catching up (GDP per capita 1973–98)

Year	Ireland	%	Spain	%	Finland	%	Portugal	%	West*	%
1973	6,867	100	8,739	100	11,085	100	7,343	100	11,534	100
1998	18,183	265	14,227	163	18,324	165	12,929	176	17,921	155

* Western Europe

Table 6.9 Mediterranean and Northern countries: GDP per capita (Western Europe = 100%) (based on Maddison, 2001: 276–8, 330)

Year	Finland	Ireland	Spain	Portugal	Greece
1950	93	75	52	45	42
1973	96	60	76	64	66
1998	102	102	79	72	63

by a relative decline during the last quarter of the century (Survey, 2000: 166).

The challenge of mixed economy and welfare state

All these developments, the requirements of structural transformation, and increased competitiveness in the globalized world system challenged the postwar West European arrangements, the mixed economy and the welfare state. This was partly a consequence of the progress of additional new and overly expensive services in the prosperous welfare states. In some cases the welfare measures became overextended and, in a way, too luxurious. According to its critics, it created too heavy a burden on the economy, too high a cost of production, which decreases competitiveness. Europe spent more than twice as much, in relative terms, on welfare expenditure as the United States or Japan. This fact became decisive when globalization sharpened international competition.

Besides, a transforming demographic situation steeply increased welfare expenditure. Demographic trends had changed dramatically by the

THE CHALLENGE OF MIXED ECONOMY AND WELFARE STATE

late twentieth century. Both mortality and birth rates dropped sharply in this period. In the early twentieth century there were 14–20 deaths/1,000 inhabitants in the West and 25–30 deaths in the South; during the twentieth century, mortality declined by one-half or one-third to 10 deaths/1,000, eliminating significant regional differences. A radical decline in infant mortality and the decisive role of improved therapy were magnified by the benefits of the welfare state, which introduced full, state-assured health insurance for all citizens in the second half of the century, and provided various benefits, including maternity leave. Several other factors also contributed: among them, improvement in housing, work conditions, nutrition, and lifestyle. Life expectancy at birth, as a consequence, increased in a spectacular fashion. At the beginning of the century it was about fifty years in the West and between 30–40 years in the South; by mid-century, Western life expectancy increased to sixty-seven years, and then, at the end of the century, to seventy-six years. The Mediterranean countries reached the Western levels at the end of the century.

Birth rates, however, 15–18/1,000 by 1950, or around 2–2.5 children per woman, declined to 1.5 children by the end of the century. England, France, Germany, and Spain counted 1.7, 1.7, 1.2, and 1.2 children per woman, respectively, in the 1990s. These figures were lower than reproduction levels, and this led to a population decrease during the last decades of the century. The last time that the fertility rate matched the level necessary for population reproduction was during the early 1970s.

Radically changing mortality and fertility rates led to significant aging of the population. While in 1950 the share of the young generation (under the age of fifteen) in Britain, Germany, France, and Italy, represented roughly one-quarter of the population, and the elderly (above sixty) represented only 14%, by 2000 the share of the young generation dropped to 17%, and the percentage of the elderly population increased to 20% (see Figure 6.11) (Livi Bacci, 2000: 171).

Because the active, productive layers of society diminished while the elderly and pensioned population grew, welfare expenditures jumped. In France, four workers financed each pensioner in 1960; by 2000, there were only two French workers for each pensioner. If demographic trends continue, by 2020 the pensioner/worker ratio will be even. According to calculations, pension expenditures in the advanced countries will double in twenty years. Without major reforms, pensions might decline by 50% in a few years. France, after confrontations between the government and the people, was forced to change its pension plan in the early twenty-first century.

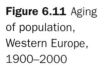

Figure 6.11 Aging of population, Western Europe, 1900–2000

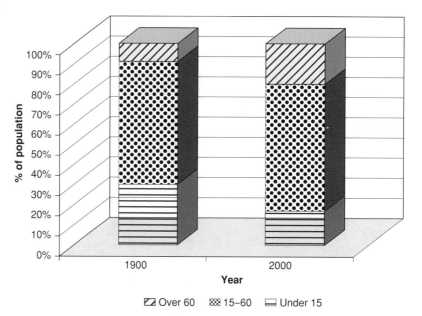

Europe, partly because of the declining population and labor force, became a continent of immigration. Immigrants, some of them illegal, made up roughly 9–10% of the population of the region at the end of the twentieth century. Poverty also increased, and became a social issue to be addressed after the mid-1970s. By the mid-1980s, 50 million people lived on incomes that were less than half of the prevailing national income level in Western Europe. This situation significantly increased the financial burdens for the welfare states. What was relatively easy to finance during high prosperity became a difficult financial burden under the new circumstances. Ticking demographic and social bombs made existing social security schemes untenable in the longer run.

Furthermore, in the globalized world economy European countries had to compete with others which had much lower wages and incomparably lower social expenditures. In the welfare states, labor costs were roughly doubled by social benefits. This situation exacerbated the problem for the European welfare systems since American and most Asian competitors had much lower social costs and a more competitive position. In the global economy,

investors will be able to seek out the most congenial environment in terms of wages, labor and environmental regulations, tax burdens, and so forth. In this way, the imperatives of market competition . . . compelling governments to reduce to the world economy's lowest common denominator the burdens and social responsibilities placed upon investors – fostering a race to the bottom. (Rupert, 2000: 80)

These changes, noted Steen Mangen,

are not merely episodic: they fundamentally undermine the long-established and, until the 1970s at least, more or less stable reconciliation of overarching welfare principles such as solidarity, equity, universality . . . Since the 1980s a growing emphasis has been placed on designing more flexible strategies . . . although these have generally meant reduction in statutory rights for recipients . . . Despite sustained efforts at cost control in the 1980s, by international comparison most European Union states remain among the highest spenders. (Mangen, 1997: 521)

The globalized, non-regulated world economy represented a serious challenge for the welfare state. State regulations and ownership, neo-liberal economics argues, are inappropriate in a cutthroat global competition. The mixed economy is not a vehicle to reach higher goals, and the welfare state, for neo-liberals, is the problem, not the solution. The neo-liberal school advocated the return to a self-regulated market system, without state regulations. It also equated freedom with a self-regulated market system. Neo-liberal ideology, advocating low taxation, appealed to Western societies.

The G-7 countries, all the leading economic powers of the world, and the international monetary institutions they created and financed, most of all the International Monetary Fund, were champions of – as Joseph E. Stiglitz, former chief economist of the World Bank and a Nobel laureate, stated – "market supremacy with ideological fervor" (Stiglitz, 2002: 12–13). "Reaganomics" was an ideologically based commitment against "big government," and in favor of drastic tax cuts and withdrawal of the state by contracting out and privatizing key public services. Several services, previously covered by the Ministry of Defence and the National Health Service (with 2,000 hospitals) in Britain, were also contracted out after the May 1979 electoral victory of Margaret Thatcher. Previously nationalized firms were reprivatized soon. Germany and Italy followed, and, from the mid-1980s, France joined as well. Within eighteen months after the electoral victory of Jacques Chirac almost all of the companies nationalized by the socialist government were reprivatized. Post-Franco Spain followed the same pattern from the mid-1980s.

This proved a serious blow to the mixed economy, and an additional ideological challenge to the welfare state (Atkinson, 1999). Privatization of state-owned sectors of the West European countries was accomplished in a few years during the 1980s and 1990s. Eliminating welfare institutions nevertheless remained a rather difficult, highly unpopular task. Elected governments had to think twice before they risked measures against the welfare system in Europe. Because of unpredictable risks and uncertainty in the unstable job market and economic situation, certain calculations showed that without welfare institutions about one-fifth of the middle class would have declined below the poverty line for at least a while in Germany and Holland in the 1980s and 1990s (Goodin et al., 1999). The welfare state as guarantor of security, even for the middle class, remained popular. It also continued to serve social peace and free access to education, a major factor of economic prosperity in modern times. As a consequence, in the most developed countries of the continent, even during the difficult last two decades of the century, social expenditure did not decline but, in several cases, increased its share of GDP. According to the 2002 Report of the OECD, the redistributive function of the welfare state reached one-quarter of the GDP even in the last decade of the century. In some cases, social benefit expenditures increased by more than 20%. The economic growth leader, Ireland, doubled its social benefit spending during the 1970s, and continued this trend during the 1980s and 1990s. The eleven members of the Eurozone increased per capita social protection benefit expenditure by 13% from the mid-1980s to the mid-1990s; Ireland increased this expenditure by 35%, while family and children benefits per head increased by 56%. Italy and France, in the same decade, increased social protection benefits by 31% and 25%, respectively. Per capita unemployment benefits increased by 37%, and old-age benefits by 14% (European Commission, 1971–80: 137; 1998–9: 150–6). Indeed, the twelve European Union countries before 1995, as an average, spent 26% of their GDP on social protection expenditures. Cultural and policy traditions, however, resulted in major differences: the Southern member countries such as Portugal, Greece, and Spain spent only about 20% of their GDP on welfare targets, while the Northern ones such as the Netherlands and Denmark spent 30–32% on the same goals. Employer contributions also exhibited a huge disparity: France, Italy, and Spain required heavy employer contributions over 50%, nearly twice as much as in Britain, and seven times higher than in Denmark.

The welfare state has been challenged and must be reformed. Trimming certain benefits, especially "luxury" benefits, increasing the retirement age, and other adjustments are on the agenda, and the process will continue. The welfare state of the twenty-first century, if it survives, will certainly be different from the one that people of the twentieth century knew.

Globalization and inequality

Globalization and European integration had a positive impact on several European countries in the core and in some of the peripheries as the free movement of capital and goods led to more production and distribution of goods and services in an integrated Europe. Allocation of resources also improved when the entire international theater was opened for entrepreneurial actions.

The nation state has become an unnatural, even dysfunctional, unit for organizing human activity and managing economic endeavor in a borderless world. It represents no genuine, shared community of economic interests; it defines no meaningful flows of economic activity. (Ohmae, 1993: 78, quoted in Rupert, 2000)

Mark Zacher speaks about

the declining pillars of the Westphalian temple . . . in which the . . . world . . . politically worshiped for over three centuries. [The system, created by the Treaty of Westphalia (1648)] recognized the state as the supreme or sovereign power within its boundaries . . . The world is in the process of a fundamental transformation from a system of highly autonomous states to one where states are increasingly enmeshed in a network of interdependencies. (Zacher, 2000: 480, 519–21)

Globalization and the massive cross-border investments of multinationals no doubt contributed to the adjustment and prosperity of Western Europe. Its established role and huge income derived from the globalized world economy, and the inter-European multinational activity often helped to revitalize ailing sectors. The British economy, for example, which endured a long struggle to restructure its economy, was greatly assisted by multinationals. The declining paper industry, in 1967 almost entirely in British hands, was renewed by huge multinational investments and technological modernization: by 1997, the industry's capacity increased by nearly 60% as American, Swedish, Finnish, and Dutch-based companies took over. The ailing British car industry underwent a similar transformation with Nissan and BMW investment.

Nissan's Sunderland factory, opened . . . in 1986, set a new benchmark for the British motor industry in labour productivity . . . While the arrival of the Japanese was the most spectacular change in the British motor industry during the 1980s, a partial renaissance was under way at the other foreign-owned companies . . . The infusion of capital and technology from overseas made a big contribution to the regeneration of the industry. (Owen, 1999: 164–5, 246, 279)

Honda, Toyota, General Motors, Ford, and Peugeot all participated in this renewal. The revitalized production of TV sets was almost entirely the consequence of Japanese, Korean, and Taiwanese multinationals, which produced 86% of British TV sets in 1996. Numerous joint ventures and multinational investments produced similar results in several other West European countries.

Enthusiasts maintain that each country profits from globalization. Capital will be invested, they argue, where it is more profitable and thus will flow into low-wage developing countries. The meaning of former categories such as "Third World," and "core and periphery" disappear. "As chains of commodity production and exchange operate above, below, and across national and regional boundaries, generating their own time-compressed spatial relations," inequalities are diminishing. Moreover, globalization gradually also globalizes social and political trends of the more advanced countries. Social convergence and global democratization follow. Some speak about the rise of a global civil society, an age when economy, politics, culture, and military organizations are all globalized, and geography ended (Lal, 1980; Dunning, 1993; Mittelman, 1995).

The concept of global advantage from globalization is, however, strongly challenged. Andrew Hurrell and Ngaire Woods emphasize an unequal relationship:

Inequality among states matters . . . Simply put, globalization affects regions of the world in different ways . . . For less powerful states in a region . . . globalization is a process, which is happening to them and to which they must respond. To some degree, they must choose either to accept the rules of the more powerful or not; although in today's world economy . . . they have little choice but to accept the rules. (Hurrell and Woods, 2000: 528–9, 531)

Certain anti-globalization concepts are much more extreme, maintaining that globalization is nothing more than imperialism, which serves only the rich countries' interests and exacerbates the exploitation and destruction of poor peripheral countries.

When two economies, at different levels of development are brought together, the natural operation of market forces tends to widen their initial inequalities . . . The polarization created by trade is deepened by factor [i.e capital and labor] movements. Attracted by higher returns, the lagging country also loses its capital and skilled labor to the advanced country. (Alam, 2000: 63)

Who is right and who is wrong? Is globalization "good" or "bad"? The critical period of the last quarter of the twentieth century undoubtedly presents dramatic evidence of further polarization. Per capita GDP during that period increased in the advanced Western world, including Western Europe and Japan, by an annual rate of roughly 2%. In Latin America, the annual growth rate was 0.99%. Africa experienced virtual stagnation, an annual 0.01% growth rate. In Central and Eastern Europe, including the successor states of the former Soviet Union, GDP declined by 1.10% per annum. Interregional disparities, or income differences, which decreased from a 15:1 ratio in 1950 to a 13:1 ratio by 1973, widened during the decades of globalization between 1973 and 1998 from 13:1 to 19:1 (Maddison, 2001: 126).

The spectacular transformation process in Central and Eastern Europe during the 1990s also generated further polarization. Premature opening of the countries' markets without previous technological–structural adjustment led to the collapse of agriculture (by up to 50%) and industry (by 25–35%). The gap between the region and advanced Western Europe broadened from a roughly 1:3 to a 1:4 ratio between 1973 and 2000 (see Figure 6.12). It took a full decade before the best-performing Central European countries recovered the losses and reached again their 1989 level of GDP. This has not yet occurred in Russia, Ukraine, and Belarus, which reached only about half of the pre-collapse GDP levels and probably will require another decade to reach the 1990 level. Statistics also give a glimpse of the social consequences: in 1989, only 2% of the Russian population lived in poverty (using the $2 per day income level as measurement); in 1998, 23.8% of Russians lived in poverty, among them half of all children. Figure 6.13 illustrates the rise in poverty levels in Central and Eastern Europe.

The growing core–periphery disparity during the second half of the century was not uniform. Lloyd Reynolds, analyzing the economic growth of the Third World, categorized thirty-seven countries into four groups, and found tremendous differences in their reaction to globalization: he distinguished among high-growth, moderate-growth, low-growth, and no-growth Third World economies. Growth disparity among the four peripheral groups was significant: the first group reached an annual average 3.5% growth, the second a 2.7% increase, the third only 1.7%, and the fourth 0.3% annual growth (Reynolds, 1985: 390–1). Over the entire last quarter of the century, Asia (excluding Japan) reached the highest growth rate: 5.46%. This was two-and-a-half times more than the Western European growth rate. Even adjusted to a per capita basis, Asian annual growth was 3.54%, enough to nearly double per capita income over the period.

Figure 6.12
Regional disparities
(GDP per capita)
1973–2000

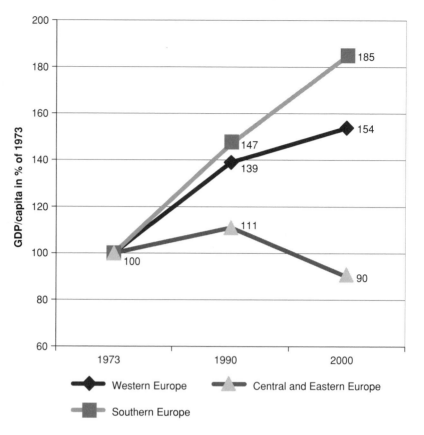

Several Asian countries of the periphery, which according to Angus Maddison's calculations had stagnated for a century (−0.11% per capita GDP growth between 1820 and 1870; 0.38% in 1870–1913; −0.02% in 1913–50), were transformed into rapidly developing countries, "small tigers," in the second half of the century, with 2.95% annual growth between 1950 and 1973, and 3.54% in 1973–98 (Maddison, 2001: 126). Japanese and American investments played a decisive role in generating this spectacular catching-up process.

European experiences reflect a similar disparity among peripheral economies in response to globalization. The traditional West European core countries reached an annual 2.03% growth rate between 1973 and 1998, while Spain and Portugal grew 2.47% and 2.88%, respectively; Ireland, a former periphery of Britain, that had a lower growth rate than Western Europe until 1973, reached 4.75% annual growth during the last quarter of the century, an increase of two-and-one-third times.

In the same period between 1973 and 1998, a striking disparity also characterized the former state socialist countries' transformation. Central European former Soviet bloc countries saw 0.73% annual growth, while the

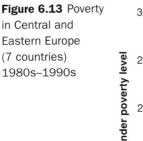

Figure 6.13 Poverty in Central and Eastern Europe (7 countries) 1980s–1990s

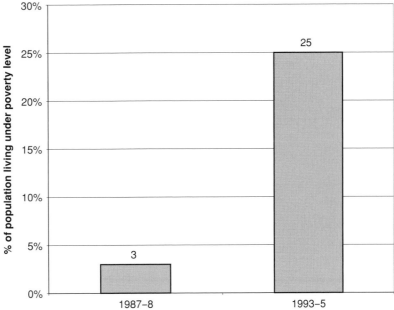

Russian Federation and Ukraine declined by an annual average of −1.08% and −2.48%, respectively.

In sum, peripheral countries by no means reacted uniformly. Some of them seemingly profited from globalization, which in the Mediterranean region and Ireland generated a spectacular catching-up process. Central Europe, profiting more from multinational investment and globalization, experienced a more successful transformation than Russia and the successor states of the Soviet Union, or the Balkan countries. The so-called multinationalization index is characteristically low in the Balkans, only 5% in Serbia and Montenegro, 6% in Bosnia–Herzegovina, 8% in Albania, and 10% in Romania, 24% in the Czech Republic, and 28% in Hungary (UNCTAD, 2003: 6).

Economic development became more successful in the more globalized Central European countries. In 1973, Poland reached only 81% of the per capita GDP level of the Russian Federation. By 1998, the Russian level dropped to 68% of the Polish one. Taken together, the former Central European state socialist countries reached only 82% of the per capita GDP level of the Soviet Union in 1973, but, by 1998, the GDP of the former Soviet Union dropped to 72% of the level of Central Europe (Maddison, 2001: 185–7).

In the success cases such as Ireland, and in the rather relative success case of Hungary (within Central and Eastern Europe), globalization, and

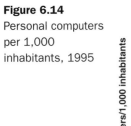

Figure 6.14
Personal computers per 1,000 inhabitants, 1995

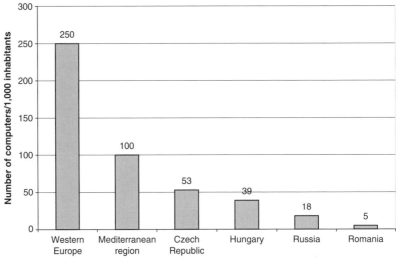

especially the role of multinationals, played the decisive role in introducing modern technology to newly established modern export sectors. Hungarian success in establishing new sectors which succeeded in Western Europe an export markets was basically the consequence of multinational investments: multinationals produced nearly half of the Hungarian value added, and 70% of total exports at the end of the century. Four multinationals, Opel, Philips, Audi, and IBM, produced 30% of Hungarian exports in 1999.

Globalization consequently does not have a generally positive or generally negative impact on less developed countries. When political stability exists, domestic infrastructure is relatively well developed, the educational system turns out a good supply of trained engineers, computer experts and skilled workers; when local value systems and religion do not work against international adjustment, globalization might have a positive impact. Certain geopolitical advantages also have an impact and can render countries or regions politically and economically more attractive. Infiltration of multinationals, investments from abroad, and a broad market opportunity granted by free trade agreements in these cases may make a difference. They may mobilize domestic resources and forces, generating high prosperity and a catching-up process with the core. These conditions existed when internationalization or the first globalization of the European economy gained impetus around the turn of the nineteenth and twentieth centuries and generated the catching-up of the Scandinavian countries. A similar development trend characterized the Mediterranean, Finnish, and Irish catching-up during the second half, especially in the last quarter of the twentieth century. It might be repeated in the first half of the twenty-first century, at least, by some of the new European Union member countries. A "peripheryless" continent, however, is yet in a distant future.

Countries with a burdensome historical legacy, dysfunctional economies, petrified societies with strong tribal features, high-level corruption, and an uneducated labor force become easy victims of globalization. Their resources are tapped and exploited by multinational companies, and their markets are occupied. Foreign direct investment in extracting branches creates foreign enclaves. The consequence of globalization in these cases may be devastating.

Historical experience, however, suggests that the most detrimental consequences may come from the lack of participation in globalization. Remaining outside cuts important economic ties to modern technology, mostly monopolized by multinational companies. It excludes the possibility of stimulation from foreign investment of subsidiaries of modern companies which creates jobs, boosts productivity, and sparks industrialization.

The globalized world economy, with all its good and bad consequences, may be more harmful without international regulation. Eliminating control over international financial markets where trillions of dollars are flowing among various countries becomes a major destabilizing force for the international economy. Capital market liberalization "entails stripping away the regulations intended to control the flow of hot money in and out of the country" (Stiglitz, 2002: 65). George Soros called attention to the danger that individual states are unable to

resist the power of global financial markets and there are practically no institutions for rule making on an international scale . . . Collective decision-making mechanism for the global economy simply does not exist . . . financial markets are inherently unstable . . . To put the matter simply, market forces, if they are given complete authority . . . produce chaos and could ultimately lead to the downfall of the global capitalist system. (Soros, 1998: xx, xxiii, xxvii)

A similar warning was repeated:

Global finance has the upper hand because [of] its power over credit creation . . . but global finance is in a parlously fragile condition. A calamitous concatenation of accidents could bring it down . . . For now . . . even the combined governments of the Group of Seven (G-7), have not been able to devise any effectively secure scheme of regulation for global finance . . . There is, in effect, no explicit political or authority structure for the global economy. There is . . . governance without government. (Cox, 1994: 48–9)

Rising global environmental considerations and regulations

One of the areas where "governance without government" turned out to be visibly dangerous was environmental destruction because of speedy economic growth. The last third of the century, however, exhibited a change in attitude toward environmental destruction.

[P]olicymakers of the 1950s and 1960s understood little if anything of the environmental implications of domestic policy or of their plans for the European Economic Community... [E]nvironment was a policy issue whose significance varied from marginal to non-existent. (McCormick, 2001: 4, 43)

From the early 1970s, the situation changed dramatically. What were the reasons behind the transformation? Some major, sometimes tragic accidents opened the eyes of the public and politicians alike. One of the earliest was the December 4–8, 1952 London smog catastrophe. In industrial centers and urban agglomerations with obsolete coal-burning heating systems, a mix of smoke and fog, dubbed "smog", proved disastrous. The 1952 smog catastrophe, however, reached extreme proportions: in a week when people could not see their own feet in the thick black smog, as many as 12,000 Londoners died and 100,000 became ill. Air pollution reached an intolerable level in the advanced industrialized world. The chronicler of the London smog catastrophe concluded:

Could modern government find the means, the desire, and the will to begin safeguarding the health and lives of its urban population – or had polluted air, sickness, and death become the inescapable price that had to be paid for the benefit of a highly industrialized society? (Wise, 1968: 38, 57, 162–3)

Ten years later, a smog crisis was repeated in the heartland of the German heavy industries, the Ruhrgebiet, where 156 people died.

The British welfare state could not afford not to act. Sir Hugh Beaver, chairman of the government Air Pollution Committee, presented the final report of investigation in November 1954 recommending the control of industrial emissions and home-heating pollution to eliminate black smoke. "Clean air should be declared a national policy . . . recognized by the government." The report recommended curbing air pollution, especially sulfur dioxide emission, by 70–80% within 10–15 years. On July 5, 1956, the Clean Air Act became law in Britain (Wise, 1968: 170, 174).

Similar attention was called to coastal water pollution by the Bravo–Ekofisk drilling rig accident in the North Sea in 1977, and by the *Amoco Cadiz* tanker accident near Brittany and the *Khark-V* accident in 1978 and

1979. A series of radiation hazards and mass sicknesses connected with nuclear power stations in the United States and the Soviet Union also contributed to environmental awareness. This was intensified by the spectacular nuclear power station accidents: the Kyshtym accident, in the Ural region of the Soviet Union, in 1957 when the failure of the cooling system contaminated nearly 60,000 hectares of land and led to the evacuation of 10,000 people, and most emphatically the deadly explosion of the Chernobyl nuclear power station in 1986, which contaminated huge areas in the Soviet Union and its neighboring countries. As the president of the Club of Rome, Aurelio Peccei, stated in 1981: society cannot "any longer trust the 'invisible hand' of classical economics, which they believed would guide them all toward an optimum level. Instead, they often find themselves kicked along by a 'mysterious boot'" (Peccei, 1981: 9).

Besides these eye-opening accidents, rapid economic growth itself made safety regulations against irresponsible pollution crucial. By the early 1970s, almost the entire European continent was industrialized. Whereas in the nineteenth century only a few "black regions" existed, now a great part of the continent was blackened. Highly polluting industries contaminated land, river, and air. Agriculture used more artificial fertilizers and pesticides than ever. Millions of cars coursed the dense network of freeways. Power consumption multiplied many times over, which meant much more coal burning and widespread use of nuclear power. Environmental danger increased exponentially: natural waters, rivers, and lakes died, forests were devastated. An urbanized Europe had to cope with millions of tonnes of waste and had to supply clean drinking water. It became evident that a rich, advanced West could no longer continue rapid economic growth by ignoring the environment. This kind of common sense is expressed by the application of the so-called Kuznets Curve, an inverted U-shape, to reflect the relationship between per capita income and pollution levels: as income began increasing, pollution first increased as well. After reaching a certain level of income, or the top of the inverted U-shape, however, pollution began to decline as income continued to rise, and society took steps to improve the environment.

If, after World War II, economic growth was the golden calf, from the early 1970s, first a handful of intellectuals, but later international institutions and governments, began worshiping the environment. The first outcry came from a private association, a group of thirty people from ten countries, who gathered in the Accademia dei Lincei in Rome in 1968. Their manifesto, *The Limits to Growth. A Report for the Club of Rome's Project on the Predicament of Mankind,* came out in 1972. The Club of Rome attacked "unlimited growth" as suicidal policy:

If the present growth trends in world population, industrialization, pollution, food production, and resource depletion continue unchanged, the limits to growth on this planet will be reached sometime within the next one hundred years. [They suggested] deliberately limiting growth . . . with that goal and that commitment, mankind would be ready now to begin a controlled, orderly transition from growth to global equilibrium. (Meadows et al., 1972: 24, 183–4)

The Club's second report, *Mankind at the Turning Point,* rephrased the argument against exponential growth in the advanced world, since its materials consumption had reached proportions of preposterous waste. In those regions there must be a relative decline. Nevertheless, they recognized the need for economic development in the less developed regions, and argued for an "organic growth, or growth with differentiation" (Mesarovic and Pestel, 1974: 3, 6).

Revolting against consumerism and growth, presenting an apocalyptic vision became fashionable in certain circles. The concept of zero growth entirely rejected the former growth idol. Conservative thinkers such as the Russian writer Alexander Solzhenitsyn in his "Letter to Soviet Leaders" in 1973 not only called for zero growth, but suggested the return to and greater use of manual labor.

The nascent "Green Movement" spread throughout Europe. In Belgium, Germany, and Switzerland Greens entered parliament in the first half of the 1980s. They soon put down roots in Austria, Finland, Italy, and Sweden. By the 1990s they existed throughout Europe. In 1997, Green parties were members of the German and French governments; by 1999 they became members of the Belgian, Italian, and Finnish governments as well, and sent thirty-seven representatives to the European Parliament. The European Green Forum argued in 1998 that environmental policy might have to penetrate the entire activity: "Pollution and other types of damage to the natural environment and human health take place in . . . agriculture, industry and transport" (Kamieniecki, 1993: 93; McCormick, 2001: 20). Environmental argumentation became a weapon of opposition movements in state socialist countries: the Hungarian *Duna Kör* attacked the regime under the banner of opposing the construction of the planned Nagymaros-Gabčíkovo Danube dam; the first major demonstration against the Bulgarian regime in the late 1980s was conducted in the name of "ecological defense."

The new interest in a globalizing world economy influenced leading international organizations. The United Nations held a conference on the human environment in Stockholm in 1972, accepting 109 non-binding recommendations. International meetings followed: in the same year, fifty-seven countries participated in a conference on the prevention of marine pollution, and then sixty-three countries met in Geneva to discuss ship pollution. Agreements, nevertheless, remained mostly bilateral.

In 1985 international efforts achieved a breakthrough: a European protocol was signed on reduction (by 30% by 1993) of sulfur emission. The Vienna Convention, followed by the Montreal Protocol, and the London, Copenhagen, and Vienna Adjustments between 1985 and 1995, concluded five decisive agreements and amendments to regulate the depletion of the ozone layer. By the 1990s, 165 countries joined, first to cap the consumption of chlorofluorocarbons (CFCs), and then to reduce it by 50%, as well as to eliminate some of the most damaging CFCs such as carbon tetrachloride, methyl, and methyl bromide chloroform (Golub, 1998: 36). In 1988 in Sofia a European agreement was accepted to reduce nitrogen emission by 1994. The following year the Basel agreement of thirty-four countries established controls for hazardous waste transportation. In 1992 in Rio de Janeiro 176 countries agreed upon influencing factors of climate change and in 1998 the Kyoto protocol decided on reducing 1990 emission levels of greenhouse gases by 8% by 2012 (Schulze and Ursprung, 2001: 246).

The German, Danish, and Dutch governments were the forerunners of environmental regulations and "cleaning up" the continent. The European Union soon followed. The heads of government of the six founder and three candidate countries of the European Community met in Paris in October 1972. They expressed the common view that economic expansion was not an end in itself and that actions to defend the environment must be accelerated. The first three-year Environmental Action Program of the European Community was adopted in November 1973, followed by the second in 1977, and three more, covering the remaining years of the century.

An environmental revolution developed during the 1970s–1980s in Europe. In 1985, the Council of Europe agreed that environmental policy must be an essential component of the activity of the Community. Two years later, the Single European Act recognized environmental protection as the legal competence of the Community, and a main policy area. The Act added Title VII (Environment) to the Treaty of Rome:

Action by the Community relating to the environment shall be based on the principles that preventive action should be taken, that environmental damage should as a priority be rectified at source, and that the polluter should pay. Environmental protection requirements shall be a component of the Community's other policies (Single Act, 1987: Article 130)

By the mid-1980s the European Union had introduced only reactive and *ad hoc* regulations. Between 1983 and 1986, however, already nearly 100 new regulations and directives were introduced. These included air quality standards, as well as limits on emissions of large industrial firms, shipments of hazardous waste, and lead content of gasoline. A whole set of regulations targeted water pollution, introducing standards for collection of urban waste water, quality objectives for inland fresh waters and drinking water, and pollution reduction directives, especially against nitrates, inorganic fertilizer, and manure. Altogether, by the end of the century, roughly 850 pieces of environmental law were enacted and a European Environmental Agency began working.

As a result, the use of artificial fertilizers and pesticides was curbed in the European Union; sales of pesticides declined by 20% during the first half of the 1990s. Production and emission of the most important pollutants such as lead and CFCs decreased – between 1990 and 1995, production of CFCs dropped by nearly 90%, and of sulfur dioxide (SO_2) emission by 30%. In Germany and Holland SO_2 emissions dropped by 60% and 45%, respectively, between 1987 and 1995. Compared with the 1980 level of emission (25 million tonnes in twelve EU countries), SO_2 emissions declined 67% by 1997. The American emission level was seven times higher than the Dutch, more than four times higher than the French, and twice as bad as the German level at the end of the century.

In less than a decade, West European lead emission from motor vehicles dropped by 25%. Lead emissions from gasoline fell by 98% in Scandinavia, and 80% in Holland and Germany. Unleaded gasoline became compulsory. Nitrogen oxide emissions dropped by nearly 20% between 1980 and 1997. The sulfur protocol of 1994 aimed at the decrease of sulfur emissions by 80–90% in Austria, Finland, France, and Germany (*Trends in Europe*, 1999: 190; McCormick, 2001: 184, 188–9, 229, 233). Carbon dioxide emissions in the European Union declined to 8,202 kilograms per person by 1995, less than half of the nearly 20,000-kilogram-per-person American level. Carbon monoxide emissions varied between 60–90 kilograms per person in Britain, Switzerland, and Holland, compared with the American 300 kilograms per person in 1995.

Badly polluted big cities became much cleaner: the average concentration of SO_2 dropped to somewhat more than one-tenth of the 1980 level in Stockholm, one-fifth in Berlin, one-third in Paris, and roughly half in London by 1995. The air in Lisbon, after Portugal joined the European Union, improved dramatically: concentration of particulates and sulfur oxides dropped by four-fifths by 1995. The environmental achievement of the European Union is unique in the world (European Commission, 1987–99: 214, 218–25).

Pollution control is an expensive practice. Although for some industries it does not surpass 1% of overall production costs, in the energy, steel, oil, paper, copper, and chemical industries it reaches 5–20% of the cost of production, and an even higher percentage of investment costs. Environmental regulations sometimes destroy certain branches of production. This was the case for the phosphate fertilizer industry in Western Europe after the 1988 regulations. Regulations increased the cost of shipping by 13–15% of total operating costs. The number of ships flying European Union flags, especially Dutch flags, significantly decreased (Golub, 1998: 6–10).

Because of a new type of core–periphery relations in the globalized world system, the advanced countries of Europe could easily find an exit from the grip of environmental regulations. They decreased production of the most polluting sectors and, similarly to very labor-intensive branches, established subsidiaries in less developed countries, mostly outside Europe. The flight of polluting industries from Europe is clearly reflected by the fact that the share of less developed countries in steel output increased from 14% to 37%, in the highly polluting tanning industry from 26% to 56%, and in fertilizer production from 20% to 45% of world output between 1979 and 1997. The advanced countries of Europe closed the most polluting stages of production while keeping the high value-added final processing at home. In the steel industry, coke ovens and sinter plants were often closed and their products imported from less developed countries. This contributed to the dramatic increase in production traded internationally between 1975 and 1997: steel from 23% to 43% and light leather from 26% to 62% (Jenkins et al., 2002: 295–9).

As an important positive outcome of strict environmental regulations, advanced countries introduced technological innovation to remain competitive by decreasing production costs. In one respect, environmental investments might be considered as long-term investment in competitiveness. European Union products meeting high green standards might be more attractive in some other markets. New green technology and services for environmental control also became saleable in foreign markets. In 1990, the world market for pollution control was $200 billion, and eco-industries created 600,000 jobs in Europe. High environmental standards also strengthened market protection by offering the possibility to exclude foreign products which violated domestic standards (Golub, 1998: 4, 5, 28).

The European Union established authority for the implementation of environmental regulations and improvement over the last two decades, but significant differences were preserved among member countries. The Dutch–German levels and the Portuguese and Greek standards are rather different. Ships flying the flags of the latter two countries registered the highest rates of environmental infractions in the Union. While the Scandinavian countries reduced SO_2 emission by 80% after 1980, Greek and Portuguese emissions increased. The Union standards, nevertheless, will gradually equalize the levels.

The most striking difference within the continent is found in Central and Eastern Europe. The countries in the region began rapid industrialization after World War II by developing coal, iron, steel, and heavy engineering, and then, from the 1960s, basic chemical industries. They built up their own "Manchesters" and "Black countries" in Katowice and throughout the infamous Black Triangle in the border area of East Germany–Czechoslovakia–Poland. Central and Eastern Europe created a strongly polluting energy-intensive industry. In 1980, energy intensity in the region was nearly eight times that of the European Union, and by 1995 pollution remained more than seven times higher. In 1995 these countries, led by Bulgaria, the Czech Republic, and Slovakia, were still among the top ten places in terms of SO_2 emissions (Turnock, 2002: 66, 96; Carter and Kantowicz, 2002: 187, 190). The economically developed Czech Republic belongs to "the most environmentally devastated countries in the whole of Europe" (Pavlínek, 2002: 119). The other countries of the region are not much better off: sulfur and nitrogen dioxide emissions, in relation to income level, were nine times higher in Hungary than the European Union average in the early 1990s. Waste treatment in Hungary reached only half the Western levels in the mid-1990s (Dingsdale et al., 2002: 161, 167, 172). Poland was the sixth most air-polluting country in Europe, and only 13% of the total Polish sewage was properly treated, compared with 50–90% in the European Union. Air pollution even doubled in Bulgaria in the first half of the 1990s.

Environmental pollution was one of the causes of the life expectancy gap in Europe. In the highly industrialized Silesia region of Poland, the concentration of respirable dust surpassed the OECD levels by nearly six times and the concentration of benzopyrene in the air was ten times higher. Consequently, respiratory diseases were 3–4 times more common. In similarly polluted Northern Bohemia during the 1960s, mortality from respiratory causes among newborns was 5–8 times higher than in moderately polluted areas (Hertzman et al., 1996: 73–4, 77).

After environmental concerns and regulations in the economically advanced West, international organizations began urging less developed countries to conform. It might be considered unfair given the time lag between the industrialization process in the core and the peripheries. There was not the same hue and cry when the Californian redwood forests were timbered as there was when Brazil cleared the rainforest in the late twentieth century. When Britain, Belgium, and later Germany established their highly polluting coal–iron–steel industries in the nineteenth century, no one cared; when China and Eastern Europe did the same in the second half of the twentieth century, they were pressured to control pollution. The main beneficiaries of this pressure, nevertheless, were the people of latecomer regions. From the 1980s, the environment became a consideration in Central and Eastern Europe as well. Several of these countries already accepted the recommendation of the United Nations Stockholm Conference in 1972, joined the international Environmental Protection Act of 1976, and joined the ozone agreement as well.

The real turning point, however, occurred with the dramatic political changes in 1989. After the collapse of state socialism in Central and Eastern Europe, the motivating dream was to join Europe. All of those countries undertook to comply with the standards of the European Union, including acceptance of the "Copenhagen Criteria" of economic, political, and environmental standards. The so-called *acquis communautaire* made the Union's environmental standards compulsory after an accepted delay of a decade or so (Baker, 2002: 31–2). Adherence to the *acquis* requires the adoption of roughly 300 pieces of EU environmental legislation, and, of course, huge investments in various programs. In Poland, 1,000 acts, decrees, and executive orders are required to realize environmental regulations. Bulgaria enacted the Law on Protection of Air, Water and Soil, Protection of Nature, Environmental Protection Law, Law on Liquid Fossil Fuel Tax, Clean Air Act, and many others during the 1990s (Pickles et al., 2002: 306). The ten new member countries must invest more than $8 billion only to bring sulfur dioxide and nitrogen oxide emissions to acceptable levels, and need $15 billion investment over twelve years to fulfill EU environmental protection standards (Turnock, 2002: 60). In the Czech Republic, $2 billion is needed to reach the EU's water standards. The PHARE program (created in 1989 to assist Poland and Hungary, and later expanded to the countries of the region) and World Bank loans assist this adjustment somewhat, and the established transition period guarantees a gradual transformation. Environmental investment in the budget of the Czech Republic, however, increased from 0.7% of the GDP in 1989 to 2.7% by 1996. In the mid-1990s, only 4% of environmental investments originated from EU sources in Poland (Carter and Kantowicz, 2002: 202).

Some first results, however, have already been recorded: lead-free gasoline became available in Hungary and Poland during the 1990s, and leaded gasoline went off the market in 1999. Several atomic power stations were upgraded, and some of them closed. Water pollution significantly decreased in the Czech Republic: instead of 27% in 1989, only 9% of waste water was discharged without any treatment by 1997. The cement industry decreased solid emissions by 97%, effected mostly through foreign investments in the decade after 1989. These are the very first steps. The new environmental policy and achievements of Europe became part of the adjustment to the end-of-century modern economic transformation.

Europe: a rising economic superpower

The gradually integrated and enlarged European Union emerged as an economic superpower during the last third of the twentieth century. An integrated – and further integrating – Europe has entered the twenty-first century to respond to the challenge of the globalized world economy. Europe of 2000 was a different continent from Europe of 1900. During the entire twentieth century, manifested in four distinctive rapid- and slow-growth periods, the West European economy increased its GDP more than tenfold, Southern Europe more than twelvefold, and Central and Eastern Europe more than sixfold; altogether Europe performed exceptionally and increased agricultural, industrial, and service production tenfold (Maddison, 1995a: 227; 2001: 273–4). This means that ten times more goods and services were produced at the end of the century than had been produced at the beginning. This has never happened before in history. Growth rates, nevertheless, were uneven among the regions during the first half of the century. Although Scandinavia joined the Western core, the Southern and Central and Eastern European peripheries lagged behind and preserved their relative backwardness. During the second half, and especially the last decades of the century, however, the core–periphery relationship underwent dramatic changes. Mediterranean Europe and the less developed Nordic countries achieved rapid growth and made impressive progress in catching up and becoming an integrated part of the West that is the European Union. Central and Eastern Europe, part of the Soviet bloc until 1989, was unable to recreate the South European or Finnish and Irish pattern of development. Instead, it experienced a deep peripheral crisis and mostly stagnated after 1973 (see Tables 6.10 and 6.11). After the collapse of state socialism, an even steeper decline followed for a while.

Table 6.10 The growth of GDP per capita (1973 = 100%) (Maddison, 2001: 185)

Year	Western Europe*	Southern Europe**	Eastern Europe***
1973	100	100	100
1990	139	147	111
1998	154	185	85

* 12 countries; ** 4 countries; *** in 1973 = 8 countries, in 1998 = 27 countries

Table 6.11 Per capita real GDP growth (Maddison, 1995a: 62; 2001: 265)

Region	1950–73	1973–98
Western Europe (12 countries)	3.8	1.8
Southern Europe (4 countries)	4.8	2.2
Eastern Europe (8 and 27 countries)	3.9	−0.9

Economic transformation, foreign investments, and economic modernization of the mid–late 1990s, however, generated a gradual recovery. Meanwhile, the Balkans and the successor states of the Soviet Union remained
further behind.

Regional disparities narrowed regarding the Southern periphery and
Ireland during the second half of the twentieth century. The countries of
the region caught up spectacularly, gradually narrowing the traditional
gap. Central and Eastern Europe and the successor states of the former
Soviet Union, however, had the worst economic performance compared
with other regions, and lost their previous positions. The gap between them
and the West opened into an abyss (see Table 6.12).

Recovery, nevertheless, began around the turn of the century. By 2004,
eight of the region's countries had become members of the European
Union, the gap between these eight and the West narrowed to 45%, and
some of the successor states of the Soviet Union also recovered part of their
losses.

Altogether, two relatively backward regions in the North and the
Mediterranean area virtually joined the core of Europe in the first or the
second half of the twentieth century. Central and Eastern Europe remained

Table 6.12 Regional disparity, GDP per capita, regions in % of the West, 1950–98 (Maddison, 2001)

Year	Western Europe* $GDP/capita %		Southern Europe** $GDP/capita %		East–Central Europe $GDP/capita %		Soviet Union & successor states $GDP/capita %	
1950	5,013	100	2,457	49	2,120	42	2,834	57
1973	12,159	100	7,651	63	4,985	41	6,058	50
1998	18,742	100	14,152	76	5,461	29	3,893	21

* 12 countries (including the Nordic countries and Italy); ** 4 countries (including Ireland)

Figure 6.15 Gross domestic product: continents, regions, 1973–2000

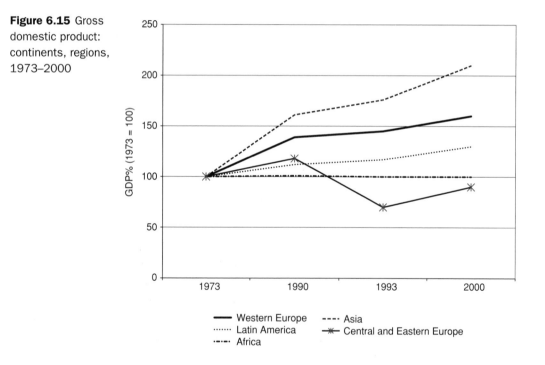

on the periphery, but eight modernized Central European countries became integrated into the European Union and the door was opened for them to begin a catching-up process. Most of the Balkans, and the former Soviet Union, nevertheless, remained far behind and reached only roughly 20% of the West European and 70% of the Central European levels. They became more peripherized than ever (Fig. 6.15).

Figure 6.16
Population and
GDP, EU–USA,
2000

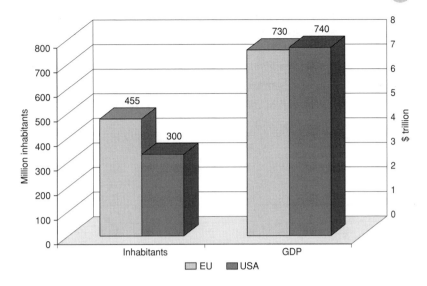

As a consequence of the exceptional economic growth, and integration, Europe became an economic superpower again. The population of the Union, after the 2004 expansion, was 455 million people, roughly 50% bigger than the American population. The total GDP of the European Union around the turn of the century, $7.3 trillion, was virtually equal to the U.S. figure of $7.4 trillion (see Figure 6.16). On a per capita basis GDP stood at only half the American level in 1950, but it rose to 75–80% of it around 2000. Differences remain which are rooted in cultural dissimilarities. The European Union of fifteen countries had only half of the American labor productivity in 1950, but reached 90% of the American productivity level by 1990 and equaled it at the end of the century. In other words, workers in the EU produce the same value per hour as workers do in the United States. Western Europe could be as rich as the United States. In terms of per capita income level, however, Europe remained roughly one-third behind the United States (see Table 6.13).

This is partly the consequence of faster American growth during the last third of the century, which checked the rapid catching-up process of Europe characteristic of the postwar decades. The major difference between the equal production of value per hour and the per capita income level, however, is mostly a consequence of the shorter European work week, more paid holidays, longer vacations, and maternity and sick leave, which is several times longer. Europe, in other words, works significantly less and preserves a welfare preference. Nevertheless, a number of European countries caught up quite dramatically with the United States between 1973 and 1998: Ireland progressed from 39% to 74% of the American GDP per

Table 6.13 The level of GDP per capita in 1990 ppp dollars, 1950–92 (Maddison, 2001: 195, 197, 228)

Countries	1950 Western Europe % of US		1973 Western Europe % of US		1998 Western Europe % of US	
Western Europe (29 countries)	4,594	48	11,534	69	17,921	66
United States	9,573	100	16,607	100	27,331	100

Figure 6.17 Labor productivity, EU–USA, 1950–90

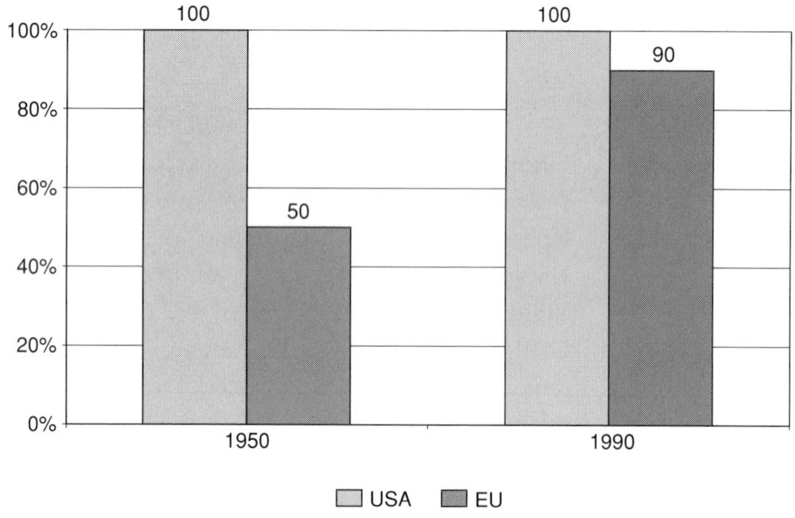

capita levels by 1998, Austria from 66% to 73%, and Norway from 63% to 87% (Survey, 2000: 161) (Fig. 6.17).

Europe also regained its leading role in world trade. Its share of world exports in 2000 was by far the largest, at roughly 43%, while the United States, Canada, and Australia combined accounted for only 19% of exports, and Asia 27%. At the beginning of the globalization process, in the 1960s–1970s, American banks and multinationals played the leading role; by the end of the century European multinational companies belonged to the main players of globalization, their role being equivalent to that of U.S. multinationals. European subsidiaries in the U.S. produced 38% of American imports from Europe, while American subsidiaries in Europe produced 33% of European imports from the U.S.

Figure 6.18 Foreign direct investment by countries of origin, 1973–2000

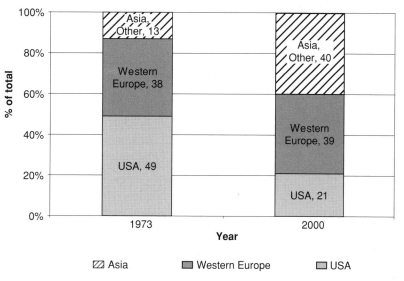

Foreign direct investment after World War II was dominated by U.S. investors. By 1973, U.S. direct investments abroad represented nearly half of the world's total, while Britain's reached only less than 13% and continental Western Europe's 25%. During the last quarter of the century, the main players grew more diverse. Japanese and European Union companies assumed an important role so that the activities of the American, Japanese, and European "triad" grew more balanced. In contrast to the postwar situation, transatlantic investment became a two-way street. In a single decade after the mid-1970s, direct investments in the United States increased by five times, and by the mid-1990s European multinationals owned nearly 60% of total foreign direct investment in the U.S., while the United States held less than half of the total FDI inflow to Europe (Pollack and Shaffer, 2001: 12–14). By the end of the 1980s, as a consequence of leveling economic power, Europe and the U.S. had equal shares in the world's FDI stocks (34% and 35%, respectively), but at the end of the century Europe's share in the world's stock of FDI far surpassed the American share and reached 39% of the total (see Figure 6.18 and Table 6.14).

FDI stocks reflect the aggregate sum of investments which were accumulated until a certain year. Regarding the present, the annual average outflow of direct investments is more expressive. Europe's share of annual outflow of FDI reached 41% of the world's total by the mid-1980s, while the U.S. accounted for only 31%. During the second half of the decade the European share became twice as great as the American (Jones and Schröter, 1993: 4, 10).

Table 6.14 Stock of foreign direct investment in 1998 (Maddison, 2001: 147)

Region/country	Total in $ million	Percent of total	Per capita in $
Western Europe	1,576,039	39	4,058
United States	875,026	21	3,234
Asia	764,746	19	217
World Total	4,088,068	100	692

The end-of-the-century world economy, however, was no longer merely a "Western" world economy. Asia emerged during the second half of the century as a major player. Japan rose to the richest group of countries. China achieved the fastest stable growth during the last third of the century. Between 1982 and 2002, China reached a 9.5% annual growth and "doubled nearly three times over since market reforms were introduced and became the second biggest economic unit in the world" (Fishman, 2005). Among the ten leading economies, China, Japan, and India represent the new Asian economic power. Asia's more than 37% share was the largest in the production of the world's GDP, and its 27% share in world exports was the second after Europe at the end of the century. Japan became an important technology leader. China and India with their 1.2–1.4 billion inhabitants comprise huge economic and intellectual potential. Their political and military importance as nuclear powers transforms the global balance of power. A three-pole international economic system is in the making, suggesting a rather different twenty-first-century world economy.

Bibliography

Alam, Shahid M., 2000. *Poverty from the Wealth of Nations. Integration and Polarization in the Global Economy since 1760*, Houndsmills: Macmillan.

Aldcroft, Derek H., 1978. *From Versailles to Wall Street 1919–1929*, Berkeley, University of California Press.

— 2001. *The European Economy, 1914–2000*, London: Routledge.

Alford, B. W. E., 1996. *Britain in the World Economy Since 1880*, London: Longman.

Andersen, Palle Schelde and Johnny Åkerholm, 1982. "Scandinavia," in: *The European Economy. Growth and Crisis*, edited by Andrea Boltho, Oxford: Oxford University Press.

Anderson, Charles W., 1970. *The Political Economy of Modern Spain. Policy-Making in an Authoritarian System*, Madison: University of Wisconsin Press.

Apel, Emmanuel, 1998. *European Monetary Integration, 1958–2002*, London: Routledge.

Archibugi, Franco, 1978. "Italian Prospects," in: *Beyond Capitalist Planning*, edited by Stuart Holland, New York: St. Martin's Press.

Arendt, Hannah, 1966. *The Origins of Totalitarianism*, Cleveland: Meridian Books.

Armengaud, André, Sidney Pollard, and Guido L. de Brabander, 1987. "Grossbritannien, Irland, Frankreich, Belgien, die Niederlände, Luxemburg 1914–1980/83," in: *Handbuch der europäischen Wirtschafts- und Sozialgeschichte*, edited by Wolfram Fischer, Stuttgart: Klett-Cotta.

Atkinson, Anthony B., 1999. *The Economic Consequences of Rolling Back the Welfare State*, Cambridge, M.A.: MIT Press.

Ausch, Sándor, 1972. *Theory and Practice of CMEA Cooperation*, Budapest: Akadémiai Kiadó.

Bairoch, Paul, 1973. "European Foreign Trade in the 19th Century," *The Journal of European Economic History*.

— 1976. "Europe's Gross National Product: 1800–1975," *Journal of European Economic History*, Vol. 5, No. 2.

Baker, Susan, 2002. "Environmental Politics and Transition," in: *Environmental Problems of East Central Europe*, edited by F. W. Carter and David Turnock, London: Routledge.

Balassa, Bela, 1961. *The Theory of Economic Integration*, Homewood: R. D. Irwin.

Baldwin, Peter, 1990. *The Politics of Social Solidarity. Class Bases of the European Welfare State 1875–1975*, Cambridge: Cambridge University Press.

Balogh, Thomas, 1978. "British Malpractice," in: *Beyond Capitalist Planning*, edited by Stuart Holland, New York: St. Martin's Press.

Barr, Nicholas, 2001. *The Welfare State as Piggy Bank. Information, Risk, Uncertainty, and the Role of the State*, Oxford: Oxford University Press.

Basch, Antonín, 1944. *The Danube Basin and the German Economic Sphere*, London: K. Paul, Trench, Trubner & Co.

Basic Statistics of the Community, 1977; 1994. Brussels: Statistical Office of the European Communities.

Basic Statistics for Fifteen European Countries, 1961. Brussels: Statistical Office of the European Communities.

Baum, Warren C., 1958. *The French Economy and the State*, Princeton: Princeton University Press.

Bazarov, V., 1928. *Planovoye Khoziaistva*, No. 2.

Beltran, Alain and Patrice A. Carré, 1991. *La fée et la servante. La société française face à l'électricité XIXe–XXe siècle*, Paris: Belin.

Berend, Ivan T., 1978. *Öt előadás gazdaságról és oktatásról*, Budapest: Magvető Kiadó.

— 1979. *A szocialista gazdaság története Magyarországon 1945–1973*, Budapest: Kossuth Kiadó.

— 1985. "Agriculture," in: *The Economic History of Eastern Europe, 1919–1945*, Vol. I, edited by Michael C. Kaser and Edward A. Radice, Oxford: Clarendon Press.

— 1990. *The Hungarian Economic Reforms 1953–1988*, Cambridge: Cambridge University Press.

— 1994. "End of Century Global Transition to a Market Economy," in *Transition to a Market Economy at the End of the 20th Century*, edited by Ivan T. Berend, Munich: Südosteuropa-Gesellschaft.

— 1996. *Central and Eastern Europe 1944–1993: Detour from the Periphery to the Periphery*, Cambridge: Cambridge University Press.

— 1998. *Decades of Crisis: Central and Eastern Europe Before World War II*, Berkeley: University of California Press.

— 2003. *History Derailed: Central and Eastern Europe in the 'Long' 19th Century*, Berkeley: University of California Press.

Berend, Ivan T. and György Ránki, 1955. *Magyarország gyáripara 1900–1914*, Budapest: Szikra Kiadó.

— 1958. *Magyarország gyáripara a II.világháború előtt és a háború éveiben, 1933–1944*, Budapest: Akadémiai Kiadó.

— 1966. *Hungary's Economy After World War I, 1919–1929*, Budapest: Akadémiai Kiadó.

— 1974. *Economic Development in East Central Europe in the 19th & 20th Centuries*, New York: Columbia University Press.

— 1982. *The European Periphery and Industrialization 1780–1914*, Cambridge: Cambridge University Press.

Berend, Ivan T. and Miklós Szuhay, 1978. *A tőkés gazdaság története Magyarországon 1848–1944*, Budapest: Kossuth Kiadó.

Berghahn, Volker Rolf, 1987. *Modern Germany: Society, Economy, and Politics in the Twentieth Century*, Cambridge: Cambridge University Press.

Bernecker, Walter L. von, 1987. "Spanien 1914–1975," in: *Handbuch der europäischen Wirtschafts- und Sozialgeschichte*, Vol. 6, edited by Wolfram Fischer, Stuttgart: Klett-Cotta.

Bernstein, Eduard, 1899. *Die Voraussetzungen des Sozialismus und die Aufgabe der Sozialdemokratie*, Stuttgart: Dietz.

Béteille, Roger, 1995. "Airbus; or, the Reconstruction of European Civil Aeronautics," in: *From Airships to Airbus. The History of Civil and Commercial Aviation*, edited by William M. Leary, Vol. 1. Washington D.C.: Smithsonian Institution Press.

Beveridge, Sir William, 1942. *Social Insurance and Allied Services*, London: His Majesty's Stationery Office.

Blaas, Wolfgang and John Foster (Eds), 1992. *Mixed Economies in Europe. An Evolutionary Perspective on their Emergence, Transition and Regulation*, Aldershot: Edward Elgar.

[The] Blue Waterway: All About the Danube–Black Sea Romanian Canal, 1984. Bucharest: Foreign Languages Press Group.

Boltho, Andrea, 1982. *The European Economy. Growth and Crisis*, Oxford: Oxford University Press.

Bovikin, V. I., 1973. "Oroszország ipari fejlődésének társadalmi-gazdasági problémái," *Történelmi Szemle*, No. 1–2, Budapest.

Braun, Hans-Joachim, 1990. *The German Economy in the Twentieth Century*, London: Routledge.

— 1995. "The Airport as Symbol: Air Transportation and Politics at Berlin-Tempelhof, 1923–1948," in: *From Airships to Airbus. The History of Civil and Commercial Aviation*, edited by William M. Leary, Vol. 1, Washington D.C.: Smithsonian Institution Press.

Brenner, Robert, 1998. "Uneven Development and the Long Downturn: Advanced Capitalist Economies from Boom to Stagnation, 1950–1998," *New Left Review*, Special Issue, May–June.

—2002. *The Boom and the Bubble: the US in the World Economy*, London: Verso.

Briggs, Asa, 1961. "The Welfare State in Historical Perspective," *Europäisches Archiv für Soziologie*, No. 2.

Broder, Albert, 1976. "Le commerce extérieur: l'échec de la conquête d'une position internationale," in: *Histoire économique et sociale de la France*. Vol. III, edited by Fernand Braudel and E. Labrousse, Paris: Presses Universitaires de France.

Brown Boveri, *75 Years of Brown Boveri, 1891–1966*, 1966. Baden: Brown Boveri & Co.

Brus, Wlodzimierz, 1986. "Institutional Change Within a Planned Economy," Chapters 23–26 in: *The Economic History of Eastern Europe 1919–1975*, Vol. 3, edited by Michael C. Kaser, Oxford: Clarendon Press.

Bukharin, Nikolai, 1971. *Economics of the Transformation Period*, New York: Bergman Publishers.

— 1982. *Selected Writings on State and the Transition to Socialism*, Armonk, N.Y.: M. E. Sharpe.

Bukharin, Nikolai and Evgeny Preobrazhensky, 1969. *The ABC of Communism*, London: Penguin Books.

Busch, Marc L. and Helen V. Milner, 1994. "The Future of the International Trading System: International Firms, Regionalism, and Domestic Politics," in: *Political Economy and the Changing Global Order*, edited by Richard Stubbs and Geoffrey R. D. Underhill, New York: St. Martin's Press.

Bussemaker, Jet, 1999. *Citizenship and Welfare State Reform in Europe*, London: Routledge.

Butschek, Felix, 1985. *Die österreichische Wirtschaft im 20. Jahrhundert*, Stuttgart: Gustav Fischer Verlag.

Byatt, I. C., 1979. *The British Electrical Industry 1875–1914*, Oxford: Clarendon Press.

Caron, François, 1979. *An Economic History of Modern France*, New York: Columbia University Press.

Carr, Edward H., 1964. *The Twenty Years' Crisis*, New York: Harper and Row.

— 1952. *The Bolshevik Revolution, 1917–1923*, Vol. 2. Baltimore: Penguin Books.

Carr, Edward H. and Robert W. Davies, 1974. *Foundation of a Planned Economy 1926–1929*, Vol. I, Harmondsworth: Pelican Books.

Carter, F. W. and David Turnock (Eds), 2002. *Environmental Problems of East Central Europe*, London: Routledge.

Carter, F. W. and Ewelina Kantowicz, 2002. "Poland" in: *Environmental Problems of East Central Europe*, edited by F. W. Carter and David Turnock, London: Routledge.

Cerny, Philip G., 2000. "The Dynamics of Financial Globalization: Technology, Market Structure, and Policy Response," in: *The New Political Economy of Globalization*, edited by Richard Higgott and Anthony Payne, Vol. 1, Cheltenham: Edward Elgar.

Chandler, Alfred D. Jr., 1977. *The Visible Hand. The Managerial Revolution in American Business*, Cambridge, M.A.: The Belknap Press of Harvard University Press.

— 1984. *The Evolution of Modern Global Competition*, Boston M.A.: Harvard Business School.

— 1986. "Technological and Organizational Underpinnings of Modern Industrial Multinational Empires: the Dynamics of Competitive Advantage," in: *Multinational Enterprise in Historical Perspective*, edited by Alice Teichova, Maurice Lévy-Leboyer and Helga Nussbaum, Cambridge: Cambridge University Press.

— 1990. *Scale and Scope: the Dynamics of Industrial Capitalism*, Cambridge, M.A.: Harvard University Press.

Churchill, Winston, 1925. In: *Parliamentary Debates: House of Commons*, Fifth Series, Vol. 183, London: H.M.S.O.

— 1974. *The Collected Works of Sir Winston Churchill*, London: Library of Imperial History.

Clegg, Armstrong H. and Theodore E. Chester, 1953. *The Future of Nationalization*, Oxford: Basil Blackwell.

Cohen, Stephen S., 1977. *Recent Development in French Planning*, Washington, D.C.: United States GPO.

Collins, Doreen, 1975. *The European Communities. The European Coal and Steel Community 1951–1970*. Vol. 1. London: Martin Robertson.

Commission, 1989. Commission of the European Communities, *European Economy* 42, Luxembourg: Office for Official Publications.

— 2000. Commission of the European Communities, *European Economy* 71. Luxembourg: Office for Official Publications.

Conklin, Alice L., 1997. *A Mission to Civilize: The Republican Idea of Empire in France and West Africa, 1895–1930*, Palo Alto: Stanford University Press.

Council of Europe, 1959. *Statistical Data*, Strasbourg: Council of Europe.

Cox, Robert W., 1994. "Global Restructuring: Making Sense of the Changing International Political Economy," in: *Political Economy and the Global Order*, edited by Richard Stubbs and Geoffrey R. D. Underhill, New York: St. Martin's Press.

Crafts, Nicholas and Gianni Toniolo (Eds), 1996. *Economic Growth in Europe Since 1945*, Cambridge: Cambridge University Press.

Crossick, Geoffrey and Serge Jaumain (Eds), 1999. *Cathedrals of Consumption. The European Department Store, 1850–1939*, Aldershot: Ashgate.

Cullen, Louis M., 1987. *An Economic History of Ireland since 1960*, London: B. T. Batsford.

Dahrendorf, Ralf, 1996. *From Europe to Europe: A Story of Hope, Trial and Error*, Cambridge, M.A.: Harvard University, Center for International Affairs.

Dalton, George, 1974. *Economic Systems and Society. Capitalism, Communism and the Third World*, Harmondsworth: Penguin Education.

Darian-Smith, Eve, 1999. *Bridging Divides: the Channel Tunnel and English Legal Identity in the New Europe*, Berkeley: University of California Press.

David, Thomas and Elizabeth Spilman, 2000. *Economic Nationalism*, (manuscript).

Declaration of the British Labour Party, 1945. "Let Us Face the Future," in: *British Labor's Rise to Power*, Herry W. Laidler, New York: League for Industrial Democracy.

De Grazia, Victoria, 1998. "Changing Consumption Regimes in Europe, 1930–1970," in: *Getting and Spending. European and American Consumer Societies in the Twentieth Century*, edited by Susan Strasser, Charles McGovern, and Matthias Judt, Cambridge: Cambridge University Press.

DeLeon, Peter, 1979. *Development and Diffusion of the Nuclear Power Reactor: a Comparative Analysis*, Cambridge, M.A.: Ballinger Publishing Co.

Delors, Jacques, 1978. "French Principles," in: *Beyond Capitalist Planning*, edited by Stuart Holland, New York: St. Martin's Press.

Dennett, Jane, Edward James, Graham Room, and Philippa Watson, 1982. *Europe Against Poverty. The European Poverty Programme 1975–80*, London: Bedford Square Press.

Denton, Geoffrey, Murray Forsyth, and Malcolm Maclennan, 1968. *Economic Planning and Policies in Britain, France and Germany*, London: Allen & Unwin.

Deutsches Zentral Archiv, 1934. January. Ausswertiges Amt. Abt. II. 41 288.

Dierikx, Marc, 1995. "Hard Work, Living off the Air: Albert Plesman's KLM in International Aviation, 1919–1953," in: *From Airships to Airbus. The History of Civil and Commercial Aviation*, Vol. 2, edited by William F. Trimble, Washington D.C: Smithsonian Institution Press.

Dingsdale, Alan, Imre Nagy, Gyorgy Perczel, and David Turnock, 2002. "Hungary," in: *Environmental Problems of East Central Europe*, edited by F. W. Carter and David Turnock, London: Routledge.

Dobb, Maurice, 1964. "Political Economy and Capitalism," quoted by Edward H. Carr, *The Twenty Years' Crisis, 1919–1939*, New York: Harper and Row.

— 1966. *Soviet Economic Development Since 1917*, London: Routledge.

Documents on German Foreign Policy 1918–1945, Series C II, page 372, Washington, D.C.: Government Printing Office, 1950.

Duchene, François and Geoffrey Shepherd (Eds), 1987. *Managing Industrial Change in Western Europe*, London: Pinter.

Dulles, Allen, 1948. *The Marshall Plan*, Providence: Berg.

Dunning, John, 1993. *The Globalization of Business. The Challenge of the 1990s*, London: Routledge.

Economic Survey of Europe, 1999. Geneva: United Nations.

— 2000. No. 2/3, Geneva: United Nations.

Eden, Lorraine, 2000. "Bringing the Firm Back In: Multinationals in International Political Economy," in: *The New Political Economy of Globalization*, edited by Richard Higgott and Anthony Payne, Vol. 1, Cheltenham: Edward Elgar.

Eichengreen, Barry, 1994 [1996]. "Institutions and Economic Growth: Europe after World War II," in: *Economic Growth in Europe since 1945*, edited by Nicholas Crafts and Gianni Toniolo, Cambridge: Cambridge University Press.

Ellman, Michael, 2000. "The Social Costs and Consequences of the Transformation Process," in: *Economic Survey of Europe. From Plan to Market: The Transition Process After 10 Years*, Geneva: United Nations.

Erhard, Ludwig, 1990. *Wohlstand für Alle*, Düsseldorf: Econ Taschenbuch Verlag.

Erlich, Alexander, 1967. *The Soviet Industrialization Debate, 1924–1928*, Cambridge, M.A.: Harvard University Press.

European Commission. *Eurostat Yearbook. A Statistical Eye on Europe*, 1971–80; 1987–99. Luxembourg: European Commission, Office for Official Publications.

European Commission,1987. *Educational Structures in the Member States of the European Communities*, Brussels: Commission of the European Communities.

Falkingham, Jane and John Hills, 1995. *The Dynamic of Welfare: The Welfare State and the Life Cycle*, Hemel Hempstead: Prentice Hall.

Feinstein, Charles H., Peter Temin, and Gianni Toniolo, 1997. *The European Economy Between the Wars*, Oxford: Oxford University Press.

Feldman, Gerald D., 1966. *Army, Industry and Labor in Germany 1914–1918*, Princeton: Princeton University Press.

Fichte, Johann Gottlieb, [1800] 1920. *Der geschlossene Handelsstaat. Ein philosophischer Entwurf als Anhang zur Rechstlehre und Probe einer künftig zu liefernden Politik*, Jena: Gustav Fischer.

Fischer, Wolfram, 1978. "Bergbau, Industrie und Handwerk," in: *Handbuch der deutschen Wirtschafts- und Sozialgeschichte*, Vol. I–II, edited by H. Aubin and W. Zorn, Stuttgart: Klett-Cotta.

— (Ed), 1992. *Die Geschichte der Stromversorgung*, Frankfurt: VWEW-Verlag.

Fishman, Ted C., 2005, *'China Inc.' How the Rise of the Next Superpower Challenges America and the World*, New York: Scribner.

Flinn, Michael, 1966. *Origins of the Industrial Revolution*, London: Longmans.

Flora, Peter and Arnold J. Heidenheimer (Eds), 1981. *The Development of Welfare States in Europe and America*, New Brunswick: Transaction Books.

Florinsky, Michael, 1936. *Fascism and National Socialism. A Study of the Economic and Social Policies of the Totalitarian State*, New York: Macmillan.

Fontaine, André, 1970. *History of the Cold War*, Vol. 2, New York: Vintage Books.

Fridlizius, Gunnar, 1963. "Sweden's Exports 1850–1960," *Economy and History*, No. 4.

Friedman, Alan, 1989. *Agnelli: Fiat and the Network of Italian Power*, New York: New American Library.

Friedman, Milton, 1959. *The Program for Monetary Stability*, New York: Fordham University Press.

— 1962. *Capitalism and Freedom*, Chicago: University of Chicago Press.

— 1963. *Inflation: Causes and Consequences*, New York: Asia Publishing House.

— 1969. *The Optimum Quantity of Money and Other Essays*, Chicago: Aldine Publishing Co.

— 1978. *The Tax Limitation, Inflation and the Role of the Government*, Dallas: Fisher Institute.

Garraty, John A., 1986. *The Great Depression*, San Diego: Harcourt Brace Jovanovich.

Geiger, Kent H., 1968. *The Family in Soviet Russia*, Cambridge, M.A.: Harvard Press.

Gendarme, René, 1950. *L'Expérience française de la nationalisation industrielle et ses enseignements économiques*, Paris: Librarire Médicis.

Gerschenkron, Alexander, 1962. *Economic Backwardness in Historical Perspective*, Cambridge, M.A.: Harvard University Press.

Gillies, James and Robert Cailliau, 2000. *How the Web was Born. The Story of the World Wide Web*, Oxford: Oxford University Press.

Girault, René, 1979. "Place et role des échanges extérieurs," in: *Histoire économique et sociale de la France*, Vol. IV, edited by Fernand Braudel and E. Labrousse, Paris: Presses Universitaires de France.

Golub, Jonathan, 1998. *Global Competition and EU Environmental Policy*, London: Routledge.

Goodin, Robert E., Bruce Headey, Ruud Muffels and Henk-Jan Dirven, 1999. *The Real Worlds of Welfare Capitalism*, Cambridge: Cambridge University Press.

Grass, Günter, 2000. *My Century*, New York: Helen and Kurt Wolff Books.

Gregor, James A., 1969. *The Ideology of Fascism. The Rationale of Totalitarianism*, New York: The Free Press.

Guerrieri, Paolo and Carlo Milana, 1990. *L'Italia e il commercio mondiale: mutamenti e tendenze nella divisione internazionale del lavoro*, Bologna: Il Mulino.

Hamilton, Alexander, 1904. *Works of Alexander Hamilton*, New York: Putnam's Sons.

Hancock, William Keith and M. Margaret Gowing, 1949. *The British War Economy*, London: Her Majesty's Stationery Office.

Hannah, Leslie, 1979. *Electricity Before Nationalization. A Study of the Development of the Electricity Supply Industry in Britain to 1948*, Baltimore: Johns Hopkins University Press.

Hardach, Karl, 1976. *The Political Economy of Germany in the Twentieth Century*, Berkeley: University of California Press.

Harrison, Joseph, 1985. *The Spanish Economy in the Twentieth Century*, London: Croom Helm.

Harrison, Mark, 1985. *Soviet Planning in Peace and War, 1938–1945*, Cambridge: Cambridge University Press.

Hayek, Friedrich A., 1944. *The Road to Serfdom*, London: Routledge.

— 1960. *The Constitution of Liberty*, Chicago: University of Chicago Press.

Heckscher, Eli F., 1954. *An Economic History of Sweden*, Cambridge: Cambridge University Press.

Heimann, Eduard, 1964. *History of Economic Doctrines. An Introduction to Economic Theory*, New York: Oxford University Press.

Helleiner, Eric, 1994. *States and the Reemergence of Global Finance: From Bretton Woods to the 1990s*, Ithaca: Cornell University Press.

— 2000. "Explaining the Globalization of Financial Markets: Bringing States Back In," in: *The New Political Economy of Globalization* edited by Richard Higgott and Anthony Payne, Vol. 1, Cheltenham: Edward Elgar.

Herlea, Alexandre, 1995. "The First Transcontinental Airline: Franco-Roumaine, 1920–1925," in: *From Airships to Airbus. The History of Civil and Commercial Aviation*, edited by William F. Trimble, Vol. 2, Washington D.C.: Smithsonian Institution Press.

Hertzman, Clyde, Shona Kelly and Martin Bobak (Eds), 1996. *East–West Life Expectancy Gap in Europe, Environmental and Non-Environmental Determinants*, Dordrecht: Kluwer.

Higgott, Richard and Anthony Payne (Eds), 2000. *The New Political Economy of Globalization*, Vols. 1–2, Cheltenham: Edward Elgar.

Higham, Robin, 1995. "A Matter of the Utmost Urgency: the Search for a Third London Airport, 1918–1992," in: *From Airships to Airbus. The History of Civil and Commercial Aviation*, Vol. 1, edited by William M. Leary, Washington D.C.: Smithsonian Institution Press.

Hitler, Adolf, [1936] 1971. *Mein Kampf*, Boston: Houghton Mifflin.

Hitler-Bormann, 1961. *The Testament of Adolf Hitler: The Hitler-Bormann Documents, February–April 1945*, edited by François Genoud, London: Icon Books.

Hobsbawm, Eric, 1968. *Industry and Empire: the Making of Modern English Society*, New York: Pantheon Books.

— 1994. *Age of Extremes. The Short Twentieth Century 1914–1991*, London: Michael Joseph.

Hobson, John A., 1902. *Imperialism: A Study*, London: K. Nisbet & Co.

Hodne, Fritz, 1975. *An Economic History of Norway 1815–1970*, Trondheim: Tapir.

— 1993. "The Multinational Companies of Norway," in: *The Rise of Multinationals in Continental Europe*, edited by Geoffrey Jones and Harm G. Schröter, Aldershot: Edward Elgar.

Hoffman, George W. (Ed), 1990. *Europe in the 1990s. A Geographic Analysis.* 6th edition, New York: John Wiley & Sons.

Hoffmann, Walther G., 1931. *Stadien und Typen der Industrialisierung*, Jena: G. Fischer.

— 1971. *Untersuchungen zum Wachstum der deutschen Wirtschaft*, Tübingen: Mohr.

Hogg, Robin L., 1986. *Structural Rigidities and Policy Inertia in Inter-War Belgium*, Brussels: Koninklijke Academie voor Wetenschappen.

Hooghe, Liesbet (Ed), 1996. *Cohesion Policy and European Integration: Building Multi-Level Governance*, Oxford: Oxford University Press.

Hopkins, Anthony G. (Ed), 2002. *Globalization in World History*, London: Pimlico.

Hungarian National Archive (Országos Levéltár), 1933 June 15. Department of Economic Policy, Ministry of Foreign Affairs. German File No. 642, Report of the Hungarian Legation of Berlin.

— 1934. Political Department, Ministry of Foreign Affairs.

— 1939. Department of Economic Policy, Ministry of Foreign Affairs.

— 1941. Department of Economic Policy, Ministry of Foreign Affairs.

— 1942. The Hungarian-German Economic Negotiations.

Hurrell, Andrew and Ngaire Woods, 2000. "Globalization and Inequality," in: *The New Political Economy of Globalization*, edited by Richard Higgott and Anthony Payne, Vol. 2, Cheltenham: Edward Elgar.

ILO, *Year Book of Labour Statistics*, 1980. Geneva: International Labour Organization.

International, 1949. *International Capital Movements During the Inter-War Period*, Geneva: United Nations.

Jacquillat, Bertrand, 1988. *Nationalization and Privatization in Contemporary France*, Stanford: Hoover Institution.

Jansen, Door A. C. M. and Marc de Smidt, 1974. *Industrie en Ruimte*, Assen: Van Gorcum.

Jenkins, Rhys, Jonathan Barton, Anthony Bartzokas, Jan Hesselberg, and Hege Merete Knutsen, 2002. *Environmental Regulation in the New Global Economy. The Impact on Industry and Competitiveness*, Cheltenham: Edward Elgar.

Johnsen, Oscar A., 1939. *Norwegische Wirtschaftsgeschichte*, Jena: G. Fischer.

Jones, Geoffrey and Harm G. Schröter (Eds), 1993. *The Rise of Multinationals in Continental Europe*, Aldershot: Edward Elgar.

Jörberg, Lennart, 1976. "Scandinavia 1914–1970," in: *The Fontana Economic History of Europe*, edited by Carlo Cipolla, Vol. 6/2, Glasgow: W. Collins Sons.

Jordi, Jean-Jacques, 2003. "The Collapse of World Dominion: the Dismantling of the European Colonial Empires and its Impact on Europe," in: *Themes in Modern European History since 1945*, edited by Rosemary Wakeman, London: Routledge.

Journal Officiel, 1936. "Journal Officiel de la Républic française, Debats parlementaires, Chambre des Députés," in: *Economic History of Europe: Twentieth Century*, edited by Shepard B. Clough, Thomas and Carol Moodie, New York: Harper and Row, 1968.

Judy, Richard W. and Virginia L. Clough, 1989. *The Information Age and Soviet Society*, Indianapolis: Hudson Institute.

Kamarás, Ferenc, Jiřina Kocourková, and Hein Moors, 1998. "The Impact of Social Policies on Reproductive Behaviour," in: *Population, Family, and Welfare. A Comparative Survey of European Attitudes*, Vol. II, edited by Rossella Palomba and Hein Moors, Oxford: Clarendon Press.

Kamieniecki, Sheldon, 1993. *Environmental Politics in the International Arena*, New York: State University Press.

Karsten, Sjoerd and Dominique Majoor (Eds), 1994. *Education in East Central Europe*, Münster: Waxmann.

Kautsky, Karl, 1914. "Der Imperialismus," *Neue Zeit* 32/2.

Kearney, A. T., 2000. "Weekly Indicators: Globalization," *The Economist*, No. 6.

Kenwood, George A. and Alan L. Lougheed, 1971. *The Growth of the International Economy 1820–1960*, London: George Allen & Unwin.

Keynes, John M., 1920. *The Economic Consequences of the Peace*, New York: Harcourt, Brace, and Howe.

— 1927. *The End of Laissez Faire*, London: Leonard and Virginia Woolf.

— 1936. *The General Theory of Employment, Interest and Money*, London: Harcourt, Brace.

— 1933. "The New York Times," quoted by John K. Galbraith, *The Age of Uncertainty*, Boston: Houghton Mifflin Co. 1977.

Khromov, Pavel A., 1950. *Ekonomicheskoe razvitie Rossii v 19–20 vekakh (1800–1917)*, Moscow: Gos. Izd-vo. polit. lit-ry.

— 1963. *Ekonomika Rossii v periode promyshlennogo kapitalizma*, Moscow: VPShi AON pri TsK KPSS.

Kimball, Warren (Ed), 1984. *Churchill and Roosevelt. The Complete Correspondence*. Princeton: Princeton University Press.

Kipling, Rudyard, 1940. *Rudyard Kipling's Verse*, Garden City, N.Y.: Doubleday & Co.

Kipping, Matthias, 1997. "European Industrial Policy in a Competitive Global Economy," in: *New Challenges to the European Union: Policies and Policy-Making*, edited by Stelios Stavridis, Elias Mossialos, Roger Morgan, and Howard Machin, Aldershot: Dartmouth Publishing Co.

Klein, Burton H., 1956. *Germany's Economic Preparations for War*, Cambridge, M.A.: Harvard University Press.

Kligman, Gail, 2000. *The Politics of Duplicity. Controlling Reproduction in Ceauşescu's Romania*, Berkeley: University of California Press.

Knox, Paul and John Agnew, 1998. *The Geography of the World Economy*, Third edition, London: Arnold.

Kohl, Jürgen, 1981. "An End to Growth? Fiscal Capacities and Containment Pressures," in: *The Development of Welfare States in Europe and America*, edited by Peter Flora and Arnold J. Heidenheimer, New Brunswick: Transaction Books.

— 1984. *Staatsausgaben in Westeuropa. Analysen zur langfristigen Entwicklung der öffentlichen Finanzen*, Frankfurt: Campus.

Kohn, Hans, 1966. *Political Ideologies of the Twentieth Century*, New York: Harper and Row.

Köllmann, Wolfgang, 1978. "Bevölkerungsgeschichte 1800–1970," in: *Handbuch der deutschen Wirtschafts- und Sozialgeschichte*, Vol. I–II, edited by H. Aubin and W. Zorn, Stuttgart: Klett-Cotta.

Korbonski, Andrzej, 1965. *Politics of Socialist Agriculture in Poland 1945–1960*, New York: Columbia University Press.

Kornai, János, 1992. *The Socialist System. The Political Economy of Communism*, Princeton: Princeton University Press.

Kostrowicka, Irena, Zbigniew Landau, and Jerzy Tomaszewski, 1966. *Historia gospodarcza polski XIX i XX wieku*, Warsaw: Wiedza.

Krantz, Olle, 1987. "Nordeuropa. Sweden, Norwegen, Dänmark, Finnland 1914–1970," in: *Handbuch der europäischen Wirtschafts- und Sozialgeschichte*, edited by Wolfram Fischer, Stuttgart: Klett-Cotta.

Kraus, Franz, 1981. "Economic Equality: The Distribution of Incomes," in *The Development of Welfare States in Europe and America*, edited by Peter Flora and Arnold J. Heidenheimer, New Brunswick: Transaction Books.

Kudrle, Robert T. and Theodor R. Marmor, 1981. "Social Security: The Importance of Socioeconomic and Political Variables," in: *The Development of the Welfare States in Europe and America*, edited by Peter Flora and Arnold J. Heidenheimer, New Brunswick: Transaction Books.

Kuznets, Simon, 1967. "Quantitative Aspects of the Economic Growth of Nations. Level and Structure of Foreign Trade. Longterm Trends," *Economic Development and Cultural Change*, No. 15/2.

Lal, Deepak, 1980. *A Liberal International Economic Order. The International Monetary System and Economic Development*, Princeton: Princeton University Press.

Lamfalussy, Alexandre, 1961. *Investment and Growth in Mature Economies*, London: St. Martin's Press.

Landes, David S., 1969. *The Unbound Prometheus. Technological Change and Industrial Development in Western Europe from 1750 to the Present*, Cambridge: Cambridge University Press.

Landesmann, Michael, 2000. "Structural Change in the Transition Economies, 1989–1999," *Economic Survey of Europe*, No. 2/3, New York: United Nations.

Lee, Joseph, 1989. *Ireland 1912–1985*, Cambridge: Cambridge University Press.

Lenin, Vladimir Ilyich, 1947. *Selected Works*, 2 vols. London: Lawrence and Wishart.

— 1971; 1974. *Selected Works*, One-Volume Edition. New York: International Publisher.

— 1988. *Imperialism, the Highest Stage of Capitalism: a Popular Outline*, New York: International Publisher.

Lévy-Leboyer, Maurice, 1968. "La croissance économique en France au XIXe siècle. Résultats préliminaires," *Annales*, É.S. C. 4.

— (Ed), 1977. *La position internationale de la France (XIXe–XXe siècles)*, Paris: Éditions de l'École des Hautes Etudes en Sciences Sociales.

Liashchenko, Petr I., 1952. *Istorija narodnogo khoziaistva SSSR*, Vol. II. Leningrad: Gos. Izd-vo polit. lit-ry.

Lieberman, Sima, 1977. *The Growth of European Mixed Economies, 1945–1970. A Concise Study of the Economic Evolution of Six Countries*, Cambridge, M.A.: Schenkman.

Linz, Juan J., 1976. "Some Notes Toward a Comparative Study of Fascism in Sociological Historical Perspective," in: *Fascism. A Reader's Guide* edited by Walter Laqueur, Berkeley: University of California Press.

List, Friedrich, [1841] 1922. *Das nationale System der politischen Ökonomie,* Jena: G. Fischer.

Livi Bacci, Massimo, 2000. *The Population of Europe. A History*, Oxford: Blackwell.

Lloyd George, David, 1932. *The Truth About Reparations and War-Debts,* Garden City, N.Y.: Doubleday.

Lodge, David, 1996. *Therapy*, London: Penguin Books.

Luckin, Bill, 1990. *Questions of Power. Electricity and Environment in Interwar Britain,* Manchester: Manchester University Press.

Luxemburg, Rosa, 1975. *Gesammelte Werke*, Band 5, Berlin: Dietz.

Lyttelton, Adrian, 1976. "Italian Fascism," in: *Fascism. A Reader's Guide,* edited by Walter Laqueur, Berkeley: University of California Press.

Mack Smith, Denis, 1959. *Italy. A Modern History*, Ann Arbor: University of Michigan Press.

Maddison, Angus, 1985. *Two Crises: Latin America and Asia 1929–38 and 1973–83,* Paris: OECD.

— 1989. *The World Economy in the 20th Century*, Paris: OECD.

— 1995a. *Monitoring the World Economy 1820–1992*, Paris: OECD.

— 1995b. *Explaining the Economic Performance of Nations. Essays in Time and Space*, Aldershot: Edward Elgar.

— 2001. *The World Economy. A Millennial Perspective*, Paris: OECD.

Mandel, Ernest, 1972. *Der Spätkapitalismus*, Frankfurt: Suhrkamp Verlag.

Mangen, Steen, 1997. "The Social Security Agenda in the post-Maastricht Union," in: *New Challenges to the European Union: Policies and Policy-Making*, edited by Stelios Stavridis, Elias Mossialos, Roger Morgan, and Howard Machin, Aldershot: Dartmouth Publishing Co.

Mann, Charles C. and Mark L. Plummer, 1991. *The Aspirin Wars. Money, Medicine, and 100 Years of Rampant Competition*, New York: Alfred A. Knopf.

Mantle, Jonathan, 1999. *Benetton. The Family, the Business and the Brand,* London: Little, Brown and Co.

Marer, Paul, J. Arvay, J. O'Connor, M. Schrenk, and D. Swanson, 1991. *Historically Planned Economies. A Guide to the Data*, Washington, D.C.: The World Bank.

Marer, Paul and Vincent Mabert, 1996. "G. E. Acquires and Restructures Tungsram: the First Six Years (1990–1995)," in: *Performance of Privatized Enterprises: Corporate Governance, Restructuring, and Profitability*, Paris: OECD.

Marshall, Thomas H., 1950. *Citizenship and Social Class and Other Essays*, Cambridge: Cambridge University Press.

Martinelli, Alberto (Ed) 1991. *International Markets and Global Firms. A Comparative Study of Organized Business in the Chemical Industry*, London: Sage Publications.

Martti, Häikiö, 2002. *Nokia: the Inside Story*, London: Pearson Education.

Marx, Karl, 2000. *Karl Marx Selected Writings*, Oxford: Oxford University Press.

Marx, Karl and Friedrich Engels, 1955. *Selected Works*, Moscow: Foreign Language Publishing House, Vol. 2.

— 1970. *The German Ideology*, New York: International Publisher.

Matejka, Harriet, 1986. "The Foreign Trade System," in: *The Economic History of Eastern Europe 1919–1975*, Vol. 3, edited by Michael C. Kaser, Oxford: Clarendon Press.

Mazover, Mark, 1998. *Dark Continent*, New York: Knopf.

McCormick, John, 2001. *Environmental Policy in the European Union*, Houndsmills: Palgrave.

Meadows, Donella H., Dennis Meadows, Jorgan Randers, and William Behrens III 1972. *The Limits of Growth. A Report for the Club of Rome's Project on the Predicament of Mankind*, New York: Universe Books.

Measuring, 1999. *Measuring Globalization. The Role of Multinationals in OECD Economies*, Paris: OECD.

Merki, Christoph Maria, 2002. *Der holprige Siegeszug des Automobils 1895–1930*, Vienna: Böhlau.

Mesarovic, Mihajlo and Eduard Pestel, 1974. *Mankind at the Turning Point. The Second Report of the Club of Rome*, New York: E. P. Dutton & Co.

Mill, John Stuart, 1946. "Considerations on Representative Government" (1861) and "On Liberty" (1859) in *Introduction to Contemporary Civilization in the West. A Source Book*, Vol. II, New York: Columbia University Press.

Milward, Alan S., 1970. *The New Order and the French Economy*, Oxford: Clarendon Press.

— 1976. "Fascism and the Economy," in: *Fascism. A Reader's Guide* edited by Walter Laqueur, Berkeley: University of California Press.

— 1979. *War, Economy and Society, 1939–1945*, Berkeley: University of California Press.

— 1984. *The Reconstruction of Western Europe 1945–51*, Berkeley: University of California Press.

Milward, Alan and S. B. Saul, 1977. *The Development of the Economies of Continental Europe 1850–1914*, London: Allen & Unwin.

Mitchell, Brian R., 1976. "Statistical Appendix," *The Fontana Economic History of Europe. Contemporary Economies*, edited by Carlo Cipolla, Vol. 6 (2), Glasgow: William Collins & Sons.

— 1998. *International Historical Statistics. Europe 1750–1993*, Fourth Edition, London: Macmillan.

Mittelman, James H., 1995. "Rethinking the International Division of Labour in the Context of Globalization," *Third World Quarterly*, 16 (2).

Molle, Willem, 1994. *The Economics of European Integration. Theory, Practice, Policy*, Aldershot: Dartmouth.

Mommen, André, 1994. *The Belgian Economy in the Twentieth Century*, London: Routledge.

Mori, Giorgio (Ed), 1977. *Il capitalismo industriale in Italia*, Rome: Editori Riuniti.

Morrison, Rodney J., 1981. *Portugal: Revolutionary Change in an Open Economy*, Boston: Auburn House.

Morrow, John H., 1993. *The Great War in the Air: Military Aviation from 1909 to 1921*, Washington D.C.: Smithsonian Institution Press.

Möser, Kurt, 1998. "World War I and the Creation of the Desire for Automobiles in Germany," in: *Getting and Spending. European and American Consumer Societies in the Twentieth Century*, edited by Susan Strasser, Charles McGovern, and Matthias Judt, Cambridge: Cambridge University Press.

Mosse, George, 1966. *The Crisis of German Ideology: Intellectual Origins of the Third Reich*, London: Weidenfeld and Nicolson.

MSzMP, 1968. *A Magyar Szocialista Munkáspárt határozatai és dokumentumai 1963–1966*, Budapest: Kossuth Kiadó.

Mueller, Bernard, 1965. *A Statistical Handbook of the North Atlantic Area*, New York: The Twentieth Century Fund.

Mühlfeld, Claus and Friedrich Schönweiss, 1989. *Nationalsozialistische Familienpolitik*, Stuttgart: Ferdinand Enke Verlag.

Mussolini, Benito, 1935. *Fascism. Doctrine and Institutions*, Rome: Ardita Publishers.

Myrdal, Gunnar, 1960. *Beyond the Welfare State. Economic Planning and Its International Implications*, New Haven: Yale University Press.

Nadal, Jorge, 1971. *La Población Española. Siglos XVI a XX*. Barcelona: Ediciones Ariel.

Nadal, Jorge, Albert Carreras, and Carles Sudrià, 1987. *La economía Espanola en el siglo XX. Una perspectiva histórica*, Barcelona: Ariel.

Nationale Wirtschaft, 1934. Hanst Ernst Posse, "Möglichkeiten der Grossraumwirtschaft," *Die Nationale Wirtschaft*. Vol. 2.

Nelson, Brent F. and Alexander C.-G. Stubb, 1998. *The European Union. Readings on the Theory and Practice of European Integration*, Boulder: Lynne Rienner.

Népszabadság, 1973. December 24.

Neufeld, Michael J., 1999. "Rocket Aircraft and the 'Turbojet Revolution': The Luftwaffe's Quest for High-Speed Flight, 1935–39," in: *Innovation and the Development of Flight*, edited by Roger D. Launius, College Station: Texas A&M University Press.

Nicholson, Michael, 1999. "How Novel is Globalization?" in: *Politics of Globalization*, edited by Martin Shaw, London: Routledge.

Nilsson, Carl-Axel, 1972. *Järn och stål i Svensk ekonomi 1885–1912. En marknadsstudie*, Lund: Gleerup.

Nove, Alec, 1977. *The Soviet Economic System*, London: Allen & Unwin.

— 1992. *An Economic History of the USSR 1917–1991*, Harmondsworth: Penguin Books.

O'Brien, Patrick K., 2004. *Colonies in a Globalizing Economy 1815–1948*, London School of Economics, Working Papers of the Global Economic History Network # 08/04.

OECD, 1987. *Structural Adjustment and Economic Performance*, Paris: OECD.

— 1999. *Measuring Globalization. The Role of Multinationals in OECD Economies*, Paris: OECD.

— 2000. *OECD Historical Statistics 1970–1999*, Paris: OECD.

Olson, Mancur, 1994. "The Varieties of Eurosclerosis: the Rise and Decline of Nations Since 1982," in: *Economic Growth in Europe Since 1945*, edited by Nicholas Crafts and Gianni Toniolo, Cambridge: Cambridge University Press.

Olšovský, R. and Vaclav Průha, 1969. *Stručný hospodářský vývoj Československa do roku 1955*, Praha: Svoboda.

Olsson, Ulf, 1993. "Securing the Markets. Swedish Multinationals in a Historical Perspective," in: *The Rise of Multinationals in Continental Europe*, edited by Geoffrey Jones and Harm G. Schröter, Aldershot: Edward Elgar.

O'Rourke, Kevin H. and Jeffrey G. Williamson, 1999. *Globalization and History. The Evolution of a Nineteenth-Century Atlantic Economy*, Cambridge, M.A.: MIT Press.

Overy, Richard J., 1982. *The Nazi Economic Recovery 1932–1938*, London: Macmillan.

Owen, Geoffrey, 1999. *From Empire to Europe. The Decline and Revival of British Industry Since the Second World War*, Hammersmith: HarperCollins.

Papadopoulos, George S., 1994. *Education 1960–1990. The OECD Perspective*, Paris: OECD.

Parliamentary Debates, 1932. "Parliamentary Debates: House of Commons," Fifth series, Vol. 261, in: *Economic History of Europe: Twentieth Century*, edited by Shepard B. Clough, Thomas and Carol Moodie, London: Harper and Row, 1968.

Pavlínek, Petr, 2002. *Environmental Transition: Transformation and Ecological Defence in Central and Eastern Europe*, London: Routledge.

Payne, Stanley, 1974. "Spain," in: *The European Right. A Historical Profile*, edited by Hans Rogger and Eugen Weber, Berkeley: University of California Press.

Peccei, Aurelio, 1981. *One Hundred Pages on the Future. Reflections of the President of the Club of Rome*, New York: Pergamon Press.

Perraton, Jonathan, David Goldblatt, David Held, and Anthony McGrew, 1997. "The Globalization of Economic Activity." *New Political Economy*, 2 (2), July.

Pesti Tőzsde, 1934. March 8.

Péteri, György, 2002. *Global Monetary Regime and National Banking. The Case of Hungary, 1921–1929*, Boulder: Social Science Monographs.

Petzina, Dietmar, 1968. *Autarkiepolitik im Dritten Reich. Der nationalsozialistische Vierjahresplan*, Stuttgart: Deutsche Verlags-Anstalt.

Pfister, Christian, 1998. "The 'Syndrome of the 1950s' in Switzerland," in: *Getting and Spending. European and American Consumer Societies in the Twentieth Century*, edited by Susan Strasser, Charles McGovern, and Matthias Judt, Cambridge: Cambridge University Press.

Picker, Henry, 1965. *Hitlers Tischgespräche im Führerhauptquartier 1941–42*, Stuttgart: Seewald.

Pickles, John, Mariana Nikolova, Caedmon Staddon, Stefan Velev, Zoya Mateeva, and Anton Popov, 2002. "Bulgaria," in: *Environmental Problems of East Central Europe*, edited by F. W. Carter and David Turnock, London: Routledge.

Piszkiewicz, Dennis, 1995. *The Nazi Rocketeers: Dream of Space and Crimes of War*, Westport: Praeger.

Plaza-Prieto, Juan, 1955. "El desarrollo del comercio exterior español desde principios del siglo XIX a la actualidad," *Revista de Económia Politica*, VI.

Plotkin, Susan L., 2000. *The Paris Metro: A Ticket to French History*, Philadelphia: Xlibris.

Poignant, Raymond, 1973. *Education in the Industrialized Countries*, The Hague: Martinus Nijhoff.

Polanyi, Karl, 1964. *The Great Transformation: The Political and Economic Origins of Our Time*, Beacon Hill: Beacon Press.

Pollack, Mark A. and Gregory C. Shaffer, 2001. *Transatlantic Governance in the Global Economy*, Lanham, M.D.: Rowman & Littlefield.

Pollard, Sidney, 1973. "Industrialization and the European Economy," *Economic History Review*, XXVI.

— 1983. *The Development of the British Economy, 1914–1980*, Caulfield East: Edward Arnold.

— 1986. *Peaceful Conquest. The Industrialization of Europe 1760–1970*, Oxford: Oxford University Press.

Posner, Michael V. and Stuart J. Woolf, 1967. *Italian Public Enterprise*, London: Gerald Duckworth.

Posse, Hans Ernst, 1934. "Möglichkeiten der Grossraumwirtschaft," *Die nationale Wirtschaft*, Vol. 2.

Pravda, 1972. August 31.

Preobrazhensky, Evgeny, 1965. *The New Economics*, Oxford: Clarendon House.

Program, 1969. "The Program of the Communist Party of Russia. Adopted at the Eighth Party Congress, held 18 to 23 March 1919," in: Bukharin, Nikolai and Evgeny Preobrazhensky, *The ABC of Communism,* London: Penguin Books.

Protokoll, 1923. *Protokoll des Ersten internationalen Sozialistischen Arbeiterkongress, Hamburg, 21 bis 25 Mai 1923*, Glashütten im Taunus: Auvermann.

Protokoll, 1927. *Sozialdemokratischer Parteitag, 1927 in Kiel. Protokoll*, Glashütten im Taunus: Auvermann.

Pryor, Frederick L., 1985. *A Guidebook to the Comparative Study of Economic Systems*, Englewood Cliffs: Prentice Hall.

Radice, Edward A., 1986. "The Second World War," in: *The Economic History of Eastern Europe 1919–1975*, vol. III, edited by Michael C. Kaser and Edward A. Radice, Oxford: Clarendon Press.

Ránki, György, 1993. *The Economics of the Second World War*, Vienna: Böhlau Verlag.

Ránki, György and Jerzy Tomaszewski, 1986. "The Role of the State in Industry, Banking and Trade," in: *The Economic History of Eastern Europe 1919–1975*, Vol. II, edited by Michael C. Kaser and Edward A. Radice, Oxford: Clarendon Press.

Ratzel, Friedrich, 1897. *Politische Geographie*, München: R. Oldenbourg.

Reagin, Nancy, 1998. "Comparing Apple and Orange: Housewives and the Politics of Consumption in Interwar Germany," in: *Getting and Spending. European and American Consumer Societies in the Twentieth Century*, edited by Susan Strasser, Charles McGovern, and Matthias Judt, Cambridge: Cambridge University Press.

Rees, Merlyn, 1973. *The Public Sector in the Mixed Economy*, London: B. T. Batsford.

Report, 1937. *The Problem of International Investment: Report by a Study Group of the Royal Institute of International Affairs*, London: Oxford University Press.

Reynolds, Lloyd G., 1985. *Economic Growth in the Third World, 1850–1980*, New Haven: Yale University Press.

Ricossa, Sergio, 1976. "Italy 1920–1970," in: *The Fontana Economic History of Europe. Contemporary Economies*, edited by Carlo Cipolla. Part I. Glasgow: William Collins.

Rupert, Mark, 2000. *Ideologies of Globalization. Contending Visions of a New World Order*, London: Routledge.

Saladino, Salvatore, 1974. "Italy," in: *The European Right. A Historical Profile*, edited by Hans Rogger and Eugen Weber, Berkeley: University of California Press.

Sánchez-Albornoz, Nicolàs, 1968. *España hace un siglo: una economía dual*, Madrid: Alianza Editorial.

Sarti, Roland, 1971. *Fascism and the Industrial Leadership in Italy, 1919–1940*, Berkeley: University of California Press.

Sassoon, Donald, 1996. *One Hundred Years of Socialism. The West European Left in the Twentieth Century*, New York: The New Press.

Schacht, Hjalmar, 1938. "Address to the Economic Council of the German Academy," quoted by Edward H. Carr, *The Twenty Years' Crisis, 1919–1939*, New York: Harper and Row, 1964.

Schlote, Werner, 1952. *British Overseas Trade from 1700 to the 1930s*, Oxford: Oxford University Press.

Schulze, Günther G. and Heinrich W. Ursprung, 2001. *International Environmental Economics*, Oxford: Oxford University Press.

Schweng, Lóránd D., 1951. *Economic Planning in Hungary Since 1938*, New York: Mid-European Studies Center of the National Committee for a Free Europe.

Sen, Amartya, 1992. *Inequality Reexamined*, Oxford: Clarendon.

Seton-Watson, Hugh, 1952. *The East European Revolution*, London: Methuen.

Šik, Ota, 1968. *Plan a trh za socializmu*, Prague: Academia.

Single Act, Article 130, 1987. (Single European Act) in McCormick, John, *Environmental Policy in the European Union*, 2001, Houndsmills: Palgrave.

Sloniger, Jerry, 1980. *The VW Story*, Cambridge: Patrick Stephens.

Smith, Adam, 1970. *The Wealth of Nations*, Harmondsworth: Penguin Books.

Soós, Károly Attila, 1986. *Terv, kampány, pénz*, Budapest: Közgazdasági és Jogi Kiadó.

Soros, George, 1998. *The Crisis of Global Capitalism*, New York: Public Affairs.

Spinelli, Altiero and Ernesto Rossi, [1985] 1998. "The Ventotene Manifesto," in: *The European Union* edited by Brent F. Nelson and Alexander C.-G. Stubb, Boulder: Lynne Rienner.

Stalin, Josif V., 1949. *Sochineniya*, Vol. 10, August–December 1927, Moscow: Politicheski Literatury.

— 1972. *The Essential Stalin: Major Theoretical Writings, 1905–1952*, edited by Bruce Franklin, Garden City, N.Y.: Doubleday.

— 1976. *Problems of Leninism*, Peking: Foreign Languages Press.

Statistical Yearbook 1990, New York: United Nations.

Statistisches Jahrbuch der Schweiz, 1950, 2001. Bern, Zürich: Bundesamt für Statistik.

Stavrianos, Leften S., [1958] 1963. *The Balkans Since 1453*, New York: Holt, Rinehart and Winston.

Steinbeck, John, 1958. *Once There Was a War*, New York: Penguin Books.

Stiglitz, Joseph E., 2002. *Globalization and its Discontents*, New York: W. W. Norton.

Stubbs, Richard and Geoffrey R. D. Underhill (Eds), 1994. *Political Economy and the Changing Global Order*, New York: St. Martin's Press.

Survey, 2000. *Economic Survey of Europe 2000*, No. 1, New York: United Nations.

— 2000a. *Economic Survey of Europe 2000*, No. 2, New York: United Nations.

Swann, Dennis, 1996. *European Economic Integration. The Common Market, European Union and Beyond*, Cheltenham: Edward Elgar.

Szuhay, Miklós, 1962. *Állami beavatkozás és a magyar mezőgazdaság az 1930-as években*, Budapest: Akadémiai Kiadó.

Taylor, Michael and David Mondey, 1983. *Daedalus: The Long Odyssey from Myth to Reality*, New York: Prentice Hall.

Thomas, Georg, 1966. *Geschichte der deutschen Wehr- und Rüstungswirtschaft 1918 bis 1943/45*, Bonn: Birkenfeld, Boppard, Boldt.

— 1987. "Portugal 1911–1974," in: *Handbuch der europäischen Wirtschafts- und Sozialgeschichte*, Vol. 6, edited by Wolfram Fischer, Stuttgart: Klett-Cotta.

Tipton, Frank B. and Robert Aldrich, 1987. *An Economic and Social History of Europe, 1890–1939*, London: Macmillan Education.

Transition Report, 2001. Energy in Transition, London: European Bank for Reconstruction and Development.

Transport, 1998. *Statistical Trends in Transport 1965–1994*, Paris: OECD.

Treitschke, Heinrich von, 1886–97. *Historische und politische Aufsätze*, Leipzig: S. Hirzel.

Trends in Europe and North America, The Statistical Yearbook of the Economic Commission for Europe 1998–99, 1999. New York: United Nations.

Trotsky, Leon, 1973. *1905*, London: Pelican Books.

Truman, Harry S., 1955–6. *Memoirs*, Vol. I–II, Garden City, N.Y.: Doubleday.

— 1968. *The Truman Administration. A Documentary History*, edited by Barton J. Bernstein and Allen J. Matusow, New York: Harper and Row.

Tsoukalis, Loukas, 1997. *The New European Economy Revisited*, Oxford: Oxford University Press.

Turnock, David, 2002. "Romania," in: Carter F. W. and D. Turnock (Eds), *Environmental Problems of East Central Europe*, London: Routledge.

UNCTAD, 2003. *World Investment Report*, New York: United Nations.

UNESCO 1963, 1999, *UNESCO Statistical Yearbook*. Paris: UNESCO.

Urwin, Derek, 1995. *The Community of Europe: a History of European Integration Since 1945*, London: Longman.

Van der Wee, Herman, 1986. *Prosperity and Upheaval: the World Economy, 1945–1980*, Berkeley: University of California Press.

Voltes, Pedro, 1974. *Historia de la economía española en los siglos XIX y XX*, Madrid: Editora Nacional.

Weimer, Wolfram, 1998. *Deutsche Wirtschafts-Geschichte. Von der Währungsreform bis zum Euro*, Hamburg: Hoffman und Campe.

Welk, William G., 1938. *Fascist Economic Policy. An Analysis of Italy's Experiment*, Cambridge, M.A.: Harvard University Press.

Weymar, Paul, 1957. *Adenauer: His Authorized Biography*, New York: Dutton.

Wildt, Michael, 1998. "Changes in Consumption as Social Practice in West Germany During the 1950s," in: *Getting and Spending. European and American Consumer Societies in the Twentieth Century*, edited by Susan Strasser, Charles McGovern, and Matthias Judt, Cambridge: Cambridge University Press.

Wilkins, Mira, 1970. *The Emergence of Multinational Enterprise*, Cambridge, M.A.: Harvard University Press.

Williams, Allan M. and Gareth Shaw, 1998. *Tourism and Economic Development. European Experience*, Chichester: John Wiley & Sons.

Wise, William, 1968. *Killer Smog. The World's Worst Air Pollution Disaster*, New York: Ballentine Books.

Wistrich, Robert, 1982. *Trotsky. Fate of a Revolutionary*, New York: Stein and Day.

Woodruff, William, 1966. *The Impact of Western Man. A Study of Europe's Role in the World Economy 1750–1960*, London: St. Martin's Press.

World Economic Conference, 1927. *The World Economic Conference: Final Report*, Geneva: League of Nations, Economic and Financial Section.

World Tables 1984–90, Washington, D.C.: The World Bank.

Zacchia, Carlo, 1976. "International Trade and Capital Movements 1920–1970," in: *The Fontana Economic History of Europe. The Twentieth Century*, Vol. 2, edited by Carlo Cipolla, Glasgow: Collins Fontana Books.

Zacher, Mark W., 2000. "The Declining Pillars of the Westphalian Temple: Implications for International Order and Governance," in: *The New Political Economy of Globalization*, edited by Richard Higgott and Anthony Payne, Vol. 1, Cheltenham: Edward Elgar.

Zamagni, Vera, 1993. *The Economic History of Italy 1860–1990*, Oxford: Clarendon Press.

Zilbert, Edward R., 1972. *Economic Institutions and Industrial Production in the German War Economy*, Ph.D. Dissertation, University of California, Los Angeles.

Zimmerman, David, 2001. *Britain's Shield: Radar and the Defeat of the Luftwaffe*, Stroud, Gloucestershire: Sutton.

Zinn, Karl Georg, 1978. "German Perspectives," in: *Beyond Capitalist Planning*, edited by Stuart Holland, New York: St. Martin's Press.

Zunkel, Friedrich, 1974. *Industrie und Staatssozialismus. Der Kampf um die Wirtschaftsordnung in Deutschland 1914–1918*, Düsseldorf: Droste.

Index

Africa 20, 22, 197, 256, 271, 307
Agnelli, Giovanni 35–6
agriculture, agricultural policy 20, 29, 30, 31, 32, 61, 77, 83, 88, 95, 102, 128, 131, 244, 260, 261, 295, employment 20, 24, 34, 37, 38, 81, 112, 131, 132, 170, 173, 242, 258, 260, 291, 299
airplanes, civil aviation 19, 81, 84, 241–2
Albania 125, 126, 151, 152, 154, 159, 166, 178, 181, 188, 309
Asia 20, 22, 23, 197, 238, 256, 271, 283, 302, 307, 324, 326
Australia 20, 40, 41, 61, 90, 278, 324
Austria 11, 16, 20, 51, 52, 54, 55, 61, 63, 64, 65, 67, 70, 71, 75, 102, 125, 175, 207, 209, 213, 220, 226, 227, 238, 256, 288, 314, 316, 323
Austria-Hungary 12, 32, 50, 54, 61
autobahn, autostrada 103, 104–5, 221, 241, 253
automotive industry, cars 19, 25, 34, 35–6, 41, 81, 82, 83, 84, 90, 103, 241, 243, 244, 250, 253, 254, 271, 283, 286, 297, 305

Balkans, Balkan countries 22, 34, 37, 38, 39, 40, 55, 88, 95, 126, 127, 150, 173, 309, 321, 322
Baltic countries 34, 54, 55, 130, 209
Battle for Grain (*Battaglia del Grano*), land reclamation 102–3
Bayer, Aspirin 26, 27–8, 271
Belgium 11, 19, 22, 25, 38, 41, 50, 52, 61, 65, 67, 68–9, 71, 196, 198,

213, 222, 227, 234, 238, 243, 248, 254, 256, 257, 274, 275, 287, 291, 314
Benelux countries 194, 198, 200, 201
Benetton 271, 274–5
Berlin 17, 19, 98, 104, 153, 167, 198, 316
Beveridge, Sir William, report 43, 81, 230, 231–2
Bolshevik Revolution 55, 96, 147, 165, 169, 279
Braun, Wernher von 122–4, 242
Bretton Woods system 43, 81, 192–3, 195, 277, 278, 281
Britain, British 10, 11, 12, 15, 17, 19, 20, 22, 23, 24, 25, 26, 28, 29, 31, 33, 38, 41, 43, 44, 45, 47, 50, 52, 56, 57, 60, 62, 63, 65, 67, 71, 81–2, 84, 90, 122, 130, 174, 192, 198, 200, 202, 207, 208, 209, 211, 212, 213, 214, 216, 217, 218, 221, 227, 228, 230, 231, 2, export 10, 11, 24, 30, industrial revolution, development 10, 11, 20, 23, 28, introduction of free trade 11
Brown Boveri Company 16–17
Budapest 17, 32, 33
Bukharin, Nikolai 138, 140, 141, 144, 145, 148, 165
Bulgaria 34, 37, 47, 51, 54, 55, 59, 66, 79, 98, 114, 127, 128, 167, 169, 170, 173, 178, 181, 185, 186, 188, 240

Canada 20, 40, 41, 61, 90, 202, 236, 250, 298, 324
capital accumulation, formation 24, 34, 178, 194, 238–9, 290

cartel agreements, compulsory cartels 66, 67, 109, 110

catching-up process 38, 39, 95, 144, 148, 149, 150, 210, 257, 295–300

Central and Eastern Europe 3, 4, 20, 30, 31, 38, 39, 40, 54, 55, 63, 64, 65, 67, 74, 80, 87, 88, 89, 90, 95, 98, 102, 126, 128, 129, 150, 151, 154, 158, 159, 166, 167, 169, 170, 171, 172, 173, 175, 176, 177, 178, 184, 187, 188, 209, 252, 275, 278, 279, 280, 293, 307, 308, 309, 320, sovietization of 151–4

Channel Tunnel 207–8

chemical industry 24, 26, 28, 29, 34, 80, 83, 103, 244, 271, 297

Churchill, Sir Winston 56, 76, 77, 151, 152, 198, 199, 203, 207

coal industry 25, 28, 81, 82, 83, 243

COCOM list 173–4

cold war 112, 123, 133, 152, 153, 154, 173, 174, 194, 196, 198, 199, 217, 230, 233, 258, 279, 295

collectivization of agriculture 148, 156, 169

colonialism, colonial empires 22, 23, 40, 41, 89, 96, 97, 98, 99, 126, 256, collapse 195–7, 263, 295

communication and service revolution 175, 182, 239, 264

consumption, consumer society 245–55, 288–9, 299, 314

corporative system 95, 97, 101, 106–8, 191, 280

Council for Mutual Economic Aid (CMEA, Comecon), see regional economic blocs

crisis and collapse of state socialism 182–5, 186, 279–80

Czechoslovakia, Czech Lands, Czech Republic 32, 54, 59, 60, 61, 66, 70, 71, 75, 98, 127, 129, 152, 159, 165, 172, 173, 175, 178, 180, 181, 188, 209, 309, 318, 319, 320

Danube–Black Sea Canal 155–6

De Gaulle, Charles 196, 205, 207, 214, 219, 223

Delors, Jacques 211, 249

Denmark 20, 28, 29, 30, 38, 47, 67, 70, 80, 207, 209, 212, 213, 227, 228, 229, 238, 242, 244, 251, 256, 261, 271, 284, 287, 304

division of labor 14, 256–7, 258, 270, 271

Dniepr hydroelectric project 147–8

Eastern Europe, see Central and Eastern Europe

economic dirigisme 92, 93, 94, 95, 99, 102, 106, 110, 114, 115, 124, 125, 130, 133, 157, 190, 191, 223

economic nationalism 40, 44, 61, 63, 93, 115, 131, 195

economic reforms in socialist Yugoslavia 178–9, Czechoslovakia 179–80, Hungary 180–1, Poland 181

education 37, 87, 88, 171–2, 236–8

electricity 17, 19, 24, 26, 29, 34, 81, 82, 83, 101, 103, 111, 139, 140, 218, 244, 295, households electrification 81–2

electro-technical industry, electronics, electro-metallurgy 26, 32, 34, 240, 287, 297–304

employment, unemployment 42, 63, 65, 93, 94, 124, 125, 185, 215, 226, 229, 280, 281, 282, 283, 293, 294, 296, 299

engineering industries 16, 26, 28, 34, 37, 80, 216, 261, 271, 286, 287, 297

environmental policy in Western Europe 309–11, in Central and Eastern Europe 318–20

equalization of income, society 170, 171, 191

European Union (European Community) 132, 133, 153, 188, 189, 193–5, 197–209, 212, 217, 234, 235, 238, 239, 240, 242, 244, 247, 248, 252, 259, 271, 272–3, 278, 279, 280, 282, 283, 284, 285, 286, 288, 291, 292, 298, 303, 304, 311, 323, 324, agricultural policy 210–11, cohesion policy 209–10, economic superpower 320–25, enlargement 292–7, 299, environmental policy 315, 316, 317, 318, monetary union 211–12

expansionism 22, 23, 40, 93, 279

exports, export industries 10, 11, 22, 24, 26, 28, 29, 32, 33, 34, 64, 66, 90, 114, 182, 243, 244, 255–6, 258, 261, 264, 267, 283, 289, 290, 297, 299, 310, export-led industrialization, export-oriented

exports, export industries (*cont.*)
economy 29, 39, 56, 87, 282, 287,
289, 297, 299, food and raw
materials, trade 22, 28, 29, 30, 31,
32, 114, 243

FIAT (Fabbrica Italiana di Automobili
Torino) 35–6
Finland 34, 54, 67, 209, 222, 240, 246,
256, 260, 261, 272, 287, 293, 298,
299, 300, 314, 316
food processing 24, 29, 32, 33, 132,
244, 297, 298
forced capital accumulation 143, 144,
146, 150, 154, 158, 169
forced industrialization and growth
133, 144, 154
foreign direct investment (FDI) 22, 24,
30, 31, 37, 62, 195, 206, 207, 259,
261, 264, 267, 270, 271, 295, 297,
305, 306, 310, 311, 325, 326
foreign trade, *see* exports
France, French 2, 11, 16, 19, 20, 22, 24,
25, 26, 28, 30, 38, 40, 41, 43, 47,
50, 52, 53, 54, 59, 61, 63, 65, 70,
71, 81, 82, 83, 90, 174, 175, 192,
194, 196, 200, 201, 203, 205, 209,
213, 214, 216, 217, 219, 221, 223,
224, 227, 230, 233, 234, 237, 238,
239, 240, 241, 242, 243, 244, 245,
246, 248, 253, 256, 257, 266, 271,
274, 275, 278, 280, 282, 283, 284,
285, 286, 287, 290, 291, 294, 301,
303, 304, 316, protectionism 68–9
Franco, Francisco 92, 97, 102, 105, 108,
109, 112, 225, 259, 279, 295
Friedman, Milton 275, 276–7, 278

GATT (General Agreement on Tariffs
and Trade) 180, 193, 259, 264
General Electric 33
Germany 2, 11, 12, 16, 19, 20, 22, 24,
25, 26, 27, 28, 30, 38, 40, 41, 42,
45, 46, 50, 51, 52, 53, 54, 55, 58,
59, 61, 62, 63, 64, 65, 70, 71, 74,
84, 90, 98, 99, 100, 102, 126, 150,
152, 153, 154, 175, 191, 194, 196,
198, 199, 200, 201, 210, 211, 213,
214, 217, 219, 220, 226, 227, 234,
238, 239, 240, 241, 242, 243, 244,
245, 246, 248, 250, 251, 253, 255,
256, 258, 270, 271, 274, 275, 280,
282, 283, 284, 285, 286, 288, 290,
291, 294, 298, 301, 303, 304, 314,

316, 318, 319, economic dirigisme
94–5, occupation of Europe 74–5,
78–9, 129–30
globalization, globalizing 15, 28, 29,
30, 37, 39, 40, 44, 262, 277, 278,
284, 287, 291, 300, 303, 305, 306,
307, 309, 310, 311, 314, catching
up 308, 309–11, and
characteristics 263–71, and
inequality 305, 306, 307
gold standard 11–12, 15, 45, 56, 63,
263, return to 56–7
Gorbachev, Mikhail 181, 279
Göring, Hermann 110, 114, 115, 129,
130
Great Depression 44, 45, 46, 61–4, 94,
95, 107, 109, 110, 112, 114, 124,
125, 130, 192, 230, 249, 276,
financial crisis 63
Greece, Greek 12, 32, 92, 97, 99, 102,
108, 111, 131, 132, 133, 151, 152,
199, 209, 210, 212, 245, 246, 258,
259, 260, 279, 293, 297, 299, 300,
304, 318
Grossraumwirtschaft, *see* regional
economic blocs

Hayek, Friedrich 275–6
heavy industries 26, 172
high-tech industries, *see* new industrial
sectors
Hitler, Adolf 55, 70, 74, 97, 99, 102,
104, 105, 106, 108, 112, 113, 114,
115, 118, 119, 127, 129, 150, 199,
201, 230
Holland, the Netherlands, Low
Countries 11, 12, 20, 22, 24, 31,
38, 41, 47, 52, 57, 61, 67, 70, 71,
82, 85, 90, 198, 211, 213, 226, 227,
238, 239, 242, 245, 248, 250, 251,
256, 257, 271, 275, 282, 283, 284,
286, 287, 288, 290, 291, 294, 298,
304, 316
Hungary, Hungarian 2, 32, 33, 34, 38,
39, 46, 47, 51, 54, 55, 59, 60, 61,
64, 66, 67, 70, 78, 79, 82, 85, 95,
98, 114, 125, 126, 127, 128, 150,
154, 156, 159, 165, 166, 167, 169,
170, 172, 173, 175, 177, 178, 179,
180, 181, 182, 184, 185, 188, 189,
209, 240, 246, 279, 280,

Iberian peninsula 37, 132, 259
illiteracy 132, 171, 236

import-substituting industrialization 29, 46, 56, 88, 103, 118, 133, 182, 195

indebtedness 184, 279

industrial employment 26, 29, 37, 38, 88, 132, 173, 243, 260, 287, 288, 291, 299

industrialization, industrial output 20, 22, 25, 28, 29, 30, 34, 37, 39, 41, 69, 76, 79, 103, 111, 151, 156, 171, 172, 173, 176, 260, 261, 282, 295, 296, 297, labor input to 169–70, 172

inflation 79, 96, 98, 111, 140, 144, 185, 186, 279, 280, 281, 282, 288, 295, 296

information technology 286, 287, 288, 297, 310

infrastructure 26, 28, 172, 241

international institutions, nineteenth century 15

International Monetary Fund (IMF) 43, 180, 192, 259, 278, 296, 303

investments 172, 183, 215–17, 238, 245, 261, 264, 282, 285, 286, 290, 294, 296, defensive investment 283, 284

Ireland, Irish 33, 39, 40, 87, 209, 210, 245, 250, 261, 262, 287, 293, 299, catching up 297–8, 299, 300, 304, 308, 309

iron and steel industry, metallurgy 25, 28, 29, 37, 80, 81, 82, 83, 103, 111, 175, 244, 283, 319

Italy 11, 12, 16, 17, 19, 26, 32, 34, 35, 36, 38, 40, 47, 51, 55, 67, 70, 95, 96, 97, 98, 99, 100, 102, 103, 106, 127, 131, 132, 175, 190, 194, 201, 209, 213, 216, 221, 225, 239, 241, 245, 246, 251, 253, 254, 256, 258, 260, 271, 274, 280, 286, 301, 303, 304

Japan 20, 22, 70, 196, 254, 275, 284, 297, 300, 307, 308, 326

Keynes, John Maynard, Keynesian economics 43–4, 53, 72–3, 74, 81, 82, 95, 203, 213, 216–17, 232, 276, 277, 280

Khrushchev, Nikita 167, 168, 178

KLM 82, 84, 85

laissez-faire, free trade 10, 11, 13, 14, 15, 39, 40, 59, 92, 95, 99, 186, 190,

221, 263, 303, decline, challenge of 42, 61, 67–8, 71, 73, 74, 79, ideology (as *Zeitgeist*) 12, 15, 275–7, 303, philosophy and economics 13, 14

Latin America 20, 183, 256, 271, 275, 278, 307

League of Nations 53, 56, 57, 58, 110, 195, 202

Lenin, Vladimir I. 23, 140, 142, 143, 145, 147, theory on socialism 137–9

List, Friedrich 46

London 17, 19, 202, 207, 228, 249, 277, 312, 315, 316

Marks and Spencer 249–50

Marshall Plan 91, 153, 193, 194, 199, 200

Marx, Karl and Friedrich Engels, theoretical legacy on socialism 133–7

Mediterranean Europe 19, 20, 30, 31, 34, 38, 39, 40, 55, 80, 89, 90, 94, 95, 98, 131, 132, 151, 175, 176, 177, 188, 206, 210, 212, 238, 242, 245, 246, 254, 257, 258, 260, 278, 281, 282, 289, 292, 293, 299, 300, 301, 309, 310, 320, 321, 322

mercantilism 12

Metaxas, John, General 92, 98, 102, 108, 111, 124, 125

migration, *see* population

Mill, John Stuart 13, 14

mixed and welfare–state economy 132, 186, 190, 191, 212, challenge of 300, state sector 203, 217–23, 238, 247

modernization, and its failure 37, 40, 79, 81, 94, 110, 132, 133, 140, 261, 286, 305, dictatorship 94, 95, 99, 110, 150, 171

Monnet, Jean 15, 200, 201, 202–3, 204, 223

multinational companies and subsidiaries 16–17, 32–3, 35–6, 120, 244, 257, 264, 268–70, 271, 285, 287, 295, 299, 305, 306, 310, 311, 324, 325

Mussolini, Benito 35, 55, 93, 96, 97, 99, 100, 101, 102, 103, 106, 107, 109, 110, 112, 117, 124, 125, 126, 221

nationalization 93, 100, 109, 112, 115, 190, 223, 303, in fascist Italy 116–17, in Franco's Spain 118, in Hitler's Germany 118, in peripheral countries 70, in the socialist regimes 139, 154, 159
NEP (New Economic Policy) 141–2
new industrial sectors, high-tech 15, 24, 25, 28, 29, 34, 81, 84, 87, 190, 200, 239, 243, 244, 284, 286, 287, 288, 295
New Zealand 20, 40, 41, 90, 278, 298, 299
Nokia 271, 272–3
non-market system 133, 144, 149, 157, 166, 169
Norway, Norwegian 11, 16, 17, 19, 28, 29, 38, 67, 71, 80, 81, 86, 129, 207, 213, 215, 222, 227, 229, 237, 238, 244, 245, 256, 261, 271
nuclear energy 239–40, 295

oil industry, production 31, 37, 116, crisis 168, 182, 184, 281, 284, 288, 289, 293, 294, 295, 296, 297

paper and pulp industry 28, 29
Paris 17, 18, 207, 250, 274, 316, Metro 18
peripheries, European 31, 32, 37, 38, 39, 40, 44, 55, 56, 69–70, 79, 86, 87, 88, 89, 94, 131, 132, 151, 195, 256, 262, 278, 280, 292, 293, 305, 306, 307, 308, 320
planning 69, 70, 105, 109, 114, 190, 223, in Franco's Spain 112, 295, in Nazi Germany 114–15, 117, 129, in Soviet Union and in the Soviet bloc 133, 140, 147, 149, 150, 154, 156, 166, 167, 168, 173, 189, 191, 280, terror as safeguard of planning 164–5, of agriculture 157–9, 163–4, system and institutions 159–63, of foreign trade 164, in mixed economies 225, 226, French planning 203, 223–5, 240, 243, Spanish planning 225
Poland 34, 38, 39, 50, 51, 54, 59, 62, 69, 70, 75, 95, 98, 102, 129, 150, 151, 154, 156, 159, 175, 176, 178, 181, 182, 183, 184, 185, 186, 188, 189, 209, 246, 279, 280, 309, 318, 319, 320

Polanyi, Karl 45, 72
population, migration 2, 3, 4, 5, 28, 41, 50, 90, 101, 105–6, 176–8, 206, 264, 295, 300–1, 302, 323
Portugal, Portuguese 11, 32, 37, 38, 39, 92, 95, 97, 99, 102, 114, 131, 132, 197, 207, 209, 210, 236, 245, 246, 259, 260, 279, 287, 295–7, 304, 316, 318, catching up 2, 246, 295–7, 300, 308
poverty 186, 302, 304, 307, 309
Preobrazhensky, Evgeny 140, 141, 143, 144, 145, 146, 165
Primo de Rivera, Miguel 92, 97, 102, 103, 108, 111
privatization, deregulation 284, 285, 303
productivity 24, 41, 85–6, 87, 90, 175–6, 177, 178, 215, 242, 245, 246, 292, 294, 295, 305, 323, 324
protectionism 12, 15, 40, 45–7, 56, 57, 58, 59, 60–1, 63, 65, 66, 68–9, 92, 95, 100, 103, 111, 112, 166, 190, 195, 259, 264, 283
public works 68, 69, 101, 103–5, 111

radar 122
railroads 15, 19, 31, 37, 59, 101, 103, 111
regional disparity within Europe and between continents 21, 23, 30, 34, 38, 39, 80, 87, 88, 89, 187, 188, 189, 300, 307, 308, 321, 322
regional economic blocs 67, 95, 111, Italian-led 125–6, German-led 114, 126–8, 166, 183, Soviet-led 153, 154, 166–9, 173, 183, 184, 185
regulated market system 42, 44, 45, 47, 72, 75, 79, 92, 95, 133, 157, 186, 190, 191
research and development (R&D) 217, 224, 285–6
Ricardo, David 13, 14
rocket and space program 118, 122–4
Romania 31, 37, 40, 47, 51, 54, 60, 61, 79, 98, 114, 127, 128, 150, 151, 152, 154, 156, 159, 167, 170, 173, 177, 309, 310
Russia 11, 12, 20, 22, 23, 31, 32, 34, 37, 38, 39, 40, 47, 50, 55, Russian Federation 293, 307, 309, 310

Salazar, António de Oliveira 92, 95, 97, 102, 114, 259, 279
Scandinavia 11, 12, 19, 20, 24, 28–30, 57, 59, 80, 81, 87, 191, 198, 229, 248, 251, 257, 261, 278, 316, 320
Schacht, Hjalmar 58, 113–14, 127
self-sufficiency, autarchy 47, 56, 61, 93, 102, 103, 110, 111, 112, 114, 116, 125, 130, 131, 133, 149, 166, 173, 190, 195, 221, 243
Serbia 32, 37, 50, 51, 75
services, service sector 19, 29, 43–4, 81, 82, 132, 175, 236, 244–5, 282, 291–2, 293, 299
Slovakia 74, 209, 318
Smith, Adam 13, 14, 42, 72
social democracy 59–60
Southern Europe, see Mediterranean Europe
Soviet Union 70, 74, 75, 84, 129, 150, 151–4, 155, 156, 157, 159, 165, 166, 167, 168, 169, 170, 171, 172, 173, 174, 175, 176, 178, 180, 184, 186, 187, 188, 199, 200, 209, 220, 246, 272, 279, 280, 298, 309, 313, 322, former 187, 321, 322, military technology 173–5, 230, 239, 260
Sozialpartnerschaft 195, 212–15
Spain, Spanish 11, 31, 32, 37, 38, 39, 40, 52, 92, 95, 103, 112, 131, 132, 133, 190, 209, 210, 225, 235, 236, 240, 245, 246, 250, 255, 258, 259, 260, 279, 293, 299, catching up 295, 299, 300, 303, 304, 308
Stalin, Josif V. 75, 145, 146, 147, 148, 149, 151, 152, 153, 154, 156, 158, 165, 166, 167, 178, "second revolution" 148, "socialism in one country" policy 146–50
state interventionism 40, 44, 60, 61, 69, 77, 79, 92, 93, 95, 99, 101, 103, 115, 190, 191, 223, 284, in fascist Italy 110, in Franco's Spain 111–12, in Nazi Germany 64, 110–11, in the Soviet bloc 157, 212, British, French 68–9
state-owned sectors, see nationalization
structural changes, crisis 79–86, 173, 175, 182, 183, 189, 226, 242–4, 245, 261, 279, 284, 286, 287, 288, 291, 292, 293, 295, 297, 298, 299
Sweden, Swedish 2, 11, 26, 28, 29, 30, 38, 57, 67, 71, 74, 75, 86, 207, 212, 213, 229, 230, 234, 237, 238, 240, 242, 244, 245, 253, 260, 261, 271, 284, 286, 287, 288, 291, 314
Switzerland, Swiss 11, 16, 17, 19, 20, 25, 26, 41, 43–4, 47, 52, 54, 57, 74, 75, 81, 82, 86, 207, 227, 230, 234, 238, 241, 246, 247, 248, 251, 253, 254, 256, 257, 265, 288, 298, 314, 316

tariffs, see protectionism
taxation 227–8, 302
technological revolution, see communication and service revolution
technology transfer 194, 239
telephone and radio 17, 81, 82, 83, 90, 250, 251, 252, 273
terms of trade 182, 282, 297
textile, and other consumer good industries 24, 25, 26, 37, 81, 82, 132, 243, 244
Tito, Josip Broz 154, 156
tourism 133, 254–5, 259, 289, 295
trade unions 93, 109, 191, 214
Trotsky, Leon 143, 144, 145, 146, 147
Tungsram, United Incandescent Lamp Co. 32–3

United Nations 112, 196, 314, 319
United States 20, 24, 25, 26, 41, 44, 46, 50, 56, 61, 62, 63, 78, 82, 85, 87, 89, 90, 91, 130, 151, 152, 153, 173–5, 192, 193, 199, 200, 203, 207, 236, 239, 245, 250, 254, 257, 259, 265, 266, 269, 271, 281, 284, 286, 287, 288, 298, 300, 313, 323, 324, 325, 326

Versailles Treaty 50, 53–5, 127
Volkswagen Werke 118, 119–20, 253

war communism 141
war preparation, war economy in World War I and II 42, 47, 70, 74–8, 82, 93, 95, 115, 130, 131, 133, 150, 154, 172, 223, British 47–9, German 49–50

Washington Consensus 278
welfare legislation, institutions 45, 68, 87, 93, 95, 110, 124–5, state socialist 165–6, 171, West European 191, 195, 226, 227, 230–6, 237, origin of welfare state 228–30, 231–2
Western Europe, Western core countries 3, 4, 11, 12, 19, 20, 22, 24, 28, 30, 31, 32, 34, 36, 37, 38, 39, 41, 60, 65, 74, 75, 79, 80, 81, 84, 86, 88, 89, 90, 112, 129, 132, 173, 175, 176, 177, 187, 188, 190, 191, 194, 196, 197, 200, 206, 213, 221, 227, 228, 231–2, 234, 236, 238, 242, 244, 245
wood, timber and paper industry 29, 244, 261
World Bank 43, 82, 193, 259, 278, 303, 319
World Trade Organization 195, 264
World Wide Web 265–66

Yugoslavia (and successors) 44, 51, 54, 58, 59, 60, 61, 66, 74, 114, 127, 128, 150, 151, 152, 154, 156, 159, 170, 176, 178, 179, 182, 184, 185, 186, 188, 209, 309